Tourist information 1:100 000 road maps

✠ Abbey / Priory	▲ Cathedral	⚓ Historic ship	☒ Museum	i To... Ce... ye...
♪ Aquarium / Dolphinarium	✝ Church	■ House	☺ Picnic area	
☐ Art collection	♛ Country park – England & Wales	◉ House and garden	⚞ Racecourse	i To... C... seasonally
☒ Art collection / Museum	♞ County show ground	⧗ Local museum	☢ Roman antiquity	
🐑 Bird sanctuary / Aviary	🚜 Farm park	⚓ Marina	☘ Safari park	— Transport collection
♜ Castle	○ Garden	◆ Maritime museum Military museum	⛟ Steam railway Miniature railway	Watermill Other place of interest
	▶ Golf course	▨ Motor racing circuit	★ Viewpoint	

Key to map pages

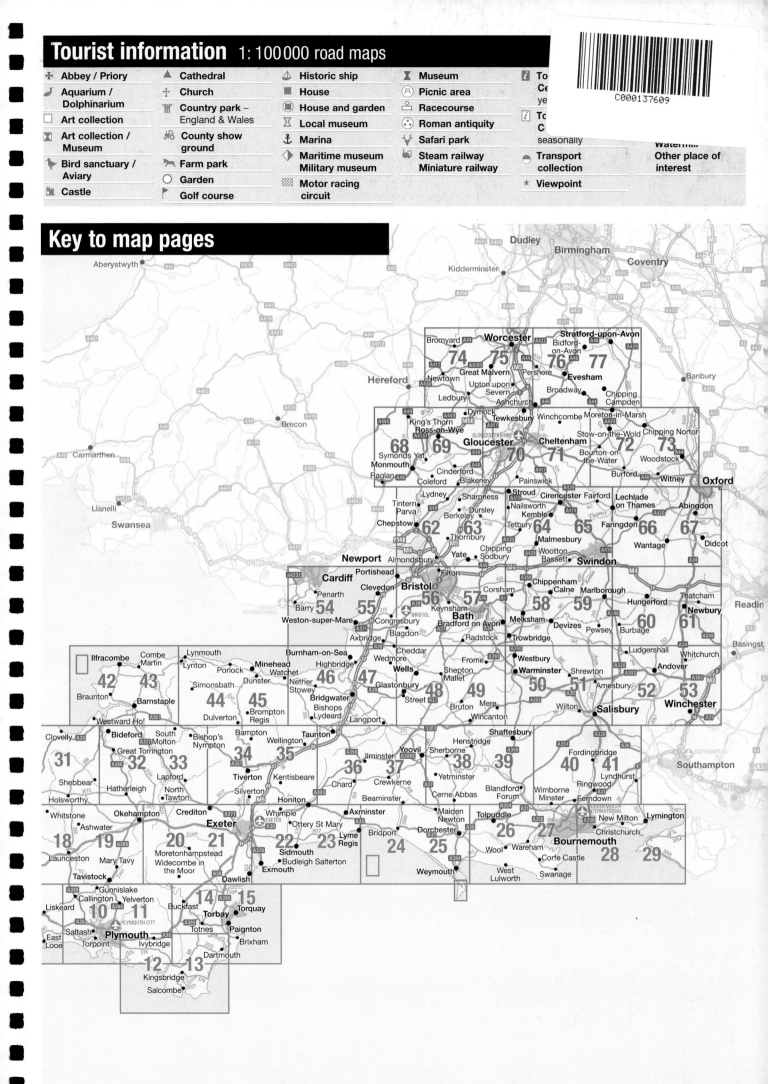

Landscape and nature

The area covered by the listings of places to visit and activities in the following pages includes the counties of Cornwall, Devon, Dorset, Gloucestershire, Somerset and Wiltshire. The region contains a wide variety of fascinating and beautiful landscapes and nationally important natural environments.

1 Bodmin Moor

Moorlands covered with small stone-walled fields and granite outcrops, as well as the scattered remains of 19th-century chalk farming.
Nature reserves NNR ☎ 01872 265710

2 Cotswolds

Mainly arable fields and some ancient woodland. Roads run from the plateau into deep coombes and through characteristic stone-built Cotswold villages and market towns.
Nature reserves NNR ☎ 01531 638500

3 Cheddar and Mendip Hills

The high limestone ridges and plateau of the Mendip Hills rear suddenly from the levels. Its ridges are slashed by deep ravines including the famous Cheddar Gorge. Holes, caverns and caves.
Nature reserves NNR ☎ 01823 283211

4 Dartmoor

Moorland covered flat topped hills with jagged tors and boggy hollows. National Park Authority ☎ 01626 832093.
Nature reserves NNR ☎ 01392 889770

5 Dorset Heaths

The core of the area, which was once all heath, is now a mixture of heathland with its associated habitats. Four significant rivers flow through the Dorset Heaths. To the north ancient woods survive.
Nature reserves NNR ☎ 01929 557450
RSPB ☎ 01929 553360

6 Exe Valley

'Deepest Devon' with red rocks and red soils. Arable fields wash over the tops of the hills and are criss-crossed by a maze of deep hedged lanes left behind by medieval colonists.
Nature reserves RSPB ☎ 01392 824614

7 Exmoor

The tallest sea cliffs in England form the northern boundary of this smallest moorland park. The grass moor of the Royal Forest is surrounded by heather-covered hills and wooded coombes. The Valley of the upper Exe separates Exmoor from the Brendon Hills at the eastern end of the park. Red deer and nightjar are representatives here of a rich diversity of wildlife. The area is also home to numerous ancient monuments with Bronze-Age burial sites, Roman fortlets, ironworks and medieval castles. The South West Coastal Path - a national trail - runs along the northern edge of the park. Exmoor National Park Authority ☎ 01398 323665
Nature reserves NNR ☎ 01823 28321

8 Isles of Scilly

The Isles of Scilly form an archipelago of more than 200 low-lying granite islands and rocks, located some 28 miles south-west of Land's End. The five main islands have a total population of just over 2000, an exceptionally mild climate, and golden sandy beaches, The unique combination of isolated south-westerly location and extreme maritime influence has resulted in the development of an island complex of international nature conservation importance. Of particular interest are the breeding seabirds and waved maritime heath.
Nature reserves NNR ☎ 01872 265710

9 Land's End

The most westerly point of the English mainland. This rocky coastline is characterised by granite cliffs, coves and headlands and possesses a number of important geological exposures. The shores of Land's End are fringed with ancient oak-woods. The cliffs are important for the study of geological processes and as breeding sites for seabirds. The larger estuaries and bays support internationally important populations of migrating and wintering birds. Marine mammals such as grey seals and harbour porpoises are also important to the area. On a clear day the Isles of Scilly are visible on the horizon.

10 Quantock Hills

Open moorland summits contrast with steep wooded slopes and valleys. Attractive villages and hamlets are scattered throughout the area.

11 Somerset Levels and Moors

The Somerset Levels and Moors are the largest area of lowland wet grassland, grazing marshes and associated wetland habitats remaining in England today.
Nature reserves NNR ☎ 01823 283211 RSPB ☎ 01458 252805

Cheddar Gorge, Somerset

Land's End, Cornwall

Sedgemoor, Somerset

12 South Hams

On Devon's south coast, south of Dartmoor. The area encompasses coastline, sweeping rivers and estuaries, and rolling countryside. In the 14th century this was the richest area in Devon. Across the hilly plateau the soils are fertile but they vary in colour. Some are sandstone based, others the creamy limestone quarried for buildings in Plymouth.

13 South Wessex Downs

South Wessex Downs are protected as an environmentally sensitive area. The most notable habitats of the South Wessex Downs are chalk grassland, chalk rivers, woodland and arable land. It contains not only the majority of England's remaining chalk grassland but also the single largest site in Northern Europe: Salisbury Plain.
Nature reserves NNR ☎ 01380 726344

Salcombe, Devon

14 Torbay

Behind the resorts, coves and cliffs lies a gentle landscape of low hills and rolling valleys filled with villages and hamlets.

15 Wiltshire Downs

Chalk downs and grasslands. Probably most famous for the Avebury World Heritage Site (NT), internationally known for its monuments from the Neolithic and Bronze age, including Stone Henge. See Ancient Monuments.
Nature reserves NNR ☎ 01380 726344

16 World Heritage / Jurassic Coast

The Dorset and east Devon coast contains a virtually complete sequence through some 200 million years of geological time and is a great fossil site. About one mile east of Lulworth Cove mud has formed around ancient tree trunks leaving donut shaped fossils. Dinosaur footprints can be seen in the thick limestones and clays known as the Purbeck Beds in Durlston Bay. The coast around Lulworth is internationally important as a living example of every stage in the development of bays and headlands.

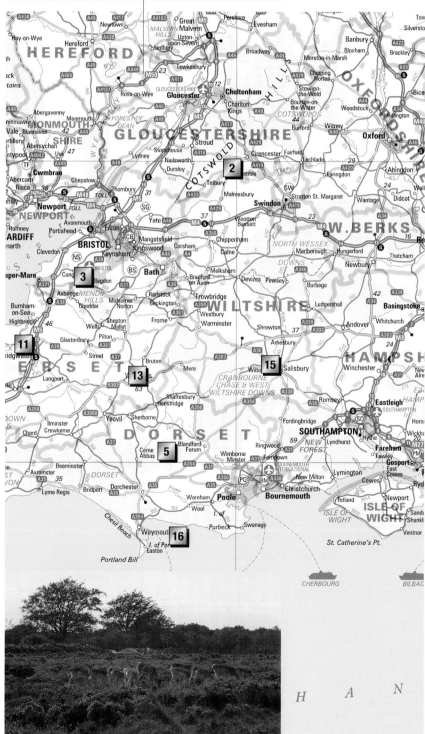

Farway, Devon

Brendon, Devon

Towns and villages

There are many charming and fascinating towns and villages in the regions covered by this atlas. What follows is a selection of some that are particularly worth visiting. As well as a description of each town, there are listings of places to visit and things to do, which can be found under various other sections in this atlas, such as Castles, Houses or Activities.

Altarnun *Cornwall* Pretty village street and 15th-century church of St Nonna, one of best churches in Cornwall. **18 D1**
Churches St Nonna

Barnstaple *Devon* Ancient port and old trading centre. Handsome old buildings and 15th-century Long Bridge. **43 D1**
Houses Arlington Court (NT)
Activities Bike Trail Cycle Hire • Exmoor Biketrail Cycle Hire • Jungleland • Lets Go Superbowl • Lynton and Barnstaple Railway • North Devon Farm Park • North Devon Karting Centre • North Devon Leisure Centre • Surf Seekers • Tarka Cruises • Tarka Trail Cycle Hire

Bath *Bath & NE S'set* Bath became a fashionable spa town in the 18th century and is famous for the Palladian elegance of its squares, terraces and crescents. Vistors can also see the famous excavated Roman baths. **57 D1**
Churches Abbey
Houses 1 Royal Crescent
Gardens Botanical Gardens • Prior Park Landscape (NT)
Historic Buildings Assembly Rooms (NT) • Guildhall • Roman Baths and Pump Room
Museums and galleries Bath Postal Museum • Bath Royal Literary and Scientific Institution • Building of Bath Museum • Burrows Toy Museum • Holburne Museum of Art • Impossible Microworld of Willard Wigan • Museum of Books • Museum of Costume • Museum of East Asian Art • Roman Baths Museum • Royal Photographic Society • Victoria Art Gallery
Activities Abbey Ales • Alice Park • Avon Valley Cyclery • Bath and Dundas Canal Co • Bath Boating Station • Bath Narrowboats • Bath Sports and Leisure Centre • Kennet & Avon Boat Trips • Royal Victoria Park

Beaminster *Dorset* Handsome place with Georgian buildings and picturesque 17th-century cottages. **37 D1**
Houses Parnham House
Gardens Horn Park Gardens • Mapperton
Activities New House Farm

Bibury *Glos* One of the most popular Cotswold villages. Home to the Arlington Row (NT) group of stone-built cottages. **65 D1**

Historic Buildings Arlington Mill
Activities Bibury Trout Farm

Blandford Forum *Dorset* Market town on the Stour. Some fine buildings of 1735-40 by John and William Bastard. **39 D1**
Churches St Peter and St Paul
Houses Milton Abbey
Museums and galleries Blandford Museum • Cavalcade of Costume Museum
Activities Blandford Leisure Centre

Bodmin *Cornwall* Traditional county town of Cornwall. Largest medieval church in Cornwall. **8 D1**
Churches St Petroc
Houses Lanhydrock (NT) • Pencarrow House
Monuments Stripple Stones
Museums and galleries Duke of Cornwall's Light Infantry Regiment
Activities Bodmin and Wenford Railway • Bodmin Jail • Camel Valley Vineyard • Glynn Valley Cycle Hire • Hengar Leisure Centre • The Dragon Leisure Centre

Boscastle *Cornwall* Has a little disused harbour (NT), flanked by steep cliffs. **17 D1**

Bourton-on-the-Water *Glos* Pretty village with river flowing down main street. **72 D1**
Activities Birdland Park & Gardens • Bourton Model Railway • Folly Farm Waterfowl • Fundays • Model Village

Bradford on Avon *Wilts* **57 D8**
Gardens The Hall • Westwood Manor (NT)
Activities Bradford on Avon Pool

Bridport *Dorset* Nice little maritime town with attractive main street and 18th-century Town Hall. Believed to have last thatch-roofed brewery in country. **24 D1**
Activities Bridport Leisure Centre • Bridport Park • Palmers Brewery

Bristol *Bristol* Old cathedral city and port with historical architecture and 19th-century university. Now vibrant centre for the arts. **56 B4**
Churches Bristol Cathedral • Lord Mayor's Chapel • St John's on the Wall • St Mary Redcliffe • Temple Church • The New Room
Houses Georgian House • Goldney House • Red Lodge
Castles Thornbury Castle
Historic Buildings Temple Church (EH) • Thomas Chatterton's house
Museums and galleries Arnolfini Arts Centre • Bristol Industrial Museum • British Empire and Commonwealth Museum • City Museum and Art Gallery
Activities Arnolfini • Bedminster • Bowlplex Bristol • Brean Leisure Park • Bristol Ice Rink • Bristol Megabowl • Bristol Zoo Aquarium • Bristol Zoo Gardens • Chew Valley Lake • Harveys Wine Museum • Hollywood Bowl • Horse World • Keynsham Park • Megabowl • Sk8 and Ride • Smiles Brewing

Clifton Suspension Bridge, Bristol

Company • St George's Park • Sustrans • The Raceway Bristol • Warner Village • Watershed • West Country Karting • West Country Waterpark • Westbury Wildlife Park

Brixham *Torbay* Resort and fishing port with beaches and attractive harbour. Good fish market. **15 D1**
Activities Brixham Leisure Centre • Brixham Sea Aquarium • Plain Sailing • Shoalstone Beach

Chagford *Devon* Quiet and charming old 'Stannary' town right in the centre of Devon; close to Dartmoor. **20 D1**
Gardens Stone Lane Gardens

Charlestown *Cornwall* Handsome harbour village. **8 D1**
Museums and galleries Shipwreck and Heritage Centre

Chipping Campden *Glos* Handsome stone buildings and picturesque High Street with styles ranging from 14th to 18th century. **77 D1**
Churches St James
Historic Buildings Chipping Campden Market Hall • Woolstaplers Hall
Activities Chipping Campden Sports Centre • Cotswold Country Cycles

Clovelly *Devon* Picturesque fishing village with steep cobbled streets and pretty white cottages. **31 D1**
Activities • The Milky Way Adventure Park

Combe Martin *Devon* Popular resort situated at the head of a sheltered valley. **43 D1**
Museums and galleries Combe Martin Motorcyle Collection
Activities Combe Martin Wildlife Park Railway • Stowford Farm

Coverack *Cornwall* Charming place. **5 D1**
Activities Coverack Windsurfing centre • Kennack Sands

Cranborne *Dorset* Known as 'Chaseborough' in novels of Thomas Hardy. **40 D1**
Gardens Cranborne Manor Gardens
Monuments Knowlton Church and Earthworks (EH)

Devizes *Wilts* Busy market town with handsome 18th-century buildings. **58 D1**
Churches St John
Museums and galleries The Kennet and Somerset Canal Museum
Activities Devizes Karting Arena • Devizes Leisure Centre

Dorchester *Dorset* County town with character. Made famous as Thomas Hardy's 'Casterbridge'. **25 D1**
Houses Hardy's Cottage (NT) • Max Gate (NT) • Wolfeton House
Castles Maiden Castle (EH)
Monuments Maiden Castle (EH) • Maumbury Rings • Poundbury Hillfort

Museums and galleries Dinosaur Museum • Dorset County Museum • Dorset Military Museum • The Keep Military Museum
Activities BHP Racing • Borough Gardens • Circuit Chevron • Clay Pigeon Kart Raceway • Dorchester Cycles • Kingston Maurward Gardens and Animal Park • Mill House Cider Museum • Thomas Hardy Brewery • Thomas Hardy Leisure Centre • Tithe Barn Children's Farm • Warmell Leisure Resort

Dunster *Somerset* Attractive place just inside Exmoor. Medieval butter cross and bridge. **45 D1**
Churches St George
Houses Dunster Castle (NT)
Historic Buildings Dunster Working Watermill (NT) • Gallox Bridge (EH) • Yarn Market EH
Activities Dunster Beach

Exeter *Devon* Historic cathedral city with medieval walls and remains of Roman roads. **21 B8**
Churches Exeter Cathedral
Houses Bowhill House EH • Killerton (NT)
Castles Exeter (Rougemont) Castle
Historic Buildings Customs House • Exeter Guildhall • Marker's Cottage (NT)
Monuments City Walls • Underground Passages
Museums and galleries Bill Douglas Centre • Royal Albert Memorial Museum and Art Gallery
Activities Clifton Hill Sports Centre • Exeter and District Ski Club • Exeter Megabowl • Grays Farm Cider • Pyramids Swimming and Leisure Centre • Riverside Leisure Centre • Saddles and Paddles • St James Sports Centre • St Peters Sports Centre • Underground Passages • Wonford Sports Centre

Fairford *Glos* Small and attractive town on the Coln. 17th and 18th-century buildings around the market place. **65 D1**
Churches St Mary
Activities Fairford Sports Centre

Fowey *Cornwall* Charming square, medieval and Tudor cottages, cobbled streets. **9 D1**
Castles St Catherine's Castle (EH)
Activities Fowey Cruising School

Gloucester *Glos* Interesting city with medieval cathedral. The historic docks have been handsomely redeveloped. **70 D2**
Churches Gloucester Cathedral
Historic Buildings Robert Raikes House
Museums and galleries City Museum and Art Gallery • Gloucester Museum and Art Gallery • Robert Opie Collection at Museum of Advertising and Packaging.
Activities Churchdown Sports Centre • Gloucester Megabowl • Gloucester Ski and Snowboard Centre • Guildhall • JDR Karting • Warehouse Climbing Centre

Ilfracombe *Devon* North Devon's most popular resort on the heritage coast. **42 D1**
Houses Chambercombe Manor
Activities Combe Martin Wildlife & Dinosaur Park • Ilfracombe (Tunnels) Beach • Seafront • Watermouth Castle Family Theme Park • Waverley Pleasure Steamers

Ivybridge *Devon* Beautifully situated town loved by Turner. **11 D1**
Activities Ivybridge Cycle Centre • South Dartmoor Leisure Centre

Launceston *Cornwall* Pleasant town. Once capital of Cornwall; historical architecture. **18 D1**
Castles Launceston Castle (EH)
Activities Hidden Valley • Launceston Steam Railway • Phoenix Leisure Centre • Roadford Lakes Angling & Watersports Centre • Tamar Otter Sanctuary • Trethorne Leisure Farm

Liskeard *Cornwall* Picturesque ancient stannery and market town with spacious town square and large perpendicular church. **9 D1**
Activities Dobwalls Family Adventure Park • Doublebois Park • Lux Park Leisure Centre • Siblyback Watersports

Looe *Cornwall* Historic little port, now a popular resort and British centre for shark fishing. **9 D1**
Activities Millendreath • Monkey Sanctuary

Lostwithiel *Cornwall* 13th century capital of Cornwall. Medieval Fowey Bridge and Stannery Court, and 1740 Guildhall. **9 D1**
Castles Restormel Castle EH

Lyme Regis *Dorset* Charming old resort overlooking Lyme Bay. Steep streets with Regency buildings. **24 D1**
Monuments Lambert's Castle (NT)
Museums and galleries Lyme Regis Museum
Activities Langmoor Gardens • Lyme Regis Marine Aquarium & Cobb History

Royal Crescent, Bath

Lacock, Wiltshire

Malmesbury *Wilts* Pleasant town above the Avon. Remains of Malmesbury Abbey, of which the historian William of Malmesbury (1090-1143) was a monk. **64 D1**
Churches The Abbey
Activities Activity Zone Leisure Centre • Lime Kiln Centre • Malmesbury Pool

Mevagissey *Cornwall* Attractive fishing village with cottages and fine harbour. **5 D1**

Newquay *Cornwall* Cornwall's most popular and lively holiday resort. 7 miles of beautiful sandy beaches. Uk's main centre for surfing. **7 D1**
Gardens Trerice (NT)
Activities Blue Lagoon Leisure • Blue Reef Aquarium • DairyLand Farm World • Dolphin Surf School • Fistral Beach • Great Western • Hendra Oasis Swimming Pool • Holywell Bay Fun Park • Lappa Valley Steam Railway • Little Western Railway, Trenance Gardens • Lusty Glaze • Mawgan Beach • Newquay Bowl • Newquay Cycle Hire • Newquay Zoo • Offshore Surfing • Porth Joke • Reef Surf School • Sealife Aquarium • Sealife Centre • Seven Bays Surf School • Springfields Fun Park & Pony Centre • Tolcarne • Trekenning Tourist Park • Trenance Leisure Park • Waterworld • West Coast Surfari

St Ives, Cornwall

Padstow *Cornwall* Fishing port with attractive medieval houses and bustling harbour. **16 D1**
Gardens Prideaux Place
Activities Berryfield Strawberry Farm • Brinhams Cycle and Tool Hire • Harlyn Bay Surf School • Mother Ivey's Bay • Old Mac Donalds Farm • Padstow Cycle Hire • Tamarisk Minature Railway

Penzance *Cornwall* On the curve of Mount's Bay. One of Cornwall's most attractive towns in terms of architecture and position. **3 D1**
Gardens Trengwainton Garden (NT)
Monuments Chysauster Ancient Village (EH) • Lanyon Quoit (NT) • Men-An-Tol
Museums and galleries National Maritime Museum Cornwall
Activities BSA National Surfing Centre • Freetime • Pedals Bike Hire • Penzance Aquarium • Penzance Jubilee Bathing Pool • St Clare Swimming Pool • The Cycle Centre

Plymouth *Devon* Major historical seaport and garrison at the head of Plymouth Sound. **10 D1**
Churches Plymouth Cathedral
Houses Saltram House (NT)
Historic Buildings Prysten House • Royal Citadel (EH)
Museums and galleries City Museum and Art Gallery • Kathleen and May boat and museum
Activities Alltrax • Arts Centre • Barbican Megabowl • Carter Boat hire • Coombe Dean Sports Centre • Dartmoor Wildlife Park • Derriford Health and Leisure Centre • Flatspot Skatepark Project • Hole, W.A. & Son • Knight Francis • Liberty Yachts Ltd • Lipson Community Sports Centre • Mayflower

Leisure Centre • Mount Batten Sailing and Watersports Centre • National Marine Aquarium • Newnham Park Outdoor Activity Centre • Phone-a-bike Breakthrough Mountain Sports • Plymouth • Plymouth Aquarium • Plymouth Boat Cruises • Plymouth Boat Cruises Ltd • Plymouth Cycle Hire.co.uk • Plymouth Dome • Plymouth Maritime Training Centre • Plymouth Megabowl • Plymouth Sailing School • Plymouth Ski Slopes & Toboggan Run • Portway Yacht Charters • Ridgeway Community Sports Centre • Southdown Yacht Club, Sea School & Charter Co. Ltd • Swiss Lake Ice Rink • Tamar Cruising • The Hoe • Tiger Moon Ltd

Polperro *Cornwall* Picturesque fishing village with colour washed cottages, known in past for smuggling. **9 D1**
Museums and galleries Smuggling Museum
Activities Land of Legend and Model Village

Polzeath *Cornwall* Sandy resort with Pentire Point (NT) to the N and Trebetherick and Daymer Bay to the S. St Enodoc church is situated in the middle of the local golf course. **16 D1**
Activities Surf's up

Poole *Poole* Old buildings and quaint narrow streets. Good beaches. Brownsea Island NT is reachable from Poole Harbour. Poole is a major port, with cross-channel ferry links to France. **27 D1**
Churches St Osmund
Activities Ashdown Leisure Centre • Baiter Skatepark • Bikes bicycles Spares Repairs • BKC Karting • Bowlplex • Cool Cats Leisure • Dolphin Swimming Pool • Gus Gorilla's Jungle Playground • Haven Sports & Leisure Centre • Lytchett Manor Sports Centre • Megabowl • Oceanos • Poole Aquarium • Poole Park • Poole Park Railway • Poole Sports Centre • Sandbanks Beach • Splashdown • The Gray Hedley Indoor Karting Centre • The Kemp Welch Leisure Centre • Tower Park

Porthtowan *Cornwall* Popular little bay. **6 D1**

Salisbury *Wilts* Cathedral city with historical buildings. **51 E8**
Churches Salisbury Cathedral • St Thomas
Houses Longford Castle • Malmesbury House • Mompesson House (NT)
Historic Buildings The North Canonry
Monuments Old Sarum (EH)
Museums and galleries Salisbury and South Wiltshire Museum • The Royal Gloucestershire, Berkshire and Wiltshire Regiment Museum
Activities Amesbury Sports and Community Centre • Avaco Karting and Laser Shooting • Cholderton Rare Breeds Farm Park • Clown About • Downton Leisure Centre • Hayball Cycle Centre • Salisbury Leisure Centre • Salisbury Swimming Pool • Stonehenge Ales • Strikers • The Rapids of Romsey • Tisbury and District Sports Centre • Westwood Sports Centre

Shaftesbury *Dorset* Picturesque old town with castle, twelve churches and four market crosses. Shaftesbury's Gold Hill looks over the picturesque Blackmore Vale of North Dorset. **39 D1**
Monuments White Sheet Hill
Activities Motcombe Park Leisure Centre • Shaftesbury Leisure Centre

Sherborne *Dorset* Handsome stone built town with a magnificent Abbey Church. **38 D1**
Houses Sherborne Castle
Activities Gryphon Leisure Centre • Worldlife and Lullingstone Silk Farm

Sidmouth *Devon* Regency style resort situated between reddish cliffs. York Terrace has balconied Georgian houses with wrought iron railings. **22 D1**
Activities Norman Lockyer Observatory • Radway • Sidmouth Sports Centre

St Ives *Cornwall* Popular resort on one of the most charming bays in England. Strong connections with artists. For example see Hepworth's house and studio in Museums and Galleries. **3 D1**
Churches St Ia
Museums and galleries Barbara Hepworth Museum and Sculpture Garden • Barnes Museum of Cinematography • Tate St Ives
Activities Godrevy • Royal • St Ives Bay • St Ives Leisure Centre

Stanway *Glos* Picturesque collection of buildings, including church, 16th/17th-century Stanway House and gatehouse. **71 D1**
Houses Stanway House

Studland *Dorset* Charming village 3m North of Swanage. Tiny Norman church, pretty bay and Studland National Trust nature reserve. **27 D1**
Activities Shell Bay

Sturminster Newton *Dorset* Historical market town by the river Stour. Home of Hardy 1876-78. **39 D1**
Activities Dorset Cycles

Swanage *Dorset* Attractive town at southern end of beautiful Studland Bay. Sandy beach. **27 D1**
Museums and galleries Tithe Barn Museum and Art Centre
Activities Bikeabout • Mowlem • Swanage Railway

Taunton *Somerset* Bustling county town dating back to Saxon times. Lies in the pretty valley of Taunton Deane, known for its apples and cider. **36 D1**
Churches St Mary Magdalene
Houses Combe Sydenham Hall
Gardens Hestercombe Gardens
Museums and galleries Somerset Cricket Museum
Activities Blackbrook Pavillion Sports Centre • Castle Sports Centre • Hollywood Bowl • Ians Cycle Centre • Kings Cycles • Sheppy's Cider Farm Centre • Staplecombe Vineyards • Taunton Aquarium Centre • The Bicycle Chain

Tewkesbury *Glos* Old riverside town in the cotswolds with half-timbered houses, great scenery and one of the best English Abbey churches. **70 D1**
Churches Abbey of St Mary
Activities Cascades Leisure Pool and Health & Fitness Suite • Kingfisher Ferries • Playzone • Pride of Avon Cruises • Talk of Tewkesbury • Telstar Hire Cruisers Ltd • Tewkesbury Sports and Leisure Centre • The Merchant's House

Tintagel *Cornwall* One of the most famous places in Cornwall. Village connected with romantic Tintagel castle and legend of King Arthur. **17 D1**
Castles Tintagel Castle
Churches St Materiana
Historic Buildings Tintagel Old Post Office (NT)

Shaftesbury, Dorset

Totnes *Devon* One of oldest and most handsome towns in England. One main street with many Elizabethan houses. **14 D1**
Castles Berry Pomeroy Castle (EH) • Totnes Castle (EH)
Historic Buildings Totnes Guildhall
Museums and galleries British Photographic Museum, Bowden House
Activities Canoe Adventures • Dartington Art • Dittisham Sailing School • Hot Pursuit • Inna River • Sharpham Vineyard • South Devon Railway • Woodland Leisure Park • Woodlands Leisure Park

Truro *Cornwall* Situated on the Fal river. Historically important as market centre and port, Truro became a cathedral city in 19th century. **4 D1**
Churches Truro Cathedral
Gardens Bosvigo House
Museums and galleries Cornwall County Museum and Art Gallery • Royal Cornwall Museum
Activities A.T.V. Motor Sports Centre • Bissoe Tramway Cycle Hire • Boscawen Park • Callestock Cider Farm • Mount Hawke Skatepark • Plaza • Skinner's Brewing Co. • Trail and Trek • Truro Cycles • Truro Leisure Centre • Truro Ten-pin Bowling Centre • World in Miniature

Wareham *Dorset* Interesting little town on the Frome. Built within Anglo-Saxon earthworks. **27 D1**
Houses Clouds Hill (NT)
Castles Corfe Castle (NT)
Museums and galleries Corfe Castle Museum • RAC Tank Museum
Activities Monkey World • Purbeck Sports

Weymouth *Dorset* Old harbour town and popular resort with late Georgian buildings. **25 D1**
Gardens Bennett's Water Gardens
Historic Buildings Nothe Fort
Activities Lakeside Superbowl • Lodmoor • Ringstead Bay • RSPB Nature Reserve, Radipole Lake • Tabor Kart Racing • The Front • Weymouth Bay Minature Railway, Lodmoor Country Park • Weymouth Sea Life Park

Wimborne Minster *Dorset* Historic market town on the Allen where it meets the Stour. Charming narrow Georgian streets and pretty squares. Near to Badbury Rings (NT). **27 D1**
Churches St Cuthburga
Houses Kingston Lacy (NT)
Gardens Deans Court Gardens
Activities Queen Elizabeth Leisure Centre

Castle Combe, Wiltshire

Churches and cathedrals

Bath & NE Somerset

Bath, Abbey *Abbey Churchyard* Site dates back to 7th-century. Gothic church built in 1499. After Dissolution church incomplete until 1864. Mostly a Victorian replica interior of a Tudor design. 57 C7

Bournemouth

Bournemouth, St Peter *Hinton Road and Parsonage Road* c1854. Tall stone tower, south aisle from earlier building. Richly restored Gothic Revival chancel and south transept. Grave of Mary Shelley. 28 B1

Bournemouth, St Stephen *St Stephens Road* Founded 1880. High bell-tower. Serene interior, organ loft above a vaulted chapel. Restored altar triptych. 28 B1

Bristol

Bristol Cathedral *Deanery Road, College Green* Unique among the English cathedrals as a 'Hall church' with aisles the same height as the main vault. Norman Chapter House, Early English Lady Chapel. 56 B4

Bristol, Lord Mayor's Chapel *St Mark, College Green* Founded c1230 as hospital chapel; 16th-century roof; some rebuilding; European medieval glass. 56 B4

Bristol, St John's on the Wall *Broad Street* Gothic church standing above gateway of old city wall. 56 B4

Bristol, St Mary Redcliffe *Redcliffe Way* 12th to 15th-century vaulted Gothic building with twin porches; Victorian stained glass and some medieval fragments. 56 B4

Bristol, Temple Church *Church Street, Temple Way* Walls and tower of 15th-century church bombed in World War II. Stands on site of 12th-century church. 56 B4

Bristol, The New Room *Horsefair* Erected in 1739 as discussion room for elders of Methodism. Simple Georgian interior. Museum of Methodism. 56 B4

Cornwall

Altarnun, St Nonna 15th-century with tall west tower. Norman font with monster carvings; 16th-century benches. 18 D1

Blisland, St Protus and St Hyacinth Partly Norman, with 15th-century tower, porch, aisles and transepts. 8 A4

Bodmin, St Petroc Largest medieval church in Cornwall. Bodmin stone. Contains unique accounts listing contributers to building. and St Petroc's casket (c1170). 8 B4

Breage, St Breaca 15th-century Cornish granite church. 15th-century mural of St Christopher and Christ. 3 E8

Come-to-Good, Quaker Meeting House Early 18th-century thatched chapel. Bare interior pine furnishings. 4 B4

Gunwalloe, St Winwaloe *Village* 15th-century 'Church of the Storms' built half on sea, half on land. Damaged by storm. 3 F9

Kilkhampton, St James Norman south doorway and carved bench-ends. 31 D5

Launcells, St Swithun 15th-century woodwork and tiles, Norman font and Gothic pulpit. Bench-ends depict Bible stories. 30 E4

Launceston, St Mary Early 16th-century. Carved granite facades, 20th-century woodwork. 18 D3

Madron, St Maddern 'Mother church of Penzance'. Contains banner made to mourn Nelson's death at Battle of Trafalgar. 2 D5

Morwenstow, St John the Baptist Church of eccentric poet Robert Hawker. Norman and early gothic with Tudor pews. 30 C4

Mullion, St Mellanus North door from 11th century, south door has dog flap for shepherd's dogs. Arts and Crafts screen. 5 G1

Mylor Churchtown, St Mylor Norman details, tallest Celtic cross in Cornwall. 4 C4

Probus, St Probus Cornwall's tallest tower. 7 F8

St Anthony-in-Roseland, St Anthony Rare Victorian restoration of a 12th-century monastic church; situated by the sea. 9 C8

St Austell, Holy Trinity Fine Gothic tower with carved statues; Norman font. 8 E3

St Buryan, St Buriana Tall granite tower and original painted rood screen. 2 E4

St Endellion, St Endelienta Carved Catacleuse Gothic altar. 16 E4

St Enodoc, St Enodoc 13th-century church in the middle of golf course. Home and resting place of poet John Betjeman. 16 E3

St Germans, St Germanus Cornwall's cathedral until c1409. Original church was seat of Saxon bishops, rebuilt as Norman outpost. 10 D3

St Ives, St Ia Early 15th-century granite church; medieval choir stalls portray local scenes; local artist Barbara Hepworth's Madonna and Child. 3 B6

St Just in Roseland, St Just in Roseland Gothic church situated in sub-tropical garden on Fal estuary; palm trees, cedars. 5 C5

St Neot, St Neot Medieval windows depict lives of the saints. Panels depict medieval ship design. 9 B6

St Enodoc church, Cornwall

Tintagel, St Materiana *Church Hill* Well-preserved Norman church on clifftop. Copy of National Gallery's Perugino altarpiece in Blessed Sacrament Chapel. 17 C6

Truro, Truro Cathedral *St Mary's Street* A fairly modern cathedral consecrated in 1887. Cruciform building completed 1910 to the design of J.L. Pearson RA in Early English style with strong French influence. Largely on site of 16th-century parish church, south aisle incorporated into new building as additional aisle to choir. Three powerful towers. The central tower rises to 250 feet and is a Cornish memorial to Queen Victoria. 4 B4

Devon

Ashton, Nr Chudleigh, St John the Baptist 15th-century church in peaceful setting. Richly decorated with much medieval. South door scarred with bullet holes from civil war. 21 E7

Bere Ferrers, St Andrew Slate tombs and granite interior. 14th-century stained glass features in east window. Ferrers monuments. 10 C5

Buckfastleigh, Buckfast Abbey Built on site from the original plan of a Cistercian monastry in 1st half of 20th century. Remains an active monastery but welcomes visitors. 14 B2

Crediton, Holy Cross Founded 12th century, mainly 15th century. Contains 20th-century works of art. Carved sedilia. 34 F1

Cullompton, St Andrew 15th century. Highly decorated tower with pinnacles and gargoyles. Richly carved, panelled ceiling. Complete colourful screen. 35 E5

Dartmouth, St Saviour Nautical town church, medieval door and Carved stone pulpit, gallery of 1633 with arms of merchant families. 15 E5

Exeter, Exeter Cathedral *Cathedral Yard and Cathedral Close* Built in Decorated style with three-storeyed west front and two great Norman transeptal towers. Famous for great west window with 14th-century tracery. Present building evolved from Norman building in middle of 13th century and displays much of the best in English Pointed architecture. The North Tower contains an ancient astronomical clock and Peter, one of the largest bells in England. The fine West Front contains many niches filled with statues. Library contains the Exon Domesday and other ancient documents. 21 B8

Hartland, St Nectan Site of Saxon abbey founded 1050. Second tallest tower in Devon, used to attract mariners at sea. 31 B5

Molland, St Mary Georgian furnishings, medieval statues. 44 F3

Ottery St Mary, Ottery St Mary Copied from Exeter Cathedral by Bishop Grandisson from 1338-42. Painted roof, fan vaulted aisle. Much original woodwork. Medieval weather vane. 22 A4

Plymouth, Plymouth Cathedral *Cecil Street and Wyndham Street* Roman Catholic Cathedral built mid-19th century in Early English style 10 E5

Tawstock, St Peter 14th-century church with wooden gallery from local Tawstock Court. Collection of Bourchier and Wrey monuments. 43 F5

Dorset

Abbotsbury, Abbotsbury Priory Buildings (EH) Remains of cloister building of Benedictine abbey, founded c1044. 25 C6

Blandford Forum, St Peter and St Paul Rebuilt 1733-9. Palladian church with square tower. Pulpit from destroyed Wren church St Antholin in London. 39 E7

Cerne Abbas, Cerne Abbey Cerne Abbey, founded AD987, consists of gatehouse, AD987 onwards, Abbey House, the hospice or guesthouse, c1450, and the abbot's porch, c1509. 38 F3

Christchurch, Priory Late 15th-century tower. North porch (1300) is largest in country; monument to Shelley. Norman nave and transepts. Decorated stone reredos representing Tree of Jesse. 28 B3

Milton Abbas, Abbey 14th-century fragment of much bigger intended building. Decorated Gothic windows. Rich altar screen of 1492. 39 F6

Sherborne, Abbey of St Mary Cathedral until 1075. 11th-century doorway at west end and four pillars survive from last Saxon church on site. South porch, crossing arch and parts of North and south transepts survive from Norman church. Remainders are 15th-century. Fan vaults cover virtually whole interior. 38 C2

Wimborne Minster, St Cuthburga Early 16th-century Flemish glass in east window. One Norman, one gothic tower. Norman font on Purbeck marble shafts. Early 14th-century astronomical clock. 27 A7

Whitchurch Cannonicorum, St Candida (St Wite) and Holy Cross Only parish church in England to retain relics and shrine of its saint. Norman font. 24 A2

Gloucestershire

Berkeley, St Mary Sandstone church. Early Gothic west front. Berkeley memorials. East window memorial to Edward Jenner. 63 C5

Bishops Cleeve, St Michael Norman church, Jacobean musician's gallery. 71 B5

Chipping Campden, St James Reputedly houses Britain's only complete set of medieval altar hangings. 77 E6

Cirencester, St John the Baptist Largest and most complex south porch in Britain. Coats of arms of patrons. Garstang chapel

surrounded by 15th-century screen. Second chapel with stone screen and timber roof. Anne Boleyn cup on display. 65 B5

Deerhurst, Odda's Chapel (EH) Rare Anglo-Saxon chapel attached to half-timbered farmhouse 70 B3

Deerhurst, St Mary Former Anglo-Saxon monastery. Restored interior with much Saxon work still evident and in good condition. Wall of tower has 8th-century relief of Madonna and Child. 70 B3

Elkstone, St John Norman church. West tower built c1370; gargoyles. Fine woodwork. Priest's dovecote. 71 E5

Fairford, St Mary Late 15th-century church. Built new from foundations. England's only complete set of medieval narrative windows. 65 B3

Gloucester, Gloucester Cathedral *Westgate Street, College Street* Romanesque building of 11th and 12th centuries with later 15th-century exterior. Beautiful Norman building with Perpendicular work on the exterior. Noted for fine 225 ft high central tower and huge 14th-century east window. Tomb of Edward II with fine canopy and figure. 70 D2

Highnam, Holy Innocents Founded 1849 Wall paintings cover the interior; iron screen and carved stone reredos. 70 C1

Kempley, St Mary (EH) Norman church. 12th to 14th-century frescoes. Roof timbers are oldest in England, c1120-50. 69 B7

Lechlade, St Lawrence 1470 church on earlier foundations. Additions in 16th century. Carvings and depictions of domestic and religious life. 66 C1

Newland, All Saints Known as 'the Cathedral of the Forest'. Sandstone church with decorated spire. 68 F5

Northleach, St Peter and St Paul 15th-century wool church with brasses of local wool merchants. Decorated two storey porch. 71 E8

Tewkesbury, Abbey of St Mary Biggest Norman tower in Europe. Decorated chapels at east end contrast with Norman work. Carved roof bosses portray life of Christ. Brasses, monuments and 14th-century windows of the choir commemorate Lords of Tewkesbury. Vestry door covered with metal taken from armour of knights killed at Battle of Tewkesbury. 70 A3

Salisbury Cathedral, Wiltshire

Culbone church, Somerset

Poole

Poole, St Osmund Built 1904-1927. Frankish turrets, Lombard arcading, Saxon patterning, Art Nouveau terracotta arch. Arts and Crafts grille. **27 B7**

Somerset

Axbridge, St John Gothic building with 17th-century fittings. Blue and white nave ceiling. **55 F8**

Brent Knoll, St Michael Norman with perpendicular additions. Satirical benchends ridiculing church authorities. 17th-century memorial to John Somerset. **47 A6**

Crewkerne, St Bartholomew Rebuilt at turn of 16th-century. Window tracery among most complicated in England. **37 E6**

Croscombe, St Mary Tower with rare Somerset spire. Jacobean woodwork. Two-storey Medieval treasury. **48 C3**

Culbone nr Porlock Weir, St Beuno Allegedly smallest church in England. Walls 12th-century or earlier. **44 B4**

Dunster, St George 12th-century priory church enlarged 13th and 15th century. Longest screen in England. **45 C6**

Farley, All Saints Rare countryside example of 17th-century brick church. Built by one of Wren's master masons. **52 F1**

Glastonbury, Glastonbury Abbey Story of abbey is mix of fact and legend, some come for ancient Christian links, others to visit legendary burial site of King Arthur. Little remains of monastic buildings. **48 D2**

Ilminster, St Mary Contains 17th-century tombs of founders of Wadham College, Oxford. Memorial brasses. **36 C5**

Isle Abbotts, St Mary Ham stone and blue lias tower with 10 original statues. Norman font and original furnishings. **36 B5**

Martock, All Saints 16th-century carved wooden 'quilted' ceiling. **37 C7**

Mells, St Andrew Rebuilt 15th century. Highly decorated church porch. **49 B6**

Muchelney, Muchelney Abbey(AM) Abbot's house is all that remains of former Benedictine monastery. Dating mainly from early 16th century contains carved woodwork, fragments of wall paintings and stonework excavated from the ruined abbey. **37 B6**

Oare, Oare Church/St Mary's Oare Church was the scene of Lorna Doone's wedding in the novel by R D Blackmore. Georgian box pews, pulpit and reading desk. 12th-century font, 15th-century chancel and nave. **44 B3**

Selworthy, All Saints Limewashed church on hilltop setting, rebuilt early 16th century. White and blue ceiling. **45 B5**

Shepton Mallet, St Peter and St Paul Original Saxon walls on present nave. 14th-century tower. Panelled wagon roof. **48 C4**

Stogumber, St Mary Chancel decorated in style of William Morris. **46 D1**

Stogursey, St Andrew Norman priory church built c1100 and seized by Henry V 1414. Rare Somerset spire. **46 C4**

Stoke Sub Hamdon, Stoke sub Hamdon Priory NT Complex of buildings including dovecote. **37 C7**

Taunton, St Mary Magdalene *Hammet Street* Sculpted tower, highest in Somerset. Oak roof and angels. **36 A2**

Washford, Cleeve Abbey (AM) One of few 13th-century monastic sites where you will see such a complete set of cloister buildings, including the refectory with its magnificent timber roof. **45 C7**

Wells, St Cuthbert *St Cuthbert Street* Largest parish church in Somerset. Carved 17th-century pulpit. Ornate roof with angels, heralds, rosettes and shields. **48 B2**

Wells, Wells Cathedral *Cathedral Green* Dates from late 12th to early 14th centuries and is renowned for majestic early English west front and great central tower. Noted features of the interior include massive but graceful inverted arches, 14th-century stained glass of the Lady Chapel and deep worn steps to the Chapter House. **48 B2**

Westonzoyland, St Mary Good tie-beam roof decorated with rosettes and crowned with quatrefoils. **47 D7**

Wiltshire

Bishops Cannings, St Mary Early gothic. Vaulted porch with Decorated ballflower. 17th-century pew beneath huge hand intended to warn occupant of sin. **58 D5**

Bishopstone, St John the Baptist Many decorated features and interesting monuments. **40 A4**

Bradford on Avon, St Lawrence Built in 10th century possibly on foundations of 8th-century church. Rediscovered 1871 after serving as barn. Simple interior with carved angels above the chancel. **57 D8**

Devizes, St John Mixture of Norman and Gothic styles. **58 D5**

Edington, St Mary, St Katherine and All Saints Late Gothic completed at time of transition from Decorated to Perpindicular church styles. **50 A3**

Inglesham, St John the Baptist Plain exterior 13th-century church saved by William Morris c1888-9. Late Saxon relief sculpture. **65 C9**

Lydiard Tregoze, St Mary Mausoleum of Caroleum art. Golden Cavalier monument. **65 F7**

Malmesbury, The Abbey Abbey founded 7th century, only 12th-century nave survives. Porch with sculptured reliefs depicting scenes from Old Testiment, Creation and Life of Christ. Norman stone carvings of apostles on interior walls of porch. Tomb of Saxon King Athelstan (died 939). **64 E3**

Salisbury, Salisbury Cathedral *The Close* Beautiful Early English building with later Decorated tower and spire. Notable west front has many niches filled with figures representing the Te Deum. **51 E8**

Salisbury, St Thomas *High Street* Most complete Doom mural in Britain. **51 E8**

Winterbourne Bassett, St Katharine and St Peter Mainly 14th-century Decorated style. Walls mainly of Sarsen stone, the ancient stone used by prehistoric man. **59 A6**

Ancient monuments

Abbot's Fish House (EH) *Meare, Somerset* well-preserved stone dwelling. **47 C9**

Adam's Grave *Alton Barnes, Wilts* Chambered long barrow.**59 D7**

Avebury Stone Circle (EH) *Avebury, Wilts* Constructed 4,000 years ago, originally using over 180 stones. **59 C7**

Badbury Rings *nr Shapwick, Dorset* Iron age hill fort with evidence of Bronze age settlement. **40 F1**

Ballowall Barrow (EH) *St Just, Cornwall* Unusual Bronze Age chambered tomb **2 D3**

Bant's Carn (EH) *St Mary's, I/Scilly* Bronze age burial mound and Roman village. **6 A3**

Barbury Castle *Wroughton, Swindon* Iron age hillfort. **65 F8**

Belas Knap (EH) *nr Winchcombe, Glos* Good example of Neolithic long barrow. **71 B6**

Blackbury Camp (EH) *Southleigh, Devon* Iron Age hillfort. **23 B6**

Bratton Camp and White Horse (EH) *Bratton, Wilts* Large Iron Age hill fort. **50 A3**

Cadbury Castle *South Cadbury, Somerset* Iron Age hill fort (reputedly 'Camelot'). Impression of a great fortress lingers. **38 A2**

Carn Brea *Redruth, Cornwall* Remains of Neolithic hillfort. **4 B2**

Carn Euny Ancient Village (EH) *Sancreed, Cornwall* Iron Age settlement, with foundations of huts and underground passage. **2 E4**

Castle An Dinas *St Columb, Cornwall* Iron Age Celtic hill fort, 200-300BC. **8 C1**

Chedworth Roman Villa (NT) *Yanworth, Glos* One of largest Romano-British villas in country. Walls plus mosaics, bathhouses, hypocausts, water-shrine and latrine. Small museum. ✆01242 890256 **71 E7**

Chysauster Ancient Village (EH) *Penzance, Cornwall* Site of Iron Age village dating from about 1 BC to the 3rd century AD. ✆07831 757934 **3 D5**

Cley Hill *Warminster, Wilts* Iron age hill fort about 300 BC. Single banked hill with two bronze age round barrows. **50 C2**

Devil's Den *Fyfield, Wilts* Chambered long barrow c4000BC. **59 C7**

The Dorset Cursus *Pentridge, Dorset* 2 Parallel banks stretching for 6 miles. Both banks flanked with barrows. **40 C3**

Ethandun Memorial *Westbury, Wilts* At Bratton Camp. Sarson stone commemorating 9-century battle. **50 A2**

Everleigh Barrows *Everleigh, Wilts* **59 F9**

Fyfield and Overton Downs *Fyfield, Wilts* Prehistoric landscape comprising an extensive field system of banks. **59 D8**

Garrison Walls (EH) *St Mary's, I/Scilly* Ramparts of walls and earthworks. **6 A3**

Giant's Grave *nr Pewsey, Wilts* Unchambered long barrow c4000BC **59 D**

Gopher Wood *Huish, Wilts* Small bronze age cemetary comprising of seven bowl barrows and a disc barrow. **59 D7**

Great Witcombe Roman Villa (EH) *Great Witcombe, Glos* Built around courtyard, luxurious bath-house. ✆01179 750700 **70 E4**

The Hurlers Stone Circle (EH) *Minions, Cornwall* Three Bronze Age stone circles in a line, some of best ceremonial standing stones in South West. **9 A8**

Halliggye Fogou (EH) *Garras, Cornwall* One of several underground tunnels, linked to Iron Age villages, unique to Cornwall. **4 F2**

Hatfield Earthworks (EH) *Marden, Wilts* Part of a Neolithic enclosure complex **59 E6**

Hound Tor (EH) *Manaton, Devon* Remains of medieval farmsteads, first occupied in Bronze Age. **20 D5**

Innisidgen Lower and Upper Burial Chambers (EH) *St Mary's, I/Scilly* Two Bronze Age cairns. **6 A3**

Jordan Hill Roman Temple (EH) *Preston, Dorset* Foundations of Romano-Celtic temple. **25 D9**

King Doniert's Inscribed Stone (EH) *St Cleer, Cornwall* Two decorated pieces of 9th-century cross believed to commemorate King of Cornwall, who drowned c875. **9 B7**

Kingston Russell Stone Circle (EH) *Abbotsbury, Dorset* Bronze Age stone circle of 18 stones. **25 C6**

Kings Weston Roman Villa *Lawrence West-on, Bristol* Possibly 3rd century AD. Bath suite, living quarters, mosaic floors, court and east wing. ✆0117 9223571 **56 A2**

Knap Hill *Alton Barnes, Wilts* Neolithic causewayed enclosure. **59 D7**

Knowlton Church and Earthworks (EH) *Cranborne, Dorset* Ruins of Norman church in middle of Neolithic earthworks. **40 D3**

Lambert's Castle (NT) *Lyme Regis, Dorset* Iron age hill fort. **24 B1**

Lanyon Quoit (NT) *Penzance, Cornwall* Fine cromlech consisting of capstone supported on three granite slabs. c1500 BC. **3 D5**

Maiden Castle (EH) *nr Dorchester, Dorset* Finest Iron Age hill fort in Britain. **25 B8**

Marden Henge *Beechingstoke, Wilts* One of largest Neolithic henge monuments in Britain. **59 E6**

Martinsell Hill *Pewsey, Wilts* Iron age hillfort enclosing 32 acres. **59 D8**

Men-An-Tol *Penzance, Cornwall* Holed Stone. **3 D5**

Merrivale Prehistoric Settlement (EH) *Dartmoor, Devon* Two rows of standing stones, remains of early Bronze Age village. **19 E7**

Merry Maidens *Lamorna, Cornwall* Circle of nineteen standing stones. **2 F4**

Maumbury Rings *Dorchester, Dorset* Originally a sacred circle of the Stone Age, the Romans later turned Rings into 'Coliseum'. **25 B8**

The Nine Stones (EH) *Winterbourne Abbas, Dorset* Remains of nine standing stones constructed about 4,000 years ago. **25 B7**

Exeter Cathedral, Devon

Notgrove Long Barrow (EH) *Notgrove, Glos* A Neolithic burial mound. **71 C8**

Nympsfield Long Barrow (EH) *Nympsfield, Glos* Neolithic long barrow **63 B8**

Offa's Dyke (EH) *Chepstow, Monmouths* Three-mile great earthwork built as a defensive boundary **62 D2**

Ogbourne Round Barrow *Ogbourne St Andrew, Wilts* A round barrow in pagan Saxon churchyard. **59 B8**

Oldbury Castle (NT) *Cherhill, Wilts* Iron age hillfort **59 B5**

Oliver's Castle *Bromham, Wilts* Iron age hill-fort with single bank and ditch. **58 C4**

Old Sarum (EH) *Salisbury, Wilts* Great earth-work with huge banks and ditch lbuilt around 500 BC. ✆01722 335398 **51 E8**

Overton Hill *West Kennett, Wilts* Bronze Age burial mounds. **59 C7**

Porth Hellick Down Burial Chamber(EH) *St Mary's, I/Scilly* Bronze Age. **6 A3**

Poundbury Hillfort *Dorchester, Dorset* Ancient entrenchment. **25 B8**

Rawlsbury Camp *Milton Abbas, Dorset* Iron age hillfort. **39 F6**

Rybury Camp *All Cannings, Wilts* Causewayed iron age enclosure. **59 D6**

St Breock Downs Monolith (EH) *nr Wadebridge, Cornwall* Prehistoric standing stone, **8 A2**

The Sanctuary (EH) *West Kennett, Wilts* Possibly 5,000 years old, Consists of two concentric circles of stones and six timber uprights indicated by concrete posts. **59 C7**

Silbury Hill (EH) *Avebury, Wilts* Largest man-made mound in ancient Europe. **59 C7**

Stanton Drew Circles (EH) *Stanton Drew, Bath & NE S'set* Three stone circles, two avenues and a burial chamber. One of finest Neolithic sites in the country. **56 D3**

Stonehenge (EH) *nr Amesbury, Wilts* Great ancient stone circle of Stonehenge stands at centre of extensive prehistoric landscape filled with remains of ceremonial and domestic structures. ✆01980 624715 **51 C8**

Stoney Littleton Long Barrow (EH) *Wellow, Bath & NE S'set* Neolithic burial mound. **57 E6**

Stripple Stones *Nr Bodmin, Cornwall* Stone circle. **8 B4**

Tregiffian Burial Chamber (EH) *St Buryan, Cornwall* Neolithic or early Bronze Age chambered tomb **2 E4**

Trencrom Hill *Penzance, Cornwall* 2nd-century BC rampart. Hut circles and well. **3 D5**

Trethevy Quoit (EH) *St Cleer, Cornwall* Cromlech or prehistoric burial place. **9 B7**

Uley Tumulus (EH) *Uley, Glos* c3000 BC, Neolithic chambered burial mound **63 C7**

Upper Plym Valley (EH) *Nr Yelverton, Devon* Scores of prehistoric and medieval sites covering six square miles. **11 B6**

West Kennett Avenue (EH) *Avebury, Wilts* Avenue of standing stones, which ran from Avebury Stone Circles to The Sanctuary, late Neolithic. **59 C7**

West Kennett Long Barrow (EH) *West Kennett, Wilts* Neolithic chambered tomb. **59 C7**

White Sheet Hill *Nr Shaftesbury, Dorset* Neolithic long barrow and Bronze age barrows. Remains of Neolithic Causeway camp and Iron Age hill fort. **39 B7**

Windmill Hill (EH) *Avebury, Wilts* Neolithic remains of three concentric rings of ditches. **59 C7**

Winterbourne Poor Lot Barrows (EH) *Winterbourne Abbas, Dorset* Part of 4,000 year old Bronze Age cemetery. **25 B7**

Woodhenge (EH) *Durrington, Wilts* Neolithic ceremonial monument 2300 BC. Entrance and long axis of the oval rings points to rising sun on Midsummer Day. **51 C8**

Zennor Cromlech *nr Zennor, Cornwall* Quoit, one of largest capstones in England **2 C5**

Lanyon Quoit, Cornwall

The places listed here are a selection of the finest houses, castles and gardens in the counties covered by this atlas. Make sure you check opening times before visiting, as many of the places listed are open only at limited times or seasons.

Houses

A La Ronde (NT) *Exmouth, Devon* c1796. ☎01395 265514 **22 D2**

Antony House (NT) *Torpoint, Cornwall* Early 18th-century house in extensive grounds. ☎01752 812191 **10 D4**

Arlington Court (NT) *Barnstaple, Devon* Noted for extensive collection of model ships, and other works of art. Gardens, and woods. ☎01271 850296 **43 E6**

Athelhampton *Puddletown, Dorset* Medieval house. Walled gardens include famous topiary pyramids. ☎01305 848363 **26 B1**

Avebury Manor (NT) *Avebury, Wilts* Present buildings date from 16th century. Topiary and flower gardens. ☎01672 539250 **59 C7**

Badminton House *Badminton, S Glos* Fine Palladian mansion; rarely open. **63 F8**

Barrington Court (NT) *Ilminster, Somerset* Tudor manor house restored 1920s. Formal garden. ☎01460 241938 **36 C5**

Bickleigh Castle *nr Tiverton, Devon* Thatched Jacobean wing, Norman chapel, moat and gardens. **34 D4**

The Bishop's Palace *Wells, Somerset* 13th-century moated palace. State rooms and gallery. ☎01749 678691 **48 B2**

Bowhill House (EH) *Exeter, Devon* 15th-century Mansion. **21 B8**

Bowood House *Calne, Wilts* 18th-century house designed by Adam. One of Capability Brown's most beautiful parks. Adventure playground. ☎01249 812102 **58 B5**

Bradley Manor (NT) *Newton Abbot, Devon* Small, 15th-century manor house. Ramparts of Berry Wood earthwork stand in the grounds. ☎01626 354513 **15 A5**

Brympton d'Evercy *nr Yeovil, Somerset* Large mansion with late 17th-century south front and Tudor west front. Extensive formal gardens with and vineyard. **37 C9**

Buckland Abbey (NT) *nr Tavistock, Devon* Originally Cistercian monastery, then home of Sir Francis Drake. Exhibitions. Elizabethan garden. ☎01822 853607 **19 F6**

Buckland Rectory *Buckland, Devon* Oldest rectory in England. **12 D4**

Cadhay *Ottery St Mary, Devon* Elizabethan manor house. Lovely garden overlooking medieval ponds. ☎01404 812432 **22 A4**

Chambercombe Manor *Ilfracombe, Devon* Late 14th and early 15th century. Herb, rose and water gardens. ☎01271 862624 **42 B5**

Chavenage House *Chavenage Green, Glos* Elizabethan house. Medieval barn. ☎01666 502329& 01453 832700 **64 C2**

Chettle House *Chettle, Dorset* Baroque Queen Anne house. ☎01258 830209 **40 D2**

Clevedon Court (NT) *nr Clevedon, N Somerset* Built c1320. One of few complete houses of this time to have survived. ☎01275 872257 **55 B8**

Clouds Hill (NT) *Wareham, Dorset* T E Lawrence's (Lawrence of Arabia) retreat. ☎01929 405616 **27 C5**

Coleridge Cottage (NT) *Nether Stowey, Somerset* Samuel Taylor Coleridge lived here 1797 to 1800. ☎01278 732662 **46 D3**

Coleton Fishacre House (NT) *Kingswear, Devon* House reflects Arts & Crafts tradition but has modern interiors. Garden has large collection of plants. ☎01803 752466 **15 E5**

Combe Sydenham Hall *Taunton, Somerset* Historic house, appointment only. Parkland open to visitors. ☎01984 656284 **36 A2**

Compton Castle (NT) *nr Paignton, Devon* Fortified manor house. ☎01803 872112 **15 C5**

Corsham Court *Corsham, Wilts* Elizabethan and Georgian house. Park and garden by Capability Brown. ☎01249 701610 **58 B2**

Cotehele House (NT) *Saltash, Cornwall* Medieval house. Formal gardens and valley garden. ☎01579 351346 **10 D4**

Court House *Painswick, Glos* Typical Cotswold manor house. **70 F3**

Dewlish House *Dewlish, Dorset* Queen Anne House erected about 1700. **26 A2**

Dodington House *Chipping Sodbury, S Glos* 18th-century Classic house designed by James Wyatt. Parkland by Capability Brown includes two lakes, nature walks. **63 F6**

Dunster Castle (NT) *Dunster, Somerset* House and medieval ruins framed with sub-tropical plants. ☎01643 821314 **45 C6**

Dyrham Park (NT) *Dyrham, S Glos* Built 1692 - 1702. Collection of Delft, paintings by Dutch masters. Formal garden, two lakes. Deer park has been here since Saxon times. ☎01779 372501 **57 A6**

Edmondsham House and Garden *Edmondsham, Dorset* Tudor/Georgian manor house . 6 acre garden and 2 acre walled garden. ☎01725 517207 **40 D4**

Endsleigh House and Gardens House *Milton Abbot, Devon* Retreat built 1811. Ornamental gardens with terraced walks. ☎01822 870248 **19 E5**

Forde Abbey *nr Chard, Somerset* 12th century Cistercian monastery converted into residence after Dissolution. Extensive grounds. ☎01460 221290 **36 E4**

Frampton Court *Frampton on Severn, Glos* Georgian stately home, dated 1732, set in beautiful gardens. ☎01452 7440267 **69 F8**

Fursdon House *Cadbury, Devon* Early manor-house with Georgian alterations. Small museum. Terraced garden. ☎01392 860860 **34 F3**

Gaulden Manor *Tolland, Somerset* Small manor of great charm. Grounds include herb and bog gardens. ☎01984 667213 **46 E2**

Georgian House *Bristol, Bristol* Georgian town house built 1790 for wealthy merchant. ☎0117 921 1362 **56 B4**

Godolphin House (NT) *Helston, Cornwall* Tudor house. ☎01736 762409 **4 E1**

Goldney House *Bristol, Bristol* Garden created in early 18th century by Quaker merchant. ☎0117 9034873 **56 B4**

Great Chalfield Manor (NT) *Bradford on Avon, Wilts* Restored 1480 moated manor house. ☎01225 782239 **57 D8**

Haldon Belvedere (Lawrence Castle) *Higher Ashton, Devon* Built 1788. **21 D7**

Hardy's Cottage (NT) *Dorchester, Dorset* Thomas Hardy born here in 1840. ☎01305 262366 **25 B8**

Hatch Court *Hatch Beauchamp, Somerset* Bath Stone Palladian mansion, surrounded by glorious parkland. ☎01823 480120 **36 B4**

Heale House *Middle Woodford, Wilts* ☎01722 782504 **51 D7**

Highcliffe Castle *Highcliffe, Dorset* Completed 1835 including stone work from Benedictine abbey in Normandy. ☎01425 270924 **28 B4**

Horton Court (NT) *Nr Chipping Sodbury, South Glos* ☎01249 730141 **63 F6**

Killerton (NT) *Exeter, Devon* Built in 1778. Collection of costumes. Hillside gardens, extensive lawns. ☎01392 881345 **21 B8**

King John's Hunting Lodge (NT) *Axbridge, Somerset* Early Tudor merchant's house now museum. ☎01934 732012 **55 F8**

Kingston Lacy (NT) *Wimborne Minster, Dorset* Completed 1665. Houses collection of Old Masters, celebrated 'Spanish Room'. ☎01202 883402 **27 A7**

Kirkham House *Paignton, Devon* 14th-century stone house with modern furniture, pottery and fabrics. ☎education officer: 0117 9750700 **15 C5**

Knightshayes Court (NT) *Tiverton, Devon* Completed 1874. Small woodland and terraced gardens. ☎01884 254665 **34 D4**

Lacock Abbey (NT) *Lacock, Wilts* Originally an abbey, converted into house 1540. ☎01249 730227 **58 C3**

Lanhydrock (NT) *Bodmin, Cornwall* Fifty rooms open to view. Wooded parkland and garden. ☎01208 73320 **8 B4**

Little Clarendon (NT) *Dinton, Wilts* Tudor house, altered 17th century with 20th-century Catholic chapel. ☎01985 843600 **50 E5**

Littledean Hall *Littledean, Glos* Norman manor house with archaeological site in grounds. Largest known Roman temple in rural Britain. ☎01594 824213 **69 E7**

Lodge Park (NT) *Aldsworth, Glos* 17th-century grandstand. Recently restored. ☎01451 844153 **72 E2**

Longford Castle *Salisbury, Wilts* Country house built at end of 16th century. **51 E8**

Longleat House *Warminster, Wilts* Early Renaissance house. Extensive landscaped park. See Activities. ☎01985 844400 **50 C2**

Lydiard Mansion *Swindon, Swindon* Fine Georgian house in 266 acre parkland. ☎01793 770401 **65 E8**

Lytes Cary Manor (NT) *Somerton, Somerset* Manor house and 14th-century chapel. Formal garden. ☎01985 843600 **47 F1**

Malmesbury House *Salisbury, Wilts* Originally 13th-century canonry. West facade designed by Wren. ☎01722 334414 **51 E8**

Max Gate (NT) *Dorchester, Dorset* Designed by poet and novelist Thomas Hardy. Tours by appointment. ☎01305 262538 **25 B8**

Midelney Manor *Drayton, Somerset* 16th-18th-century manor house. Gardens, walks and heronry. ☎01458 251229 **37 B6**

Milton Abbey *Blandford Forum, Dorset* Georgian Gothic house built on site of former Benedictine abbey. ☎01258 880489 **39 E7**

Mompesson House (NT) *Salisbury, Wilts* Turnbull collection of English 18th-century drinking glasses. Walled garden. ☎01722 335659 **51 E8**

Montacute House (NT) *Montacute, Somerset* Late Elizabethan house. Portraits from National Portrait Gallery. Beautiful gardens. ☎01935 823289 **37 C7**

Mount Edgcumbe *Torpoint, Cornwall* House and furniture restored. Colourful 18th-century gardens. Landscaped park, woodland and coastal walks. ☎01752 822236 **10 D4**

Dyrham Park, South Gloucestershire

Newark Park (NT) *Ozleworth, Glos* Tudor hunting lodge, converted into house by Wyatt. ☎01453 842644 **63 D7**

Overbecks (NT) *Salcombe, Devon* Edwardian house contains local photographs; inventions by Otto Overbeck. Secret room for children. Beautiful garden. ☎01548 842893 **13 E5**

Owlpen Manor *Uley, Glos* Cotswold manor house 15th- 18th centuries. Terraced gardens. ☎01453 860261 **63 C7**

Painswick House *Painswick, Glos* Fine example of Palladian architecture. **70 F3**

Parnham House *Beaminster, Dorset* Fine Tudor manor house. Extensive grounds and gardens. ☎01308 862645 **37 F7**

Pencarrow House *Bodmin, Cornwall* Georgian mansion. ☎01208 841369 **8 B4**

Philipps House (NT) *Dinton, Wilts* Neo-Grecian house completed 1820. Landscaped park . ☎01985 843600 **50 E5**

Powderham Castle *Powderham, Devon* Medieval castle built c1390. Georgian interiors. Gardens. ☎01626 890243 **22 D1**

Priest's House (NT) *Muchelney, Somerset* Late medieval house. Occupied and furnished by tenants. ☎01458 252621 **37 B6**

Pythouse *Tisbury, Wilts* Palladian-style Georgian mansion. ☎01747 870210 **50 F3**

Red Lodge *Bristol, Bristol* Last surviving suite of 16th-century rooms in Bristol. Tudor-style garden. ☎0117 921 1360 **56 B4**

1 Royal Crescent *Bath, Bath & NE S'set* First house to be built here. Fine example of Palladian architecture. ☎01225 428126 **57 C7**

Saltram House (NT) *Plymouth, Devon* Former Tudor mansion. Tree and shrub garden. ☎01752 333500 **10 E5**

Sheldon Manor *nr Chippenham, Wilts* Manor house. 15th-century detached chapel. Terraced gardens. **58 B3**

Sherborne Castle *Sherborne, Dorset* 16th-century house built for Raleigh. Grounds by Capability Brown. ☎01935 813182 **38 C2**

Shute Barton (NT) *Shute, Devon* Important surviving non-fortified manor house from Middle Ages. ☎01297 34692 **23 A7**

Snowshill Manor (NT) *Snowshill, Glos* Tudor manor house with early 18th-century facade. Famous forcollection of musical instruments, clocks and toys. ☎01386 852410 **76 F4**

Stanway House *Stanway, Glos* Jacobean manor house in 20 acres of landscaped grounds. Important 14th-century tithe barn. ☎01386 584469 **71 A7**

Stourhead (NT) *Nr Warminster, Wilts* Built in 1722 and later enlarged. Grounds are famous example of early 18th-century landscape movement. ☎01747 841152 **50 C2**

Sudeley Castle *Winchcombe, Glos* Last home and burial place of Katherine Parr. Art collection, award winning gardens, adventure playground. ☎01242 602308 **71 B6**

Tintinhull House (NT) *nr Yeovil, Somerset* 17th-century house. 4 acres of formal gardens and with orchard. ☎01935 822545 **37 E8**

Tiverton Castle *Tiverton, Devon* Historic castle built 1106. ☎01884 253200 **34 D4**

Torre Abbey Mansion *Torquay, Torbay* Founded in 1196 as a monastery. House built in 18th century. Medieval monastic remains. ☎01803 293593 **15 C6**

Treasurer's House (NT) *Martock, Somerset* Small house dating from 13th and 14th centuries. ☎01985 843600 **37 C7**

Trerice (NT) *Nr Newquay, Cornwall* Small Elizabethan manor house with gabled facade. Pleasant gardens. ☎01637 875404 **7 C7**

Ugbrooke House *Chudleigh, Devon* House and church built c1200. Capability Brown landscaped park . ☎01626 852179 **21 E7**

Watersmeet House (NT) *Lynmouth, Devon* Fishing lodge. ☎01598 753348 **44 B1**

Westwood Manor (NT) *Bradford on Avon, Wilts* 15th-century manor house. ☎01225 863374 **57 D8**

Wilton House *Wilton, Wiltshire* Acres of fine lawns. ☎01722 746720 **51 E6**

Wolfeton House *Dorchester, Dorset* Medieval and Elizabethan house. Cider house. ☎01305 263500 **25 B8**

Castles

Berkeley Castle *Berkeley, Glos* Completed 1153 at command of Henry II. Castle now stately home.Terraced Elizabethan gardens. ☎01453 810332 **63 C5**

Berry Pomeroy Castle (EH) *Totnes, Devon* Combines medieval castle with flamboyant courtier's mansion. ☎01803 866618 **14 C4**

Bickleigh Castle *Tiverton, Devon* 14th-century fortified manor on site of Norman castle. **34 D4**

Carn Brea Castle *Carn Brea, Cornwall* Possibly 15th-century hunting lodge. **4 B1**

Castle Drogo (NT) *Nr Exeter, Devon* Last castle to be built in Britain, now 20th-century home. ☎01647 433186 **21 B8**

Christchurch Castle and Norman House (EH) *Christchurch, Dorset* Built late 11th century. ☎01202 495127 **38 C2**

Corfe Castle (NT) *Wareham, Dorset* Magnificent ruins of 1000-yr-old castle dominate Isle of Purbeck. ☎01929 481294 **27 C5**

Cromwell's Castle (EH) *Tresco, Scilly Isles* 17th-century round tower. **6 A2**

Dartmouth Castle (EH) *Dartmouth, Devon* Defensive castle. ☎01803 833588 **15 E5**

Daws Castle (EH) *Watchet, Somerset* Site of Saxon refuge. **45 C8**

Exeter (Rougemont) Castle *Exeter, Devon* Started in 1068. County Court built on site in 18th century. **21 B8**

Farleigh Castle (EH) *Farleigh Hungerford, Somerset* 14th-century castle with chapel . ☎01225 754026 **57 E8**

Harry's Walls (EH) *St Mary's, I/Scilly* Incomplete 16th-century fort. **6 A3**

King Charles's Castle (EH) *Tresco, I/Scilly* Castle remains. **6 A2**

Launceston Castle (EH) *Launceston, Cornwall* Set on the motte of a Norman castle. ☎01566 772365 **18 D3**

Ludgershall Castle and Cross (EH) *Ludgershall, Wilts* Ruins of early 12th-century royal hunting palace with late-medieval cross. ☎01264 790404 **52 A2**

Lulworth Castle (EH) *Wareham, Dorset* Early 17th-century hunting lodge. 18th-century house in parkland. ☎01929 400352 **27 C5**

Lydford Castle (EH) *Lydford, Devon* Late 12th-century keep with rectangular bailey. Earthworks of original Norman fort are to the south. **19 D7**

Nunney Castle (EH) *Nunney, Somerset* Small castle built 14th-century with moat. **49 B6**

Okehampton Castle (EH) *Okehampton, Devon* Ruins of largest castle in Devon with Norman motte and keep's jagged remains. ☎01837 52844 **20 B1**

Old Wardour Castle (EH) *Tisbury, Wilts* Ruins of 14th-century castle with landscaped grounds. ☎01747 870487 **50 F3**

Pendennis Castle (EH) *Falmouth, Cornwall* End of chain of castles built by Henry VIII along coast. ☎01326 316594 **4 D4**

Portland Castle (EH) *Portland, Somerset* One of best preserved of Henry VIII's coastal forts. ☎01305 820539 **48 D1**

Parnham House, Dorset

Restormel Castle (EH)*Lostwithiel, Cornwall* One of oldest and best Norman motte-and-bailey castles in Cornwall. Founded 1100. ☎01208 872687 **9 D5**

St Catherine's Castle (EH) *Fowey, Cornwall* Small fort built by Henry VIII. **9 E5**

St Mawes Castle (EH) *St Mawes, Cornwall* Built by Henry VIII. Stands in sub-tropical gardens. ☎01326 270526 **4 D4**

St Michael's Mount (NT) *Marazion, Cornwall* Spectacular castle on rocky island dates from 14th century. ☎01736 710507 **3 D7**

Sherborne Old Castle (EH) *Sherborne, Dorset* Ruins of early 12th-century castle. ☎01935 812730 **38 C2**

Sudeley Castle *Winchcombe, Glos* Tudor building once home of Katherine Parr. Royal relics. Fine gardens and wildlife reserve. ☎01242 603197 **71 B6**

Tintagel Castle (EH) *Tintagel, Cornwall* Remains of medieval castle, thought to date from 13th century. Associated with King Arthur. ☎01840 770328 **17 C6**

Totnes Castle (EH) *Totnes, Devon* Superb Norman motte and bailey castle. ☎01803 864406 **14 C4**

Wardour Old Castle *nr Salisbury, Wilts* Hexagonal castle builtin 1392. Partly blown up in Civil War, remains may be seen in Wardour Park. **51 E8**

Nunney Castle, Somerset

Gardens

Many houses and castle listed elsewhere on these page also have fine and important gardens.

Abbotsbury Sub-Tropical Gardens *Abbotsbury, Dorset* Victorian walled gardens in 20 acres of woodland valley. Children's play area. Nature trail. ☎01305 871387 **25 C6**

Aurelia Gardens *nr Ferndown, Dorset* **40 F4**

Barnsley Park *Barnsley, Glos* Herb garden, vegetable garden and fruit trees. ☎01285 740561 **65 A6**

Batsford Park Arboretum *Moreton-in-Marsh, Glos* Established 1880s. Over 50 acres with 1500 different species. Waterfall. ☎01386 701441 **72 A3**

Bennett's Water Gardens *Weymouth, Dorset* 6 acres of ponds, including collection of over 150 types of lilies. ☎01305 785150 **25 E8**

Bicton Gardens *East Budleigh, Devon* Historic gardens. Play areas, museum. Train rides. ☎01395 568465 **22 D3**

Bosvigo House *Truro, Cornwall* Enclosed and walled gardens surrounding Georgian house. ☎01872 275774 **4 B4**

Botanical Gardens *Bath, Bath & NE S'set* Over 5,000 varieties of plants. Rock garden and pond. ☎01225 482624 **57 C7**

Broadleas Gardens Charitable Trust Ltd *Devizes, Wilts* Eight acres of beautiful garden and woodland. ☎01380 722035 **58 D5**

Burncoose Gardens and Nursery *Gwennap, Cornwall* 30 acre woodland garden. ☎01209 860316 **4 B2**

Burrow Farm Gardens *Dalwood, Devon* 7 acre site, part of which created from ancient Roman clay pit. ☎01404 831285 **36 F2**

Caerhays Castle Gardens *St. Austell, Cornwall* Informal woodland garden extending to some 60 acres. ☎01872 501310 **8 E3**

Castle Hill *Filleigh, Devon* Early 18th-century landscaped park and woodland. **43 F8**

Claverton Manor *Claverton, Bath & NE S'set* The grounds of American Museum are copy of George Washington's formal flower garden at Mount Vernon. ☎01225 460503 **57 D7**

Compton Acres Gardens *Canford Cliffs, Dorset* Series of themed gardens over 15 acres of land. ☎01202 700778 **27 C8**

Corfe Castle Model Village and Gardens *Corfe Castle, Dorset* Detailed model of Corfe Castle and village. Old English country garden. ☎01929 480415 **27 D6**

Cothay *nr Wellington, Somerset* Virtually untouched since Edward IV. Small individual gardens. **35 B7**

The Courts (NT) *Holt, Wilts* English garden style at its best. Garden includes topiary, water features. ☎01225 782340 **58 D2**

Cranborne Manor Gardens *Cranborne, Dorset* ☎01725 517248 **40 D3**

Dartington Hall *Dartington, Devon* Large garden of trees and shrubs. ☎01803 862367 **14 C3**

Deans Court Gardens *Wimborne Minster, Dorset* 13 acres of gardens. Peacocks and monastery fish pond. **27 A7**

East Lambrook Manor *South Petherton, Somerset* Notable garden. Many unusual plants. ☎01460 240328 **37 C6**

Escot Country Park and Gardens *Ottery St Mary, Devon* Wild gardens in 250 acres of landscaped parkland. Currently has the only otters in East Devon. Wild boar enclosures and birds of prey. Eight acres of wetlands, adventure playground. ☎01404 822188 **22 A4**

Glendurgan Garden (NT) *Mawnan Smith, Cornwall* One of best sub-tropical gardens of South West. ☎01812 862090 **4 E3**

Hazelbury Manor Gardens *Crewkerne, Somerset* 186 acres of which 8 acres are landscaped gardens. ☎01225 812088 **37 E6**

Hestercombe Gardens *nr Taunton, Somerset* Formal garden. ☎01823 413923 **36 A2**

Hidcote Manor Garden (NT) *Hidcote Bartrim, Glos* Arts and Crafts garden on a hilltop. ☎01386 438333 **77 D6**

Horn Park Gardens *Beaminster, Dorset* ☎01308 862212 **37 F7**

Iford Manor Garden *Frome, Somerset* Italian style manor garden. ☎01225 863146 **49 B7**

Kiftsgate Court Garden *Mickleton, Glos* Rare plant garden. ☎01386 438777 **77 D6**

Knoll Gardens and Nursery *Hampreston, Dorset* A nationally acclaimed modern garden. ☎01202 873931 **27 A8**

Lee Ford *Budleigh Salterton, Devon* 40 acres of parkland, formal and woodland gardens. ☎01395 445894 **22 D3**

Longcross Victorian Garden *Trelights, Cornwall* Victorian garden in 2 1/2 acres. Maze, pet's corner. ☎01208 880243 **16 E4**

Lost Gardens of Heligan *Pentewan, Cornwall* Over 80 acres including kitchen garden, fruit houses. ☎01726 845100 **8 F3**

Luckington Court *Luckington, Wilts* Three acre garden with ornamental trees and shrubs. ☎01666 840205 **63 F8**

Lydney Park *Lydney, Glos* Extensive gardens. Roman temple site and museum. ☎01594 842027 **62 B4**

Mapperton Gardens *Beaminster, Dorset* Terraced hillside gardens with ancient fishponds and summerhouse. ☎01308 862645 **37 F7**

Marwood Hill *Marwood, Devon* 18 acre garden, bog garden. ☎01271 342528 **43 D5**

Minterne Gardens *Minterne Magna, Dorset* Large shrub garden. Fine Japanese cherry display in spring. ☎01300 341370 **38 F3**

Miserden Park Gardens and Plant Centre *Miserden, Glos* Well established garden. Topiary. ☎01285 821303 **70 F4**

Moreton Gardens *Moreton, Dorset* 3.5-acre landscaped garden, Lawrence of Arabia is buried nearby. ☎01929 405084 **26 C3**

Painswick Rococo Garden *Painswick, Glos* Ponds, woodland walks, maze, kitchen garden. ☎01452 813204 **70 F3**

Pine Lodge Gardens and Nursery *St Austell, Cornwall* 30 acres with over 6,000 plants. ☎01726 73500 **8 E3**

Prideaux Place *Padstow, Cornwall* Deer park and restored garden ☎01841 532411 **16 E3**

Prior Park Landscape (NT) *Bath, Bath & NE S'set* Beautiful and intimate 18th-century landscaped garden. ☎01225 833422 **57 C7**

Royal Horticultural Society's Rosemoor Garden Great *Torrington, Devon* ☎01805 624067 **32 C2**

Stapehill Abbey Gardens *Stapehill, Dorset* Award winning gardens in grounds of restored monastery. ☎01202 861686 **40 F4**

Stone Lane Gardens *Chagford, Devon* 5-acre landscaped arboretum and water garden. ☎01647 231311 **20 C4**

Stourton House Flower Garden *Stourton, Wilts* Over 4 acres of flower gardens. ☎01747 840417 **49 E7**

Trebah Garden *Mawnan Smith, Cornwall* 25 acre wooded ravine garden in grounds to private beach. ☎01326 250448 **4 E3**

Trelissick Garden (NT) *nr Truro, Cornwall* Artistically planted garden and orchard. ☎01872 862090 **4 B4**

Trengwainton Garden (NT) *Penzance, Cornwall* Shrub and woodland garden. ☎01736 363021 **3 D5**

Tresco Abbey Gardens *Tresco, I/Scilly* Sub-tropical gardens and remains of Benedictine priory. ☎01720 424105 **A2**

Trerice (NT) *Nr Newquay, Cornwall* Summer garden, orchard. ☎01637 875404 **7 C7**

Westbury Court (NT) *Westbury-on-Severn, Glos* Formal water garden with canals and yew hedges. ☎01452 760461 **69 E8**

Westonbirt Arboretum *Westonbirt, Glos* 600 acres. ☎01666 880220 **64 E2**

Historic Buildings

Agincourt House *Dartmouth, Devon* Restored 14th-century merchants house. ☎01804 32472 **15 E5**

Arlington Mill *Bibury, Glos* Wool and corn mill, now a museum. **65 A7**

Ashleworth Tithe Barn (NT) *Ashleworth, Glos* Stone-tiled 15th-century tithe barn. ☎01684 855300 **70 B2**

Assembly Rooms (NT) *Bath, Bath & NE S'set* Designed by John Wood the Younger 1769. ☎01225 477789 **57 C7**

Barton Tithe Barn (EH) *Bradford on Avon, Wilts* Medieval stone-built barn. **57 D8**

Bayard's Cove Fort (EH) *Dartmouth, Devon* A small artillery fort built c1534. **15 E5**

Beckford's Tower *Bath, Bath & NE S'set* Built 1827 now museum. Spiral staircase and panoramic view ☎01225 422212 **57 C7**

Blaise Hamlet (NT) *Henbury, Bristol* Picturesque cottages. ☎01985 843600 **56 A3**

Branscombe Old Bakery, Manor Mill and Forge (NT) *Seaton, Cornwall* ☎01297 680333 (OB), 01392 881691 (MM), 01297 680481 (F). **10 E2**

Chipping Campden Market Hall *Chipping Campden, Glos* Built 1627. **77 E6**

Clifton Observatory *Clifton, Bristol* Former snuff mill now with camera obscura. **56 B3**

Cornish Mines and Engine houses (NT) *Pool, Cornwall* Two great beam engines. ☎01209 315027 **4 B1**

Customs House *Exeter, Devon* 1680-81, oldest surviving substantial brick building in Exeter. ☎01643 821759 **21 B8**

Dunster Working Watermill (NT) *Dunster, Somerset* 18th century. **45 C6**

Dupath Holy Well (EH) *Callington, Cornwall* c1500 and almost complete. **10 B3**

Cotehele House Gardens, Cornwall

Exeter Guildhall *Exeter, Devon* 16th-century oak roof. ☎01392 665500 **21 B8**

Gallox Bridge (EH) *Dunster, Somerset* Stone packhorse bridge. **45 C6**

Glastonbury Tribunal (EH)*Glastonbury, Somerset* Well-preserved medieval town house. ☎01458 832954 **48 D2**

Greenway (NT) *Galmpton, Devon* Estate on banks of River Dart. ☎01803 842382 **12 D4**

Guildhall *Bath, Bath & NE S'set* 18th century. ☎01225 477724 **57 C7**

Little Fleece Bookshop (NT) *Painswick, Glos* 17th-century building, restored in 'Arts & Crafts' style 1935. Now bookshop. ☎01452 812103 **70 F3**

Loughwood Meeting House (NT) *Dalwood, Devon* c1653. ☎01392 881691 **36 F2**

Marker's Cottage (NT) *Exeter, Devon* Medieval cob house. ☎01392 461546 **21 B8**

Newhall Equestrian Centre (NT) *Broadclyst, Devon* Traditional farm-buildings. ☎01392 462453 **22 B1**

The North Canonry *Salisbury, Wilts* Largest Tudor domestic building in city. ☎01722 555121/0/3 **51 E8**

Nothe Fort *Weymouth, Dorset* Restored Victorian fort with ramparts and gun decks. ☎01305 766626 **25 E8**

Pittville Pump Room *Cheltenham, Glos* Built between 1825 and 1830. Spa waters still available. ☎01242 523852 **71 C5**

Prysten House *Plymouth, Devon* 15th-century priest's house. ☎01752 661414 **10 E5**

Robert Raikes House *Gloucester, Glos* Home of founder of Sunday School. **70 D2**

Roman Baths and Pump Room *Bath, Bath & NE S'set* Baths are fed by only hot springs in Britain. The Pump Room is 18th-century. ☎01225 477785 **57 C7**

Royal Citadel (EH) *Plymouth, Devon* 17th-century fortress. ☎01752 775841 **10 E5**

Stembridge Tower Mill (NT) *High Ham, Somerset* Last thatched windmill in England. ☎01458 250818 **47 E8**

Temple Church (EH) *Bristol, Bristol* Tower and walls are 15th-century. **56 B4**

Thomas Chatterton's house *Bristol, Bristol* Home of 18th-Century poet. **56 B4**

Tintagel Old Post Office (NT) *Tintagel, Cornwall* 14th-century stone house with thick slate roof. ☎01840 770024 **17 C6**

Totnes Guildhall *Totnes, Devon* Part of Benedictine priory. ☎01803 862147 **14 C4**

Treasurer's House (NT) *Martock, Somerset* c13th century. ☎01935 843600 **37 C7**

Wesley's Cottage *Trewint, Cornwall* 18th-century cottage, Wesley stayed and preached here. ☎01566 86158 **10 C1**

Westbury College Gatehouse (NT) *Westbury on Trym, Bristol* 15th-century gatehouse. ☎01985 843600 **56 A3**

West Pennard Court Barn (NT) *Nr Glastonbury, Somerset* 15th-century barn. ☎01985 843600 **48 D2**

White Mill (NT) *Sturminster Marshall, Dorset* Rebuilt in 1776. ☎01258 858051 **27 A6**

Woolstaplers Hall *Chipping Campden, Glos* Built 1340. Now museum. **77 E6**

Yarn Market (EH) *Dunster, Somerset* A 17th-century octagonal market hall. **45 C6**

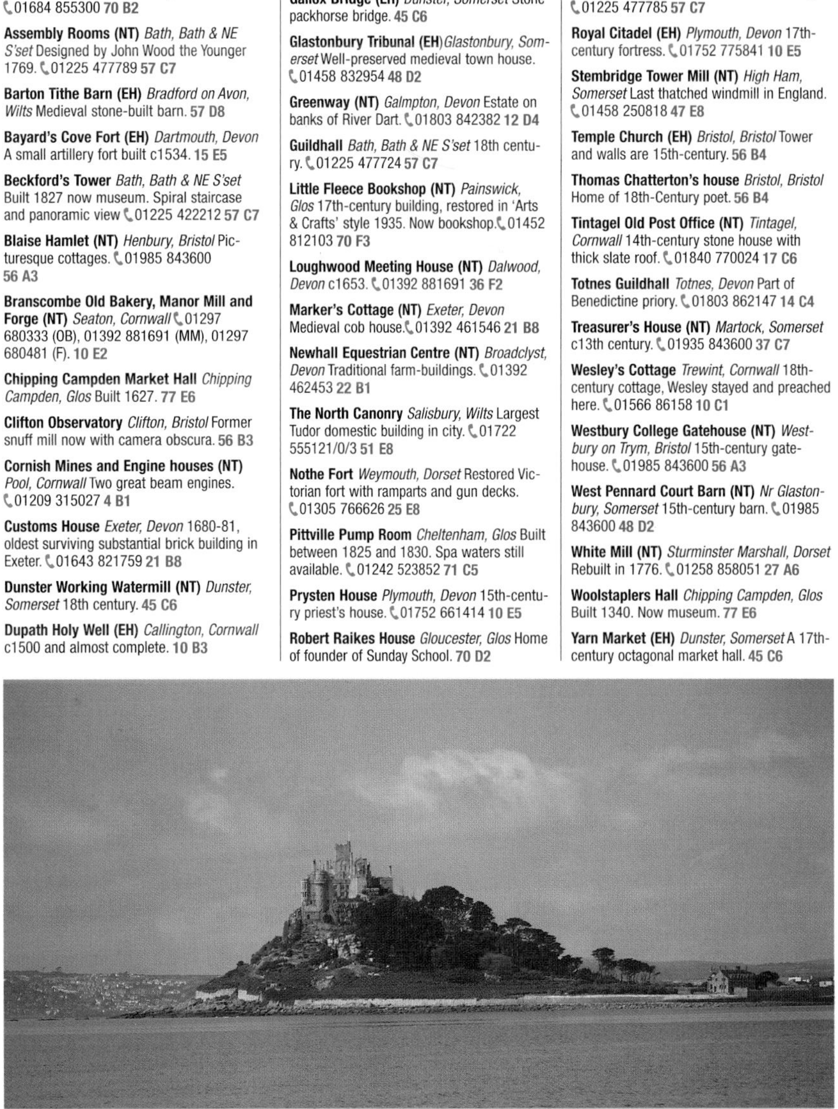

St Michael's Mount, Cornwall

Museums and galleries

Alexander Keilor Museum *Avebury, Wilts* Collection of important local prehistoric material. ☎01672 539250 **59 C7**

American Museum in Britain *Claverton, Bath & NE S'set* In Claverton Manor. Development of North American decorative arts. Native American and folk art. See Gardens ☎01225 460503 **57 D7**

Arnolfini Arts Centre *Bristol, Bristol* Visual arts centre. ☎0117 9299191 **56 B4**

Atwell-Wilson Motor Museum Trust *Calne, Wilts* Vintage and classic cars. Classic motorbikes. ☎01249 813119 **58 B5**

Automobilia *St Stephen, Cornwall* Over 50 vehicles dating from 1904 to 1960s. Automobilia . ☎01726 823092 **8 E1**

Barbara Hepworth Museum and Sculpture Garden *St Ives, Cornwall* Sculptures in bronze, stone and wood, paintings and drawings. Studio and garden run by Tate Gallery. ☎01736 796226 **3 B6**

Bath Postal Museum *Bath, Bath & NE S'set* 4,000 years of communication from Sumarian clay tablets to the present day. ☎01225 460333 **57 C7**

Bath Royal Literary and Scientific Institution *Bath, Bath & NE S'set* Geology, natural history, ethnology, archaeology, art and history artefacts. ☎01225 312084 **57 C7**

Big Four Railway Museum *Bournemouth, Bournemouth* Collection of railway items and working model railway ☎ **28 B1**

Bill Douglas Centre *Exeter, Devon* History of cinema. ☎01392 264321 **21 B8**

Blandford Museum *Blandford Forum, Dorset* History of Blandford Forum and neighbouring villages. ☎01258 450388 **39 E7**

Bournemouth Aviation Museum *Christchurch, Dorset* Comprehensive display of aircraft models. ☎01202 580858 **28 B3**

British Cycling Museum *Camelford, Cornwall* History of cycles and cycling memorabilia from 1818. ☎01840 212811 **17 D7**

British Empire and Commonwealth Museum *Bristol, Bristol* ☎0117 9254983 **56 B4**

British Photographic Museum, Bowden House *Totnes, Devon* ☎01803 863664 **14 C4**

Bristol Industrial Museum *Bristol, Bristol* Vehicles, shunting engine and Fairbairn steam crane. Bristol Harbour Railway; steam tug 'Mayflower' and other boats. New exhibition about the Bristol Slave Trade. ☎0117 9251470 **56 B4**

Building of Bath Museum *Bath, Bath & NE S'set* History of transformation of Bath from small provincial spa, into Georgian splendour. ☎01225 333895 **57 C7**

Burrows Toy Museum *Bath, Bath & NE S'set* Dolls, toys, books and games ☎ **57 C7**

Cavalcade of Costume Museum *Blandford Forum, Dorset* Historical costumes covering a 250 year period. ☎01258 453006 **39 E7**

Camborne School of Mines *Redruth, Cornwall* Local geological collection of minerals and ores. Art exhibition featuring the works of local artists. ☎01209 714866 **4 B2**

Cheltenham Art Gallery and Museum *Cheltenham, Glos* Nationally important Art and Crafts movement collection; furniture, paintings, ceramics, jewellery and local history. ☎01242 237431 **71 C5**

City Museum and Art Gallery *Bristol, Bristol* Art and archaeology, geology and natural history, housed in a magnificent early 20th-century building. ☎0117 9223571 **56 B4**

City Museum and Art Gallery *Gloucester, Glos* Local history and small collection of British paintings.☎01452 524131 **70 D2**

City Museum and Art Gallery *Plymouth, Devon* Paintings, ceramics, archaeology, natural history. **10 E5**

Cobbaton Combat Collection *Cobbaton, Devon* World War II British and Canadian military equipment. ☎01769 540740 **43 F7**

Coldharbour Mill Museum *Uffculme, Devon* Displays of Victorian spinning, carding and weaving machines. ☎01884 840960 **35 D6**

Combe Martin Motorcycle Collection *Combe Martin, Devon* Over 60 motorcycles, scooters and carriages. ☎01271 882346 **43 B6**

Corinium Museum *Cirencester, Glos* Extensive collection of Romano-British antiquities from Corinium. ☎01285 655611 **65 B5**

Cotswold Motoring Museum and Toy Collection *Cheltenham, Glos* Thirty cars and motorcycles on display with a selection of prams, toys and pedal cars. Over 800 vintage advertising signs. Also Toy collection. ☎01451 821255 **71 C5**

County Museum and Art Gallery *Truro, Cornwall* Local painters, small selection of English pictures and a number of continental works, chiefly late 14th-century Italian. **4 B4**

Morwellham Quays, Devon

Dartington Glass Centre *Great Torrington, Devon* Tours of the factory, displays of glass making techniques. Exhibition on history of glass. ☎01805 22321 **32 C2**

Dartmouth Museum *Dartmouth, Devon* Historic and maritime museum in former merchant's house 1640. ☎01803 832923 **15 E5**

Dinosaur Museum *Dorchester, Dorset* Fossils, skeletons, reconstructions, interactive computer displays and videos. ☎01305 269880 **25 B8**

Dorset County Museum *Dorchester, Dorset* Local wildlife, rocks, fossils, archaeology and displays on Dorset writers. ☎01305 262735 **25 B8**

Dorset Military Museum *Dorchester, Dorset* Modern military museum with creative displays. ☎01305 264066 **25 B8**

Duke of Cornwall's Light Infantry Regiment *Bodmin, Cornwall* History of Cornwall's county regiment from 1702-1959. ☎01208 72810 **8 B4**

Exeter Maritime Museum *Exeter, Devon* One of the largest collections of old working boats in the world. **21 B8**

Fleet Air Arm Museum *RNAS Yeovilton, Somerset* Over 40 aircraft and many models and equipment. ☎01935 840565 **37 B8**

Geevor Tin Mine Museum *Trewellard, Cornwall* Heritage centre. Tells story of production of tin and of miners. ☎01736 788662 **2 D3**

Gloucester Folk Museum *Gloucester, Glos* Local history exhibits, including stake at which Bishop Hooper allegedly burned. ☎01452 396467 **70 D2**

Gloucester Museum and Art Gallery *Gloucester, Glos* Archaeology, geology, natural history ☎ **70 D2**

Great Western Railway Museum *Swindon, Wilts* Collection of famous GWR locomotives. ☎01793 466646 **65 E8**

Haynes Motor Museum *Yeovil, Somerset* Britain's largest collection of automobilia. ☎01963 440804 **37 C9**

The Helicopter Museum *Weston-Super-Mare, N Somerset* Examples from around the world with displays. ☎01934 635227 **55 D6**

Holburne Museum of Art *Bath, Bath & NE S'set* 17th/18th century fine and decorative art. Old Masters including Gainsborough, Stubbs, Turner. ☎01225 466669 **57 C7**

Holst Birthplace Museum *Cheltenham, Glos* Original piano and manuscripts. ☎01242 524846 **71 C5**

Impossible Microworld of Willard Wigan *Bath, Bath & NE S'set* Gallery of micro sculptures with award winning viewing stations. Sculptures include Statue of Libery in the eye of a needle. ☎01225 333003 **57 C7**

Isles of Scilly Museum *St Mary's, I/Scilly* Geology, archaeology, history and natural history. ☎01720 422337 **6 A3**

Jenner Museum *Berkeley, Glos* Georgian house and gardens. Home of Dr Edward Jenner, smallpox vaccination pioneer. ☎01453 810631 **63 C5**

Kathleen and May *Plymouth, Devon* Last of the west country's wooden trading schooners, now museum. **10 E5**

The Keep Military Museum *Dorchester, Dorset* History of infantry, cavalry and artillerymen of the counties of Devon and Dorset. ☎01305 264066 **25 B8**

The Kennet and Somerset Canal Museum *Devizes, Wilts* ☎01380 721279 **58 D5**

Longstone Heritage Centre *St Mary's, I/Scilly* History of Isles from prehistoric times. Also 'Papers Past at Longstone' - displays of original newspapers, c1793 onwards, including special birthpapers to buy. ☎01720 422924 **6 A3**

Lyme Regis Museum *Lyme Regis, Dorset* Winner of Museum of South-west prize and Gulbenkian Prize. ☎01297 443370 **24 B1**

Camborne Tin Mines,

Maritime Museum *Appledore, Devon* North Devon's maritime history illustrated by models, photographs etc ☎01237 422064 **35 D6**

Morwellham Quays *Tavistock, Devon* See Activities. ☎01822 832766 **19 F6**

Museum of Books *Bath, Bath & NE S'set* Exhibition of first and early editions of Bath authors. Includes Charles Dickens and Jane Austen. ☎01225 466000 **57 C7**

Museum of Costume *Bath, Bath & NE S'set* More than 150 complete outfits on display. ☎01225 477785 **57 C7**

Museum of East Asian Art *Bath, Bath & NE S'set* 5 galleries and over 500 art treasures from East Asia. ☎01225 464640 **57 C7**

Museum of Smuggling *Polperro, Cornwall* Exhibits and photographs dating from 18th century ☎01503 273005 **9 E7**

National Waterways Museum *Gloucester Docks, Glos* Located in listed Victorian warehouse. ☎01452 318054 **70 D2**

National Maritime Museum Cornwall *Penzance, Cornwall* Launched June 2002. National small boat collection, galleries, remote-controlled models, live demonstrations. ☎01326 313388 **3 D5**

Nature in Art *Twigworth, Glos* Located in Wallsworth Hall. Museum dedicated to art inspired by nature. ☎01452 731422 **70 C2**

Newlyn Art Gallery *Newlyn, Cornwall* Changing exhibitions of contemporary art by leading artists. ☎01736 363715 **2 E5**

Paul Corin's Magnificent Music Machines *St Keyne, Cornwall* Includes cafe organ, player pianos, American Wurlitzer theatre pipe organ. ☎01579 343108 **9 C7**

Priest's House Museum *Wimborne Minster, Dorset* Award winning museum in Elizabethan Town House. ☎01202 882533 **27 A7**

RAC Tank Museum *Wareham, Dorset* WWI walk-through trench experience. Vehicle collection. ☎01929 405096 **27 C5**

Robert Opie Collection at Museum of Advertising and Packaging. *Gloucester, Glos* World's largest collection of British advertising images. ☎01452 302309 **70 D2**

Roman Baths Museum *Bath, Bath & NE S'set* Roman temple and bathing complex. ☎01225 477785 **57 C7**

Royal Cornwall Museum *Truro, Cornwall* World-famous mineral collection, Old Master drawings, archaeology, paintings by Newlyn School. ☎01872 272205 **4 B4**

The Royal Gloucestershire, Berkshire and Wiltshire Regiment Museum *Salisbury, Wilts* Collections include medals, uniforms, and militaria. ☎01722 414536 **51 E8**

Royal Photographic Society *Bath, Bath & NE S'set* 18th-century chapel. Gallery and museum. ☎01225 462841 **57 C7**

Royal Signals Museum *Blandford Camp, Dorset* Displays include ENIGMA, Special Operations Executive, SAS. Many displays for children. ☎01258 482248 **39 E8**

Russel-Cotes Art Gallery and Museum *Bournemouth, Bournemouth* Victorian art collection, Japanese art and artefacts, contemporary art. ☎01202 451800 **28 B1**

Salisbury and South Wiltshire Museum *Salisbury, Wilts* Includes Stonehenge, settlers from Stone Age to Saxons, Old Sarum and Salisbury, Wedgwood, pre-NHS surgery, costumes. ☎01722 332151 **51 E8**

Shipwreck and Heritage Centre *Charlestown, Cornwall* Houses largest shipwreck artefact collection in UK. ☎01726 69897 **8 E3**

Soldiers of Gloucestershire Museum *Gloucester Docks, Glos* ☎01452 522082 **70 D2**

Somerset Cricket Museum *Taunton, Somerset* Historic barn containing cricket memorabilia. ☎01823 275893 **36 A2**

Tate St Ives *St Ives, Cornwall* Over 200 works of modern art as well as special exhibitions from the other Tate galleries. ☎01736 796226 **3 B6**

Tolpuddle Martyrs Museum *Tolpuddle, Dorset* Story of the six workers transported to Australia in 1834 as punishment for forming a trade union. ☎01305 848237 **26 B2**

Totnes Motor Museum *Totnes, Devon* Vintage sports cars, racing cars, trophies and toy cars. ☎01803 862777 **14 C4**

TV, Radio and Memorabilia Musuem *Montacute, Somerset* Vintage to modern day radios; film, TV and children's books and toys; televisions, household appliances; advertising signs and packaging. ☎01935 823024 **37 C7**

Victoria Art Gallery *Bath, Bath & NE S'set* Paintings, drawings etc. Artists include Gainsborough, Turner, and Sickert. ☎01225 477233 **57 C7**

Wellington Aviation Museum *Moreton-in-Marsh, Glos* ☎01608 650323 **72 A3**

Chalk Horses

Chalk horses are a well-known feature of the south-western landscape. The list here names them and gives the dates they were created.

Alton Barnes	1812
Hackpen Hill	1838
Broad Town	1863
Cherhill	1780
Marlborough	1873
Pewsey	1937
Devizes	1999

Fleet Air Arm Museum, Yeovilton

Activities

Listed here is a wide range of selected activities for both children and adults – and many are suitable for both. Some do not need advance booking, but it is always best to telephone first to check both availability and opening times.

Animals

AQUARIA

Aqualand *Torquay, Torbay* Local and exotic-marine life. ☎01803 294439 **15 C6**

Blue Reef Aquarium *Newquay, Cornwall* Undersea safari. ☎01637 878134 **7 C7**

Bristol Zoo Aquarium *Bristol, Bristol* Variety of species, Large landscaped displays from around the world. ☎01179 738951 **56 B4**

Brixham Sea Aquarium *Brixham, Torbay* ☎01803 882204 **15 D6**

Lyme Regis Marine Aquarium & Cobb History *Lyme Regis, Dorset* Dorset's waters. ☎01297 444230 **24 B1**

Mevagissey Aquarium *Mevagissey, Cornwall* Displays of the fish found in local waters. ☎01726 843305 **5 B8**

National Marine Aquarium *Plymouth, Devon* Sharks, seahorses, deep reef displays etc. ☎01752 600301 **10 E5**

Oceanarium *Bournemouth, Bournemouth* Ocean displays of climates and wildlife from around the world. ☎01202 311993 **28 B1**

Penzance Aquarium *Penzance, Cornwall* ☎01736 64857 **3 D5**

Plymouth Aquarium *Plymouth, Devon* ☎01752 633333 **10 E5**

Poole Aquarium & Serpentarium *Poole, Poole* Houses sharks, piranhas, freshwater and marine species. Serpentarium - one of few places in country licensed to keep venomous snakes. Crocodile pool and Insectarium. ☎01202 686712 **27 B7**

Sea Discovery Centre *Axmouth, Devon* ☎01297 24774 **23 B7**

Sealife Aquarium *Newquay, Cornwall* Over 30 displays. Sea horse feeding and demonstrations. ☎01637 878134 **7 C7**

Sealife Centre *Newquay, Cornwall* Home to over 3,000 creatures. Over 30 displays, special touch pools. ☎01637 872822 **7 C7**

Seashore Centre *Goodrington, Torbay* Walk-in rock-pools etc ☎01803 528841 **15 D5**

Taunton Aquarium Centre *Taunton, Somerset* ☎01823 350169 **36 A2**

Wembury Marine Centre *Wembury, Devon* Interactive displays of rock pools and Devon's sea. ☎01752 862538 **11 F6**

Weston-super-Mare Sea Life Centre *Weston-super-Mare, N Somerset* ☎01934 613361 **55 D6**

Weymouth Sea Life Park *Weymouth, Dorset* Seal sanctuary, tropical shark nursery, blue-whale splash pool, stingrays, and otters' centre. ☎01305 788255 **25 E8**

BIRDS

Abbotsbury Swannery *Abbotsbury, Dorset* World famous swan sanctuary. ☎01305 871858 **25 C6**

Birdland Park & Gardens *Bourton-on-the-Water, Glos* Seven acres inhabited by over 500 birds, flamingos, pelicans and penguins. Also tropical, temperate and desert houses. ☎01451 820480 **72 C2**

Cotswold Falconry Centre *Moreton-in-Marsh, Glos* Breeding and conservation. Eagles, hawks, owls and falcons. ☎01386 701043 **72 A3**

Exmoor Falconry and Animal Farm *Allerford, Somerset* Animal handling, flying displays, falconry days, and riding. ☎01643 862816 **45 B5**

Folly Farm Waterfowl *nr Bourton-On-the-Water, Glos* Also farm animals, llamas and rheas. ☎01451 820940 **72 C2**

National Birds of Prey Centre *Newent, Glos* Over 110 aviaries with 85 species. World's leader in captive breeding. ☎01531 820286 **69 B8**

Paradise Park *Hayle, Cornwall* Collection of rare birds. ☎01736 753365 **3 C7**

Prinknash Bird and Deer Park *Cranham, Glos* Unusual birds from all over the world. Other animals, such as deer and African Pygmy Goats. ☎01452 812727 **70 E3**

Rode Bird Gardens *Rode, Somerset* 17 acres of gardens with 1200 birds, 200 species. Children's play area. ☎01373 830326 **58 F8**

Screech Owl Sanctuary *Nr Newquay, Cornwall* Care and rehabilitation for sick and injured owls. ☎01726 860182 **7 C7**

Wildfowl and Wetlands Centre *Slimbridge, Glos* World's largest collection of exotic, rare and endangered wildfowl. Also Hanson's Discovery Centre, Cheng-Kim Loke Wildlife Art Gallery, Tropical House and Sustainable Garden. ☎01453 890333 **63 B6**

OPEN FARMS AND PETTING ZOOS

Animal Farm Adventure Park *Burnham on Sea, Somerset* Farm animals and pets corner. Play areas. ☎01278 751628 **47 B6**

Bibury Trout Farm *Bibury, Glos* Working trout farm.'Catch your own' fishery, plant sales. ☎01285 740215 **65 A7**

Big Sheep *Bideford, Devon* Farm based attraction with indoor play area. ☎01237 472366 **42 F3**

Bush Farm Bison Centre *West Knoyle, Wilts* Herds of bison, wapiti and red deer. Gallery of North American wildlife and artefacts. ☎01747 830263 **50 E2**

Butts Farm Rare Farm Animals *South Cerney, Glos* A working farmstead with a wide variety of animals. Petting and feeding. ☎01285 862205 **65 C5**

Canonteign Falls and Farm Park *Nr Chudleigh, Devon* England's highest natural waterfall. Wildlife and woodland nature reserve. ☎01647 252434 **21 E7**

The Cheese Farm *Upton Cross, Cornwall* Milking, calf-rearing and farmyard activities; cheese-making; animal park and nature walk; museum. ☎01579 362244 **9 A8**

Cholderton Rare Breeds Farm Park *Salisbury, Wilts* Winner of the 'Best Family Attraction in Wiltshire' award in 1998 and 2000. ☎01980 629438 **51 E8**

Cotswold Farm Park *Cheltenham, Glos* Rare breeds conservation. Adventure playground, pets corner. ☎01451 850307 **71 C5**

Court Farm Country Park *Banwell, N Somerset* 25,000 sq ft indoor play areas, animals. ☎01934 822383 **55 E8**

DairyLand Farm World *Newquay, Cornwall* Winner of 4 national awards. Real working farm. Adventure playground, milking parlour, horse-rides and nature trails. ☎01872 510246 **7 C7**

Farmer Giles Farmstead *Teffont, Wilts* Working dairy farm. Pets' corner and adventure play area. ☎01722 716338 **50 E4**

Farmer Palmer's Farm Park *Organford, Dorset* Feeding, milking demonstrations. Tractor-trailer ride. Indoor and outdoor play areas. ☎01202 622022 **27 B5**

Ferne Animal Sanctuary *Chard, Somerset* Home to 300 abandoned animals, set in 50 acres of countryside. ☎01460 65214 **36 E4**

Folly Acres *Stroud, Glos* Working farm, Rural Conservation area. ☎01453 766822 **64 A2**

Folly Farm Waterfowl *nr Bourton-On-the-Water, Glos* Waterfowl, farm animals, llamas and rheas. ☎01451 820940 **72 C2**

Heaven's Gate Farm Animal Rescue Centre *nr Langport, Somerset* Rehoming centre for variety of animals and fowl. ☎01458 252656 **47 F8**

Home Farm *Minehead, Somerset* Small livestock farm. ☎01984 640817 **45 B6**

Miniature Pony and Animal Farm *Moretonhampstead, Devon* Animals and adventure play area. ☎01647 432400 **20 C5**

National Animal Welfare Trust, Heavens Gate Farm *Nr Langport, Somerset* Rescue and re-homing centre for domestic and farm animals. ☎01458 252656 **47 F8**

New House Farm *Beaminster, Dorset* Llama Trekking. ☎01308 868674 **37 F7**

North Devon Farm Park *Barnstaple, Devon* 15th-century farm house. Farm park and rare breeds centre. ☎01271 830255 **43 E6**

Pennywell Farm & Wildlife Centre *Buckfastleigh, Devon* Shire horses, falconry displays, pets corner and play areas. ☎01364 642023 **14 B2**

Porfell Animal Land *Nr Lanreath, Cornwall* Wild and domestic animals in natural environments. ☎01503 220211 **9 D6**

Putlake Adventure Farm *Langton Matravers, Dorset* Bottle feed lambs. Picnic and play areas, farm trail, pony rides and trailer rides. Barn owls and ferret racing. ☎01929 422917 **27 E6**

Quince Honey Farm *South Molton, Devon* Watch honey bees at work through glass booths. ☎01769 572401 **33 A7**

Rode Bird Gardens, Somerset

Roves Farm Visitors Centre *Swindon, Glos* Bottle feed and see a variety of farm animals. ☎01793 763939 **70 B4**

Skinners Ash Farm *Honiton, Devon* Pony rides, rare breeds, pets' area. Wild birds and hatcheries. ☎01404 850231 **35 F7**

Sorley Tunnel *Kingsbridge, Devon* Farm animals and pets' corner, play area and pony rides. ☎01548 85771 **13 D5**

South West Hedgehog Hospital *Newton Abbot, Devon* 01626 62319 ☎ **15 A5**

Tamar Valley Donkey Park *Gunnislake, Cornwall* Children's Centre; petting area and donkey rides. ☎01822 834072 **10 A4**

Tithe Barn Children's Farm *Dorchester, Dorset* Ancient barn and children's farm animal petting area ☎01305 871817 **25 B8**

Trenouth Farm and Rare Breeds Centre *Wadebridge, Cornwall* Animals, virtual climbing wall, roller blading, crazy golf, pony rides, soft play area, ten pin bowling, shire horse rides, golf course. ☎01841 540606 **8 A2**

Trethorne Leisure Farm *Launceston, Cornwall* Massive indoor play area, ten pin bowling, rare breeds. ☎01566 86324 **18 D3**

Woodland Leisure Park *Totnes, Devon* Biggest indoor adventure centre in the UK. 5 floors, 3 watercoasters, arctic sledges etc. Falconry centre, hundreds of animals and birds. ☎01803 712598 **14 C4**

The World of Country Life *Exmouth, Devon* Falconry displays, deer park safari. Farm centre, petting area and nursery. Historical exhibits. ☎01395 274533 **22 D2**

HORSES

There are numerous stables and riding schools located throughout the south-west. Consult local directories or information centres.

Horse World *Bristol, Bristol* Equine rescue centre. ☎01275 540173 **56 B4**

National Shire Horse Centre *Yealmpton, Devon* More than 40 shire horses on 60 acre farm. Butterfly house, pet's area and adventure playground. ☎01752 880268 **11 E7**

Shires Family Adventure Park *Wadebridge, Cornwall* Shire horse centre and family adventure park. ☎01841 541215 **8 A2**

Shire Horse Farm and Carriage Museum *Treskillard, Cornwall* All 3 breeds of heavy English horses. Over 40 horse-drawn vehicles. ☎01209 713606 **4 C1**

Springfields Fun Park & Pony Centre *Nr Newquay, Cornwall* Large all weather family fun centre. Pony rides and farm animals. ☎01637 881224 **7 C7**

Tamar Valley Donkey Park *Gunnislake, Cornwall* ☎01822 834072 **10 A4**

ZOOS AND WILDLIFE PARKS

Alstone Wildlife Park *Highbridge, Somerset* ☎01278 782405 **47 B6**

Bristol Zoo Gardens *Bristol, Bristol* ☎0117 9738951 **56 B4**

Buckfast Butterfly Farm and Dartmoor Otter Sanctuary *Buckfastleigh, Devon* Tropical garden housing exotic butterflies and moths. Large landscaped otter enclosures. ☎01364 642916 **14 B2**

Combe Martin Wildlife & Dinosaur Park *Ilfracombe, Devon* Safari park. 20 acres home to otters, gibbons etc. Life-size dinosaur models including a 22 ft Tyrannosaurus Rex. ☎01271 882486 **42 B5**

Cricket St Thomas Wildlife Park *Chard, Somerset* Famous country estate where animals and birds live naturally. Safari trains and walks. ☎01460 30111 **36 E4**

Dartmoor Wildlife Park *Plymouth, Devon* Over 1000 creatures in 30 acres Devonshire countryside. ☎01752 837645 **10 E5**

Exmoor Wildlife Park *Bratton Fleming, Devon* 170 species. ☎01598 763352 **43 D7**

International Animal Rescue *Ash Mill, Devon* 60 acre animal sanctuary with a wide range of rescued animals. Rare plant nursery. ☎01769 550277 **33 B8**

Jungleland *Barnstaple, Devon* Chipmunks, terrapins, birds and fish in exotic settings under cover. ☎01271 343884 **43 E6**

Kingston Maurward Gardens and Animal Park *Dorchester, Dorset* Children can feed unusual animals. ☎01305 215003 **25 B8**

Longleat *Warminster, Wilts* Safari park. Adventure castle, King Arthur's Mirror Maze, safari boats, Longleat railways, butterfly gardens, world's longest hedge maze and pet's corner. ☎01985 844400 **50 C2**

Monkey Sanctuary *Looe, Cornwall* ☎01503 262532 **9 E8**

Monkey World Ape Rescue Centre *Wareham, Dorset* ☎01929 462537 **27 C5**

National Seal Sanctuary *Gweek, Cornwall* Britain's largest seal rescue facility. ☎01326 221361 **4 E2**

Newquay Zoo *Newquay, Cornwall* Feedings and displays. ☎01637 873342 **7 C7**

Paignton Zoo and Environmental Park *Paignton, Devon* One of England's largest zoos with more than 1,300 animals, and more than 300 species within 75 acres. ☎01803 527936 **15 C5**

Secret World Badger & Wildlife Reserve Centre *East Huntspill, Somerset* ☎01278 783250 **47 C6**

Shaldon Wildlife Trust *Shaldon, Devon* Many rare and endangered species. ☎01626 872234 **15 A6**

Tamar Otter Sanctuary *Launceston, Cornwall* ☎01986 893470 **18 D3**

Tropiquaria *Minehead, Somerset* Indoor tropical rainforests. Exotic creatures. Farm animals, pirate ship adventure playground, trampolines etc. ☎01984 640688 **45 B6**

Westbury Wildlife Park *Bristol, Bristol* ☎0117 9500439 **56 B4**

Worldlife and Lullingstone Silk Farm *Sherborne, Dorset* Conservation and environmental displays. Tropical jungle with butterflies. Silk farm. ☎01935 474608 **38 C2**

World-wide Butterflies and Wildlife *nr Yeovil, Somerset* Living butterflies and unique silk farm in Elizabethan Compton House. ☎01935 474608 **37 C9**

Children's activities

ADVENTURE AND PLAY CENTRES AND PARKS

The Alice in Wonderland Family Park *Hurn, Dorset* 7 acres of landscaped park with variety of activities. ☎01202 483444 **28 A2**

Animal Farm Adventure Park *Burnham on Sea, Somerset* See Open Farms **47 B6**

Ashcombe Adventure Centre *Ashcombe, Devon* 20 acre woodland site for paintball, 12 miles of quad bike tracks and clay pigeon shooting. ☎01626 866766 **21 E8**

Ballyhoo Leisure Ltd *Cheltenham, Glos* Children's play centre. ☎01242 252205 **71 C5**

Bens Play World *St Austell, Cornwall* Adventure centre. ☎01726 815553 **8 E3**

Longleat, Wiltshire

Brean Leisure Park *Bristol, Bristol* Pool complex with four water shutes. Funfair. ☎01278 751595 **56 B4**

Brocklands Adventure Park *Kilkhampton, Cornwall* Adventure park and wildlife centre. Two-seater super-carts, 'Supa Bouncer' for all ages, bumper-boats, train rides, pony rides, paddle boats, ride-on racing cars, crazy golf, trampolines. Mini assault course. ☎01288 321920 **31 D5**

Brocklands Adventure Park *Holsworthy, Devon* Crazy golf, pony rides, ball pools, pixie village etc. ☎01288 321225 **31 F6**

Butlins *Minehead, Somerset* Traditional funfair, waterworld etc. ☎01643 703331 **45 B6**

Cattle Country Adventure Park *Berkeley, Glos* Large outdoor park and indoor slides. ☎01453 810510 **63 C5**

Clown About *Salisbury, Wilts* Children's adventure playground, ball pools, aerial slides, soft play area and children's ten-pin bowling. ☎01722 413121 **51 E8**

Crealy Adventure Park *Clyst St Mary, Devon* ☎01395 233200 **22 A1**

Dick Whittington Family Leisure Park *Little London, Glos* Play zone/adventure park, pets corner. ☎01452 525125 **69 D8**

Diggerland *Willand, Devon* Adventure park with JCBs and Dumper Trucks. ☎08700 344437 **35 D5**

Dobwalls Family Adventure Park *Dobwalls, Cornwall* Miniature train rides, adventure park, art exhibition. ☎01579 320325 **9 B7**

Flambards Village Theme Park *Helston, Cornwall* Recreation of Victorian and wartime street. Cornwall Aero Park and Exploratorium. Rides include log flume and rollercoasters. ☎01326 573404 **4 E1**

Fundays *Bourton-on-the-Water, Glos* Large indoor children's adventure playground. Special evenings for teenagers and adults. ☎01451 822999 **72 C2**

Fun Factory *Torquay, Torbay* Indoor adventure centre. ☎01803 201606 **15 C6**

Gus Gorilla's Jungle Playground *Poole, Poole* Adventure playground for children up to 12 years old. Spiral slides, aerial walkways, tube slides, tarzan ropes, roller challenge, ball pool. ☎01202 717197 **27 B7**

Hidden Valley *Launceston, Cornwall* Treasure hunt centre. Also 9 hole golf course, nature reserve, farm animals, miniature railway and play area. ☎01566 86463 **18 D3**

Holywell Bay Fun Park *Newquay, Cornwall* Pitch and putt, kid's go-karting, rides, bumper boats, maze, indoor adventure area. ☎01637 830531 **7 C7**

The Jolly Roger Adventure Children's indoor play area. *Swindon, Glos* ☎01793 522044 **70 B4**

Jungle Jungle *Yeovil, Somerset* Jungle playground. ☎01935 433833 **37 C9**

K's *Minehead, Somerset* Children's play area and soft play area. ☎01643 703044 **45 B6**

Kids Kingdom *St Austell, Cornwall* Soft play area for tots and toddlers. Monster hut maze, gladiator rings etc. ☎01726 77377 **8 E3**

Killarney Springs *Bude, Cornwall* Adventure playground, boating lake, BMX track, basketball. Fishing lake, white-water rapids etc. ☎01288 331475 **30 E4**

Milford Adventure Playground *Yeovil, Somerset* 01935 411325 **37 C9**

The Milky Way Adventure Park *Clovelly, Devon* Rollercoasters; adventure play area; archery; golf driving; railway; bird and sheep dog displays etc. ☎01237 431255 **31 B6**

Once Upon a Time *Woolacombe, Devon* Children's adventure playground, ages 3-11. ☎01271 867474 **42 C4**

Pecorama Pleasure Gardens *Beer, Devon* Minature train. Aviary, crazy golf, children's activity area. ☎01297 21542 **23 A6**

Playzone *Tewkesbury, Glos* ☎01684 7738730 **70 A3**

Rainbow Fun House *Torquay, Torbay* ☎01803 296926 **15 C6**

Rug Ratz *Yeovil, Somerset* Children's play centre ☎01935 476989 **37 C9**

Shires Family Adventure Park *Tredinnick, Cornwall* ☎01841 540215 **2 D4**

Smugglers Barn *Abbotsbury, Dorset* Undercover play area for the under 11s. ☎01305 871817 **25 C6**

Sorley Tunnel Adventure Farm *Kingsbridge, Devon* Dairy farm, indoor play zones (including soft play areas for toddlers), pony rides, railway tunnel walk and craft shops. ☎01548 854078 **13 D5**

Springfields Fun Park & Pony Centre *Newquay, Cornwall* Large family fun centre. Pony rides and farm animals. ☎01841 541215 **7 C7**

Tower Park *Poole, Poole* Indoor playworld. UCI cinema, Megabowl, Quasar and amusement arcade. ☎01202 747533 **27 B7**

Trenouth Farm Rare Breeds Centre *Wadebridge, Cornwall* See Open Farms **8 A2**

Trethorne Leisure Farm *Launceston, Cornwall* See Open Farms **18 D3**

Watermouth Castle Family Theme Park *nr Ilfracombe, Devon* Rides, adventure playground, mini golf, mazes, model railway, tube slides, crazy snooker, gnomeland and swing boats. ☎01271 867474 **42 B5**

Woodlands Leisure Park *Totnes, Devon* See Open Farms **14 C4**

Wookey Hole Caves *Wells, Somerset* Mirror maze, cave museum, paper making, and treasure hunts, See also Interactive Historical. ☎01749 672243 **48 B2**

General interest

BREWERY TOURS

Abbey Ales *Bath, Bath & NE S'set* Pre-booking required. ☎01225 444437 **57 C7**

Badger Brewery *Blandford St Mary, Dorset* Phone for details. ☎01258 452141 **39 E7**

Bird in Hand *Hayle, Cornwall* Tours by appointment. ☎01736 753974 **3 C7**

Hopback Brewery *Downton, Hants* Tours by appointment. ☎01725 510986 **28 B5**

J.C & R.H. Palmer *Bridport, Dorset* Tours by appointment. ☎01308 422396 **24 B4**

Palmers Brewery *Bridport, Dorset* One of the few traditional breweries left in Britain. ☎01308 427500 **24 B4**

St Austell Brewery Co. *St Austell, Cornwall* Tours and tastings. ☎01726 66022 **8 E3**

Skinner's Brewing Co. *Truro, Cornwall* Tours by appointment ☎01872 271885 **4 B4**

Smiles Brewing Company *Bristol, Bristol* Tours and tastings. ☎01275 375894 **56 B4**

Stonehenge Ales *Salisbury, Wilts* Tours by appointment. ☎01980 670631 **51 E8**

Tally Ho *Okehampton, Devon* 15th-century coaching inn with own brewery. Tours by appointment. ☎01837 810306 **20 B1**

Thomas Hardy Brewery *Dorchester, Dorset* Pre-book tours. ☎01305 251251 **25 B8**

Tuckers Maltings *Newton Abbot, Devon* Traditional working malthouse open to the public. ☎01626 334734 **15 A5**

The Wickwar Brewing Company *Wickwar, S Glos* Tours by appointment. ☎01454 294168 **63 E6**

CIDER

Avalon Vineyard *East Pennard, Somerset* Organic wine, mead, cider and tasting. Walks in vineyard. ☎01749 860393 **48 D3**

Bridge Farm Cider *East Chinnock, Somerset* Pre-book tours. ☎01935 862387 **37 D7**

Brimblecombe Cider *Dunsford, Devon* 400 year old cider barn. ☎01647 252783 **21 C6**

Burrow Hill Cider *Kingsbury Episcopi, Somerset* ☎01460 240782 **37 B6**

Callestock Cider Farm *Truro, Cornwall* Museum, farm shop, animals, orchard rides. ☎01872 573356 **4 B4**

Clawford Cider *Clawton, Devon* Working vineyards and orchards, lake and walks. ☎01409 254177 **18 A4**

Coombes Somerset Cider *Nr Highbridge, Somerset* Cider museum, videos, play area and tastings. ☎01278 641265 **47 B6**

Countryman Cider *Tavistock, Devon* Tours of orchard mill and press in 15th-century stables; tastings. ☎01822 870226 **19 F6**

Grays Farm Cider *Exeter, Devon* Oldest cider making firm in Devon. Visitors welcome. ☎01647 61236 **21 B8**

Green Valley Cyder *Clyst St George, Devon* Visitors welcome. ☎01392 876658 **22 C1**

Hancock's Devon Cider *South Molton, Devon* Self-guided tours of cider press house. ☎01769 572678 **33 A7**

Hecks Farmhouse Cider *Street, Devon* Makers of cider and apple juice. Sampling and small museum. ☎01458 442367 **23 C5**

The Lyme Bay Winery *Shute, Devon* Cider and wine tastings. ☎01297 551355 **23 A7**

Mill House Cider Museum *Nr Dorchester, Dorset* ☎01305 852220 **25 B8**

Parson's Choice Cider *West Lyng, Somerset* Birds of Prey, tours. ☎01823 490978 **47 F6**

Perry's Cider Mills *Ilminster, Somerset* Presses and cider making equipment on view. Sampling. ☎01460 52681 **36 C5**

Saul's Farmhouse Cider *Wembworthy, Devon* Orchard and vineyard tours by arrangement. ☎01769 580750 **33 E6**

Sheppy's Cider Farm Centre *Taunton, Somerset* Cider shop and sampling, museum, nature walks and tours of the distillery. ☎01823 461233 **36 A2**

Somerset Distillery - Somerset Cider Brandy Company Ltd *Martock, Somerset* Sample cider and Cider Brandy. Orchard trail. ☎01460 240782 **37 C7**

Stancombe Cider *Sherford, Devon* ☎01548 531634 **13 D6**

Torre Cider *Washford, Somerset* Cider-tasting. Orchard and tree nursery. Farm wagons and traditional cider-making equipment. Farm animals. ☎01984 640004 **45 C7**

Veryan Vineyard *Portloe, Cornwall* Tours, working vineyard, orchards and winery. ☎01872 501404 **5 C6**

INTERACTIVE AND HISTORICAL ATTRACTIONS

Babbacombe's Model Village *Torquay, Torbay* ☎01803 315315 **15 C6**

Beer Quarry Caves *Beer, Devon* Caverns dating from Roman times. Tours and exhibits. ☎01297 20986 **23 A6**

Bodmin Jail *Bodmin, Cornwall* Former county prison dating back to 1776. Dungeons, plus displays. ☎01208 76292 **8 B4**

Bygones *Torquay, Torbay* Victorian street. ☎01803 326108 **15 C6**

Charmouth Heritage Coast Centre *Charmouth, Dorset* Discovering fossils with guided walks, theatre and displays. ☎01297 560772 **24 B2**

Eden Project *St Austell, Cornwall* Vast conservatories with controlled environments. Interactive learning. ☎01726 811911 **8 E3**

Finch Foundry NT *Sticklepath, Devon* 19th-century water-powered forge. Regular demonstrations. ☎01837 840046 **20 B2**

Flambards Village Theme Park *Helston, Cornwall* See Children's Activities **4 E1**

Gaia Energy Centre *Delabole, Cornwall* On site of UK's first commercial windfarm. Displays and tours of environmentally friendly energy sources. ☎01840 213321 **17 D6**

Goonhilly Earth Station *Helston, Cornwall* Largest satellite earth station in the world. Guided tours, interactive displays and film shows. ☎0800 679593 **4 E1**

The Gnomes Reserve and Pixie Kiln *Princetown, Devon* ☎01364 631412 **20 F1**

Kents Cavern *Torquay, Torbay* Prehistoric remains, and the life of the Caveclan. Guided tours. ☎01803 215136 **15 C6**

Land of Legend and Model Village *Polperro, Cornwall* Internationally famous model village. **9 E7**

The Merchant's House *Tewkesbury, Glos* One of row of restored cottages built around 1450. Restored to show medieval merchant's shop and house. ☎01684 297174 **70 A3**

Model Village *Bourton-on-the-Water, Glos* Copy of village. ☎01451 820467 **72 C2**

Morwellham Quay *Tavistock, Devon* Underground train-ride, horse drawn carriage rides and costumes. ☎01822 832766 **19 F6**

New Barn Field Centre *Bradford Peverell, Dorset* Iron Age Homestead authentically recreated. Working pottery, with opportunity to 'throw' a pot, and a wild flower reserve. ☎01305 267463 **25 B8**

Norman Lockyer Observatory *Sidmouth, Devon* Victorian telescopes, planeterium and displays. Visits by arrangement. ☎01395 579941 **22 C4**

Peat Moors Centre *Glastonbury, Somerset* Reconstruction of Iron Age roundhouses. ☎01458 860697 **48 D2**

Plymouth Dome *Plymouth, Devon* Interactive displays covering 400 years of Plymouth history. ☎01752 600608 **10 E5**

Poldark Mine *Wendron, Cornwall* Underground workings with guided tour. Children's play area. ☎01326 573173 **4 D1**

Prehistoric Hilltop Settlement *Capton, Devon* Reconstruction of a prehistoric hill settlement. Produce for sale. ☎01803 712452 **14 E4**

Spirit of the West *Nr Newquay, Cornwall* American themed park, American town recreations. ☎01637 881160 **7 C7**

Underground Passages *Exeter, Devon* City medieval passageways, built to carry water into city centre. Exhibition, and guided tour. ☎01392 665887 **21 B8**

Wookey Hole *Wookey, Somerset* Spectacular caves and legendary home of Witch of Wookey. See also Children's Activities ☎01749 672243 **48 B2**

World of Country Life *Exmouth, Devon* See Open Farms **22 D2**

Scenic minature train rides

VINEYARDS

Camel Valley Vineyard *Bodmin, Cornwall* Award-winning Cornish vineyard. Guided tours. ☎01208 77959 **8 B4**

Castle Cary Vineyard and Winery *Castle Cary, Somerset* 5 acre vineyard. Tours by appointment. ☎01963 351507 **48 E4**

Clawford Vineyard *Clawton, Devon* Fishing lake, 35 acres of vines and 20 acres of cider apple trees. ☎01409 254177 **18 A4**

Down St Mary Vineyard *Crediton, Devon* Tour of the winery and vineyard, wine tasting. ☎01363 82300 **34 F1**

Dunkery Vineyard *Minehead, Somerset* 7 acres in Exmoor National Park. Tours by appointment. ☎01643 841505 **45 B6**

Manstree Vineyard *Shillingford, Devon* ☎01392 832218 **34 B4**

Moorlynch Vineyard *Bridgwater, Somerset* Sample award winning still and sparkling wines. ☎01458 210393 **47 D5**

Polmassick Vineyard *St Ewe, Cornwall* Self-guided tours through secluded valley vineyard. ☎01726 842239 **5 A7**

Sharpham Vineyard *Totnes, Devon* Self-guided vineyard trail and river walk with wine tastings. ☎01803 732203 **14 C4**

Staplecombe Vineyards *Taunton, Somerset* Self-guided tours and free tastings of wines. ☎01823 451217 **36 A2**

Three Choirs Vineyard *Newent, Glos* Wine tastings and tours. ☎01531 890223 **69 B8**

Whatley Vineyard and Herb Garden *Frome, Somerset* ☎01373 836467 **49 B7**

Wortld in Minature *Goonhavern, Cornwall* Minature versions of the world's landmarks ☎01872 572828 **7 E6**

Wraxall Vineyard *Shepton Mallet, Somerset* Tours available. ☎01749 860331 **48 C4**

Railways

MINIATURE RAILWAYS

Bickington Steam Railways *Stover, S Glos* ☎01626 821111 **63 F5**

Blaise Castle *Henbury, Bristol* **56 A3**

Brean Central Minature Railway, Brean Leisure Park *Brean, Somerset* ☎01278 751595 **55 E5**

Brockland Adventure Park *Bude, Cornwall* See Children's Activities **30 E4**

Bourton Model Railway *Bourton-on-the-Water, Glos* ☎01451 820686 **72 C2**

Buckfastleigh Minature Railway *South Devon Railway Station, Devon* ☎01364 642338 **14 B2**

Clevedon Miniature Railway *Clevedon, N Somerset* **55 B8**

Coate Water Park Miniature Railway *Swindon, Glos* ☎01793 531117 **70 B4**

Combe Martin Wildlife Park Railway *Combe Martin, Devon* ☎01271 882486 **43 B6**

Cricket St.Thomas Railway, Wildlife Park *Nr Chard, Somerset* See Zoos **36 E4**

Dobwalls Family Adventure Park *Liskeard, Cornwall* See Children's Activities **9 C8**

Gorse Blossom Minature Railway *Liverton, Devon* ☎01626 821361 **21 E6**

GWR Museum Miniature Railway *Coleford, Devon* ☎01594 833569 **33 F8**

Hidden Valley *Launceston, Cornwall* See Children's Activities **18 D3**

Hunters Rest Minature Railway *Clutton Hill, Bath & NE S'set* ☎01761 452303 **56 E4**

Jungle Express, Paignton Zoo Environmental Park *Paignton, Devon* ☎01803 697500 **15 C5**

World in Minature, Cornwall

Little Western Railway, Trenance Gardens *Newquay, Cornwall* **7 C7**

The Lynbarn fundraiser railway, Milky Way Adventure Park *Bideford, Devon* To help rebuilding of Lynton & Barnstaple Railway. ☎01237 431255 **42 F3**

Moors Valley Railway *Nr Ringwood, Hants* ☎01425 471415 **41 E6**

Paradise Park *Hayle, Cornwall* ☎01736 753365 **3 C7**

Pecorama–Beer Heights Light Railway *Beer, Devon* ☎01297 21542 **23 A6**

Perrygrove Railway *Coleford, Devon* ☎01594 834991 **33 F8**

Pixieland Fun Park *Kilkhampton, Cornwall* ☎01288 321225 **31 D5**

Plymouth Minature Steam Locomotive Society *Southway, Plymouth* **11 C5**

Poole Park Railway *Poole, Poole* ☎01202 683701 **27 B7**

Rode Woodland Railway, Rode Bird Gardens *Rode, Somerset* ☎01373 830326 **58 F8**

Salthouse Fields *Clevedon, N Somerset* Crazy golf, miniature railway, bouncy castle, tennis, putting, bowls and rides. **55 B8**

Seaton and District Electric Tramway *Seaton, Cornwall* Miniature tramway system. ☎01297 20375 **10 E2**

Tamarisk Minature Railway *Nr Padstow, Cornwall* ☎01841 540829 **16 E3**

Weston Miniature Railway *Weston-super-Mare, N Somerset* ☎01934 643510 **55 D6**

Weymouth Bay Minature Railway, Lodmoor Country Park *Weymouth, Dorset* ☎01305 785747 **25 E8**

STEAM AND NOVELTY RAILWAYS

Avon Valley Railway *Bitton, S Glos* Along former branch of old Midland Railway. Wide variety of main line, industrial steam and diesel locomotives. ☎0117 932 5538 **57 C5**

Bicton Woodland Railways *East Budleigh, Devon* ☎01395 658465 **22 D3**

Dean Forest Railway *Lydney, Glos* Steam railway running between Lydney and Parkend. ☎01594 845840 **62 B4**

Bideford and Instow Railway Group *Bideford, Devon* Brake van rides. **42 F3**

Bodmin and Wenford Railway *Bodmin, Cornwall* Restored steam engines and rides. ☎01208 73666 **8 B4**

Dartmoor Railway *Crediton, Devon* Operates on the route of the old Southern Railway line from Crediton to Okehampton and Meldon Quarry. ☎01837 55637 **34 F1**

Devon Railway Centre *Bickleigh, Devon* Operating 2' gauge railway, as well as short 71/4" gauge train ride. ☎01884 855671 **11 C7**

East Somerset Railway *Cranmore, Somerset* Strawberry Line through the Mendip Hills. Locoshed, museum, art gallery, and play area. ☎01749 880417 **49 C5**

Exmoor Steam Railway *Bratton Fleming, Devon* Unique half size railway running within Exmoor National Park. Highest narrow gauge railway in England. ☎01598 710711 **43 D7**

Gloucestershire Warwickshire Steam Railway *Toddington, Glos* ☎01242 621405 **71 A6**

Lappa Valley Steam Railway *Newquay, Cornwall* ☎01872 510317 **7 C7**

Launceston Steam Railway, *Launceston, Cornwall* ☎01566 775665 **18 D3**

Lynton and Barnstaple Railway *Barnstaple, Devon* ☎01598 763487 **43 E6**

Lynton Cliff Railway *Lynton, Devon* Oldest working water operated cliff railway. ☎01598 753486 **44 B1**

Morwellham Quay *Tavistock, Devon* Underground train. See also Interactive Historical ☎01822 832766 **19 F6**

Paignton and Dartmouth Steam Railway *Paignton, Devon* ☎01803 555872 **15 C5**

Plym Valley Railway *Plympton, Plymouth* Steam and diesel locomotives. **11 D6**

Seaton Tramway *Seaton, Cornwall* Tramway running through the Axe valley. ☎01297 20375 **10 E2**

South Devon Railway *Totnes, Devon* Historic line follows the scenic River Dart. ☎08453 451420 **14 C4**

Swanage Railway *Swanage, Dorset* Line currently operates between Swanage and Norden. ☎01929 425800 **27 E7**

Swindon and Cricklade Railway *Nr Swindon, Wilts* ☎01793 771615 **65 E7**

West Somerset Railway *Minehead, Somerset* Britain's longest steam railway. ☎01643 704996 **45 B6**

Sports and games

BICYCLE HIRE

Aldridge Cycles *Camborne, Cornwall* ☎01209 714970 **3 B9**

Alltrax *nr Plymouth, Devon* ☎01752 863553 **10 E5**

Avon Valley Cyclery *Bath, Bath & NE S'set* ☎01225 442442 **57 C7**

Bath and Dundas Canal Co *Bath, Bath & NE S'set* Day boat hire, canoe hire, bike hire. ☎01225 722292 **57 C7**

The Bicycle Chain *Taunton, Somerset* ☎01823 252499 **36 A2**

Bideford Bicycle Hire *Bideford, Devon* ☎01237 424123 **42 F3**

Bikeabout *Swanage, Dorset* ☎01929 425050 **27 E7**

Bikes Bicycles Spares Repairs *Poole, Poole* ☎01202 769202 **27 B7**

Bike Services *Helston, Cornwall* Sales, repair, and hire. ☎01326 564654 **4 E1**

Bike Trail Cycle Hire *Barnstaple, Devon* ☎01271 372586 **43 E6**

Bissoe Tramway Cycle Hire *Truro, Cornwall* Sales, servicing, hire. ☎01872 870341 **4 B4**

Bluebell Cycle Hire *Bridgwater, Somerset* ☎01278 722123 **47 D5**

Bournemouth Mountain Bikes Centre *Bournemouth, Bournemouth* ☎01202 514344 **28 B1**

Bridge Bike Hire *Wadebridge, Cornwall* ☎01208 813050 **8 A2**

Bridge Cycle Hire *Wadebridge, Cornwall* ☎01208 814545 **8 A2**

Brinhams Cycle and Tool Hire *Padstow, Cornwall* ☎01841 532594 **16 E3**

Camel Trail Cycle Hire *Wadebridge, Cornwall* ☎01208 814104 **8 A2**

Cannington Countryside Visitors Centre *Cannington, Somerset* Pitch and putt, cycle hire. ☎01278 655007 **46 D5**

Compass Holidays *Cheltenham, Glos* ☎01242 250642 **71 C5**

Cool Cats Leisure *Poole, Poole* ☎01202 701100 **27 B7**

Cotswold Country Cycles *Chipping Campden, Glos* ☎01386 438706 **77 E6**

Cotswold Water Park & Keynes Country Park *Cirencester, Glos* 132 Lakes. Angling, sailing, jet-skiing, water skiing, children's beaches, bike and boat hire all available. ☎01285 861459 **65 B5**

Country Lanes Cycle Centre *Moreton-in-Marsh, Glos* ☎01608 650065 **72 A3**

Crabtree's *Cheltenham, Glos* ☎01242 515291 **71 C5**

Cycle *Honiton, Devon* ☎01404 47211 **35 F7**

The Cycle Centre *Penzance, Cornwall* ☎01736 351671 **3 D5**

Cycle Clinic *Stroud, Glos* ☎01453 835200 **64 A2**

Cycle Hire *Newquay, Cornwall* ☎01637 874040 **7 C7**

Cyclehire *Paignton, Devon* ☎01803 521068 **15 C5**

Cycle Nucleus *St Austell, Cornwall* ☎01726 68569 **8 E3**

Dartmoor Cycles *Tavistock, Devon* ☎01822 618178 **19 F6**

Dartmoor Cycle Hire Centre *Tavistock, Devon* ☎01822 618189 **19 F6**

Diventure *Salcombe, Devon* ☎01548 843663 **13 E5**

Don't Push it *Bude, Cornwall* ☎01288 359555 **30 E4**

Dorchester Cycles *Dorchester, Dorset* ☎01305 776977 **25 B8**

Dorset Cycles *Sturminster Newton, Dorset* ☎01963 362476 **39 D5**

Elm Farm Cycle Hire *Redruth, Cornwall* ☎01209 891498 **4 B2**

Exmoor Biketrail Cycle Hire *Barnstaple, Devon* ☎01598 763263 **43 E6**

Forest Adventure *Coleford, Devon* ☎01594 834661 **33 F8**

GH Cycle Centre *Burnham on Sea, Somerset* ☎01278 782350 **47 B6**

Giffords Cycles *Holsworthy, Devon* ☎01409 254020 **31 F6**

Glynn Valley Cycle Hire *Bodmin, Cornwall* ☎01208 74244 **8 B4**

Hayball Cycle Centre *Salisbury, Wilts* ☎01722 411378 **51 E8**

Hayle Cycles *Hayle, Cornwall* ☎01736 753825 **3 C7**

Hot Pursuit *Totnes, Devon* ☎01803 865174 **14 C4**

Ians Cycle Centre *Taunton, Somerset* ☎01823 365917 **36 A2**

Ivybridge Cycle Centre *Ivybridge, Devon* ☎01752 258944 **11 D8**

Kings Cycles *Taunton, Somerset* ☎01823 352272 **36 A2**

Kings Cycles *Wellington, Somerset* ☎01823 662260 **35 B7**

Knobblies *Exmouth, Devon* ☎01395 270182 **22 D2**

Langport and River Parrett Visitors Centre and Cycle Hire, Langport, *Langport, Somerset* Cycle hire and trails. ☎01458 250350 **47 F8**

The Lock Inn Cottage *Bradford on Avon, Wilts* ☎01225 868068 **57 D8**

Newquay Cycle Hire *Newquay, Cornwall* ☎01637 874040 **7 C7**

North Coast Cycles *Bude, Cornwall* ☎01288 352974 **30 E4**

Bicton Woodland Railway, Devon

Oceanos *Poole, Poole* ☎01202 706166 **27 B7**

Okehampton Cycles *Okehampton, Devon* ☎01837 53248 **20 B1**

Onabike *Newton Abbot, Devon* ☎01626 334664 **15 A5**

Otter Cycle Hire *Braunton, Devon* ☎01271 813339 **42 D4**

Padstow Cycle Hire *Padstow, Cornwall* ☎01841 533533 **16 E3**

Pedals Bike Hire *Penzance, Cornwall* ☎01736 360600 **3 D5**

Pentewan Valley Cycle Hire *St Austell, Cornwall* ☎01726 844242 **8 E3**

P.G.Hayes Garages *Minehead, Somerset* ☎01643 705363 **45 B6**

Phone-a-bike Breakthrough Sports *Plymouth, Devon* ☎01752 795419 **10 E5**

Plymouth Cycle Hire.co.uk *Plymouth, Devon* ☎01752 258944 **10 E5**

Roger Joseph Cycles *Bridgwater, Somerset* ☎01278 663545 **47 D5**

Saddles and Paddles *Exeter, Devon* Canoe and bike hire. ☎01392 424241 **21 B8**

Somerset Cycles *Bridgwater, Somerset* ☎01278 653334 **47 D5**

Sustrans *Bristol* Cycle hire and specially designed cycle routes. ☎0117 9628893 **56 B4**

Tarka Trail Cycle Hire *Barnstaple, Devon* ☎01271 324202 **43 E6**

Tavistock Cycles *Tavistock, Devon* ☎01822 617630 **19 F6**

Trail and Trek *Truro, Cornwall* ☎01872 561124 **4 B4**

Truro Cycles *Truro, Cornwall* ☎01872 271703 **4 B4**

Westham Cycles *Westham, Dorset* ☎01305 776977 **25 E8**

CRAZY GOLF / PITCH AND PUTT

Abbey Park *Torquay, Torbay* Crazy golf. ☎01803 201201 **15 C6**

Arnold Palmer Putting Course Golf Courses *Exmouth, Devon* ☎01395 226226 **22 D2**

Atlantic Village *Bideford, Devon* Mini golf. ☎01237 422544 **42 F3**

Berryfield Strawberry Farm *Padstow, Cornwall* ☎01841 520178 **16 E3**

Blue Anchor Park *Minehead, Somerset* Crazy golf. ☎01643 821360 **45 B6**

Borough Gardens *Dorchester, Dorset* Tennis, putting, bowls. ☎01305 262691 **25 B8**

Boscombe Chine Gardens *Boscombe, Bournemouth* Crazy golf **28 B2**

Bristol Megabowl *Bristol, Bristol* Indoor adventure golf, ten-pin bowling, children's play house. ☎0117 953 8538 **56 B4**

Brockland Adventure Park *Kilkhampton, Cornwall* See Children's Activities **31 D5**

Bude Haven Recreation Ground *Bude, Cornwall* Crazy golf and tennis. ☎01288 352974 **30 E4**

Butlins *Minehead, Somerset* Crazy golf, funfair, waterworld. ☎01643 708171 **45 B6**

Cannington Countryside Visitors Centre *Cannington, Somerset* See Bike Hire **46 D5**

Cheddar Crazy Golf *Cheddar, Somerset* In Cheddar Gorge. ☎01934 743661 **56 F1**

Coate Water Country Park *Swindon, Glos* Crazy golf, outdoor pool. ☎01793 490150 **70 B4**

Colliford Lake Park *St Neot, Cornwall* ☎01208 821469 **9 B6**

Combe Grove Manor *Monkton Combe, Bath & NE S'set* ☎01225 835533 **57 D7**

Cotswolds Honburne *Cirencester, Glos* Crazy golf. ☎01285 860216 **65 B5**

Dawlish Obstacle Golf *Dawlish, Devon* ☎01626 863873 **22 E1**

Doublebois Park *Liskeard, Cornwall* Crazy golf. ☎01502 500500 **9 C8**

Falmouth beach *Falmouth, Cornwall* Crazy golf and jet ski hire. **4 D4**

Fantasy Island Fun Park *Bideford, Devon* Crazy golf. ☎01237 422992 **42 F3**

Hidden Valley *Launceston, Cornwall* See Children's Activities **18 D3**

Hoburne Park *Christchurch, Dorset* Crazy Golf. ☎01425 273379 **28 B3**

The Hoe *Plymouth, Devon* Crazy golf. **10 E5**

Holywell Bay Fun Park *Newquay, Cornwall* See Children's Activities **7 C7**

Ladram Bay *Otterton, Devon* Crazy golf. **22 C3**

Langmoor Gardens *Lyme Regis, Dorset* Crazy golf. ☎01297 442053 **24 B1**

Lappa Steam Railway *Newquay, Cornwall* Crazy golf. ☎01872 510317 **7 C7**

Lower Gardens *Bournemouth, Bournemouth* Crazy golf. ☎01202 765150 **28 B1**

Old Mac Donalds Farm *Padstow, Cornwall* ☎01841 540829 **16 E3**

Mawgan Beach *Newquay, Cornwall* Crazy golf. **7 C7**

Merlin's Magic Land *Lelant, Cornwall* ☎01736 752885 **3 C6**

Mole Cottage *Chittlehamholt, Devon* 10 hole crazy golf. ☎01769 540471 **33 B5**

Once Upon a Time *Woolacombe, Devon* Crazy Golf. ☎01271 863879 **42 C4**

Pecorama *Beer, Devon* See Children's Activities **23 A6**

Poole Park *Poole, Poole* Crazy golf. **27 B7**

Quaywest *Paignton, Devon* Crazy golf. ☎01803 555550 **15 C5**

Rowlands Wait Touring Park *Bere Regis, Dorset* Crazy golf. ☎01929 71958 **26 A3**

Royal Victoria Park *Bath, Bath & NE S'set* Mini golf, tennis. **57 C7**

St Michaels Park *Cirencester, Glos* Crazy golf. ☎01285 659182 **65 B5**

Salthouse Fields *Clevedon, N Somerset* See Miniature Railways **55 B8**

Sandbanks Beach *Poole, Poole* Crazy golf. **27 B7**

Seadown Park *Charmouth, Dorset* Mini golf. **24 B2**

Seafront *Ilfracombe, Devon* Crazy golf. **42 B5**

Seafront *Paignton, Devon* Crazy golf. ☎01803 558010 **15 C5**

Seafront *Teignmouth, Devon* Crazy golf. **15 A6**

Stowford Farm *Combe Martin, Devon* Crazy golf. ☎01271 882476 **43 B6**

Swanpool beach *Falmouth, Cornwall* Crazy golf. **4 D4**

Trekenning Tourist Park *Newquay, Cornwall* ☎01637 880462 **7 C7**

Trenance Leisure Park *Newquay, Cornwall* ☎01637 872884 **7 C7**

Trenouth Farm Rare Breeds Centre *Wadebridge, Cornwall* See Open Farms **8 A2**

World in Miniature *Truro, Cornwall* 9 hole crazy golf. ☎01872 572828 **4 B4**

World of Country Life *Exmouth, Devon* Crazy golf. ☎01395 274533 **22 D2**

Yeovil Recreation Ground *Yeovil, Somerset* Crazy golf. ☎01935 411120 **37 C9**

GO-KARTING

ACF Hospitality *Wrington, N Somerset* Racing minis, dune buggies, karts, shooting, paintball, ballooning. ☎01934 862305 **56 D1**

A.T.V. Motor Sports Centre *Truro, Cornwall* ☎01872 560 753 **4 B4**

Avaco Karting and Laser Shooting *Salisbury, Wilts* ☎01794 884693 **51 E8**

BHP Racing *Dorchester, Dorset* ☎01305 262211 **25 B8**

BKC Karting *Poole, Poole* ☎01202 666557 **27 B7**

Churston Go-Karts *Churston Ferrers, Torbay* ☎01803 842779 **15 D6**

Circuit Chevron *Dorchester, Dorset* Outdoor Circuit. ☎01300 348499 **25 B8**

Clarke's Leisure *Burnham on Sea, Somerset* ☎01278 751829 **47 B6**

Clay Pigeon Kart Raceway *Dorchester, Dorset* Outdoor. ☎01935 83713 **25 B8**

Combe Karting *Chippenham, Wilts* Outdoor. ☎01249 783010 **58 B3**

Cornwall Karting *Wadebridge, Cornwall* ☎01637 860160 **8 A2**

Devizes Karting Arena *Devizes, Wilts* ☎01380 729016 **58 D5**

Formula Fun *Swindon, Glos* ☎01793 434234 **70 B4**

Formula K Raceways Ltd *Minehead, Somerset* ☎01643 708949 **45 B6**

Go-Karting & Leisure Services *Chippenham, Wilts* ☎01249 446503 **58 B3**

Grand Prix Go Karts *Dawlish, Devon* ☎01626 862521 **22 E1**

The Gray Hedley Indoor Karting Centre *Poole, Poole* **27 B7**

Holywell Bay Fun Park *Newquay, Cornwall* See Children's Activities **7 C7**

Hullavington *Nr Corston, Bath & NE S'set* Outdoor. ☎01305 774047 **57 C5**

Indoor Karting Centre *Christchurch, Dorset* ☎01202 570022 **28 B3**

JDR Karting *Gloucester, Glos* ☎01452 311211 **70 D2**

Jeepers Fun Carts *Hayle, Cornwall* ☎01736 754960 **3 C7**

Karting World (Southwest) Ltd *Bridgwater, Somerset* ☎01278 431919 **47 D5**

Kids Karting Cheltenham *Cheltenham, Glos* ☎01242 516464 **71 C5**

Leisure Sales and Activities *Newton Abbot, Devon* ☎01626 864315 **15 A5**

Middlemoor Water Park *Woolavington, Somerset* Water-skiing, jet-skiing and biking, pro karting. ☎01278 685578 **47 C7**

Newnham Park Outdoor Activity Centre *Plymouth, Devon* ☎01752 338544 **10 E5**

North Devon Karting Centre *Barnstaple, Devon* ☎01271 328460 **43 E6**

Powerhouse Karting *Camborne, Cornwall* ☎01209 711993 **3 B9**

The Raceway Bristol *Bristol, Bristol* Indoor. ☎01275 817011 **56 B4**

Raceworld Indoor Circuit *Aylesbeare, Devon* ☎01395 233397 **22 B2**

Sedgemoor Karting *Bridgwater, Somerset* ☎01278 691953 **47 D5**

South West Indoor Karting *Cheddar, Somerset* ☎01934 744459 **56 F1**

Tabor Kart Racing *Weymouth, Dorset* ☎01305 774074 **25 E8**

West Country Karting *Bristol, Bristol* Outdoor. ☎01454 202666 **56 B4**

Winners Actiondrome *Swindon, Glos* Indoor. ☎01793 814340 **70 B4**

ICE SKATING AND ROLLER SKATING

Bristol Ice Rink - John Nike Leisuresport *Bristol, Bristol* ☎0117 9292148 **56 B4**

Brocklands Adventure Park *Bude, Cornwall* See Children's Activities **30 E4**

Link Centre *Swindon, Glos* State of the art climbing wall and ice-skating rink. ☎01793 445566 **70 B4**

Swiss Lake Ice Rink *Plymouth, Devon* ☎01752 222200 **10 E5**

Trenouth Farm Rare Breeds Centre *Wadebridge, Cornwall* See Open Farms **8 A2**

Riverside Leisure Centre *Exeter, Devon* Leisure pool (waterslides and fountains), badminton, five-a-side, table tennis, roller skating etc. ☎01392 221771 **21 B8**

Stratford Park Leisure Centre *Stroud, Glos* Swimming pool (indoor, outdoor), badminton, squash, tennis. ☎01453 766771 **64 A2**

SKATEPARKS

Baiter Skatepark *Poole, Poole* **27 B7**

Bedminster *Bristol, Bristol* Outdoor **56 B4**

Bridport Park *Bridport, Dorset* **24 B4**

Flatspot Skatepark Project *Plymouth, Devon* Indoor. ☎01752 222213 **10 E5**

The Front *Weymouth, Dorset* Outdoor, with roof. ☎01305 771301 **25 E8**

Keynsham Park *Bristol, Bristol* **56 B4**

Mount Hawke Skatepark *Truro, Cornwall* Indoor. Video games. ☎01209 890705 **4 B4**

St George's Park *Bristol, Bristol* Outdoor concrete park. **56 B4**

Saltash Skatepark *Saltash, Cornwall* Outdoor, concrete bowl. **10 D4**

Seaton Skatepark *Seaton, Cornwall* Near sea front. Outdoor. **10 E2**

Sk8 and Ride *Bristol, Bristol* 5,000sqft indoor. ☎0117 907 9995 **56 B4**

Skate Rock Park *Newport, Cornwall* 10,000sqft outdoor. Indoor kidney bowl. Dirt jumps. ☎01271 372027 **18 C3**

Torpoint Sk8park *Torpoint, Cornwall* **10 D4**

SKIING

Avon Ski Centre *Sandford, Devon* ☎01934 852335 **34 F1**

Christchurch Ski & Leisure Centre *Christchurch, Dorset* ☎01202 499155 **28 B3**

Exeter and District Ski Club *Exeter, Devon* ☎01392 211422 **21 B8**

Gloucester Ski and Snowboard Centre *Gloucester, Glos* ☎01452 414300 **70 D2**

High Action - Outdoor Pursuits Centre *Churchill, Devon* Skiing, snow boarding, tobogganing, pony-trekking, archery, rifle shooting. ☎01934 852335 **36 F3**

Plymouth Ski Slopes & Toboggan Run *Plymouth, Devon* ☎01752 600220 **10 E5**

Torquay Alpine Sky Club *Torquay, Torbay* ☎01803 313350 **15 C6**

Torquay Alpine Ski Club *Torquay, Torbay* ☎01803 313350 **15 C6**

Wellington Sports Centre *Wellington, Somerset* ☎01823 663010 **35 B7**

Yeovil Ski Centre *Yeovil, Somerset* ☎01935 421702 **37 C9**

SPORTS AND LEISURE CENTRES

Acorn Leisure Centre *Torquay, Torbay* ☎01803 328819 **15 C6**

Activity Zone Leisure Centre *Malmesbury, Wilts* ☎01666 822583 **64 E3**

Amesbury Sports and Community Centre *Salisbury, Wilts* ☎01980 622173 **51 E8**

Archway Sports Centre *Stroud, Glos* ☎01453 767374 **64 A2**

Ashdown Leisure Centre *Poole, Poole* ☎01202 604224 **27 B7**

Ashmoor Recreation Centre *Newton Abbot, Devon* ☎01364 654303 **15 A5**

Axe Valley Sports Centre *Axminster, Devon* ☎01297 35235 **23 A7**

Backwell Leisure Centre *Backwell, N Somerset* ☎01275 463726 **56 C1**

Canoeing, Plymouth

Bath Sports and Leisure Centre *Bath, Bath & NE S'set* ☎01225 462563 **57 C7**

Beaufort Sports Centre *Tuffley, Glos* ☎01452 303256 **70 D2**

Berkeley Vale Leisure Centre *Berkeley, Glos* ☎01453 511617 **63 C5**

Bishop's Cleeve Sports Centre *Cheltenham, Glos* ☎01242 673581 **71 C5**

Blackbrook Pavillion Sports Centre *Taunton, Somerset* ☎01823 333435 **36 A2**

Blandford Leisure Centre *Blandford Forum, Dorset* ☎01258 455566 **39 E7**

Blue Lagoon Leisure *Newquay, Cornwall* ☎01637 850741 **7 C7**

Bournside Sports Centre *Cheltenham, Glos* ☎01242 239123 **71 C5**

Bradley Stoke Leisure Centre *Bradley Stoke, S Glos* ☎01454 867050 **62 F4**

Bridport Leisure Centre *Bridport, Dorset* ☎01308 427464 **24 B4**

Brixham Leisure Centre *Brixham, Torbay* ☎01803 883388 **15 D6**

Broadmeadow Sports Centre *Teignmouth, Devon* ☎01626 775940 **15 A6**

Broadstone Leisure Centre *Broadstone, Poole* ☎01202 605222 **27 A7**

Brockworth Sports Centre *Brockworth, Glos* ☎01452 863518 **70 D3**

Bucklers Mead Sports Centre *Yeovil, Somerset* ☎01935 431716 **37 C9**

Budehaven Leisure Centre *Bude, Cornwall* ☎01288 356191 **30 E4**

Budehaven Leisure Centre *Bude, Cornwall* ☎01288 353714 **30 E4**

Callington Community Sports Centre *Callington, Cornwall* ☎01579 383477 **10 B3**

Camelford Sports Centre *Camelford, Cornwall* ☎01840 213188 **17 D7**

Carn Brea Recreation Centre *Redruth, Cornwall* ☎01209 714766 **4 B2**

Castle Place Leisure Centre *Trowbridge, Wilts* ☎01225 762711 **58 E1**

Cascades Leisure Pool and Health Suite *Tewkesbury, Glos* ☎01584 293740 **70 A3**

Castle Sports Centre *Taunton, Somerset* ☎01823 322934 **36 A2**

Cheltenham Recreation Centre *Cheltenham, Glos* ☎01242 528764 **71 C5**

Chilton Trinity Sports Centre *Bridgwater, Somerset* ☎01278 429119 **47 D5**

Chipping Campden Sports Centre *Chipping Campden, Glos* ☎01386 841595 **77 E6**

Christie Miller Sports Centre *Melksham, Wilts* ☎01225 702826 **58 D3**

Churchdown Sports Centre *Gloucester, Glos* ☎01452 855994 **70 D2**

Churchill Leisure Centre *Churchill, Devon* ☎01934 852303 **36 F3**

Cleeve Sports and Fitness Centre *Cleeve, Glos* ☎01242 673581 **69 E8**

Clifton Hill Sports Centre *Exeter, Devon* ☎01392 253353 **21 B8**

Colin Tooze Sports Centre *Ottery St Mary, Devon* ☎01404 814317 **22 A4**

Colyton Sports Centre *Colyton, Devon* ☎01297 552000 **23 B6**

Coombe Dean Sports Centre *Plymouth, Devon* ☎01752 307000 **10 E5**

Cotswold Leisure Centre *Cirencester, Glos* ☎01285 654057 **65 B5**

Cresta *Chard, Somerset* ☎01460 64084 **36 E4**

Cricklade Leisure Centre *Cricklade, Wilts* ☎01793 750011 **65 D6**

Croft Sports Centre *Swindon, Glos* ☎01793 526622 **70 B4**

Culm Valley Sports Centre *Cullompton, Devon* ☎01884 32853 **35 E5**

David Lloyd Leisure Ltd *Bournemouth, Bournemouth* ☎01202 394333 **28 B1**

Dawlish Leisure Centre *Dawlish, Devon* ☎01626 863873 **22 E1**

Derriford Health and Leisure Centre *Plymouth, Devon* ☎01752 792840 **10 E5**

Devizes Leisure Centre *Devizes, Wilts* ☎01380 728894 **58 D5**

Dorcan Recreation Centre *Swindon, Glos* ☎01793 524489 **70 B4**

Downton Leisure Centre *Salisbury, Wilts* ☎01725 513668 **51 E8**

Dursley Swimming Pool and Sports Centre *Dursley, Glos* ☎01453 543832 **63 C7**

The Dragon Leisure Centre *Bodmin, Cornwall* ☎01208 75715 **8 B4**

Dyrons Leisure Centre *Newton Abbot, Devon* ☎01626 260426 **15 A5**

East Bridgwater Sports Centre *Bridgwater, Somerset* ☎01278 456087 **47 D5**

Exmouth Sports Centre *Exmouth, Devon* 2 ☎01395 266381 **22 D2**

Fairford Sports Centre *Fairford, Glos* ☎01285 713786 **65 B8**

Ferndown Leisure Centre *Ferndown, Dorset* ☎01202 877468 **40 F4**

Frome Leisure Centre *Frome, Somerset* ☎01373 465445 **49 B7**

Five Acres Leisure Centre *Coleford, Devon* ☎01594 835388 **33 F8**

Gillingham Leisure Centre *Gillingham, Dorset* ☎01747 822026 **49 F8**

Glastonbury Leisure Centre *Glastonbury, Somerset* ☎01458 830090 **48 D2**

Gloscat Leisure Centre *Cheltenham, Glos* ☎01242 532119 **71 C5**

Goldenstones Pools and Leisure Centre *Yeovil, Somerset* ☎01935 474166 **37 C9**

Gordano Sports Centre *Portishead, N Somerset* ☎01275 843942 **56 A1**

Gryphon Leisure Centre *Sherborne, Dorset* ☎01935 814011 **38 C2**

Haven Sports & Leisure Centre *Poole, Poole* ☎01202 700211 **27 B7**

Haydon Wick Community & Leisure Centre *Swindon, Glos* ☎01793 706666 **70 B4**

Helston Sports Centre *Helston, Cornwall* ☎01326 563320 **4 E1**

Heywood Leisure Centre *Cinderford, Glos* ☎01594 824008 **69 E7**

Highworth Recreation Centre *Swindon, Glos* ☎01793 762602 **70 B4**

Holsworthy Leisure Centre *Holsworthy, Devon* ☎01409 254013 **31 F6**

Honiton Sports Centre *Honiton, Devon* ☎01404 42325 **35 F7**

Huish Episcopi Sports Centre *Langport, Somerset* ☎01458 251055 **47 F8**

Hutton Moor Leisure Centre *Weston-Super-Mare, N Somerset* . ☎01934 635347 **55 D6**

Keynsham Town Council Sports *Keynsham, Bath & NE S'set* ☎0117 986 8683 **57 C5**

King Alfred's Sports Centre *Burnham on Sea, Somerset* ☎01278 786868 **47 B6**

King of Wessex Leisure Centre *Cheddar, Somerset* ☎01934 744939 **56 F1**

Kingswood Leisure Centre *Kingswood, Glos* ☎01454 865700 **63 D6**

The Kemp Welch Leisure Centre *Poole, Poole* ☎01202 738787 **27 B7**

Launceston Leisure Centre *Launceston, Cornwall* ☎01566 772551 **18 D3**

Leighton Recreation Centre *Westbury, Wilts* ☎01373 824448 **50 A2**

Lime Kiln Centre *Malmesbury, Wilts* ☎01793 852197 **64 E3**

Link Centre *Swindon, Glos* ☎01793 445566 **70 B4**

Lipson Community Sports Centre *Plymouth, Devon* ☎01752 263284 **10 E5**

Lords Meadow Leisure Centre *Crediton, Devon* ☎01363 776190 **34 F1**

Lux Park Leisure Centre *Liskeard, Cornwall* ☎01579 342544 **9 C8**

Lytchett Manor Sports Centre *Poole, Poole* ☎01202 632765 **27 B7**

Marlborough Leisure Centre *Marlborough, Wilts* ☎01672 513161 **59 C8**

Mayflower Leisure Centre *Plymouth, Devon* ☎01752 564564 **10 E5**

Millendreath Holiday Village *Looe, Cornwall* ☎01503 263281 **9 E8**

Motcombe Park Leisure Centre *Shaftesbury, Dorset* ☎01747 854486 **39 B7**

Nailsworth Recreation Centre *Stroud, Glos* ☎01453 836951 **64 A2**

Newent Sports Centre *Newent, Glos* ☎01531 821519 **69 B8**

North Devon Leisure Centre *Barnstaple, Devon* ☎01271 373361 **43 E6**

Oasis Leisure Centre *Swindon, Glos* ☎01793 445566 **70 B4**

Parish Wharf Leisure Centre *Portishead, N Somerset* ☎01275 848494 **56 A1**

Patchway Sports Centre *Almondsbury, S Glos* ☎01454 865890 **62 F3**

Pewsey Leisure Centre *Pewsey, Wilts* ☎01672 562469 **59 D8**

Phoenix Leisure Centre *Launceston, Cornwall* ☎01566 772551 **18 D3**

Pinehurst Sports Centre *Swindon, Glos* ☎01793 611612 **70 B4**

Polkyth Leisure Centre *St Austell, Cornwall* Swimming, squash. ☎01726 223344 **8 E3**

Poole Sports Centre *Poole, Poole* ☎01202 777788 **27 B7**

Preston Sports Centre *Yeovil, Somerset* ☎01935 471131 **37 C9**

Purbeck Sports Centre *Wareham, Dorset* ☎01929 556454 **27 C5**

Pyramids Swimming and Leisure Centre *Exeter, Devon* ☎01392 265898 **21 B8**

Quayside Leisure Centre *Kingsbridge, Devon* ☎01548 857100 **13 D5**

Queen Elizabeth Leisure Centre *Wimborne Minster, Dorset* ☎01202 888208 **27 A7**

Rednock Sports centre *Dursley, Glos* ☎01453 543832 **63 C7**

Ridgeway Leisure Centre *Swindon, Glos* ☎01793 813280 **70 B4**

Ridgeway Community Sports Centre *Plymouth, Devon* ☎01752 335612 **10 E5**

Riverside Leisure Centre *Exeter, Devon* See Roller Skating **21 B8**

The Rock Climbing and Caving Centre *Chudleigh, Devon* ☎01626 852717 **21 E7**

St Benedicts Sports and Community Centre *Cheltenham, Glos* ☎01242 226299 **71 C5**

St Ives Leisure Centre *St Ives, Cornwall* ☎01736 797006 **3 B6**

St James Sports Centre *Exeter, Devon* ☎01392 460789 **21 B8**

St Michaels Hall *Yeovil, Somerset* ☎01935 431715 **37 C9**

St Peters Sports Centre *Exeter, Devon* ☎01392 265877 **21 B8**

Salisbury Leisure Centre *Salisbury, Wilts* ☎01722 339966 **51 E8**

Salisbury Swimming Pool *Salisbury, Wilts* ☎01722 339373 **51 E8**

Saltash Leisure Centre *Saltash, Cornwall* ☎01752 840940 **10 D4**

Sandford Park Lido *Cheltenham, Glos* ☎01242 524430 **71 C5**

Scotch Horn Leisure Centre *Nailsea, N Somerset* ☎01275 856965 **56 B1**

Shelton Sports Hall *Badminton, S Glos* ☎01249 651056 **63 F8**

Shepton Mallet Leisure Centre *Shepton Mallet, Somerset* ☎01749 346644 **48 C4**

Sidmouth Sports Centre *Sidmouth, Devon* ☎01395 577679 **22 C4**

Shaftesbury Leisure Centre *Shaftesbury, Dorset* ☎01747 854637 **39 B7**

Ships & Castle *Falmouth, Cornwall* ☎01326 212129 **4 D4**

Sir David English Sports Centre *Bournemouth, Bournemouth* ☎01202 859503 **28 B1**

South Dartmoor Leisure Centre *Ivybridge, Devon* ☎01752 896999 **11 D8**

Springfield Leisure Centre *Corsham, Wilts* ☎01249 712846 **58 B2**

Stanchester Sports Centre *Stoke sub Hamdon, Somerset* ☎01935 825261 **37 C7**

Stratford Park Leisure Centre *Stroud, Glos* See Roller Skating **64 A2**

Stratton St Margaret Sports & Leisure *Swindon, Glos* ☎01793 825525 **70 B4**

Strode Leisure Centre *Clevedon, N Somerset* ☎01275 879242 **55 B8**

Swiss Valley Sport Centre *Clevedon, N Somerset* ☎01275 877182 **55 B8**

Tetbury Sports and Leisure Centre *Tetbury, Glos* ☎01666 505805 **64 D2**

Tewkesbury Sports Centre *Tewkesbury, Glos* ☎01684 293953 **70 A3**

Thomas Hardy Leisure Centre *Dorchester, Dorset* ☎01305 266772 **25 B8**

Thornbury Leisure Centre *Thornbury, Devon* ☎01454 865777 **31 E8**

Tisbury and District Sports Centre *Tisbury, Wilts* ☎01747 871141 **50 F3**

Tiverton Pool *Tiverton, Devon* ☎01884 254221 **34 D4**

Torbay Leisure Centre *Paignton, Devon* ☎01803 522240 **15 C5**

Torquay Squash Centre *Torquay, Torbay* ☎01803 323491 **15 C6**

Torridge Pool & Fitness Centre *Bideford, Devon* ☎01237 471794 **42 F3**

Torrington Sports Hall and Pool *nr Barnstaple, Devon* ☎01805 624767 **43 E6**

Trowbridge Sports Centre *Trowbridge, Cardiff* ☎01225 764342 **54 A4**

Truro Leisure Centre *Truro, Cornwall* ☎01872 261628 **4 B4**

Two Riversmeet Leisure Centre *Christchurch, Dorset* ☎01202 477987 **28 B3**

Verwood Leisure Centre *Verwood, Dorset* ☎01202 825005 **40 E4**

Wadebridge Sports Centre *Wadebridge, Cornwall* ☎01208 814980 **8 A2**

Warehouse Climbing Centre *Gloucester, Glos* ☎01452 302351 **70 D2**

Warmell Leisure Resort *Dorchester, Dorset* ☎01305 852911 **25 B8**

Warminster Sports Centre *Warminster, Wilts* ☎01985 212946 **50 C2**

Wellington Sports Centre & Pool *Wellington, Somerset* ☎01823 663010 **35 B7**

Wells Leisure Centre *Wells, Somerset* ☎01749 670055 **48 B2**

West Somerset Sports and Leisure Centre *Minehead, Somerset* ☎01643 708815 **45 B6**

Westwood Sports Centre *Salisbury, Wilts* ☎01722 329717 **51 E8**

Whitecross Leisure Centre *Lydney, Glos* ☎01594 842383 **62 B4**

White Horse Leisure Centre *Calne, Wilts* ☎01249 814032 **58 B5**

Wincanton Sports Centre *Wincanton, Somerset* ☎01963 824400 **49 F6**

Withypool Activity Centre *Minehead, Somerset* ☎01460 55081 **45 B6**

Wonford Sports Centre *Exeter, Devon* ☎01392 253453 **21 B8**

Wotton-Under-Edge Joint Sports Centre *Wotton under Edge, Glos* ☎01453 842626 **63 D7**

Yate Leisure Centre *Yate, S Glos* ☎01454 865800 **63 F6**

Yeovil Recreation Centre *Yeovil, Somerset* ☎01935 411120 **37 C9**

TEN-PIN BOWLING

AMF Bowling *Torquay, Torbay* ☎01803 201230 **15 C6**

Arena One *Bristol, Bristol* ☎0117 9537310 **56 B4**

Barbican Megabowl *Plymouth, Devon* ☎01752 252171 **10 E5**

Blue Lagoon Leisure *See Sports Centres* **7 C7**

Bournemouth Bowlplex *Bournemouth, Bournemouth* ☎01202 638238 **28 B1**

Bournemouth Superbowl *Bournemouth, Bournemouth* ☎01202 291717 **28 B1**

Bowlplex Bristol *Bristol, Bristol* ☎0117 9610000 **56 B4**

Bowlplex *Poole, Poole* ☎01202 765489 **27 B7**

Bridgwater Mega Bowl *Bridgwater, Somerset* ☎01278 427519 **47 D5**

Dolphin Bowl *Weston-Super-Mare, N Somerset* ☎01934 626480 **55 D6**

Exeter Megabowl *Exeter, Devon* ☎01392 439090 **21 B8**

Gloucester Megabowl *Gloucester, Glos* ☎01452 616262 **70 D2**

Hayle Bowl *Hayle, Cornwall* ☎01736 752595 **3 C7**

Hollywood Bowl *Bristol, Bristol* ☎0117 9771777 **56 B4**

Hollywood Bowl *Taunton, Somerset* ☎01823 444144 **36 A2**

LA Bowl *Newton Abbot, Devon* ☎01626 355455 **15 A5**

Lakeside Superbowl *Weymouth, Dorset* ☎01305 781444 **25 E8**

Lets Go Superbowl *Barnstaple, Devon* Bowling, Quasar. ☎01271 321123 **43 E6**

Lyneham Lanes *Chippenham, Wilts* ☎01249 890381 **58 B3**

Megabowl *Bristol, Bristol* ☎0117 9538538 **56 B4**

Megabowl *Poole, Poole* ☎01202 715907 **27 B7**

Megabowl *Swindon, Glos* ☎01793 886886 **70 B4**

Newquay Bowl *Newquay, Cornwall* ☎850741 **7 C7**

Ozzell Bowl *St Austell, Cornwall* ☎01726 77766 **8 E3**

Plymouth Megabowl *Plymouth, Devon* ☎01752 336666 **10 E5**

St Mawgan Bowl *Wadebridge, Cornwall* ☎01841 540560 **8 A2**

Strikers *Salisbury, Wilts* ☎01722 413121 **51 E8**

Swindon Superbowl *Swindon, Glos* ☎01793 886886 **70 B4**

Tower Park *Poole, Poole* See Children's Activities **27 B7**

Trenouth Farm Rare Breeds Centre *Wadebridge, Cornwall* See Open Farms **8 A2**

Trethorne Leisure Farm *Launceston, Cornwall* See Open Farms **18 D3**

Truro Ten-pin Bowling Centre *Truro, Cornwall* ☎01872 222333 **4 B4**

TENNIS

See Also Sports Centres

Alice Park *Bath, Bath & NE S'set* **57 C7**

Borough Gardens *Dorchester, Dorset* Tennis, putting, bowls. ☎01305 262691 **25 B8**

Boscawen Park *Truro, Cornwall* ☎01872 74766 **4 B4**

Bude Haven Recreation Ground *Bude, Cornwall* See Crazy Golf **30 E4**

Coronation Lake and Park *Helston, Cornwall* ☎01326 572144 **4 E1**

Delta Tennis Centre *Swindon, Glos* ☎01793 445555 **70 B4**

East Devon Tennis Centre *Exmouth, Devon* ☎01395 223355 **22 D2**

Eastover Park Tennis Centre *Bridgwater, Somerset* ☎01278 444480 **47 D5**

Irnham Road Recreation Ground *Minehead, Somerset* **45 B6**

Longstone Park *Saltash, Cornwall* ☎01579 341345 **10 D4**

Poltair Park *St Austell, Cornwall* ☎01726 61585 **8 E3**

Royal Victoria Park *Bath, Bath & NE S'set* See Crazy Golf **57 C7**

Salthouse Fields *Clevedon, N Somerset* See Miniature Railway **55 B8**

Trenance Leisure Park *Newquay, Cornwall* ☎01637 872884 **7 C7**

Tuckingmill Pavilion *Camborne, Cornwall* ☎01209 714766 **3 B9**

Victoria Park *Redruth, Cornwall* ☎01209 216019 **4 B2**

Water sports

BOAT HIRE

Bath and Dundas Canal Co. *Bath, Bath & NE S'set* Day boat hire, canoe hire, bike hire. ☎01225 722292 **57 C7**

Bath Boating Station *Bath, Bath & NE S'set* Hire a rowing boat, punt or canoe. ☎01225 466407 **57 C7**

Bath Narrowboats *Bath, Bath & NE S'set* ☎01225 447276 **57 C7**

Carter Boat hire *Plymouth, Devon* ☎01752 872189 **10 E5**

Eves of St Mawes & Bluebell Classic Sailing Ltd *St Mawes, Cornwall* Traditional sailing boats. ☎01326 270000 **4 D4**

Glevum Boat Hire *Stroud, Glos* Self-drive narrowboat hire ☎01453 882048 **64 A2**

Grand Western Horseboat Co. *Tiverton, Devon* Horse-drawn barge trips. Rowing/dayboat hire. ☎01884 253345 **34 D4**

Hole, W.A. & Son *Plymouth, Devon* ☎01752 664650 **10 E5**

Knight Francis *Plymouth, Devon* ☎01752 823827 **10 E5**

Killarney Springs *Bude, Cornwall* See Children's Activities **30 E4**

Liberty Yachts Ltd *Plymouth, Devon* ☎01752 227911 **10 E5**

Plymouth Boat Cruises Ltd *Plymouth, Devon* ☎01752 822797 **10 E5**

Sailing in the South West

Portway Yacht Charters *Plymouth, Devon* ☎01752 606999 **10 E5**

Professional Boatman's Association Ltd *Kingsbridge, Devon* ☎01548 531678 **13 D5**

River Maid Motor Launch Service *Kingsbridge, Devon* ☎01548 853525 **13 D5**

Roadford Lakes Angling & Watersports Centre *Nr Launceston, Cornwall* Canoeing, sailing, windsurfing and archery. Rowing boats to hire. ☎01409 211507 **18 D3**

Salcombe Boat Hire *Salcombe, Devon* ☎01548 844475 **13 E5**

Siblyback Watersports *Nr Liskeard, Cornwall* Play area, sailing, trout fishing, wind surfing, sailing, canoeing, rowing boats for hire. ☎01579 346522 **9 C8**

Stithians Lake *Redruth, Cornwall* Windsurfing, canoeing, trout fishing, boat hire, sailing. ☎01209 860301 **4 B2**

Southdown Yacht Club, Sea School & Charter Co. Ltd *Plymouth, Devon* ☎01752 822925 **10 E5**

Tamar Cruising *Plymouth, Devon* ☎01752 822105 **10 E5**

Tiger Moon Ltd *Plymouth, Devon* ☎01752 815059 **10 E5**

Tightlines *Kingsbridge, Devon* ☎01548 844475 **13 D5**

Tucker Boat Hire *Kingsbridge, Devon* ☎01548 842840 **13 D5**

Whitestrand Boat Hire *Salcombe, Devon* ☎01548 843818 **13 E5**

Handsam Boat Co *Evesham, Worcs* Motor boat hire. ☎07860 895416 **76 D3**

Cotswold Water Park & Keynes Country Park *Cirencester, Glos* See Bike Hire **65 B5**

Pittville Boating Lake *Cheltenham, Glos* ☎01242 260706 **71 C5**

Chew Valley Lake *Bristol, Bristol* Boat hire available. ☎01275 333345 **56 B4**

CANOEING

Bath and Dundas Canal Co *Bath, Bath & NE S'set* See Boat Hire **57 C7**

Bath Boating Station *Bath, Bath & NE S'set* See Boat Hire **57 C7**

Canoe Adventures *Totnes, Devon* ☎01803 365301 **14 C4**

Cotswold Water Park *Cirencester, Glos* See Bike Hire **65 B5**

Inna River *Totnes, Devon* Offers Canadian canoe trips. ☎01364 643516 **14 C4**

Mill on the Brue Outdoor Activity Centre *Bruton, Somerset* Rock climbing, archery, gliding, canoeing, formula one, grass skiing, shooting, abseiling, camping and grass tobogganing. ☎01749 812307 **49 E5**

Saddles and Paddles *Exeter, Devon* See Bike Hire **21 B8**

Ships & Castle Leisure Pool *Falmouth, Cornwall* See Sports Centres **4 D4**

Siblyback Watersports *Nr Liskeard, Cornwall* See Boat Hire **9 C8**

Skern Lodge Appledore *Bideford, Devon* Powerboat rides, surfing, climbing, canoeing. ☎01237 475992 **42 F3**

Stithians Lake *Redruth, Cornwall* See Boat Hire **4 B2**

Roadford Lakes Angling & Watersports Centre *Nr Launceston, Cornwall* See Boat Hire **18 D3**

Tamar Watersports Centre *Kilkhampton, Cornwall* Sailing, windsurfing and canoeing . ☎01288 321712 **31 D5**

West Country Waterpark *Bristol, Bristol* Windsurfing, jet and water skiing, shooting and canoeing. ☎01454 773599 **56 B4**

RIVER CRUISES AND BOAT RIDES

Bath Narrowboats *Bath, Bath & NE S'set* ☎01225 447276 **57 C7**

Dart Pleasure Craft *Dartmouth, Devon* Coast and river boat trips. ☎01803 834488 **15 E5**

Exmoor Boat trips *Lynmouth, Devon* Along heritage coastline. ☎01598 752509 **44 B1**

Grand Western Horseboat Co *Tiverton, Devon* See Boat Hire **34 D4**

Kennet & Avon Boat Trips *Bath, Bath & NE S'set* ☎01373 813957 **57 C7**

Kingfisher Ferries *Tewkesbury, Glos* ☎01684 294088 **70 A3**

Knight Francis Boat Trips *Plymouth, Devon* ☎01752 823827 **10 E5**

Plymouth Boat Cruises *Plymouth, Devon* ☎01752 822797 **10 E5**

Pride of Avon Cruises *Tewkesbury, Glos* ☎01684 275906 **70 A3**

Salcombe Powerboat School *Salcombe, Devon* Offers four days trips to the Isles of Scilly and return as well as Channel Islands or France for three or four days. Once a year Round Britain RIB Cruise. ☎01548 842727 **13 E5**

Stuart Line Cruises *Exmouth, Devon* ☎01395 279693 **22 D2**

Talk of Tewkesbury *Tewkesbury, Glos* Cruises ☎01684 292981 **70 A3**

Tamar Cruising *Plymouth, Devon* ☎01752 822105 **10 E5**

Tarka Cruises *Barnstaple, Devon* Cruises on the Taw and Torridge Estuary ☎01237 476191 **43 E6**

Telstar Hire Cruisers Ltd *Tewkesbury, Glos* Cruises along the River Avon. ☎01684 294088 **70 A3**

Viking Warrior *Bath, Bath & NE S'set* Cruises between Putney Weir and Bathampton Weir. Also available for private charter for a crew of up to 10 people ☎01225 460831 **57 C7**

Whitestrand Boat Hire *Salcombe, Devon* Cruises and self-drive boats available. ☎01548 842482 **13 E5**

Waverly Excursions Ltd *Minehead, Somerset* Pleasure cruise steam ships Waverley and Balmoral licensed for up to 800 passengers. ☎0141 2218152 **45 B6**

Waverley Pleasure Steamers *Ilfracombe, Devon* ☎01271 865655 **42 B5**

LEISURE POOLS

Aquasplash Leisure Centre *Minehead, Somerset* Slides and wave pool. Also gym, sauna. ☎01643 708000 **45 B6**

Blue Lagoon Leisure *Newquay, Cornwall* See Sports Centre **7 C7**

Carn Brea Recreation Centre *Redruth, Cornwall* See Sports Centres **4 B2**

Cascades Leisure Pool and Health Suite *Tewkesbury, Glos* See Sports Centres **70 A3**

Cirencester Open Air Swimming Pool *Cirencester, Glos* ☎01285 653947 **65 B5**

Crewkerne Aqua Centre *Crewkerne, Somerset* ☎01460 77665 **37 E6**

Coate Water Country Park *Swindon, Glos* See Crazy Golf **70 B4**

Dolphin Swimming Pool *Poole, Poole* ☎01202 677217 **27 B7**

Greenbank Swimming Pool *Street, Devon* Heated outdoor swimming pool. ☎01458 442468 **23 C5**

Hengar Leisure Centre *Bodmin, Cornwall* ☎01208 850382 **8 B4**

Lux Park Leisure Centre *Liskeard, Cornwall* ☎01579 342544 **9 C8**

Malmesbury Pool *Malmesbury, Wilts* Open air heated pool. ☎01666 822329 **64 E3**

Oasis Leisure Centre *Swindon, Glos* See Sports Centres **70 B4**

The Olympiad Leisure centre *Chippenham, Wilts* ☎01249 444144 **58 B3**

Polkyth Leisure Centre *St Austell, Cornwall* ☎01726 223344 **8 E3**

The Rapids of Romsey *Salisbury, Wilts* Water park including water canons, tropical rain showers. ☎01794 830333 **51 E8**

Riviera Centre *Torquay, Torbay* Fun Pool with flume ride. ☎01803 299992 **15 C6**

River Dart Country Park *Ashburton, Devon* Heated outdoor pool. ☎01364 652511 **14 B3**

Riverside Leisure Centre *Exeter, Devon* See Roller Skating **21 B8**

Sandford Parks Lido *Cheltenham, Glos* 50m heated outdoor pool, children's small pool, table tennis. ☎01242 524430 **71 C5**

Sedgemoor Splash Leisure Pool *Bridgwater, Somerset* Fun pool with wave machine, two slides, various water features. ☎01278 425636 **47 D5**

Ships & Castle Leisure Pool *Falmouth, Cornwall* See Sports Centres **4 D4**

South Dartmoor Leisure Centre *Ivybridge, Devon* See Sports Centres **11 D8**

The Splash Leisure Pool *Bude, Cornwall* ☎01288 356191 **30 E4**

Stratford Park Leisure Centre *Stroud, Glos* Roller skating, indoor and outdoor pool, badminton. ☎01453 766771 **64 A2**

Tisbury and District Sports Centre *Salisbury, Wilts* Outdoor swimming pool in the summer. ☎01747 871141 **51 E8**

Tropicana *Weston-Super-Mare, N Somerset* Outdoor pool. ☎01934 626581 **55 D6**

Truro Leisure Centre *Truro, Cornwall* ☎01872 261628 **4 B4**

SAILING

Calvert Trust Watersports Centre *South Molton, Devon* Sailing and trout fishing. ☎01288 321262 **33 A7**

Chew Valley Lake *Bristol, Bristol* Sailing club, visitors' centre and bird hides. ☎01275 333345 **56 B4**

Cornish Cruising *Falmouth, Cornwall* Yachts available. ☎01386 211800 **4 D4**

Cornish Day Sailing *Falmouth, Cornwall* ☎01326 211800 **4 D4**

Cotswold Water Park & Keynes Country Park *Cirencester, Glos* See Bike Hire **65 B5**

Dartmouth Yacht Cruise School *Bussage, Glos* Yacht hire. ☎01803 863162 **64 B2**

Dart Sailing School *Dartmouth, Devon* ☎01803 833973 **15 E5**

Devon and West Yacht School *Hillhead, Cornwall* ☎01803 883718 **8 C4**

Dittisham Sailing School *Totnes, Devon* Sailing tuition. Daily and weekly hire of boats and dingies. ☎01803 883716 **14 C4**

Eves of St Mawes & Bluebell *St Mawes, Cornwall* See Boat Hire **4 D4**

Falmouth School of Sailing *Falmouth, Cornwall* ☎01326 211311 **4 D4**

Fowey Cruising School *Fowey, Cornwall* Skippered holidays. ☎0172 6832129 **9 E5**

Island Cruising Club *Salcombe, Devon* Tuition and boat hire. ☎01548 843481 **13 E5**

Windsurfing off the Dorset coast

John Clift Powerboat School *Salcombe, Devon* Sailing, powerboating and canoeing. ☎01548 842727 13 E5

Liberty Yachts *Plymouth, Devon* Personal tuition. ☎01752 227911 10 E5

Mountain Water Experience *Salcombe, Devon* Sailing tuition and boat hire, canoeing, archery, assault courses etc. ☎01548 550675 13 E5

Mount Batten Sailing and Watersports *Plymouth, Devon* ☎01752 404567 10 E5

Mylor Sailing School *Falmouth, Cornwall* Tuition in dinghies, powerboats or keelboats. Holiday courses, children's expedition days, day cruises. ☎01326 377633 4 D4

Outdoor Adventure *Bude, Cornwall* Surfing, windsurfing, sailing, mountainbiking, kayaking, canoeing, climbing, abseiling and kites. ☎01288 361312 30 E4

Plain Sailing *Brixham, Torbay* Channel crossings, weekend breaks. ☎01803 853843 15 D6

Plymouth Maritime Training Centre *Plymouth, Devon* ☎01752 265695 10 E5

Plymouth Sailing School *Plymouth, Devon* ☎01752 667170 10 E5

Sail West 'Irene Jack' Traditional Sailing *Falmouth, Cornwall* ☎01326 563987 4 D4

Start Point Sailing *Ringmore, Devon* ☎01548 810917 12 C4

Roadford Lakes Angling & Watersports Centre *Nr Launceston, Cornwall* See Boat Hire 18 D3

Stithians Lake *Redruth, Cornwall* See Boat Hire 4 B2

Siblyback Watersports *Nr Liskeard, Cornwall* See Boat Hire 9 C8

Tamar Watersports Centre *Kilkhampton, Cornwall* See Canoeing 31 D5

Trysail *Falmouth, Cornwall* ☎01326 212320 4 D4

West Country Waterpark *Bristol, Bristol* See Canoeing 56 B4

Wimbleball Lake *Dulverton, Somerset* Sailing, fishing, camping. ☎01398 371372 45 F5

SURFING

BSA Approved surfing schools.

Adventure Sports *Redruth, Cornwall* ☎01209 218962 4 B2

Beam House PGL Adventure *Nr Bideford, Devon* ☎01805 622992 42 F3

Big Blue Surf School *Bideford, Devon* ☎01288 331764 42 F3

BSA National Surfing Center *Penzance, Cornwall* ☎01637 850737 3 D5

Dolphin Surf School *Newquay, Cornwall* ☎01637 873707 7 C7

ESF Surf School *Perranporth, Cornwall* ☎01872 571259 7 E6

Freeride Surf School *Nr Newquay, Cornwall* ☎01872 240723 7 C7

Freetime *Penzance, Cornwall* ☎01736 871302 3 D5

Harlyn Bay Surf School *Padstow, Cornwall* ☎01841 533076 16 E3

Offshore Surfing *Newquay, Cornwall* ☎01637 877083 7 C7

Outdoor Adventure *Bude, Cornwall* See Sailing 30 E4

Red River Surf School *Hayle, Cornwall* ☎01209 713687 3 C7

Reef Surf School *Newquay, Cornwall* ☎07071 234455 7 C7

St George House *Georgeham, Devon* ☎01271 890755 42 D4

Second Skin Surf School *Braunton, Devon* ☎01271 812195 42 D4

Sennen Surfing Centre *Sennen, Cornwall* ☎01736 871458 2 E3

Seven Bays Surf School *Newquay, Cornwall* ☎01841 521314 7 C7

Shore Surf School *St Ives Bay, Cornwall* ☎01736 755556 3 B6

Surfrider Action Holidays *Woolacombe, Devon* ☎01271 870365 42 C4

Surf Seekers *Barnstaple, Devon* ☎07977 924588 43 E6

Surf South West *Croyde Bay, Devon* ☎01271 890400 42 D3

Surf's up *Polzeath, Cornwall* ☎01208 862003 16 E3

West Coast Surfari *Newquay, Cornwall* ☎01637 876083 7 C7

WATER PARKS

Blue Lagoon Leisure *Newquay, Cornwall* See Sports Centre 7 C7

Brean Leisure Park *Bristol, Bristol* See Children's Activities 56 B4

Bude Splash Centre Bude, Cornwall Slides, wave machine and tropical temperatures. u01288 356191 30 E4

Butlins *Minehead, Somerset* See Crazy Golf 45 B6

Hendra Oasis Swimming Pool *Newquay, Cornwall* Flumes, rapids and water rides. Outdoor pool. ☎01637 875778 7 C7

QuayWest *Paignton, Devon* Britains only outdoor waterpark. ☎01803 555550 15 C5

The Splash *Bridgwater, Somerset* Waterslide, waves, rapids. ☎01278 425636 47 D5

Splashdown *Poole, Poole* ☎01202 716123 27 B7

Waterworld *Newquay, Cornwall* Waterslides. ☎01637 853828 7 C7

Woodlands Leisure Park *Totnes, Devon* See Open Farms 14 C4

JET SKI AND WATER SKI HIRE

Cotswold Water Park & Keynes Country Park *Cirencester, Glos* See Bike Hire 65 B5

Falmouth beach *Falmouth, Cornwall* 4 D4

Middlemoor Water Park *Woolavington, Somerset* See Go-Karting 47 C7

Spring Lakes *South Cerney, Glos* Sheltered lake forwaterskiing. ☎01285 860606 65 C5

West Country Waterpark *Bristol, Bristol* See Canoeing 56 B4

WINDSURFING

Coverack Windsurfing centre *Coverack, Cornwall* Holidays and courses to all standards. ☎01326 280939 5 G3

Stithians Lake *Redruth, Cornwall* See Boat Hire 4 B2

Siblyback Watersports *Nr Liskeard, Cornwall* See Boat Hire 9 C8

Roadford Lakes Angling & Watersports Centre *Nr Launceston, Cornwall* See Boat Hire 18 D3

Outdoor Adventure *Bude, Cornwall* See Sailing 30 E4

Tamar Watersports Centre *Kilkhampton, Cornwall* See Canoeing 31 D5

West Country Waterpark *Bristol, Bristol* See Canoeing 56 B4

Cotswold Water Park, Keynes Country Park *Cirencester, Glos* See Bike Hire 65 B5

Picture credits

All pictures courtesy Southwest Tourism, with thanks, except p.II right, p.IV top, p.VI bottom left and p. VII top James Hughes.

Beaches and resorts

Bude *Bude, Cornwall* Small unspoilt resort town. Popular beaches for families and surfers. Annual jazz festival. 30 E4

Carbis Bay *Carbis Bay, Cornwall* Sheltered bay ideal for families and surfers. 3 C6

Constantine Bay *Constantine, Cornwall* Wide beach with pale sands. 4 E2

Crackington Haven *Crackington Haven, Cornwall* Coastal village with good beach and cliff walks. Cornwall's highest coastal point. 17 A7

Crantock *Crantock, Cornwall* Long, peaceful sandy beach backed by sand dunes. Good for surfing. 7 C6

Crinnis, Carlyon Bay *Nr St Austell, Cornwall* Popular sandy beach backed by cliffs. 8 E3

Duporth *Duporth, Cornwall* Shingle and rocky beach in a sheltered bay. 8 E3

Fistral Beach *Newquay, Cornwall* Sandy beach partly sheltered by dunes. One of the top surfing spots in Europe. 7 C7

Gyllyngvase *Falmouth, Cornwall* Main resort beach for Falmouth. Small, wide sandy beach. 4 D4

Godrevy *St Ives, Cornwall* Extensive sandy beach to east of St Ives Bay, lighthouse island featured in Virginia Wolfe's To the Lighthouse. 3 B6

Great Western *Newquay, Cornwall* Popular family beaches in sheltered coves. 7 C7

Holywell Bay *Newquay, Cornwall* Sandy beach with dunes. Good surfing. 7 C7

Kennack Sands *Nr Coverack, Cornwall* Two sheltered sandy beaches. Part of National Nature Reserve. 5 G3

Kynance Cove (NT) *Lizard, Cornwall* Famed beauty spot. Sheltered sandy coves and caves at low tide. 5 H2

Millendreath *Looe, Cornwall* Lively beach resort. 9 E8

Mother Ivey's Bay *Padstow, Cornwall* Isolated rural beach accessible by coastal path. 16 E3

Parr Sands *Nr St Austell, Cornwall* Extensively sandy beaches. 8 E3

Pendower *Roseland, Cornwall* Long sandy beach. Cliffs and rock pools. 9 C8

Perranporth *Perranporth, Cornwall* Lively beach resort. Village End beach and Penhale Sands are both sandy beaches with good surfing in places. 7 E6

Porth Joke *Newquay, Cornwall* Attractive bay with sandy beach. 7 C7

Porthpean *Nr St Austell, Cornwall* Safe sandy cove. Popular with families. 8 E3

Porthtowan *Porthtowan, Cornwall* North coast rural family resort. 6 F4

Portwrinkle *Nr Torpoint, Cornwall* Sandy beach with rocks in a rural setting. Popular with surfers. 10 D4

St Ives Bay *St Ives, Cornwall* 6 km of golden sandy beaches bordered by fishing resort of St Ives. The best stretches include Carbis Bay and Porthminster Beach, with Godrevy Lighthouse. 3 B6

Swanpool *Falmouth, Cornwall* Small sand and pebble beach. 4 D4

Tolcarne *Newquay, Cornwall* One of Newquay's most popular beaches close to the town centre. 7 C7

Treyarnon Bay *Treyarnon, Cornwall* Wide sandy bay in an Area of Outstanding Natural Beauty. 16 F2

Vault Beach *Gorran Haven, Cornwall* Gently shelving sandy beach on National Trust land. Good for families. 5 B8

Watergate *Watergate, Cornwall* 2 miles of golden sands. Lots of activities and rival to Fistral Bay for surf. 17 D7

Widemouth Bay *Bude, Cornwall* Large sandy beach. Low cliffs and rock formations. Good surfing due to reef. 30 E4

Bantham *Bantham, Devon* Sandy beach backed by sand dunes. Popular with surfers. 12 D4

Bigbury-on-Sea *Bigbury-on-Sea, Devon* Sandy beach at the mouth of the South Devon Avon. Connected to Burgh Island by a causeway at low tide; at high tide a sea tractor transports passengers. 12 D4

Blackpool Sands *Blackpool, Devon* One of the most picturesque beaches in Devon. Crescent sands backed by cliffs and fields. European blue flag award, Seaside awards. 15 F5

Challaborough *Challaborough, Devon* Sheltered sandy cove. Rock pools at low tide. 12 C3

Exmouth Beach *Exmouth, Devon* Exmouth has remained a popular resort since Victorian heyday. The sandy beach is backed by a wide promenade. 22 D2

Hope Cove *Nr Salcombe, Devon* Sandy beach. Safe swimming area. 13 E5

Ilfracombe (Tunnels) Beach *Ilfracombe, Devon* Grey sand and shingle backed by cliffs with small bays and rock pools. Swimming and scuba diving. 42 B5

Meadfoot *Torquay, Torbay* Sandy beach to the east of Torquay in the middle of popular resort. 15 C6

Ness Cove *Shaldon, Devon* Sandy cove backed by red sand cliffs. 15 A6

Oddicombe and Maidencombe Bay *Torquay, Torbay* Known as 'the English Riviera', Torquay and its surrounding coast are popular due to mild climate and golden sands. 15 C6

Plymouth *Plymouth, Devon* Sandy beach. Watersports available. 10 E5

Putsborough Sands *Putsborough, Devon* 3 miles of Golden sands. Excellent surfing towards the two headlands. 42 C3

Slapton Sands *Slapton, Devon* Long, straight shingle beach backed by Slapton Ley freshwater lake (NT). 13 C7

Salcombe North and South Sands *Salcombe, Devon* Sandy, family beach. 13 E5

Saunton Sands *Saunton, Devon* Superb beaches with miles of sand dunes. 42 D4

Shoalstone Beach *Brixham, Torbay* Gently shelving shingle beach. Open air swimming pool 15 D6

Thurlestone South *Thurlestone, Devon* Owned by the National Trust. Popular sandy beach. 12 D4

Wembury Beach *Wembury, Devon* Small cove surrounded by low cliffs. 11 F6

Woolacombe Village Beach *Woolacombe, Devon* 2 1/4 miles of golden sands backed by hills and downs. Water sports. Regular surfing competitions. Woolacombe Sands is within the Heritage Coastline and is backed by National Trust land. 42 C4

Bournemouth *Bournemouth, Bournemouth* One of the most popular resorts in the South. Bournemouth town has lots to do and has numerous sandy beaches. See Activities and Museums and Galleries for things to do in Bournemouth. 28 B1

Charmouth *Charmouth, Dorset* Ideal for family holidays. Sandy beach with cafe and beach huts nearby, as well as Heritage Coastal Centre. Famous worldwide for its fossils. 24 B2

Christchurch Friars Cliff and Highcliffe Castle *Christchurch, Dorset* Sand and gravel beaches. Backed by promenade and beach huts. 28 B3

Church Ope Cove *Portland, Somerset* Sheltered beach with limestone pebbles. Private beach huts. 48 D1

Durdle Door *Nr Wareham, Dorset* Famous for Durdle Door Arch, a naturally formed arch in the headland. The beach is narrow and shingly. 27 D5

Golden sands at Poole

Kimmeridge Bay *Kimmeridge, Dorset* Sandy beach with fossil-bearing shale. Popular with surfers. 27 E5

Lyme Regis *Lyme Regis, Dorset* Known as the Jurassic Coast due to number of fossils in area. Site from which ships sailed to meet the Spanish Armada. 24 B1

Sandbanks, Harbour Lake. *Poole, Poole* Popular sandy beaches. 27 B7

Shell Bay *Studland, Dorset* Beautiful beach on tip of Studland Peninsula. Part of Purbeck Heritage Coast. 27 D7

West Bay *West Bay, Dorset* Ideal location for family holidays. 24 B4

Burnham-on-Sea *Burnham on Sea, Somerset* Traditional family resort. 7 miles of sandy beaches with sand dunes. 47 B6

Dunster Beach *Dunster, Somerset* Quiet sandy beach. Safe for children. 45 C6

Minehead *Minehead, Somerset* Boasts a sandy beach and seafront. Varied choice of entertainments and shopping facilities nearby. 45 B6

Weston-Super-Mare *Weston-Super-Mare, N Somerset* Resort with wide sandy beach. 55 D6

National route planning

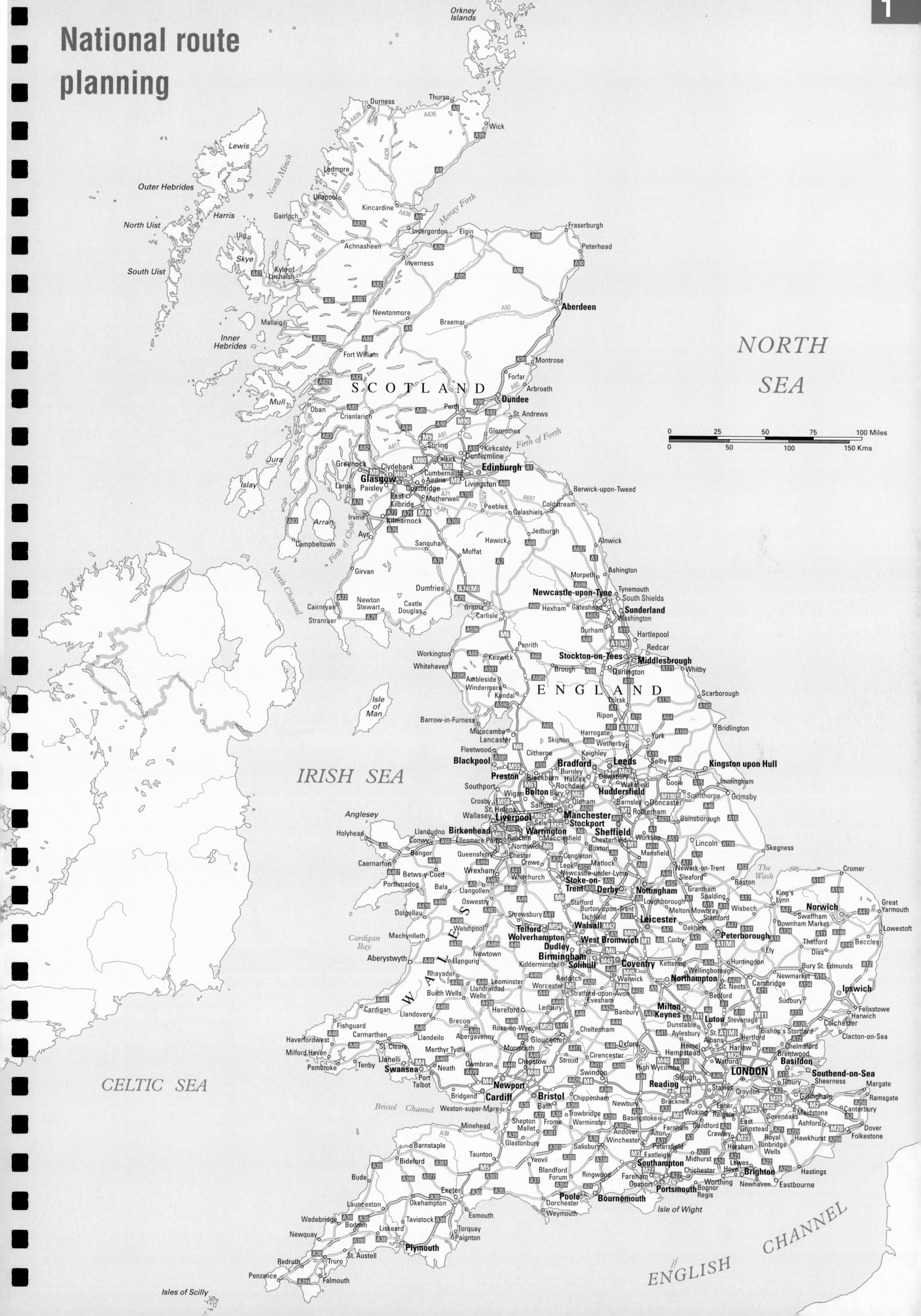

SCOTLAND

ENGLAND

WALES

NORTH SEA

IRISH SEA

CELTIC SEA

ENGLISH CHANNEL

North Minch

Moray Firth

Firth of Forth

Firth of Clyde

North Channel

Cardigan Bay

Bristol Channel

The Wash

Orkney Islands

Outer Hebrides

Inner Hebrides

Lewis

Harris

North Uist

South Uist

Skye

Mull

Jura

Islay

Arran

Anglesey

Isle of Man

Isle of Wight

Isles of Scilly

| 0 | 25 | 50 | 75 | 100 Miles |
| 0 | 50 | 100 | | 150 Kms |

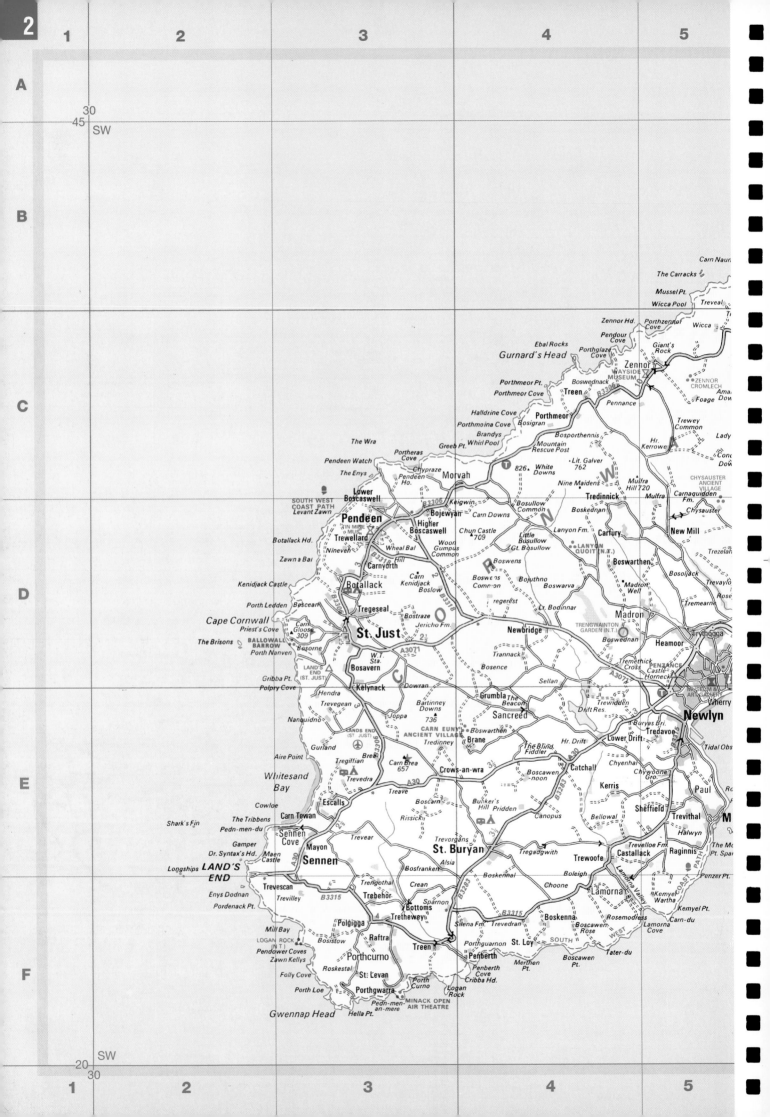

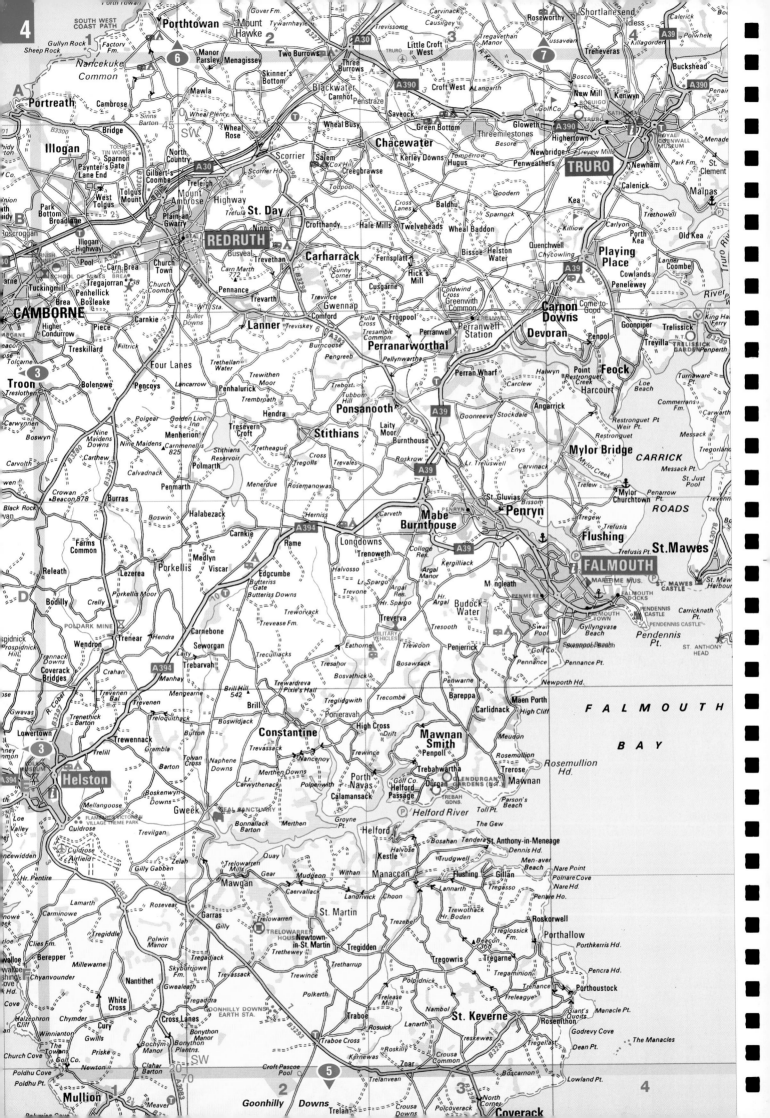

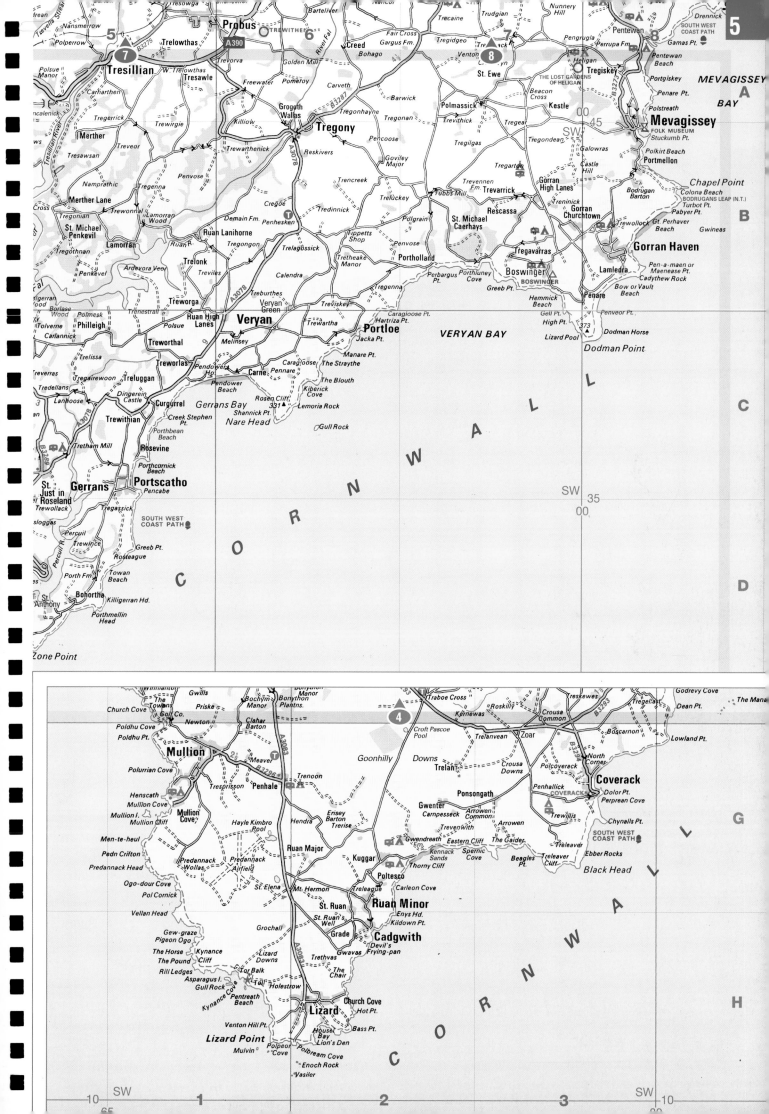

1   **2**   **3**   **4**

A

Men-a-vaur
Round I.
White I.
Golden Ball
Didley's Pt.
Porth
St. Helen's
Plumb I.
Morran
Shipman Hd.
St. Helen's
Pool
Tean
Lower
St. Martin's Bay
St. Martin's Hd.
Tean Sd.
Town
CROMWELL'S
KING CHARLES' CASTLE
Middle Town
CASTLE I.
Northwethel
Hell Bay
Northward
Old Grimsby
ST.
Higher Town
BRYHER
New
BLOCKHOUSE
MARTIN'S
Scilly Rock
Grimsby
TRESCO
Cruther's Pt.
English I.
Nornour
Hanjague
Gweal
Lizard Pt.
Guther's I.
I   S   L   E   S
Gt. Ganilly
Black Rocks
Pentle Bay
Lit. Ganilly
Maiden Bower
Pool
Gt. Pool
O   F
Eastern Is.
Seal Rock
Samson
TRESCO
Gt. Innisvouls
Castle
Hill 138
ABBEY
Gt. Ganinick
Illiswilgig
Bryher
Tresco
GARDENS
Lit.
Menawethan
Flats
VALHALLA FIGUREHEAD COLLECTION
Gt.
Ganinick
Arthur
Bollard Pt.
Puffin I.
Crow Pt.
Crow Sound

B

Mincarlo
Samson
Bar Pt.
Stony I.
BANTS CARN BURIAL
INNISIDGEN
White I.
Samson
CHAMBER A.M.
BURIAL CHAMBERS
Flats
Green I.
The
Watermill Cove
Freshwater
South Hill
Road
Gull
Cb.
Toll's I.
Castinicks
S   C   I   L   L   Y
Maypole
Pelistry Bay
Lit. Minalto
Gt. Minalto
Porthfoo
Holy
Deep Pt.
Rocky
Vale
Hill
Hugh Town
ST. MARY'S
St. Mary's Pool
A3710
PORTH HELLICK DOWN
Star Castle
MARY'S
BURIAL CHAMBERS
PENZANCE 2:40
The Garrison
WALLS
ST. MARY'S
(APR-NOV)
SV
10
Woolpack Pt.
Old Town
SV
10
85
Porth
95
Cressa
St. Mary's Sound
Inner Hd.
Peninnis Hd.
Outer Hd.

C

Gunners
Haycocks
Annet Hd.
Kittern Rock
Annet
Smith Sound
Gugh
Burnt I.
Dropnose Pt.
Hellweathers
The Cove
Hoe Pt.
Castinicks
Isinvrank
Brothers
Wingletang
Gt. Crebawethan
ST. AGNES
Bay
Lit. Crebawethan
Muncoy Neck
hop Rock
Jacky's Rock
Melledgan
Rosevear
Western Rocks
Rosevean
Daisy
Corregan
Gilstone

D

E

Bawden Rocks
PE
Gree
Newdowns Hd.
Trevellas
Crams
Porth
St. Agnes Head
Trevaunance
Cove
New Downs
Higher
Bal
Tubby's Hd.
St. Agnes
SW
ST AGNES BEACON
50
628
55
Chapel Porth
Goonvrea
Mingoose
Porth Towan
Towan
Cross
SOUTH WEST
Gover
COAST PATH
Porthtowan
Mount H
Gullyn Rock
Factory
Manor
Sheep Rock
Fm.
Parsley Menagissey
Nancekuke
Common
Gull Rock
Sk
Portreath
Cambrose
Mawla
Bc

1   **2**   **3**   **4**   **5**

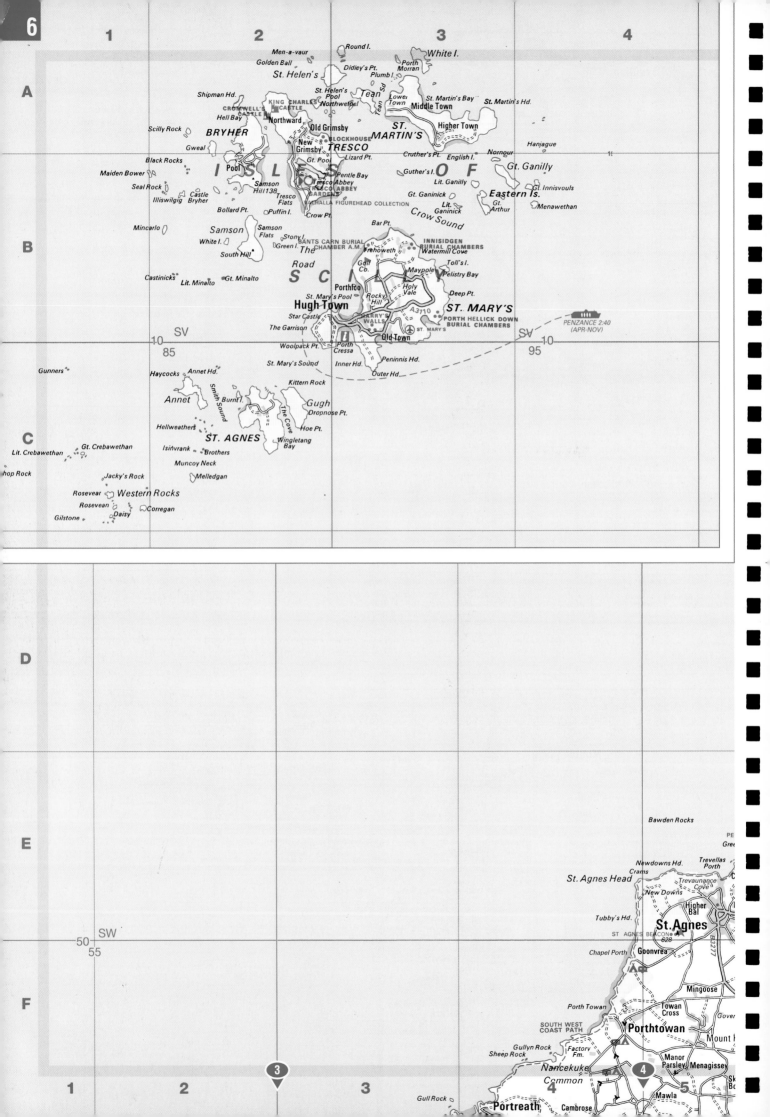

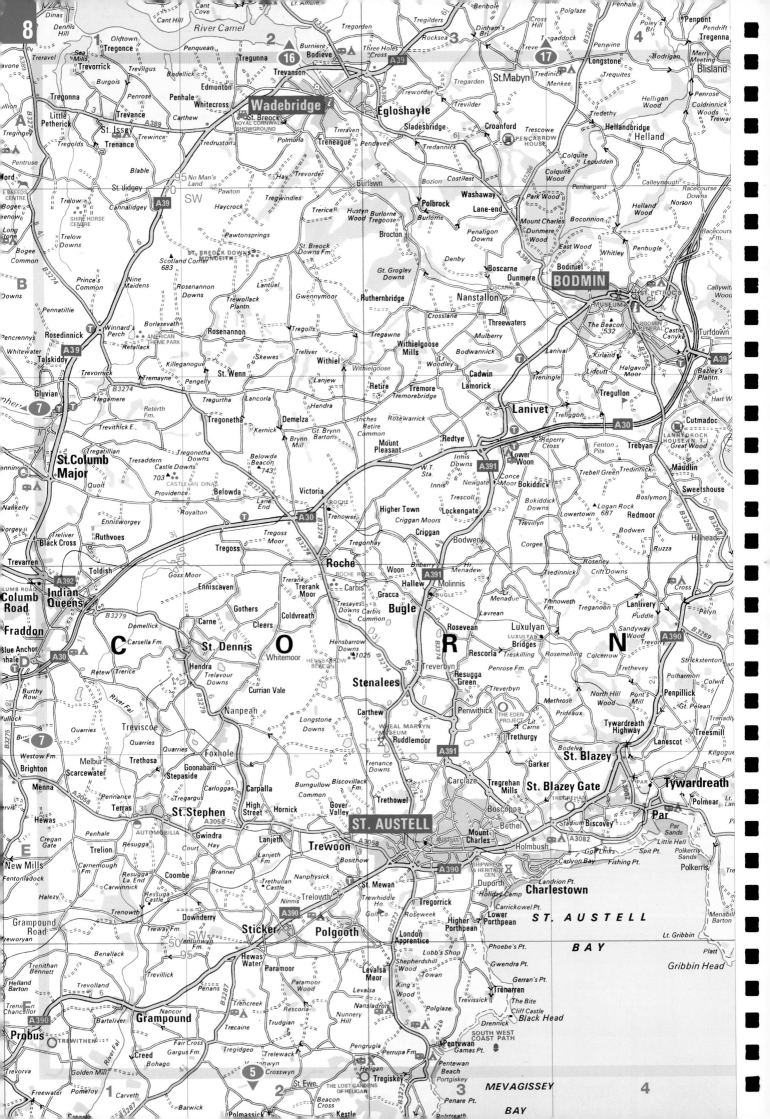

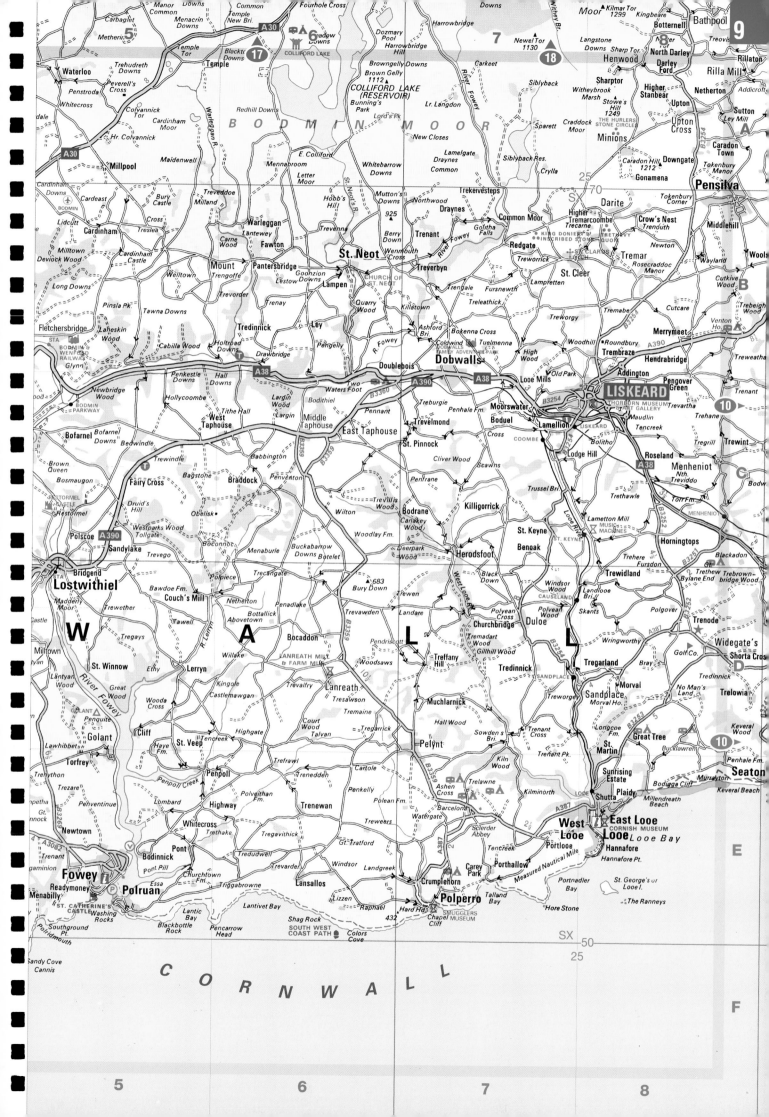

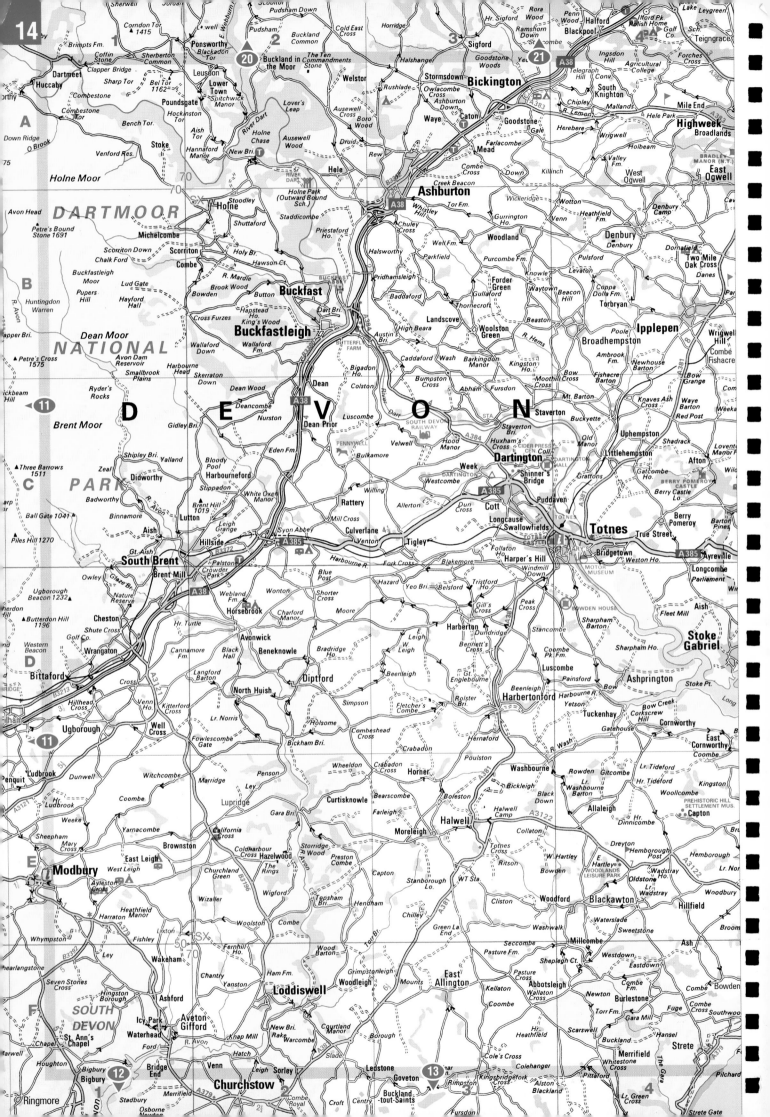

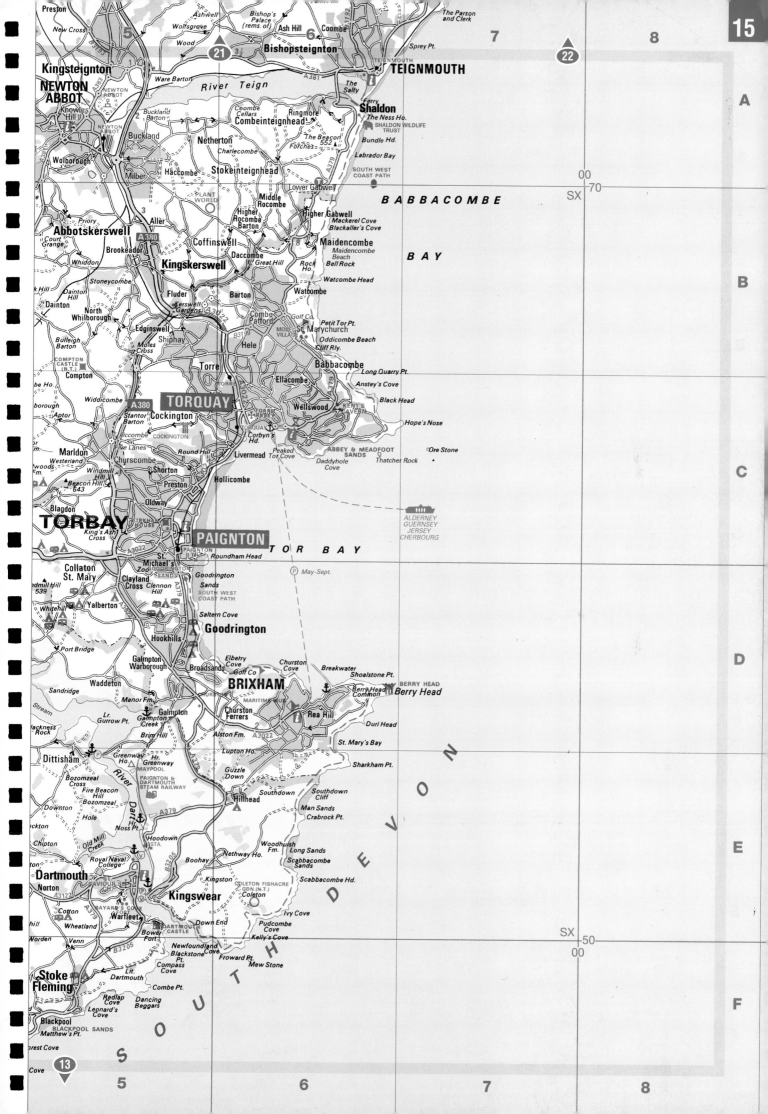

85
00
SW

A

B

C

D

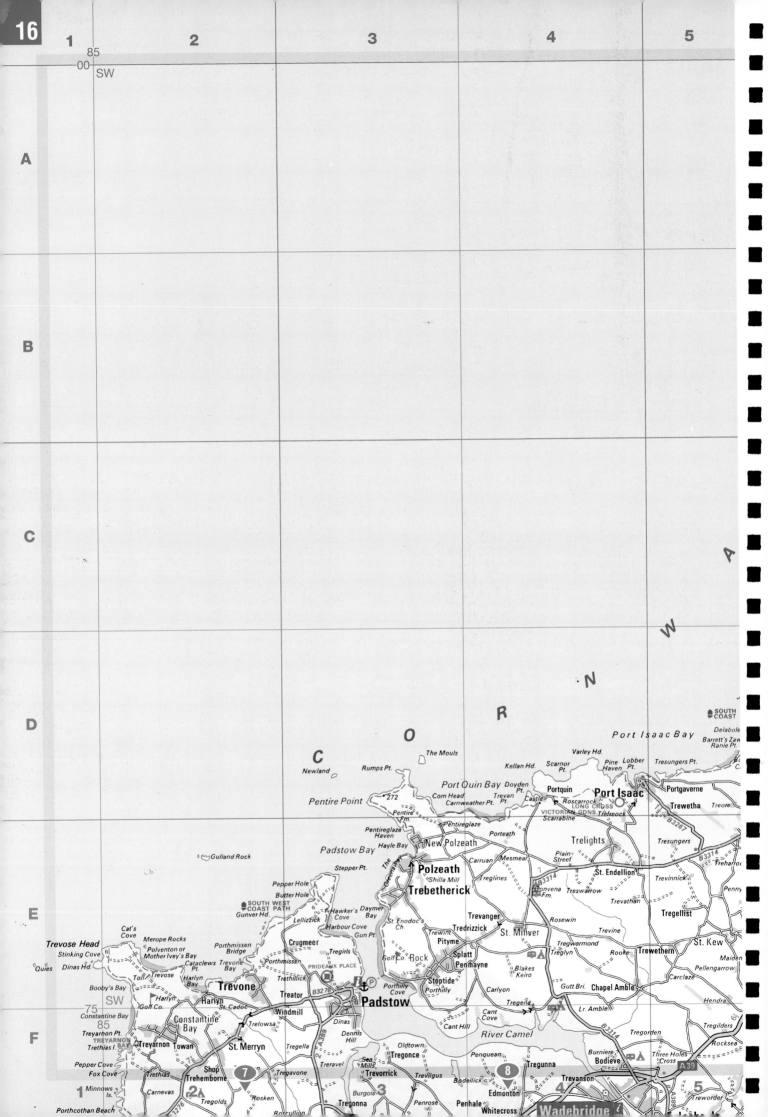

SOUTH
COAST

Port Isaac Bay   Delabole
Barrett's Zawn
Ranie Pt.

C O R N W A

The Mouls
Newland   Rumps Pt.   Kellan Hd.   Scarnor   Varley Hd.   Pine   Lobber   Tresungers Pt.
                                                      Pt.   Haven   Pt.
Pentire Point   •272   Com Head   Doyden   Portquin   Port Isaac   Portgaverne
                   Carnweather Pt.   Trevan   Pt.   Roscarrock   Trewetha
Port Quin Bay   Castle   Pt.   VICTORIAN GDNS   LONG CROSS   Treore
                                                Scarrabine   Trefreock   B3267

Pentire   Treharrou
Fm.   Pentireglaze   Trelights   Penny
Pentireglaze
Haven   Porteath   Trevinnick
Gulland Rock   Hayle Bay   New Polzeath   Mesmear   Plain   St. Endellion   Tresungers
Padstow Bay   Carruan   Street   B3314
                              The   Polzeath   Treglines   B3314   Treswarrow   Trevathan
Stepper Pt.   Shilla Mill   Trebetherick   Convena   Treglan   Tregellist
Pepper Hole   Fm.
Butter Hole   Trevanger   Trevine
SOUTH WEST   Hawker's   Daymer   St. Enodoc's   Tredrizzick   Rosewin   Tregwarmond
COAST PATH   Cove   Bay   Ch.   St. Minver   Tregwarmond   Trewethern   St. Kew
Gunver Hd.   Lellizzick   Harbour Cove   Trewint   Pityme   Treglyn   Rooke
Cat's   Gun Pt.   Golf Co.   Rock   Splatt   Maiden
Cove   Merope Rocks   Crugmeer   Penmayne   Blakes   Treglyn   Pellengarrow
Trevose Head   Polventon or   Tregirls   Keiro   Gutt Bri.   Carclaze
Stinking Cove   Mother Ivey's Bay   Porthmissen   Stoptide   Chapel Amble
Quies   Dinas Hd.   Bridge   Trevone   Porthilly   Hendra
          Cataclews   Bay   Golf Co.   Stoptide   Carlyon   Lr. Amble
          Pt.   Trethillick   Porthilly Cove   Tregena
Toll   Trevose   Porthmissen   PRIDEAUX PLACE   Rock   Tregilders
Booby's Bay   Harlyn   B3314
          Harlyn Bay   Treator   B3276   Padstow   Cant   Gutt Bri.   Tregorden
Golf Co.   St. Cadoc   Windmill   Cove   Burniere   Rocksea
Constantine Bay   Harlyn   Dinas   Cant Hill   River Camel   Three Holes
          Trelowsa   Dennis   Tregunna   Bodieve   Cross   A39
Treyarnon Pt.   Constantine   Hill   Oldtown   Penquean   Trevanson
Trethias I.   Bay   Treyarnon Towan   St. Merryn   Tregella   Tregonce   Trevilgus   Tregena
Pepper Cove   Shop   Tregavone   Sea   Trevorrick   Badellick   Edmonton   Wadebridge
Fox Cove   Trehemborne   Mills
Minnows   Carnevas   Rosken   Burgois   Tregonna   Penrose   Penhale   Whitecross   Treworder
Is.   Tregolds
Porthcothan Beach   7   3   8   4   5

75
85
SW

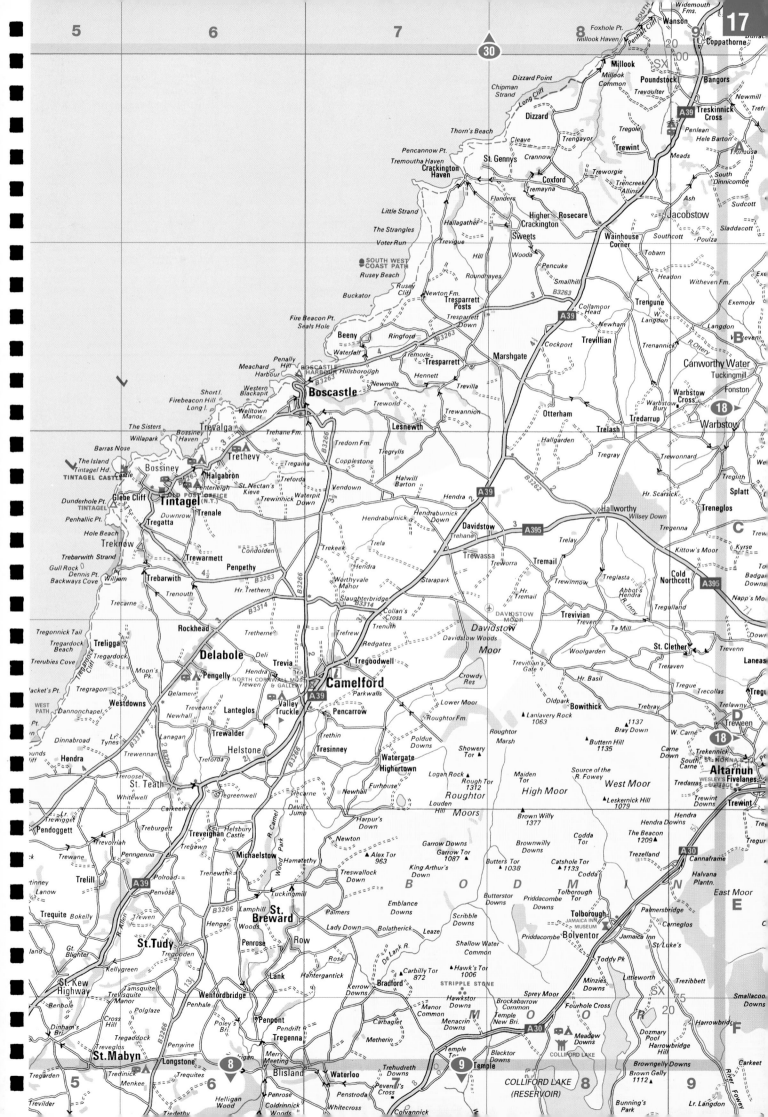

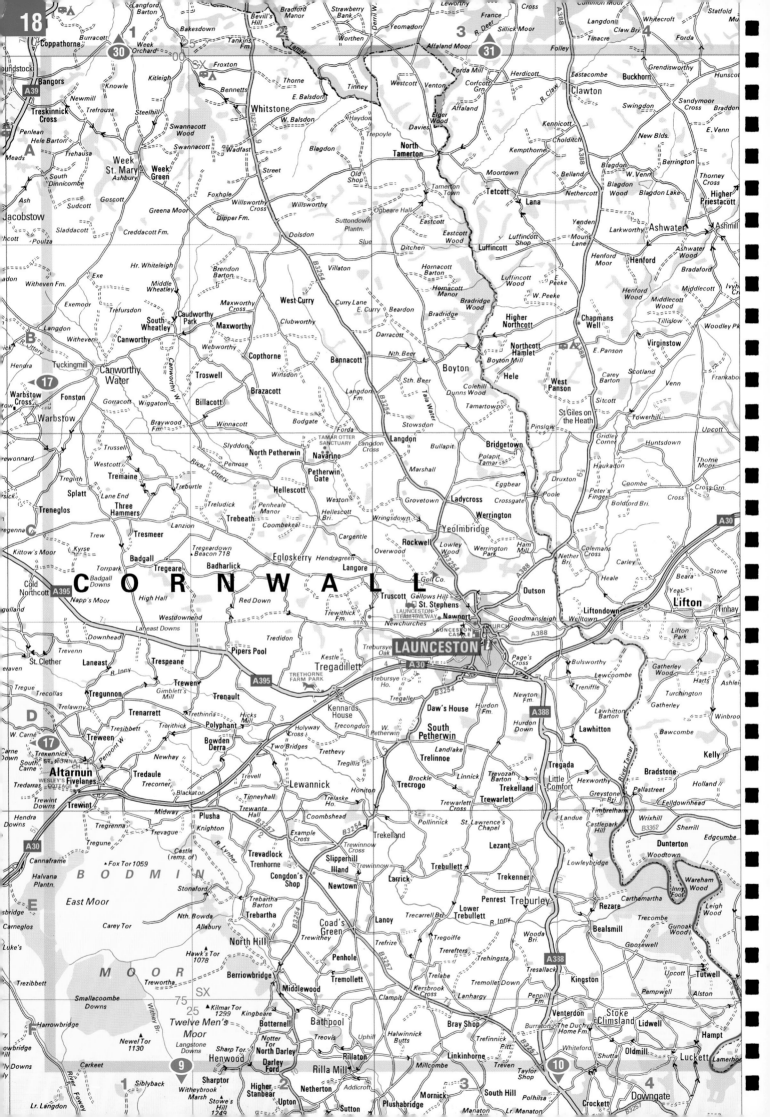

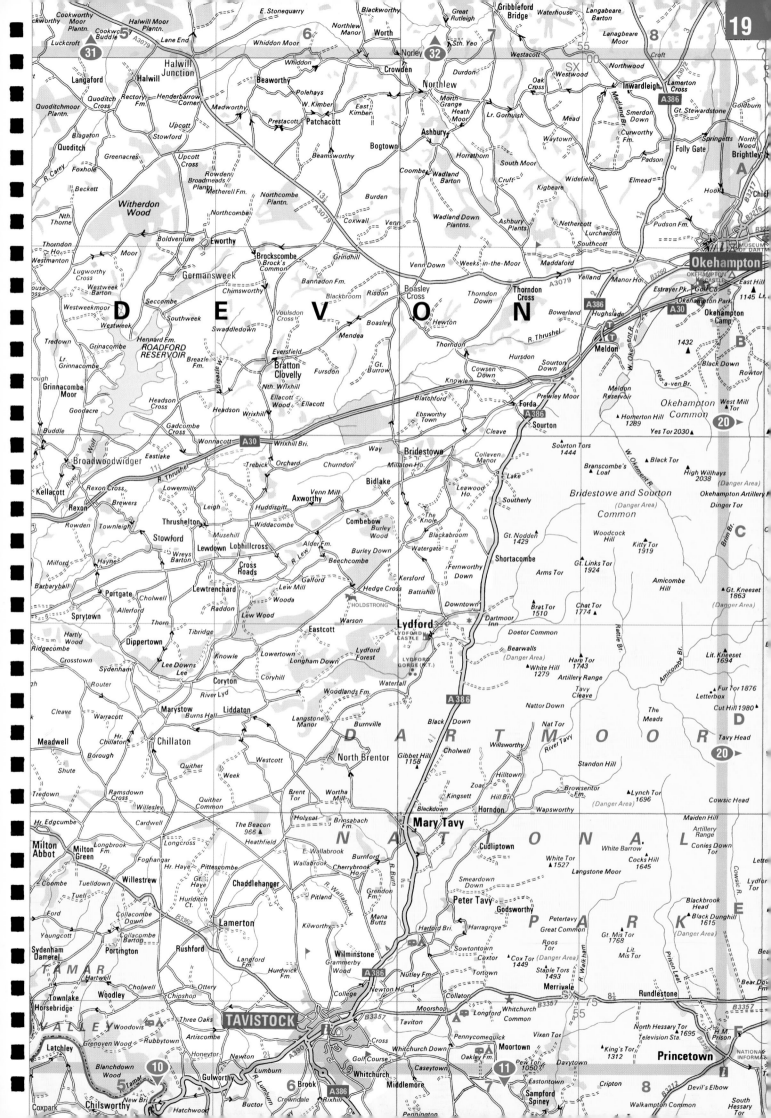

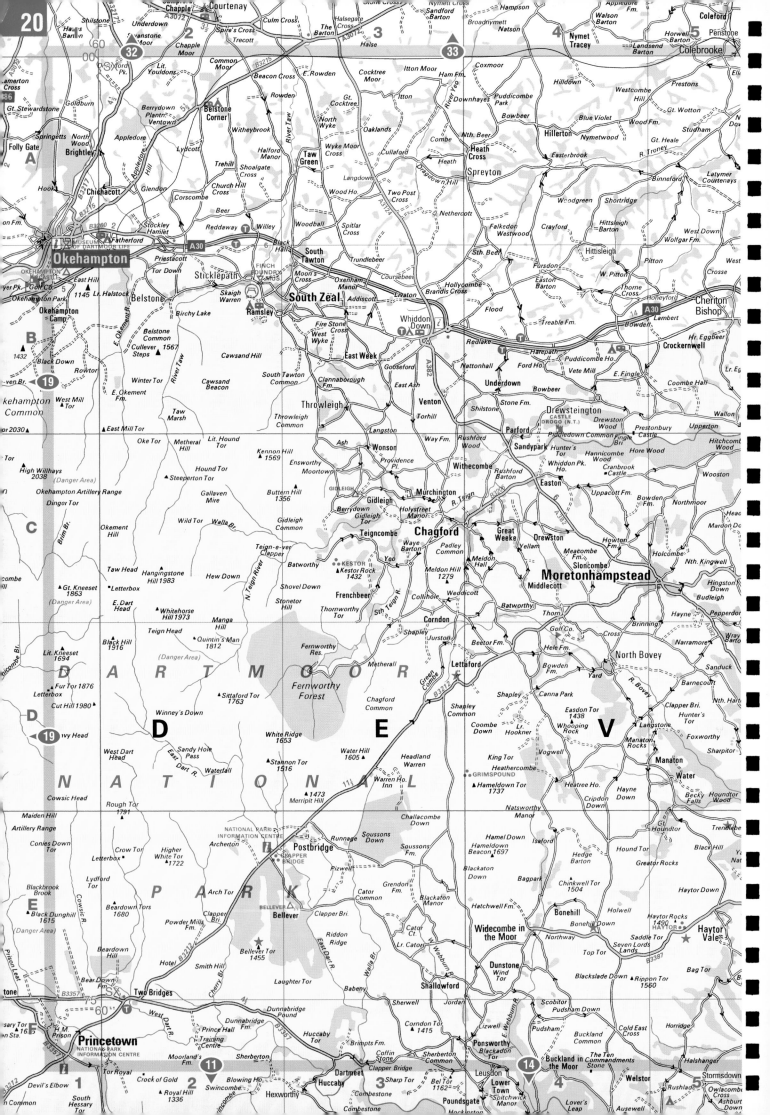

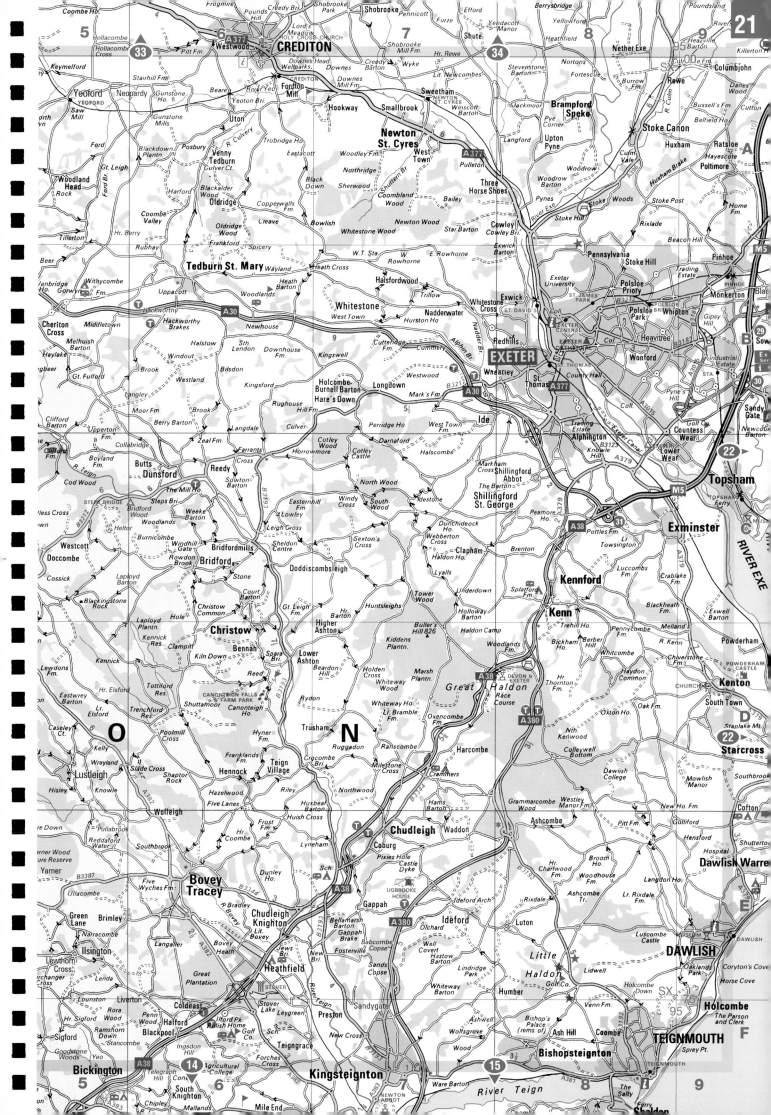

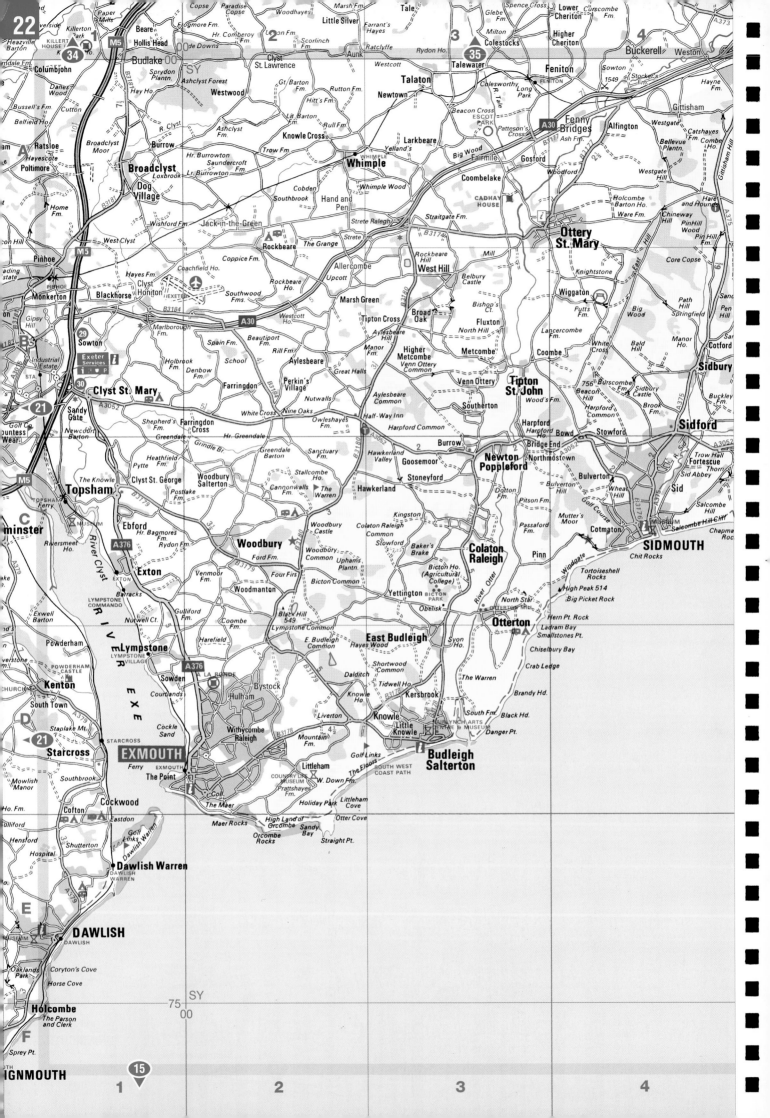

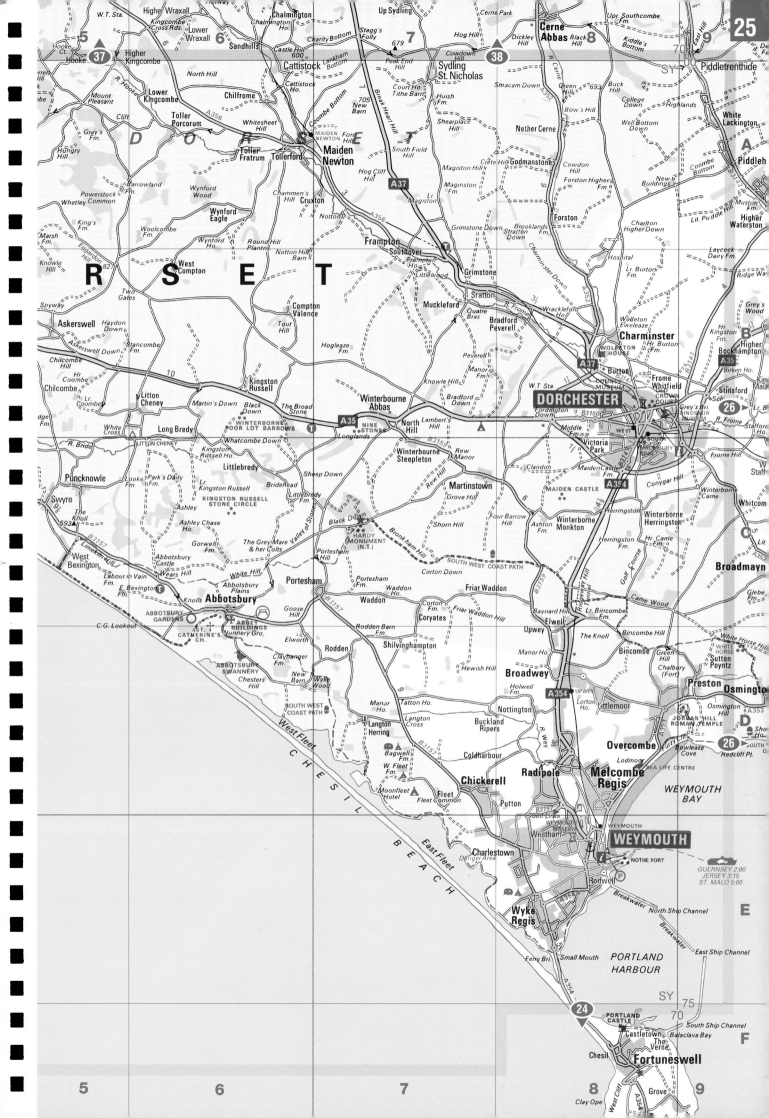

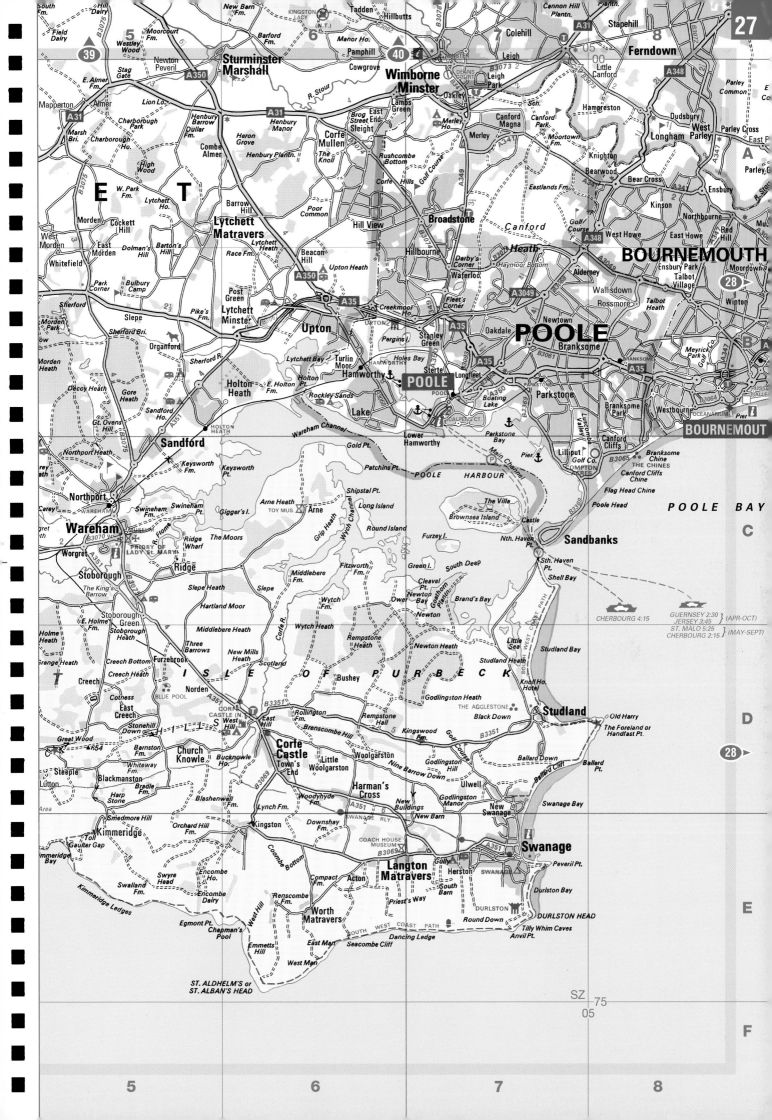

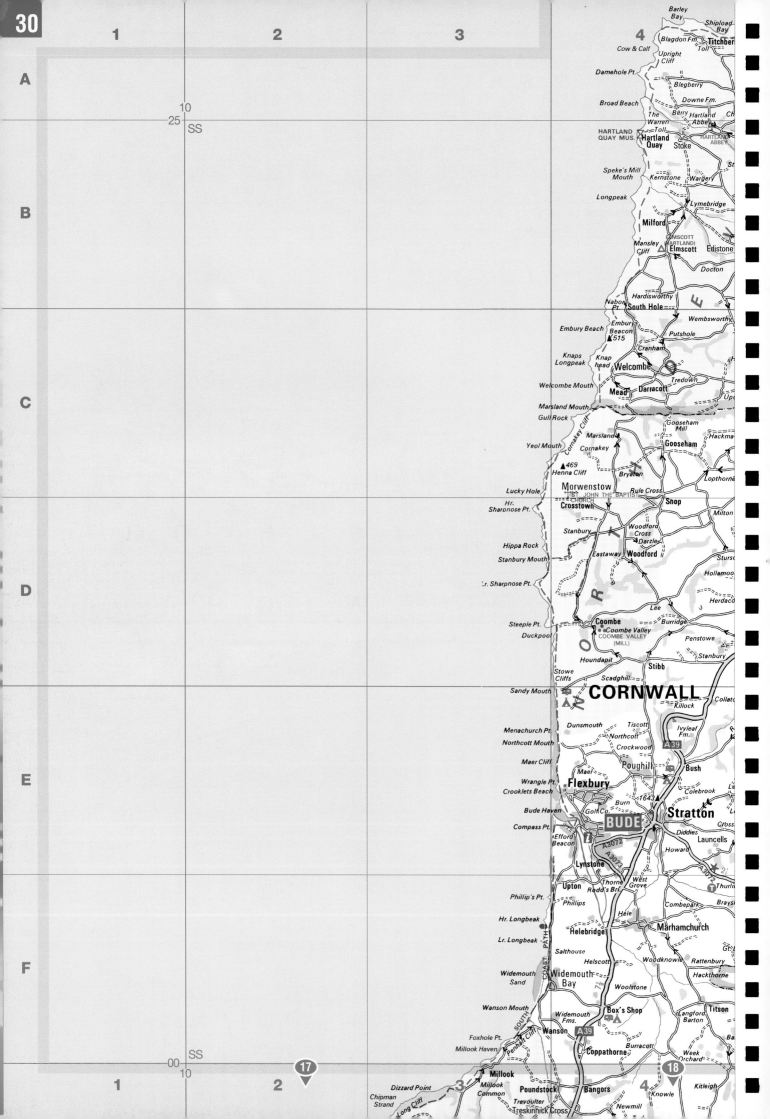

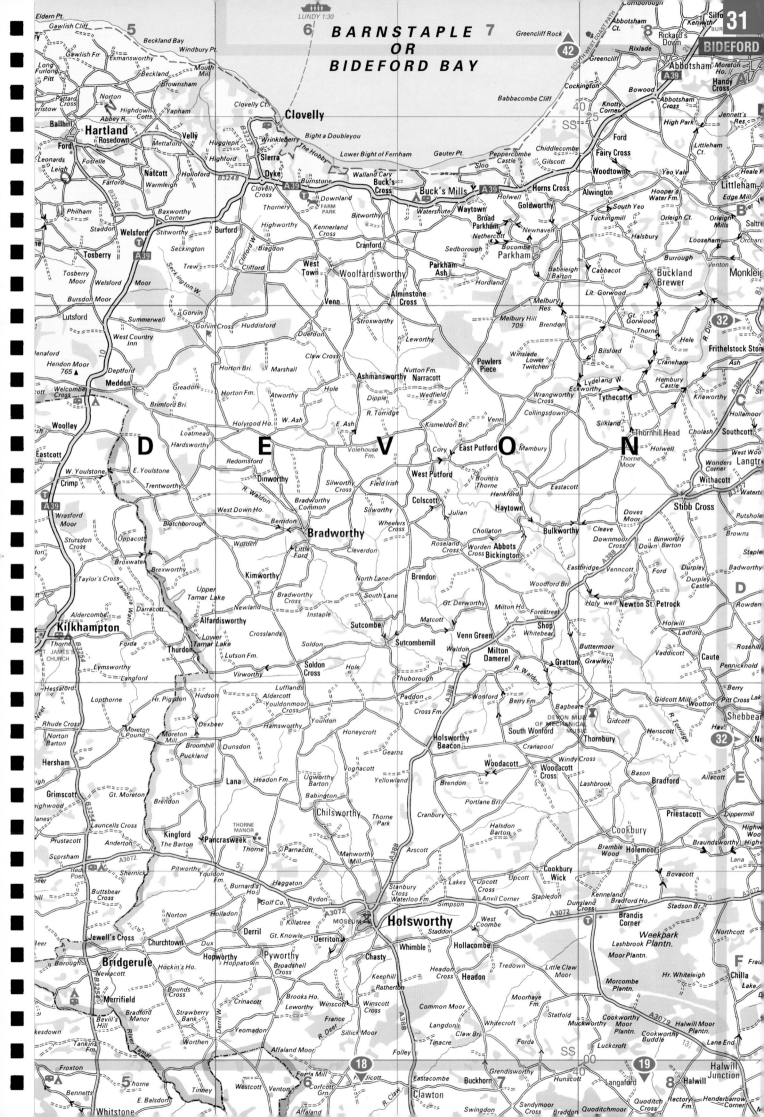

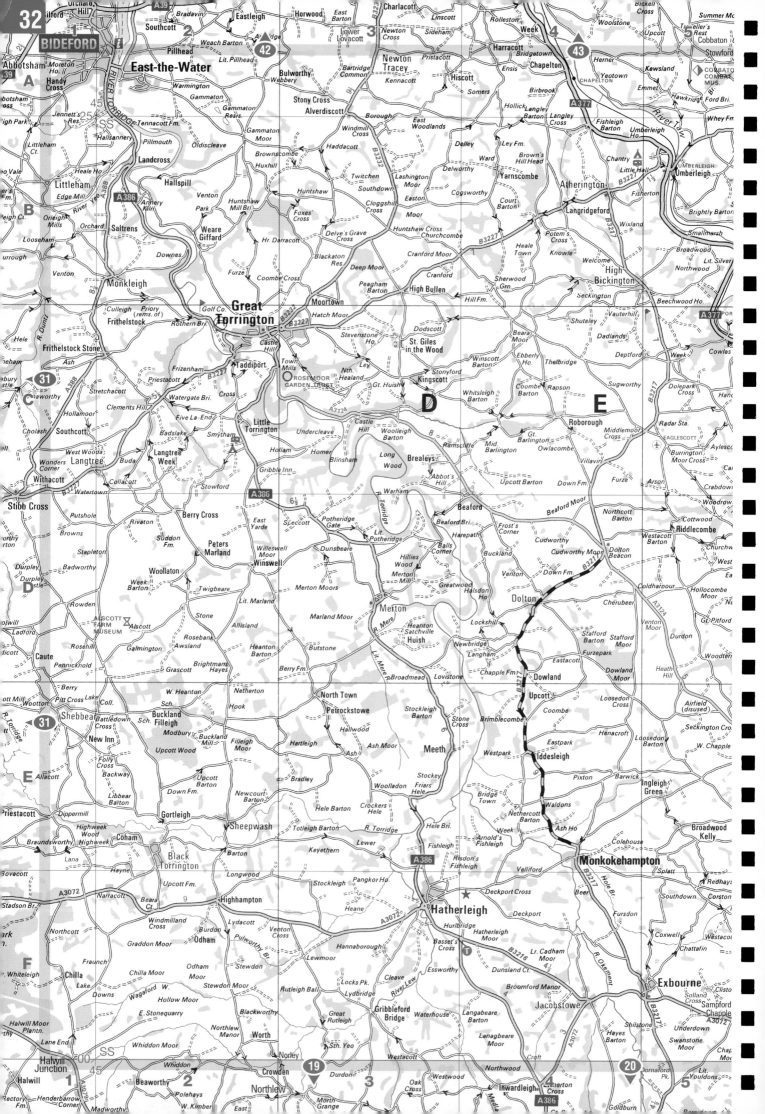

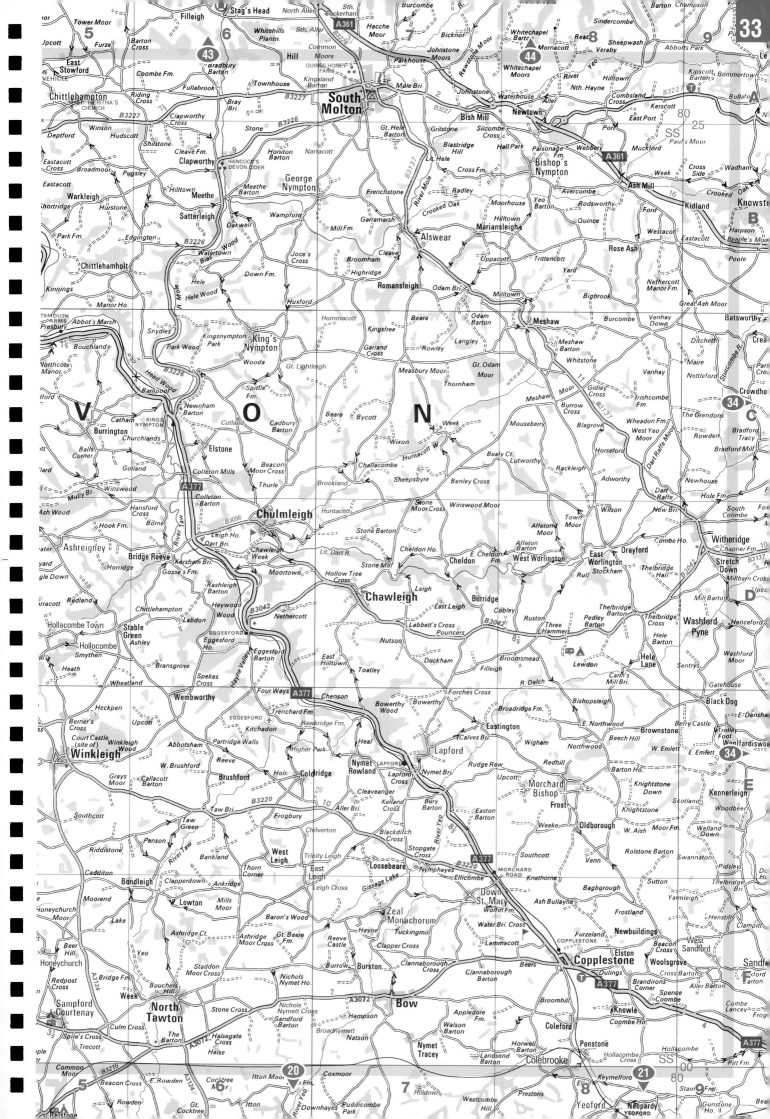

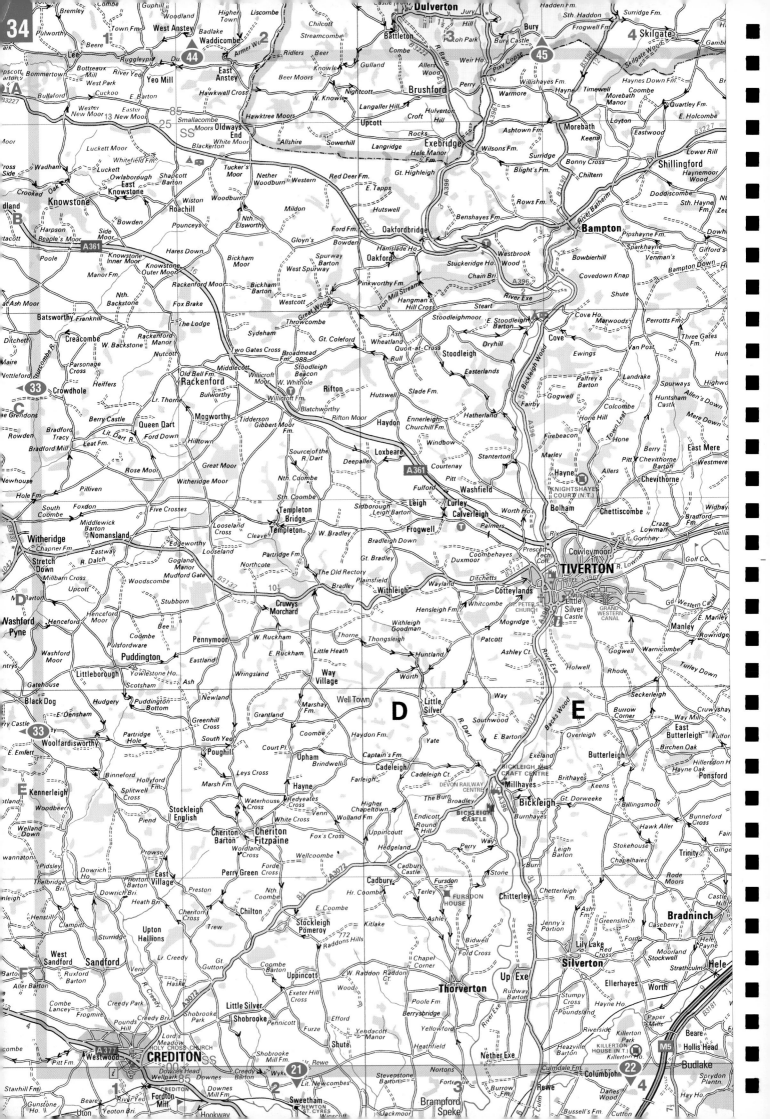

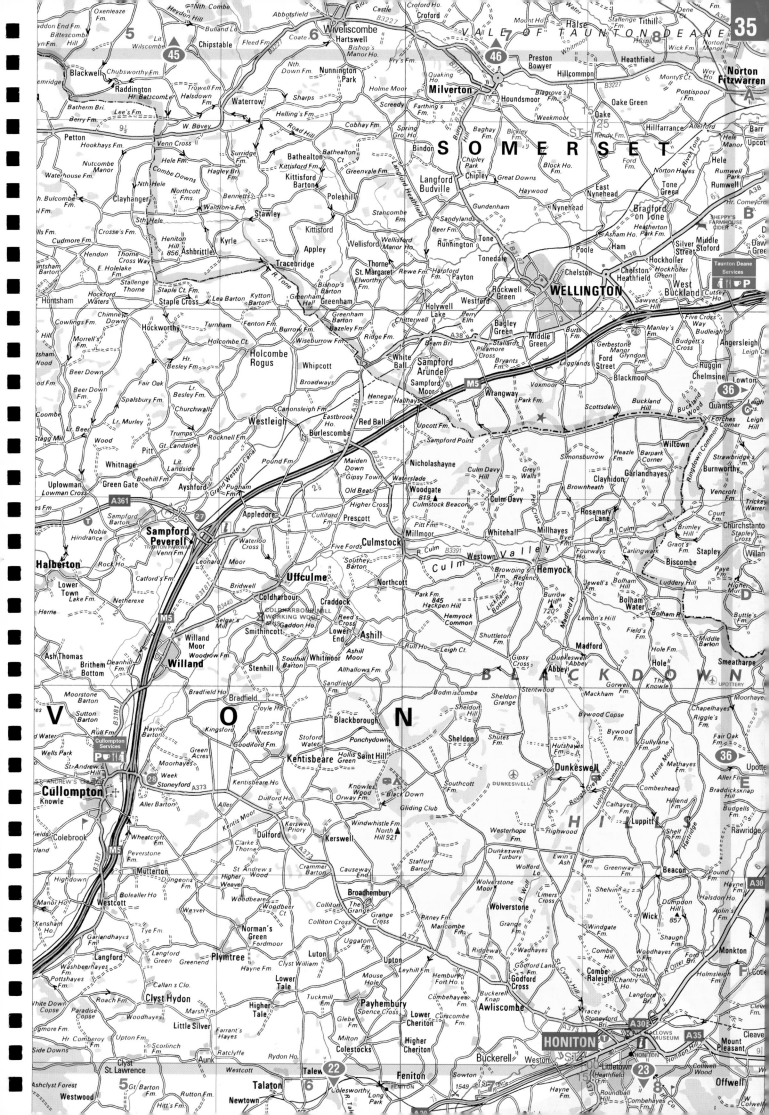

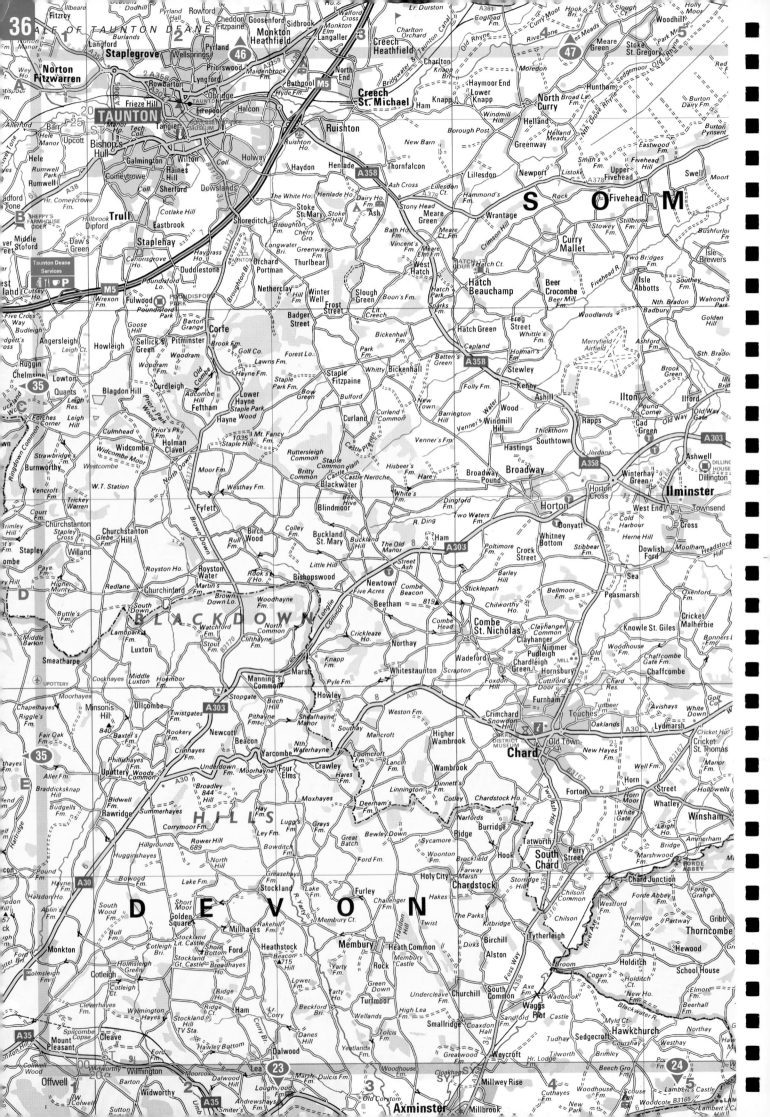

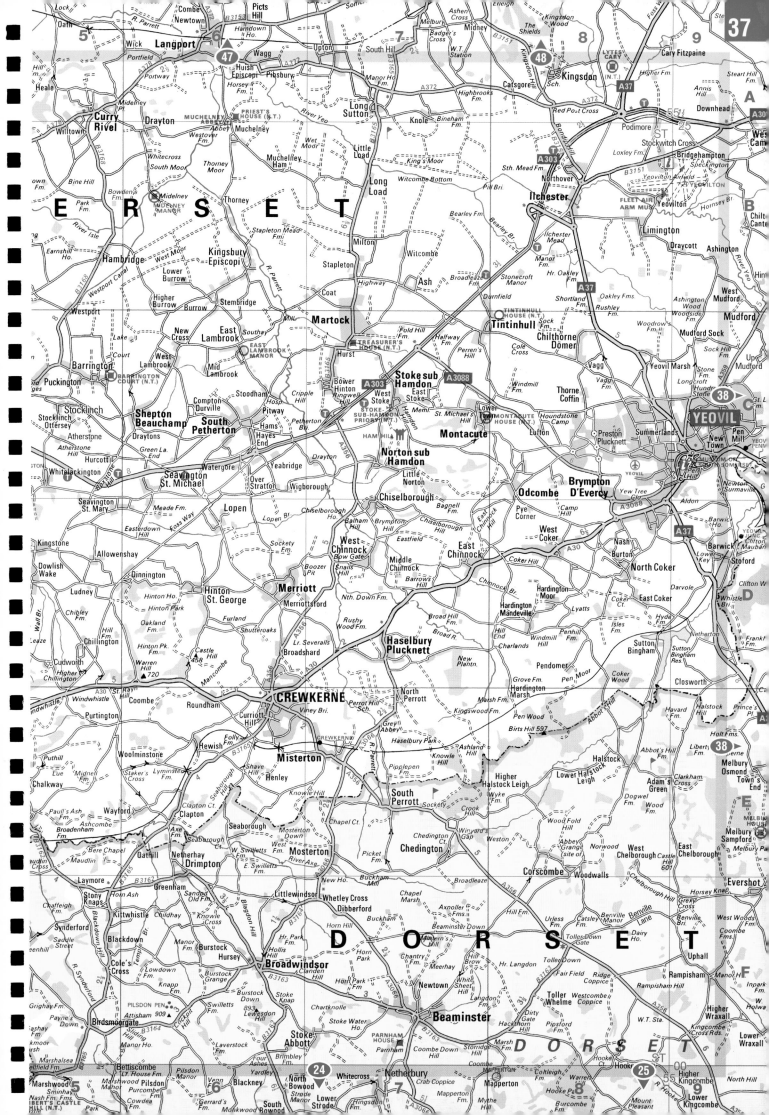

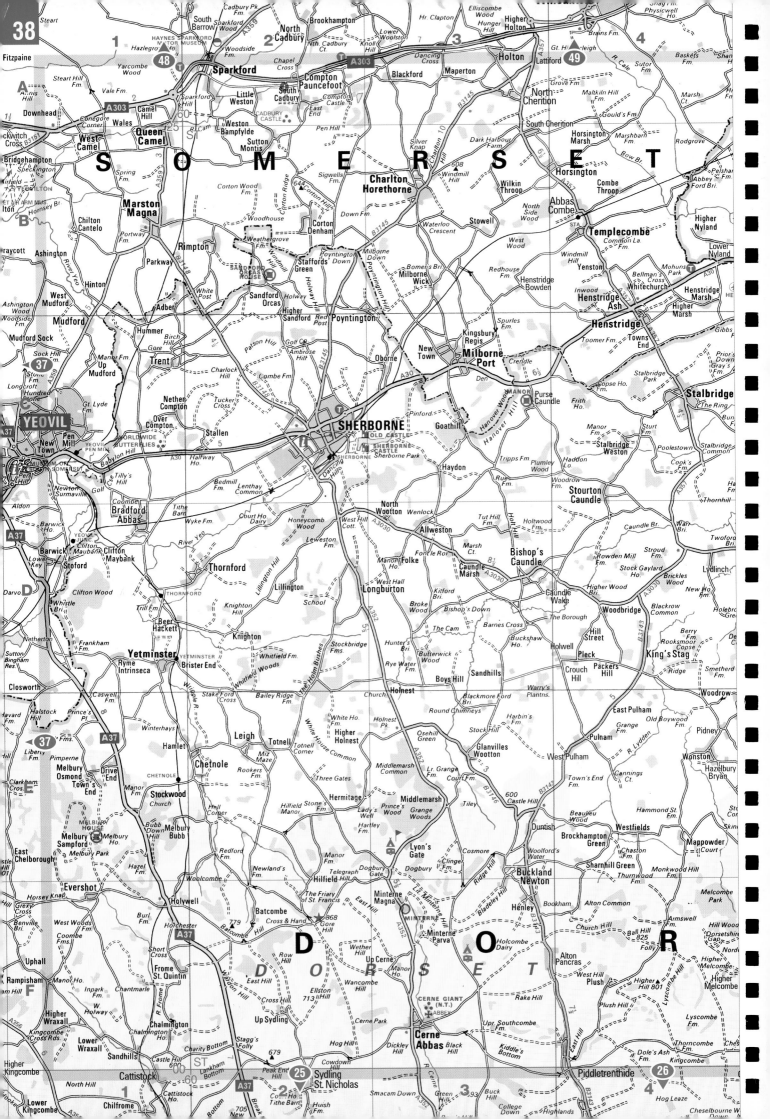

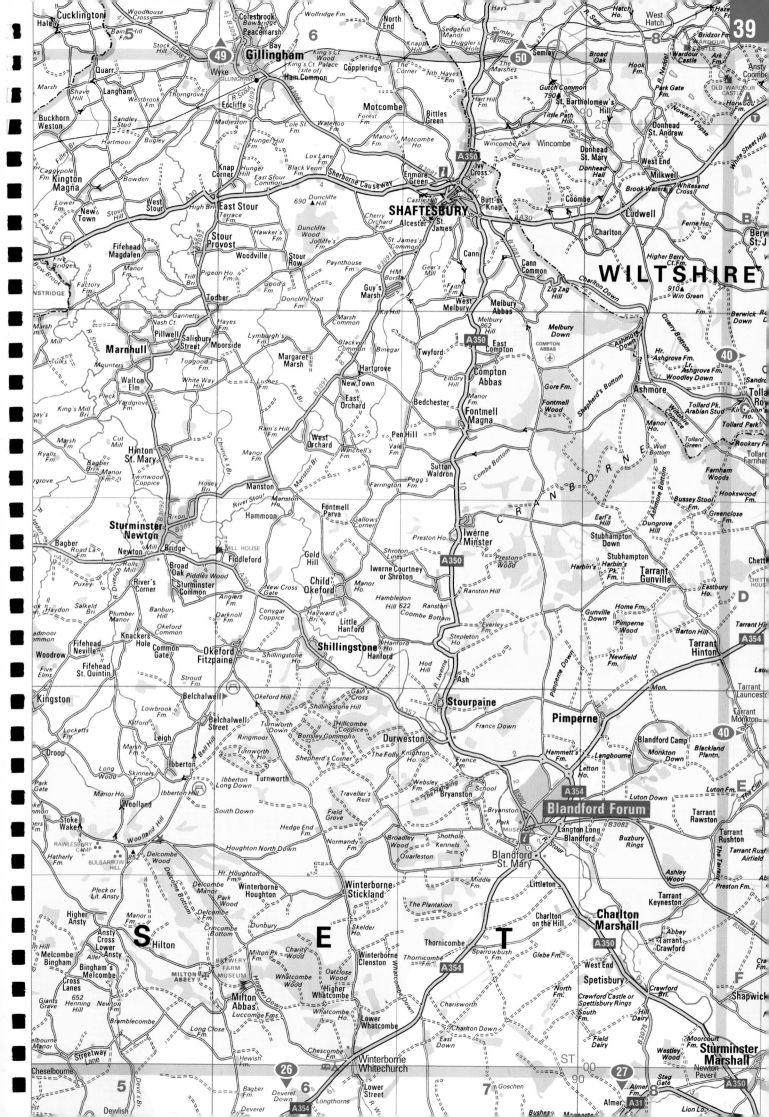

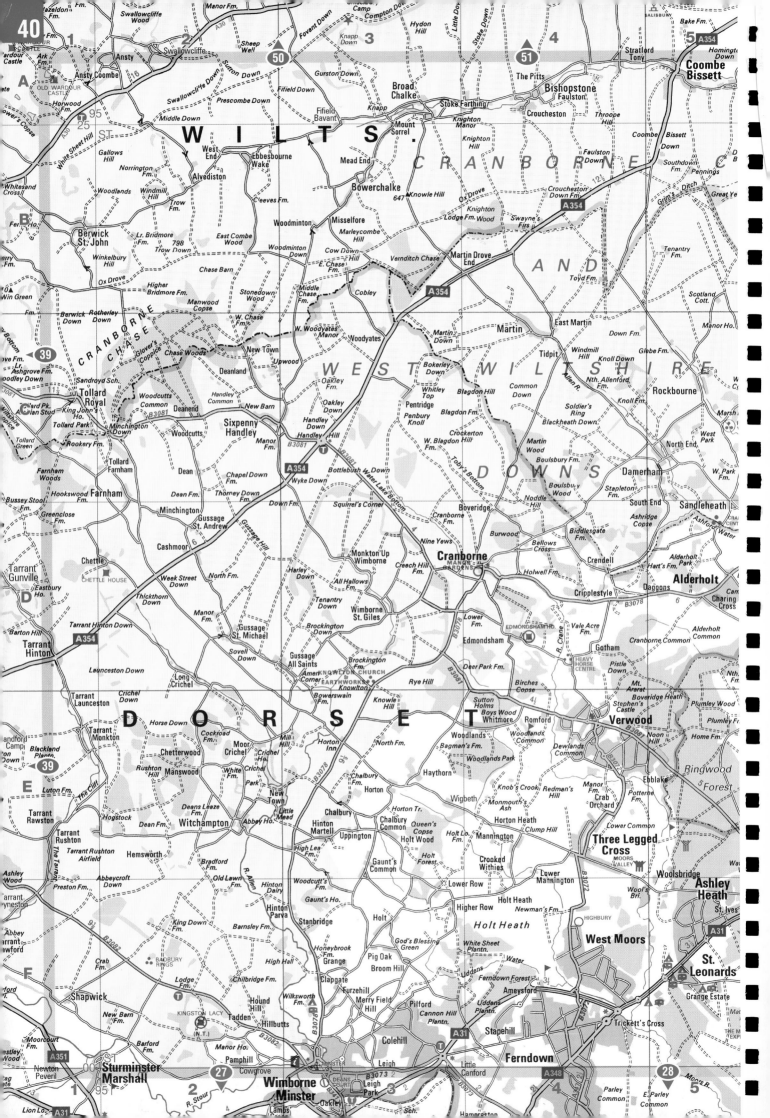

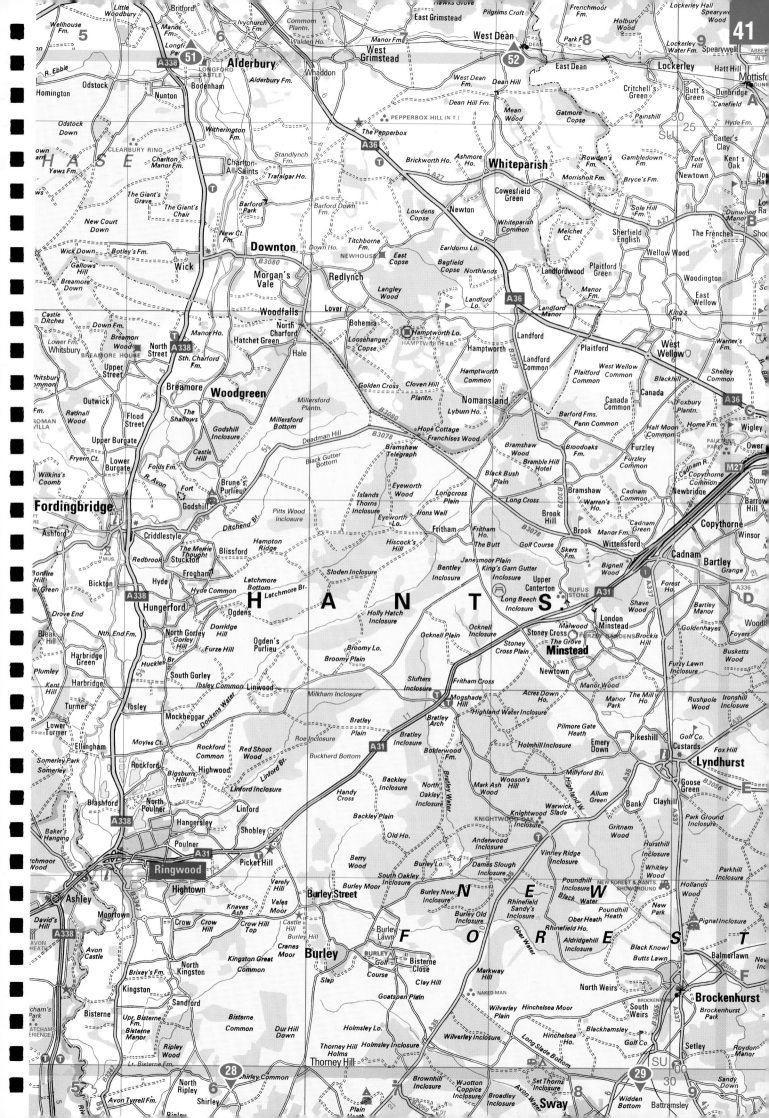

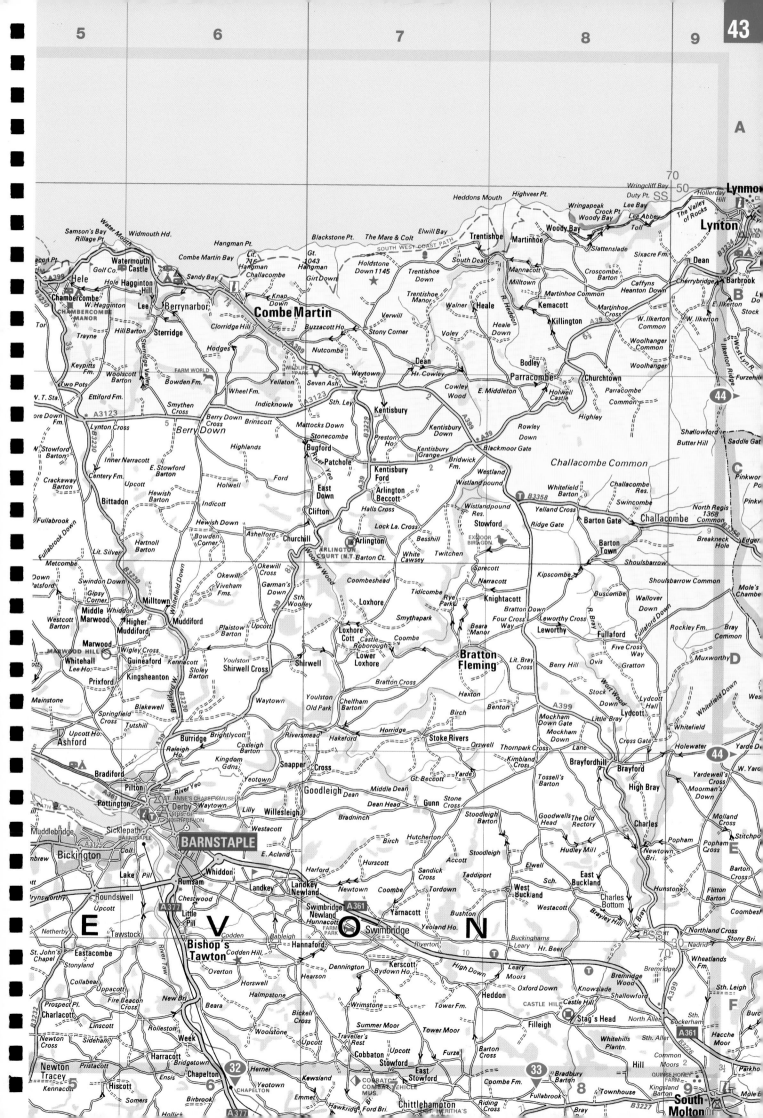

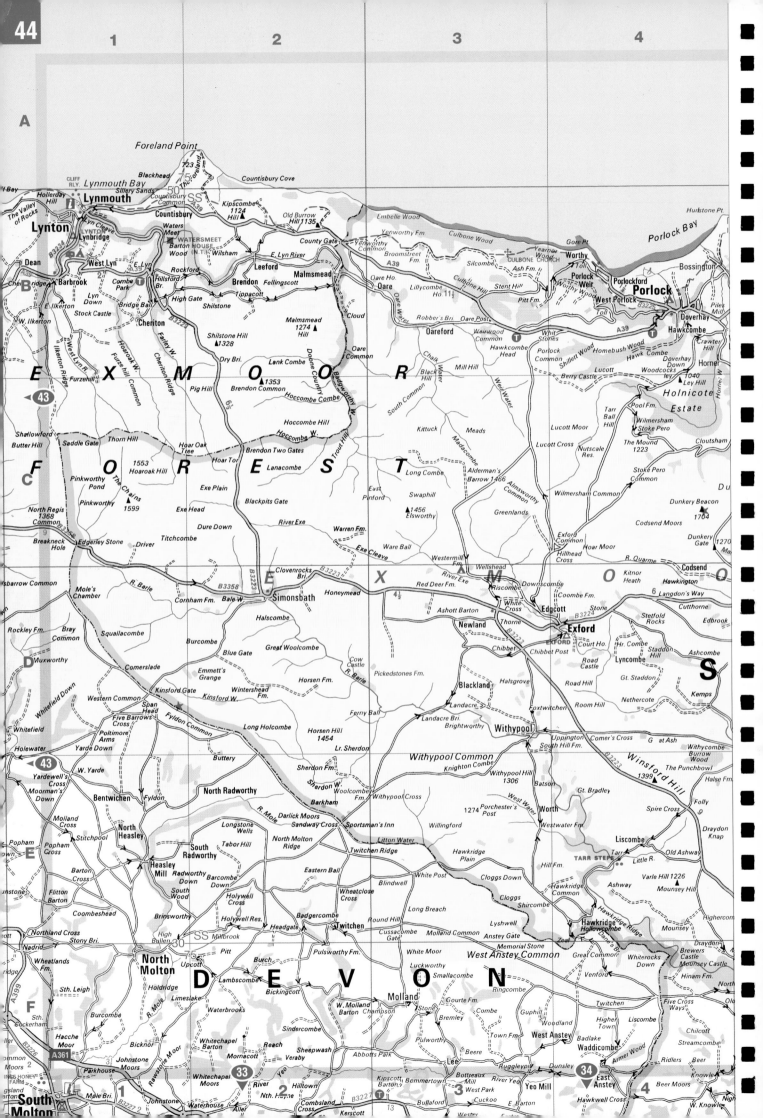

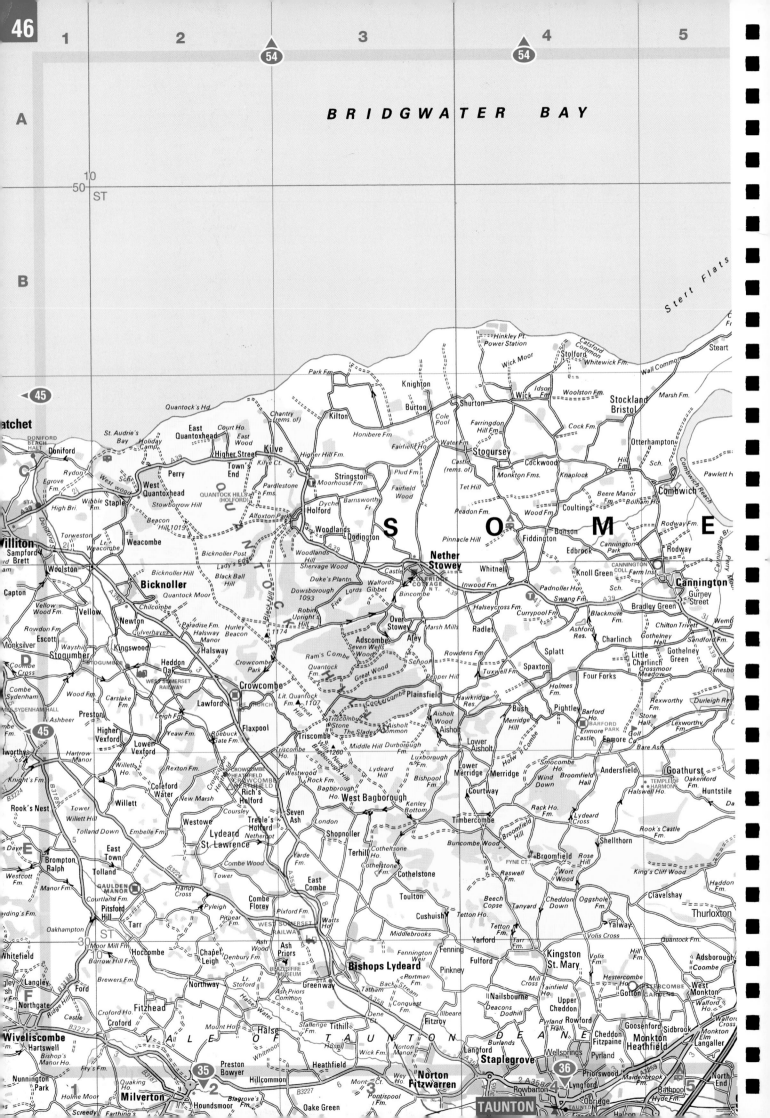

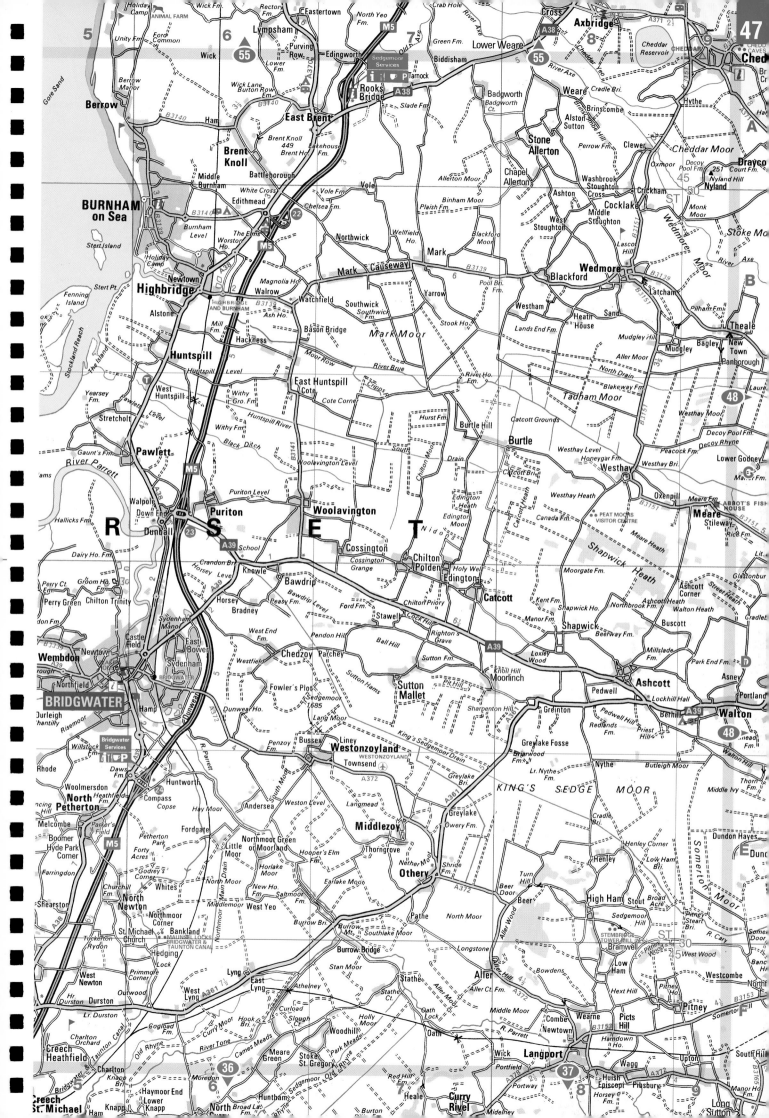

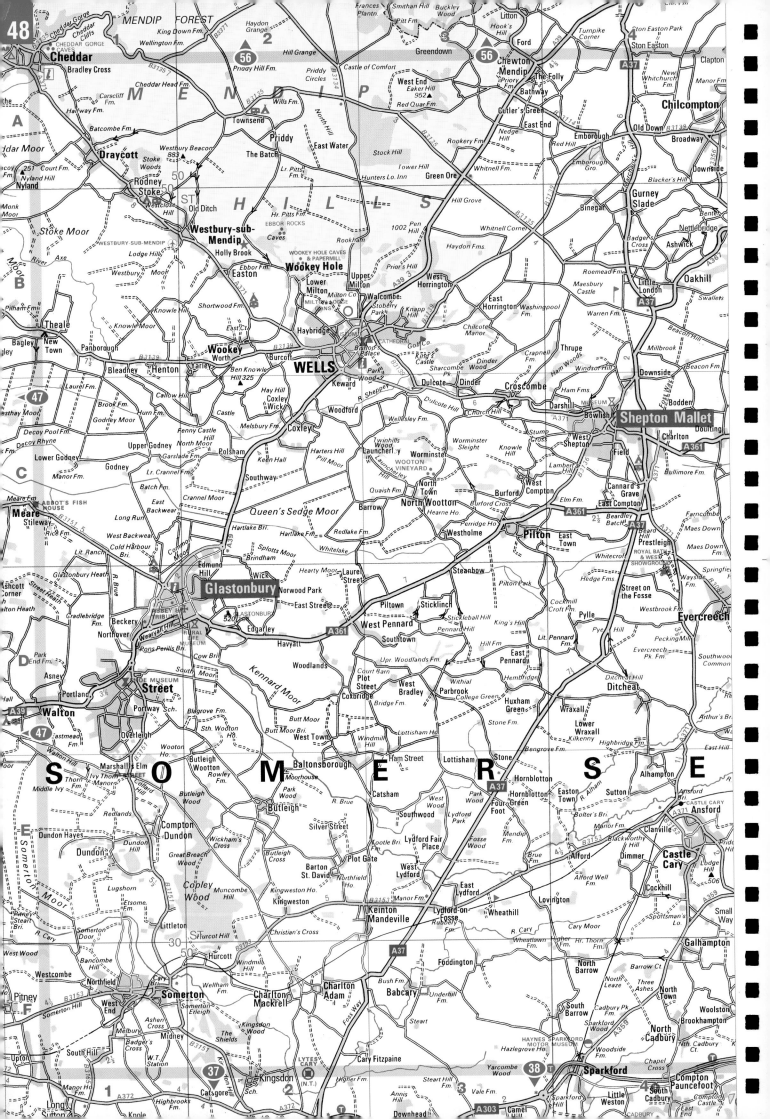

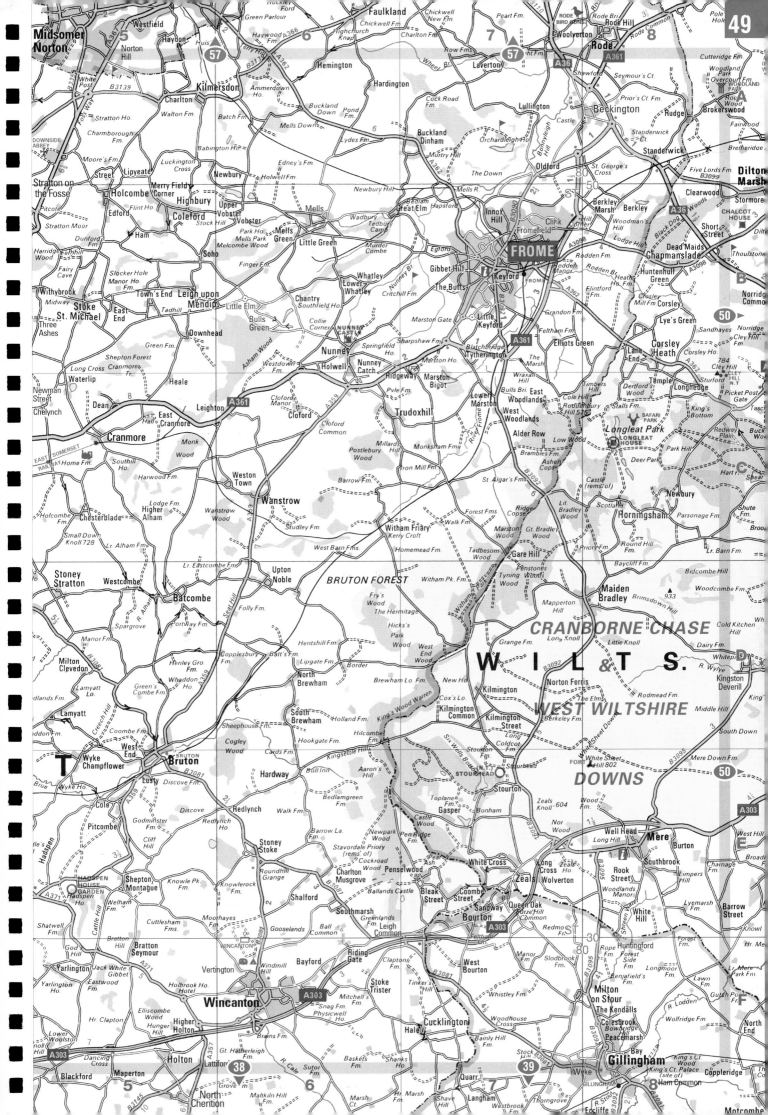

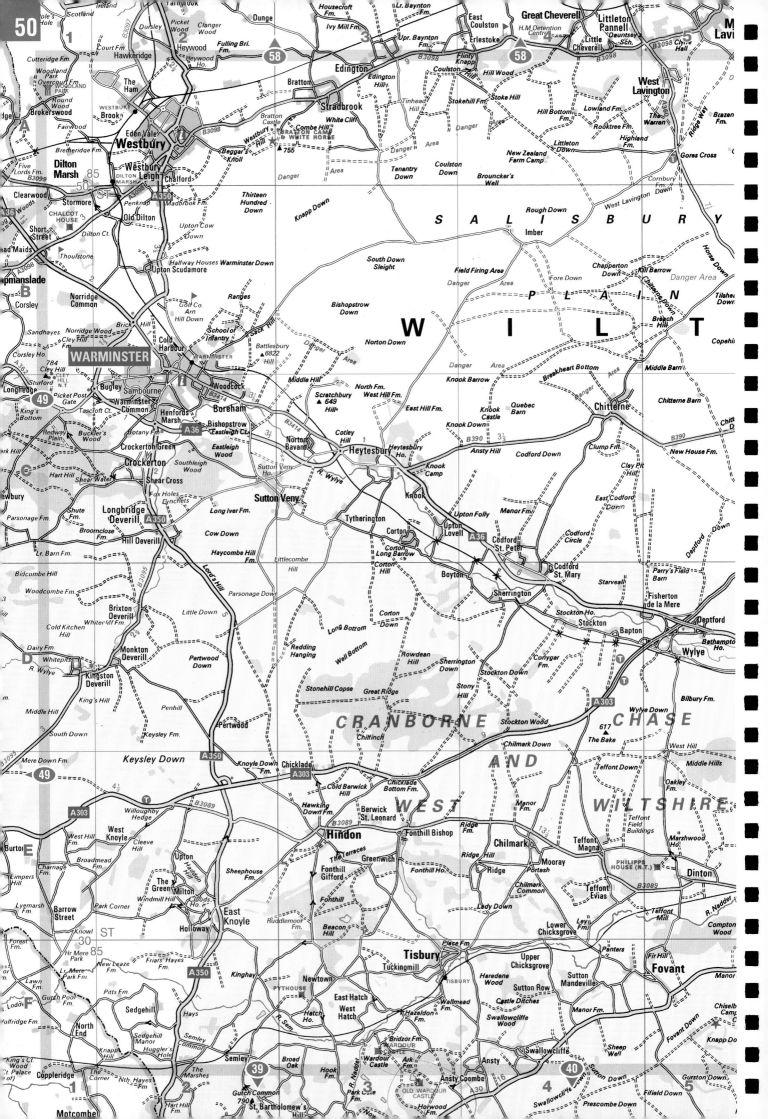

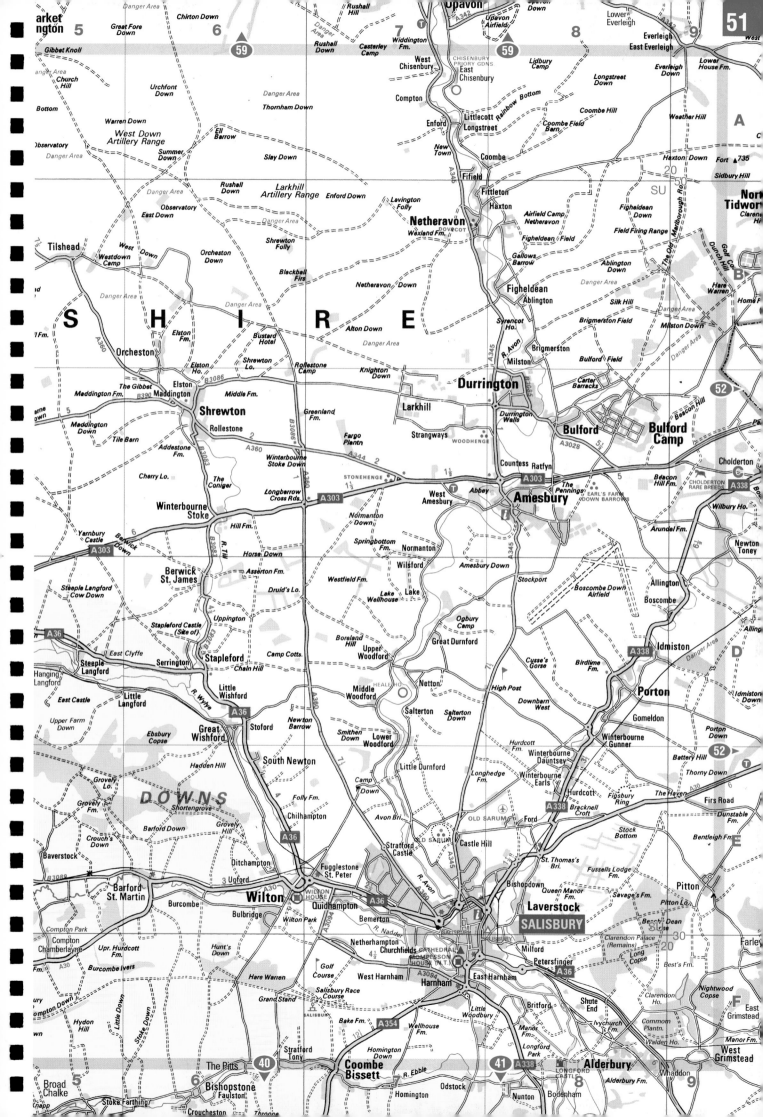

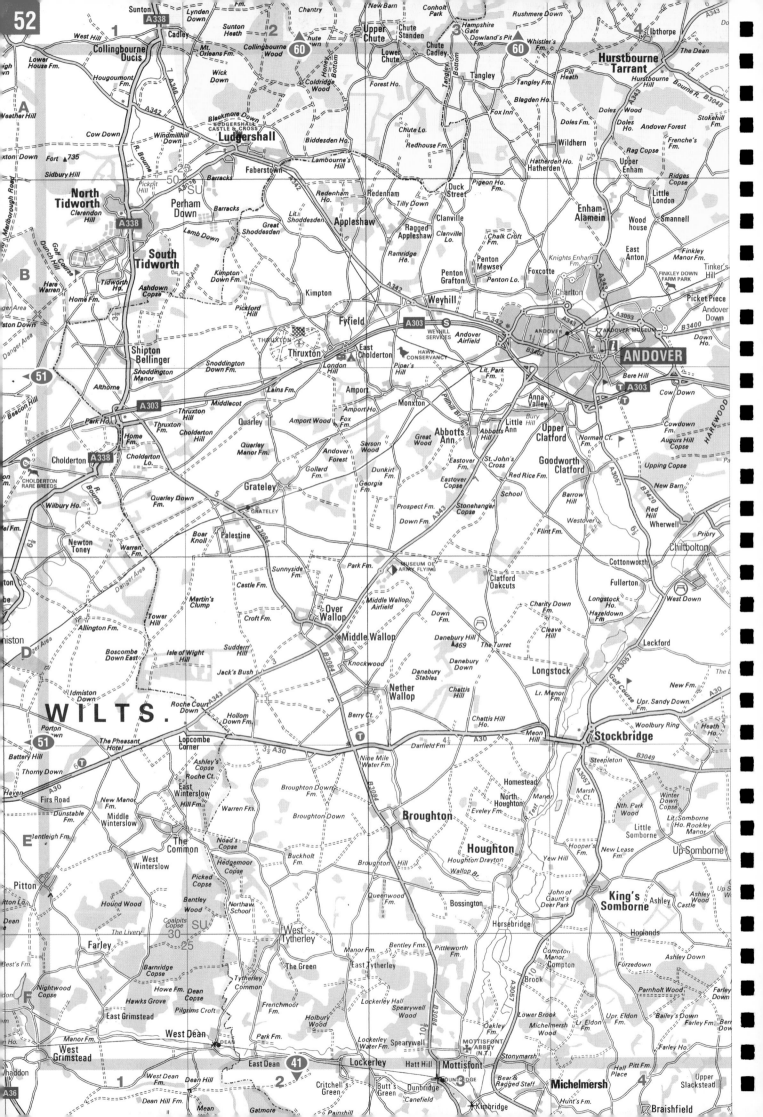

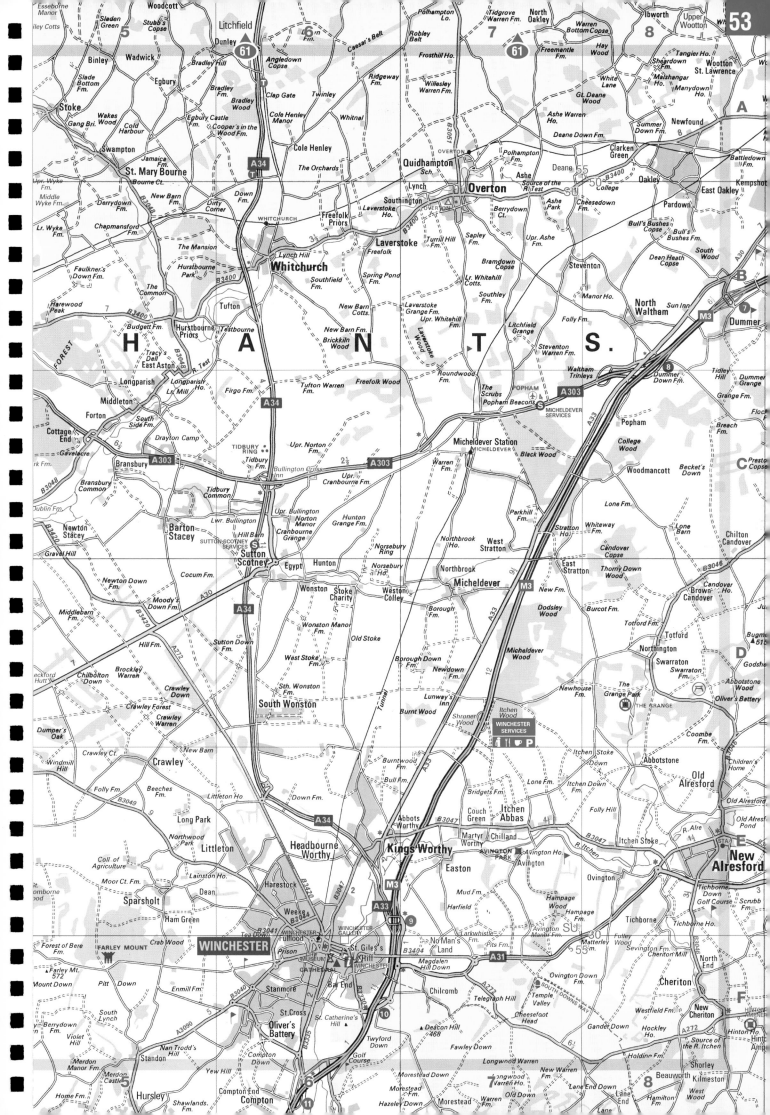

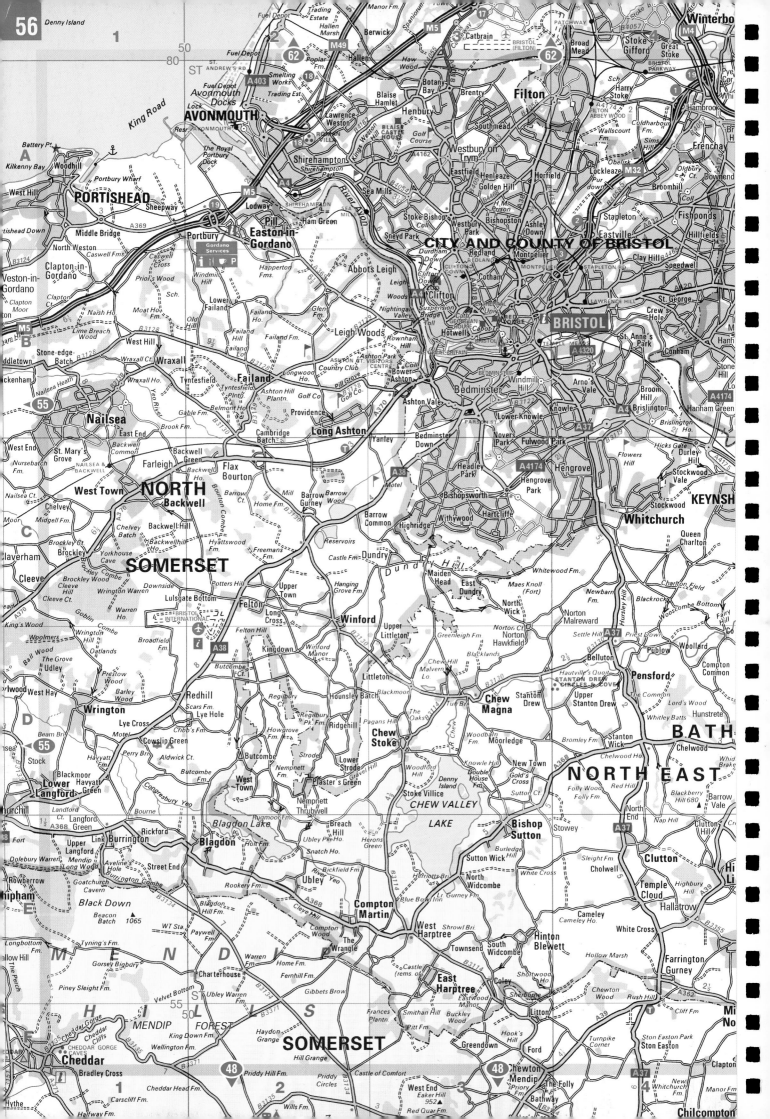

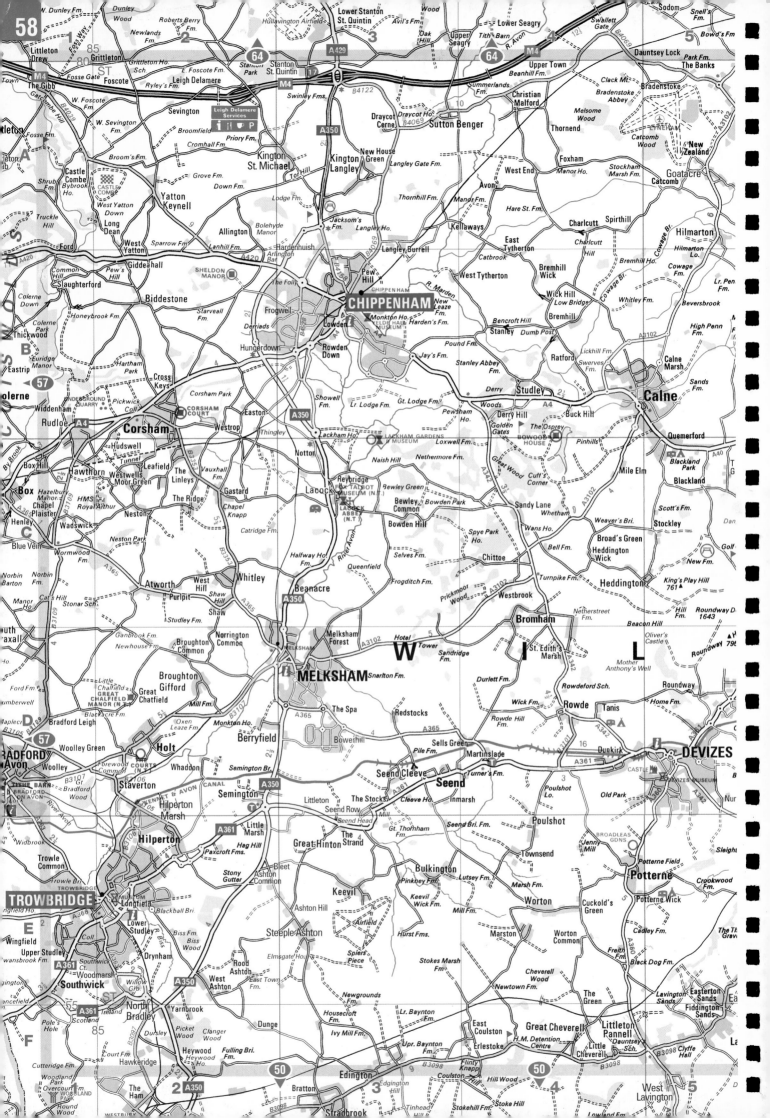

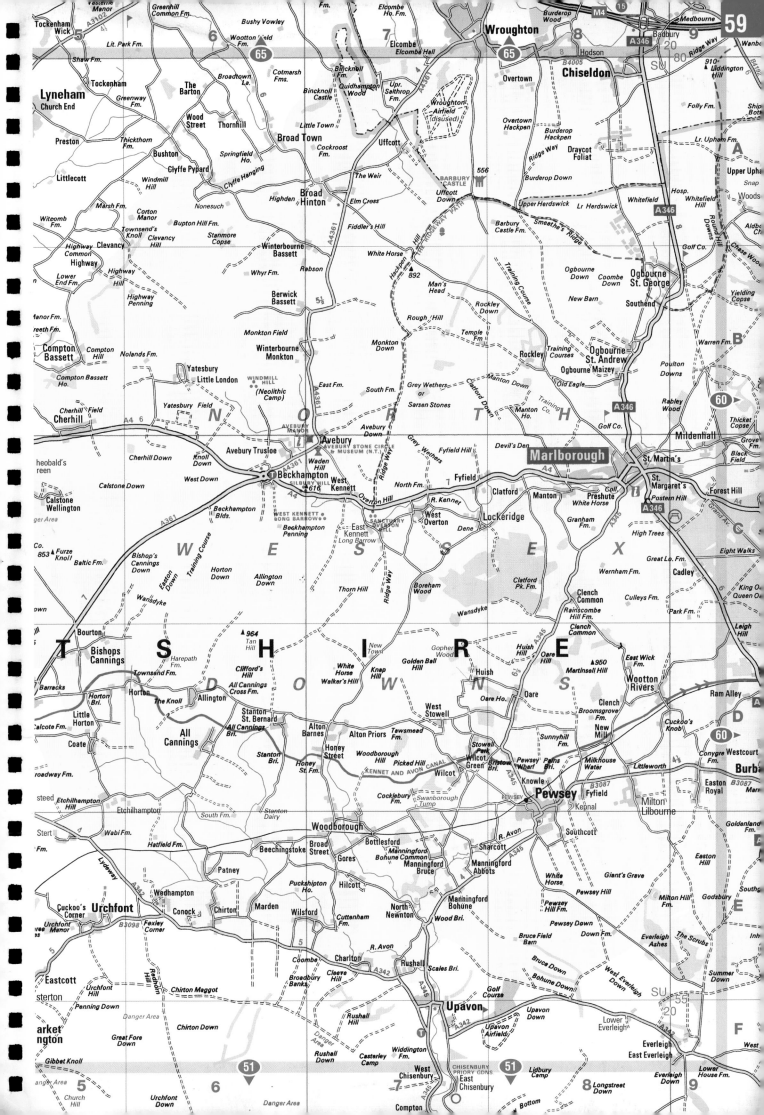

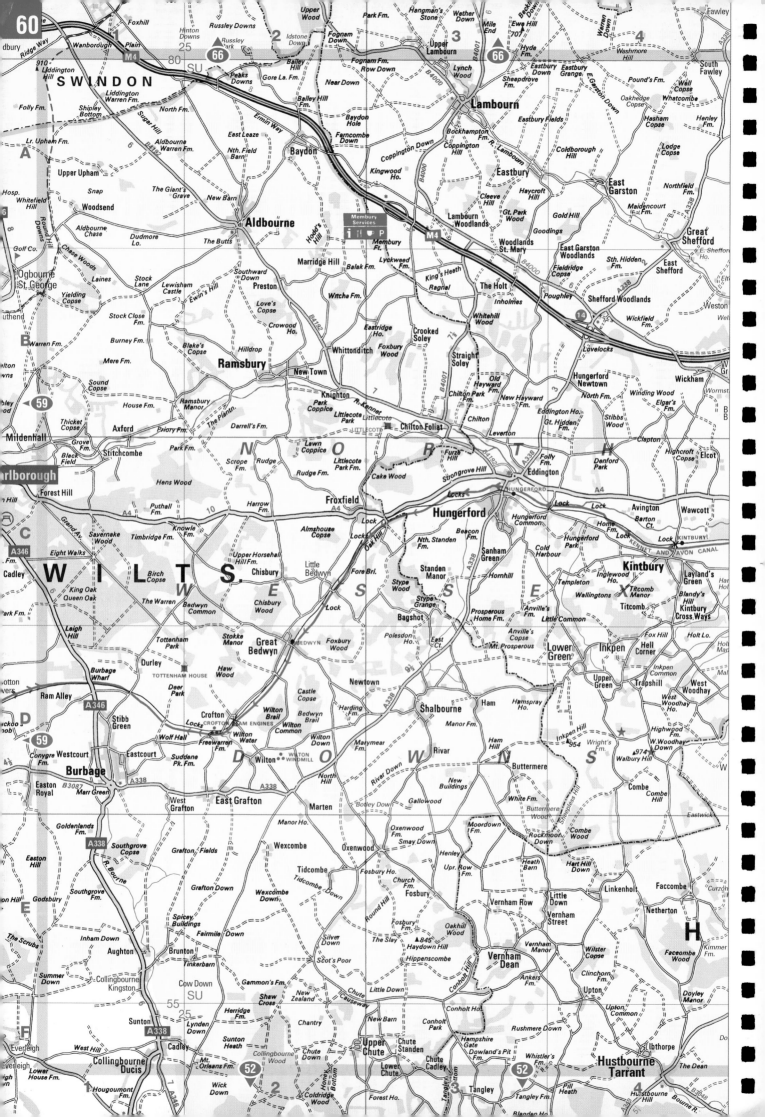

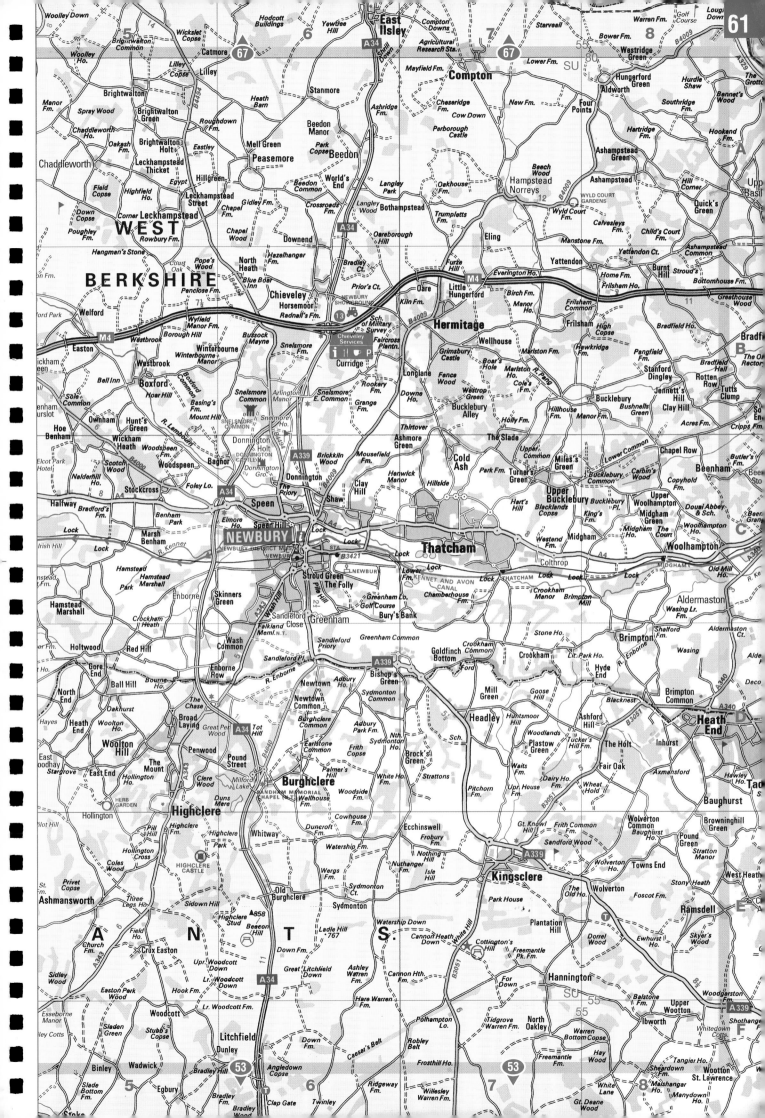

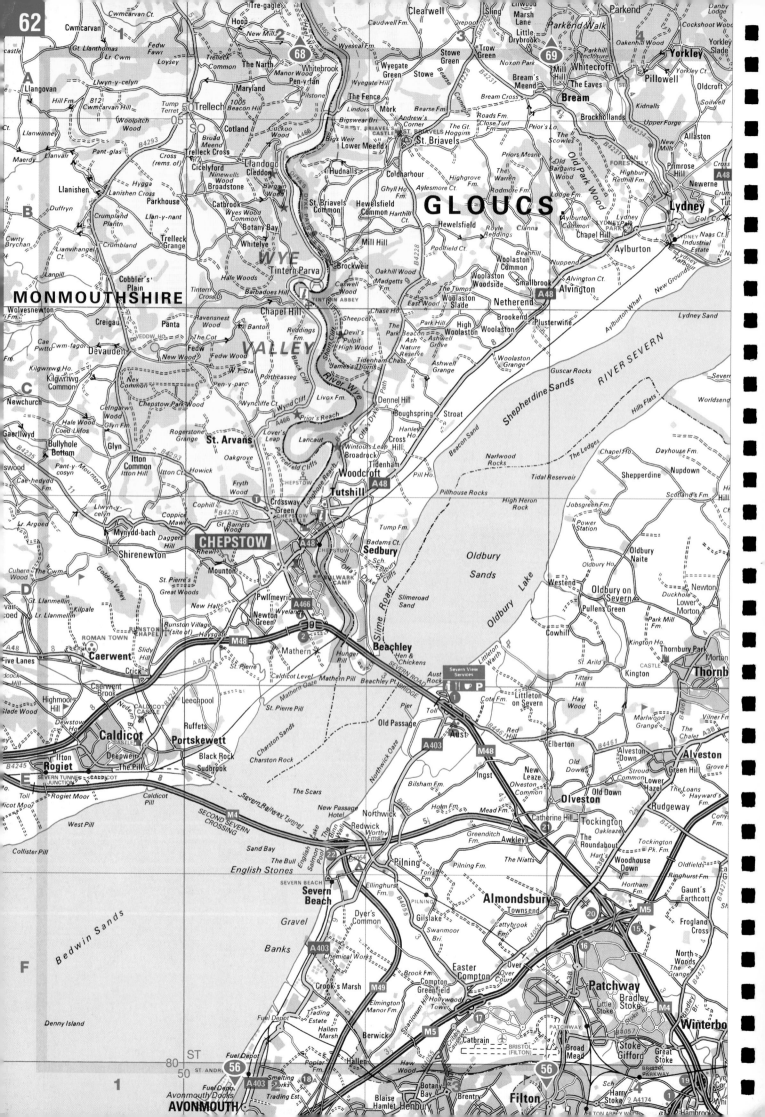

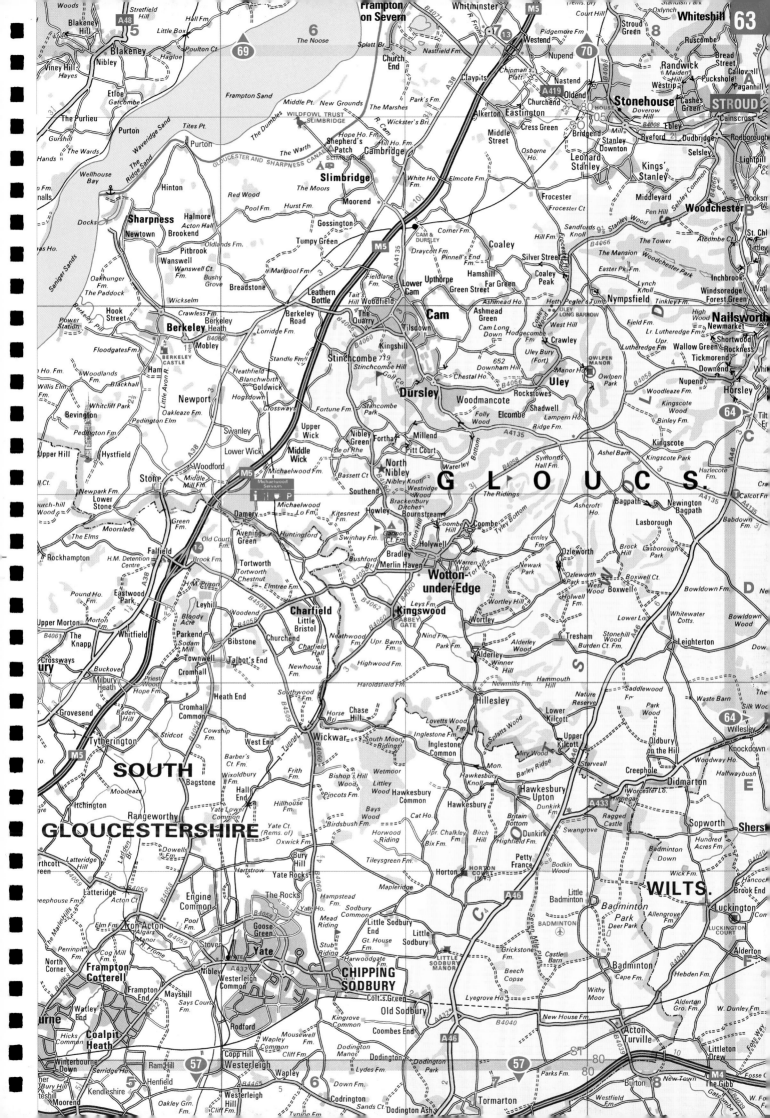

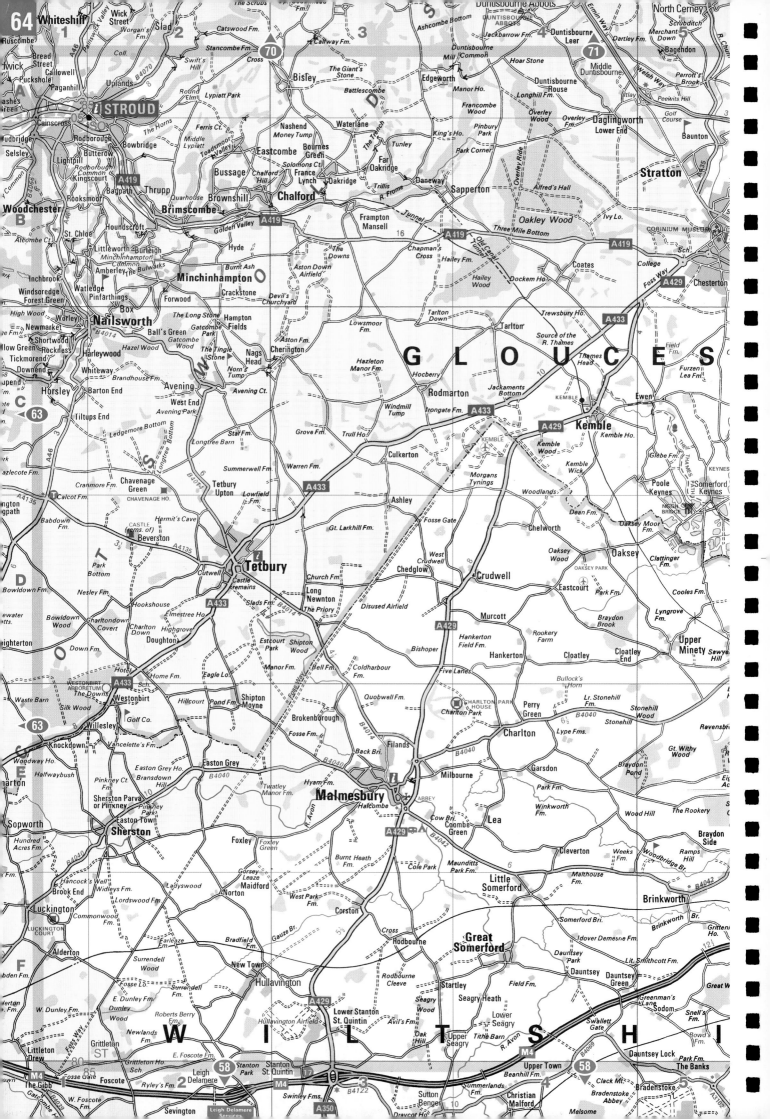

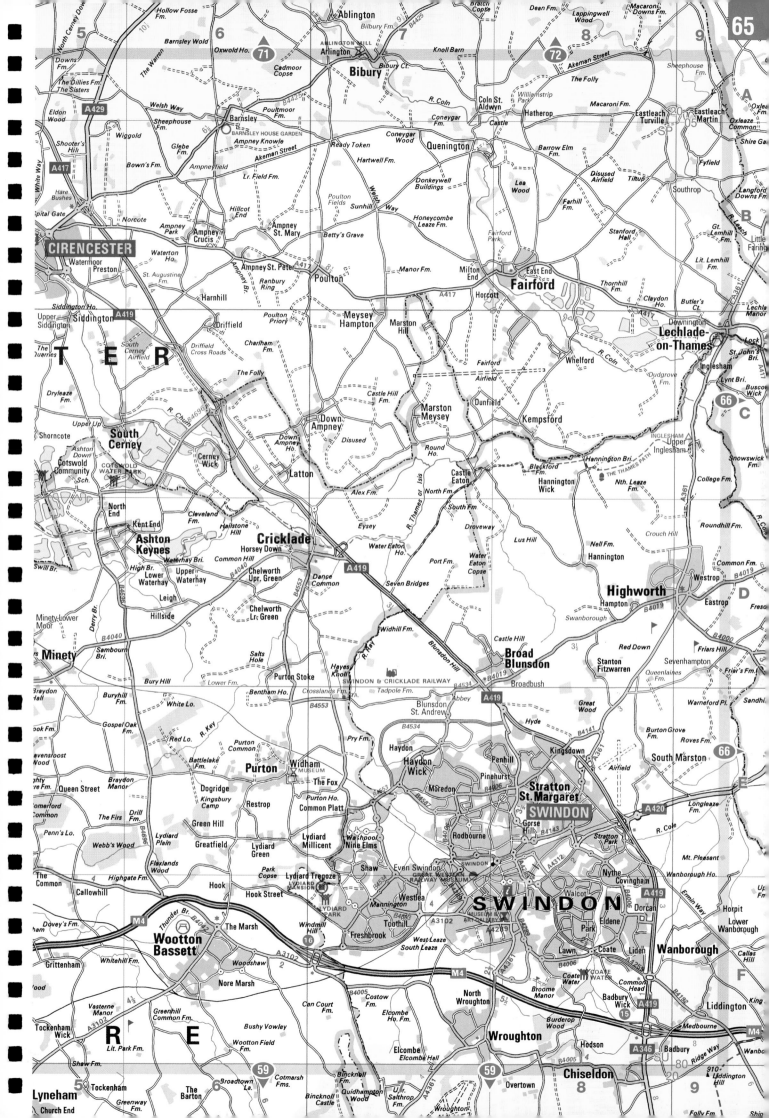

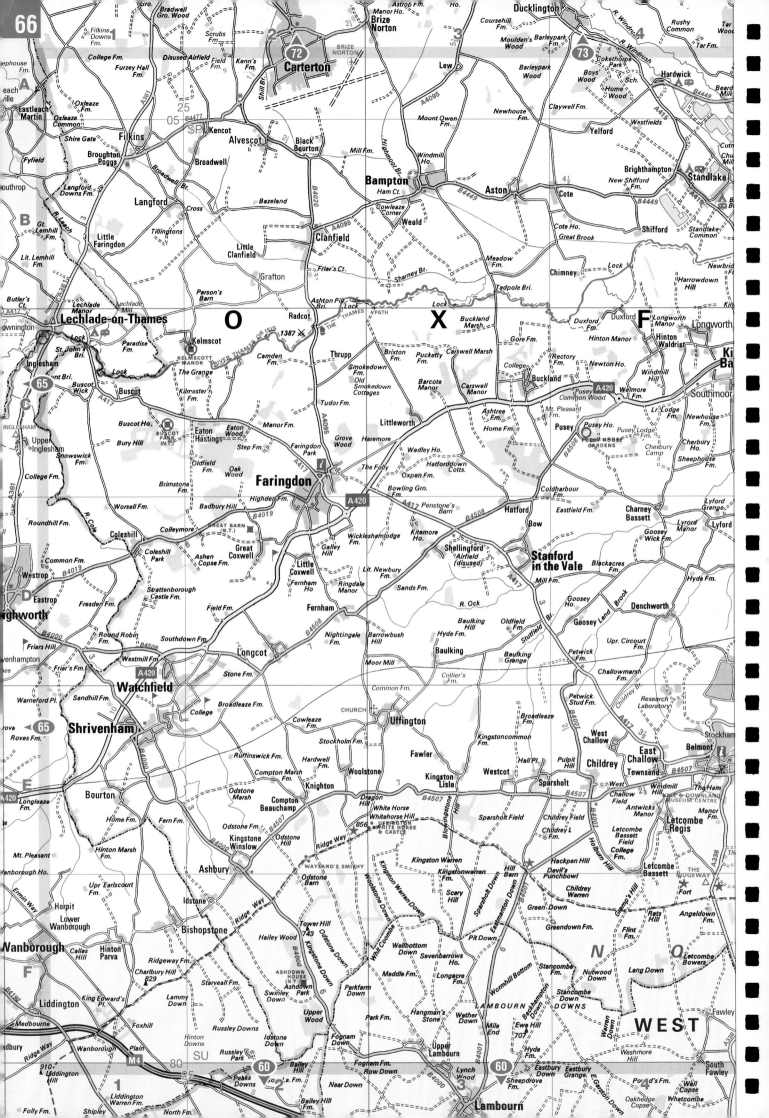

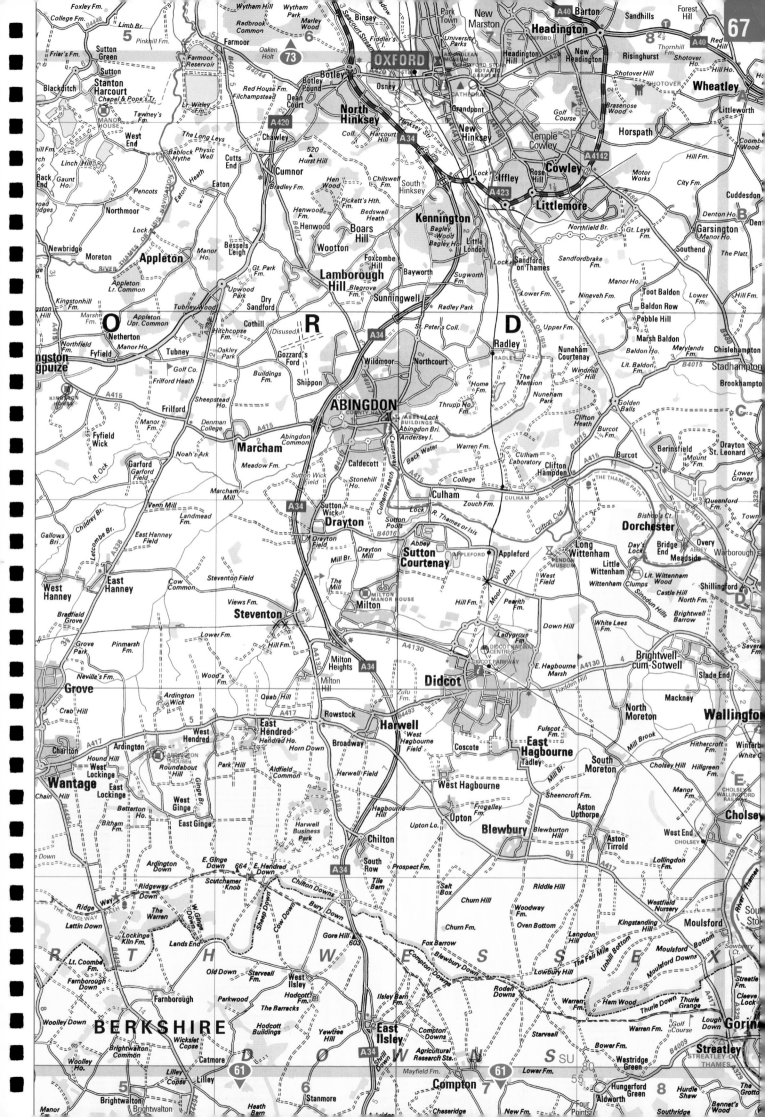

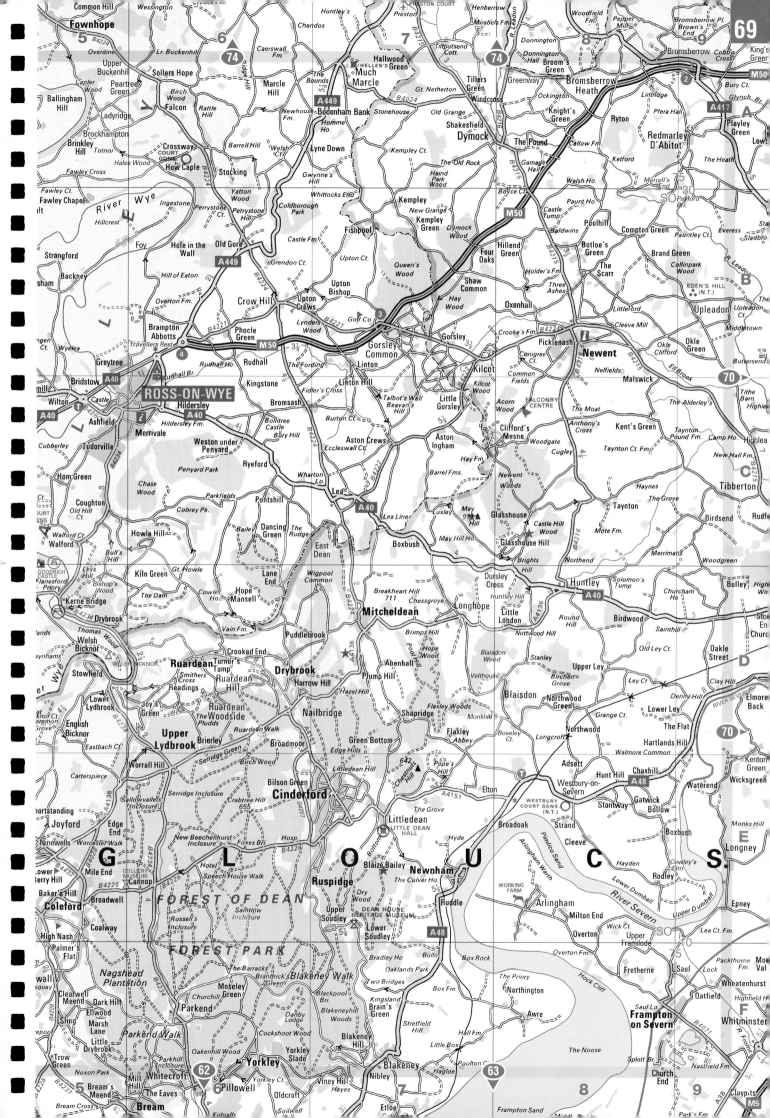

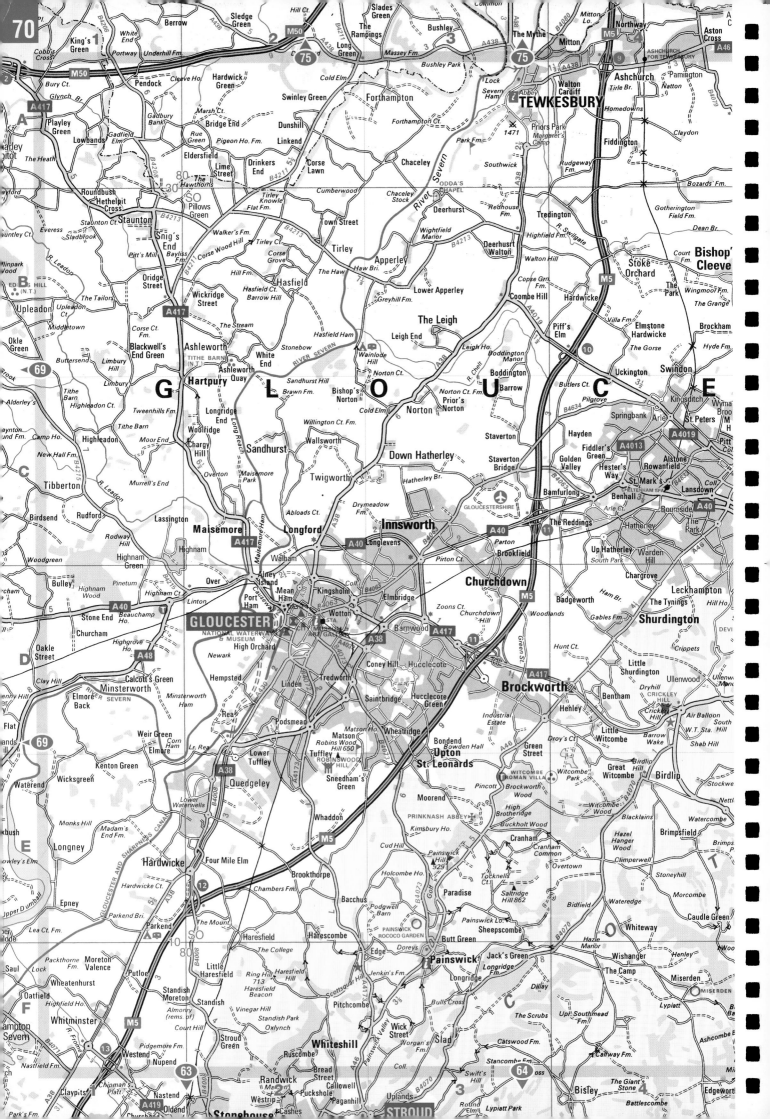

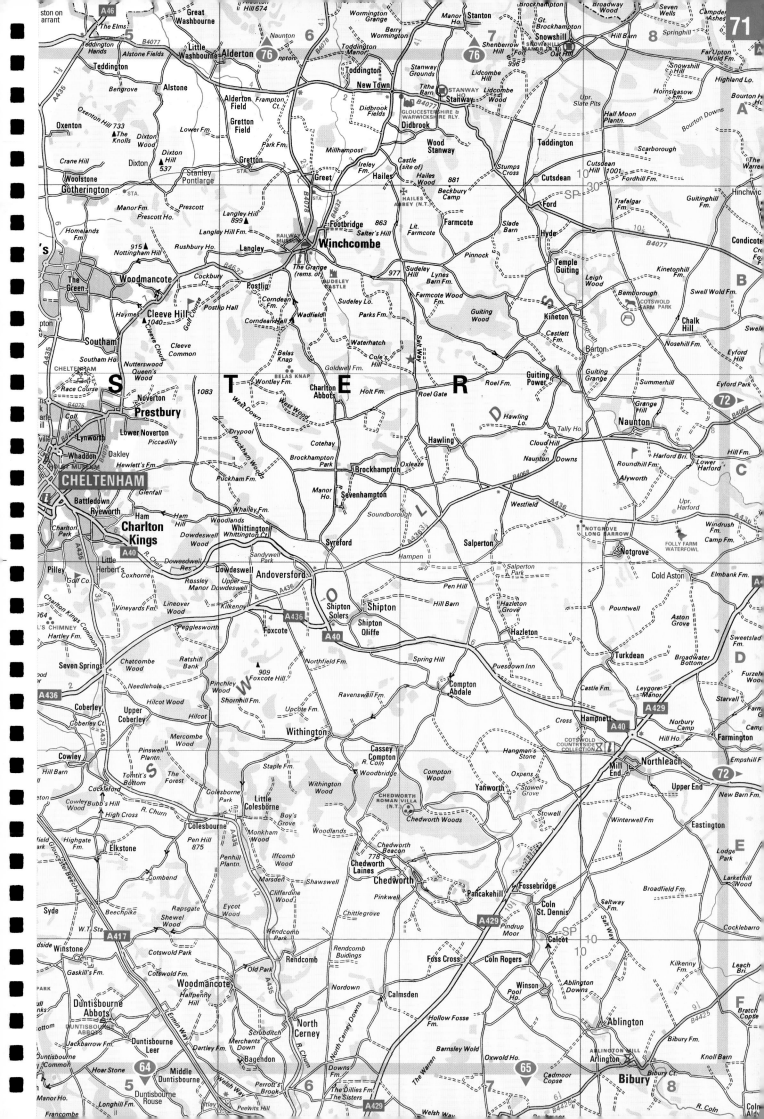

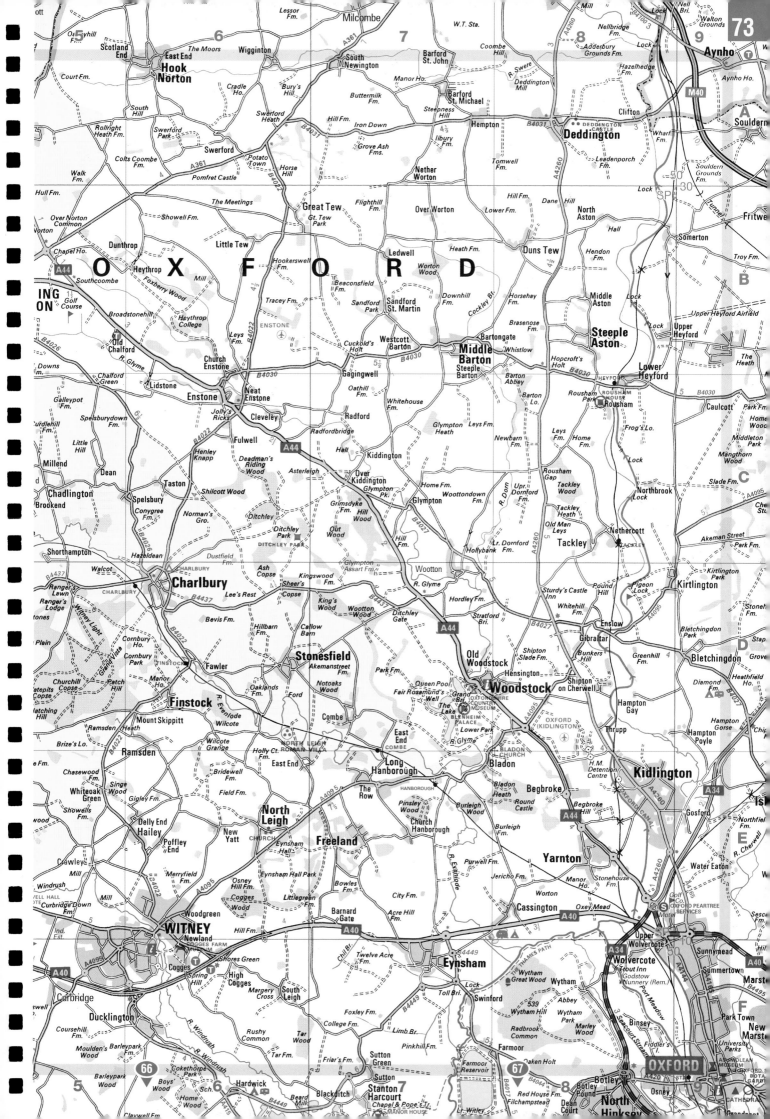

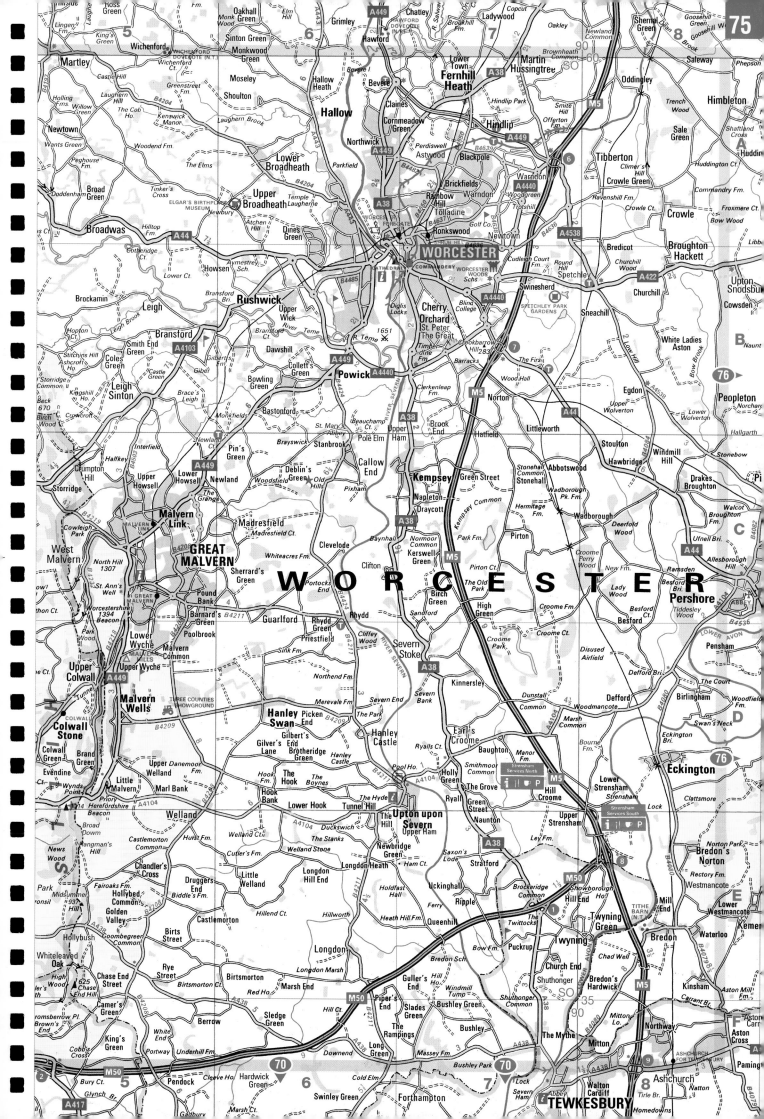

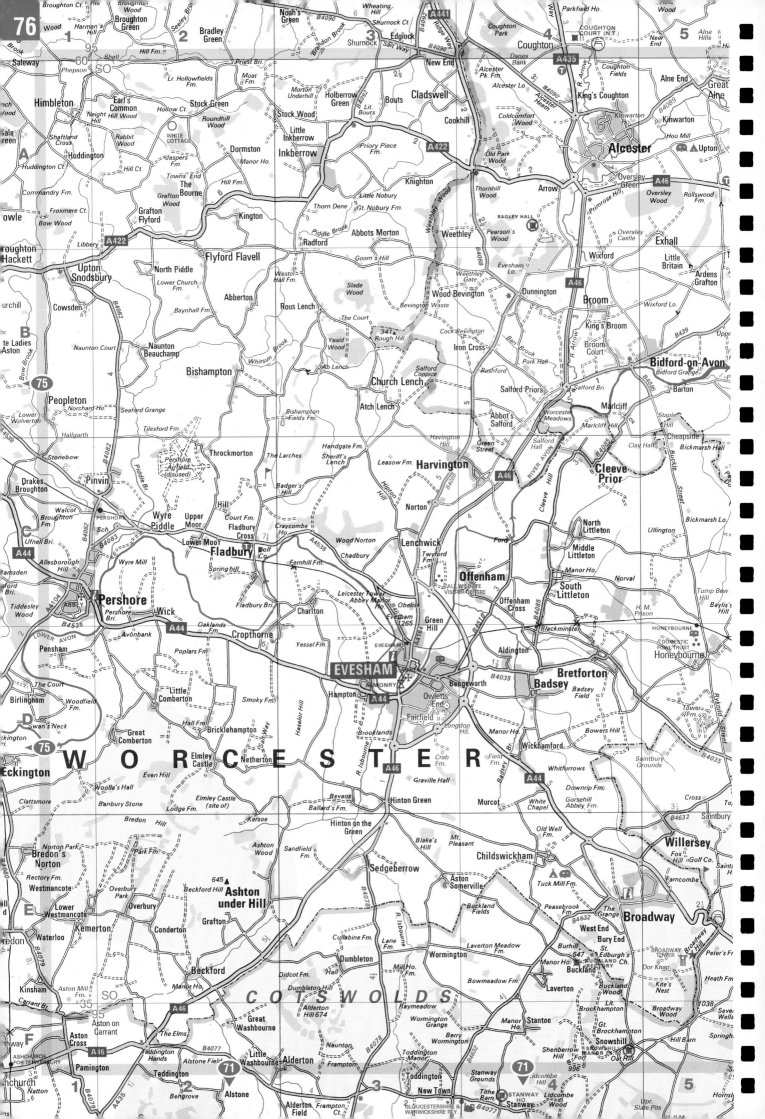

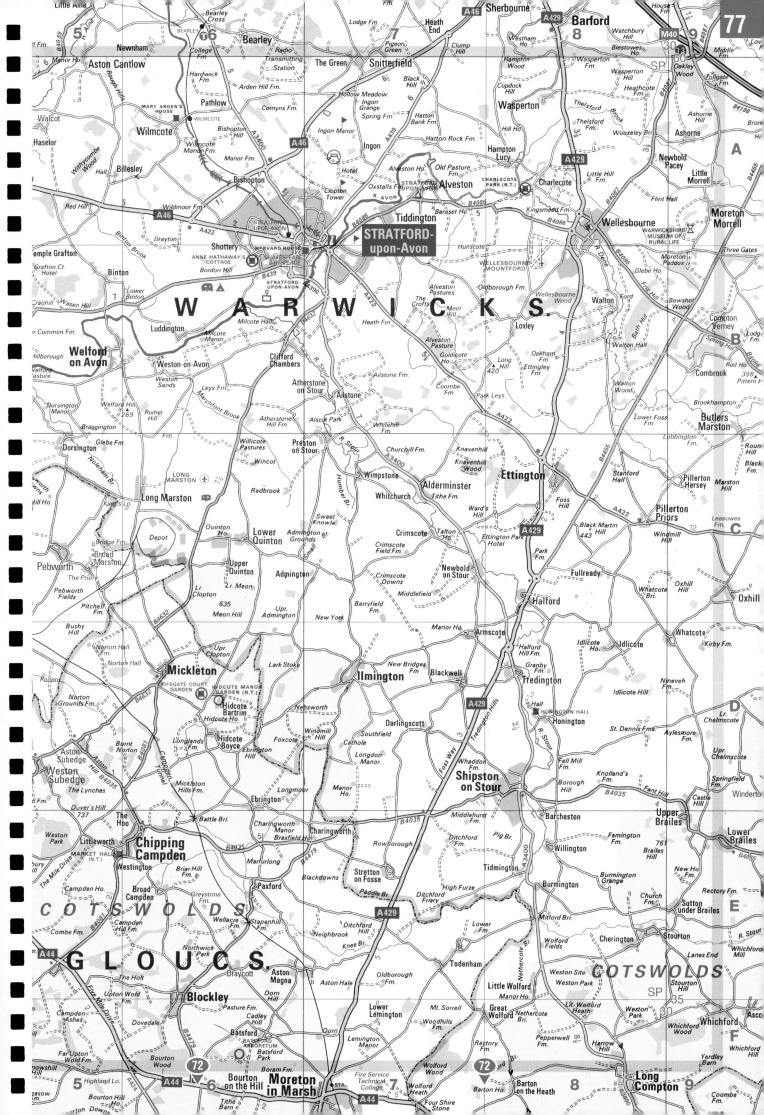

Key to Town Plan Symbols

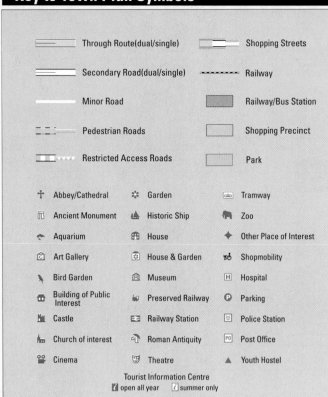

	Through Route(dual/single)		Shopping Streets
	Secondary Road(dual/single)	----	Railway
	Minor Road		Railway/Bus Station
---	Pedestrian Roads		Shopping Precinct
	Restricted Access Roads		Park

† Abbey/Cathedral ⁘ Garden 🚋 Tramway
🏛 Ancient Monument ⚓ Historic Ship 🐘 Zoo
Aquarium 🏠 House ◆ Other Place of Interest
Art Gallery House & Garden ♿ Shopmobility
Bird Garden 🏛 Museum H Hospital
Building of Public Interest Preserved Railway P Parking
Castle Railway Station Police Station
Church of interest Roman Antiquity PO Post Office
Cinema Theatre ▲ Youth Hostel

Tourist Information Centre
open all year   summer only

Bath

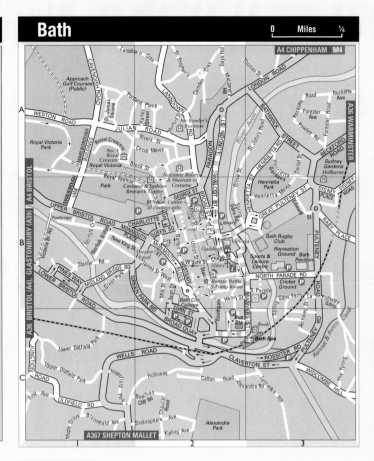

0   Miles   ¼

A4 CHIPPENHAM M4

Bath

Alexandra Park. . . C2
Alexandra Rd . . . C2
Approach Golf Courses (Public) . A1
Archway St C3
Assembly Rooms and Museum of Costume . . A2
Avon St B2
Barton St B2
Bath Abbey † . . B2
Bath City College . B2
Bath Pavilion . . . B3
Bath Rugby Club . B3
Bath Spa Station C3
Bathwick St . . . A3
Beechen Cliff Rd . C2
Bloomfield Ave. . . C1
Book Mus . . . C3
Broad Quay C2
Broad St B2
Brock St. A1
Bus Station C2
Calton Rd C2
Camden Cres . . . A2
Cavendish Rd. . . . A1
Charlotte St . . . B2
Chaucer Rd C2
Cheap St B2
Circus Mews . . . A2
Claverton St. . . . C2
Corn St C2
Costume and Fashion Research Centre B2

Cricket Ground. . . B3
Daniel St A3
Edward St A3
Ferry Lane B3
First Ave C1
Forester Ave. . . . A3
Forester Rd A3
Gays Hill A2
George St B3
Great Pulteney St. B3
Green Park. B1
Green Park Rd . . B2
Grove St. B3
Guildhall B2
Harley St A2
Hayesfield Park . . C1
Henrietta Gdns . . A3
Henrietta Mews . . B3
Henrietta Park . . B3
Henrietta Rd. . . . A3
Henrietta St . . . B3
Henry St. B2
Holburne Mus . . B3
Holloway C2
Information Ctr . B2
James St West. . . B2
Julian Rd A1
Junction Rd C1
Kipling Ave C2
Lansdown Cres . . A1
Lansdown Rd. . . . A2
Library B2
London Rd. A3
London St B2
Lower Bristol Rd . B1
Lower Oldfield Park. C1
Lyncombe Hill . . . C3

Manvers St. B3
Maple Grove C1
Margaret's Hill . . A2
Marlborough Buildings A1
Marlborough Lane B1
Midland Bridge Rd B1
Milk St B2
Milson St B2
Monmouth St. . . B2
Morford St A2
Mr Bowler's Business A2
New King St B1
No. 1 Royal Crescent . . . A1
Norfolk Bldgs. . . A1
Norfolk Cres. . . . B1
North Parade Rd . B3
Oldfield Rd C1
Paragon A2
Pines Way A1
Police Station . B3
Portland Pl. A2
Post Office . . . B2
Postal Museum B2
Powlett Rd. A3
Prior Park Rd . . . C3
Pulteney Gdns . . . B3
Pulteney Rd B3
Queen Sq. B2
Raby Place. B3
Recreation Ground B3
Rivers St A2
Rockliffe Ave . . . A3
Rockliffe Rd A3
Roman Baths & Pump Room . . B2

Rossiter Rd C3
Royal Ave. A1
Royal Cres A1
Royal Victoria Park A1
RPS National Centre of Photography . B2
St James Sq A1
St John's Rd A3
St Stephen's A2
Shakespeare Ave C2
Southgate C2
South Parade. . . . B3
Sports & Leisure Centre B3
Spring Gdns C3
Spring Gdns Rd . . B2
Stall St. B2
Stanier Rd A1
Sydney Gdns . . . A3
Sydney Place . . . B3
Theatre Royal . B2
The Tyning C3
Thomas St A3
Union St B2
Upper Bristol Rd . B1
Upper Oldfield Park. C1
Victoria Art Gallery B2
Victoria Bridge Rd B1
Walcot St B2
Wells Rd C1
Westgate St B2
Weston Rd A1
Widcombe Hill . . . C3

Bristol

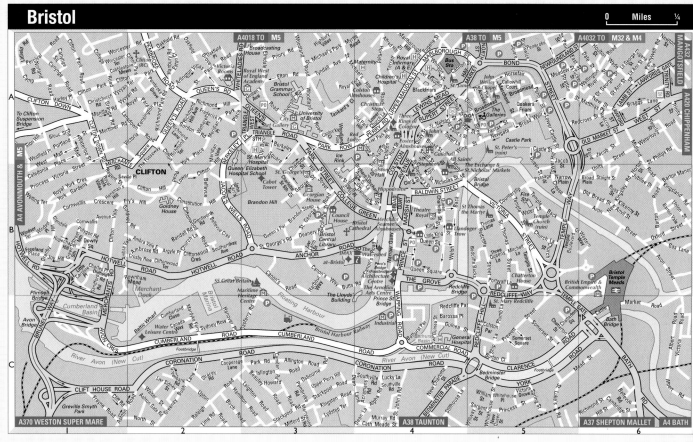

0 Miles ¼

Bristol

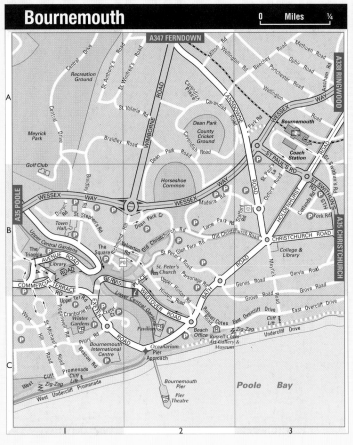

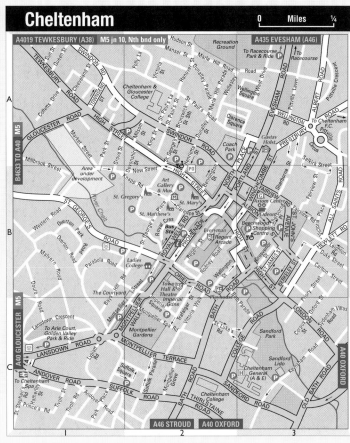

Bournemouth

Ascham Rd A3	Durrant Rd B1	Oxford Rd B3
Avenue Rd B1	East Overcliff	Park Rd A3
Bath Rd C2	Drive C3	Parsonage Rd B2
Beacon Rd C1	Exeter Cres C1	Pavilion 🏛 C2
Beechey Rd A3	Exeter Rd C1	Pier Approach . . . C2
Bournemouth	Gervis Place B1	Pier Theatre 🏛 . . . C2
International Ctr . C1	Gervis Rd B3	Police Station 🚨 . B3
Bournemouth Pier C2	Glen Fern Rd B2	Poole Bay C3
Bournemouth	Golf Club A1	Portchester Rd . . . A3
Station ≈ A3	Grove Rd B3	Post Office 🏤 . . . B1
Braidley Rd A1	Hinton Rd B2	Priory Rd C1
Cavendish Place . . B1	Holdenhurst Rd . . B3	Recreation Ground A1
Cavendish Rd A2	Horseshoe	Richmond Hill Rd . B1
Central Drive A1	Common B2	Russell Cotes
Christchurch Rd . . B3	Information Ctr ℹ . B2	Art Gallery
Cliff Lift C1/C3	Lansdowne Rd . . . A2	& Museum 🏛 . . . C2
Coach Station . . . A3	Lorne Park Rd . . . B2	Russell Cotes Rd . C2
College & Library . B3	Lower Central	St Anthony's Rd . . C1
Commercial Rd . . B1	Gdns B2	St Michael's Rd . . C1
Cotlands Rd B3	Madeira Rd B2	St Paul's Lane . . . B3
County Cricket	Methuen Rd A3	St Paul's Rd B3
Ground A2	Meyrick Park A1	St Peter's
Cranborne Rd . . . C1	Meyrick Rd B3	Church 🏛 B2
Dean Park A2	Milton Rd A2	St Peter's Rd B2
Dean Park Cres . . B2	Oceanarium ✦ . . . C2	St Stephen's Rd . . B1
Dean Park Rd A2	Old Christchurch	St Swithun's Rd . . A3
	Rd B2	St Swithun's
	Ophir Rd A3	Rd South B3

St Valerie Rd A2	
St Winifred's Rd . . A2	
Stafford Rd B3	
Terrace Rd B1	
The Square B1	
The Triangle B1	
Town Hall B1	
Tregonwell Rd . . . C1	
Underclliff Drive . . C3	
Upper Central	
Gardens B1	
Upper Hinton Rd . B2	
Upper Terr Rd . . . C1	
Wellington Rd . . . A3	
Wessex Way B2	
West Cliff	
Promenade C1	
West Hill Rd C1	
West Underclliff	
Promenade C1	
Westover Rd B2	
Wimborne Rd A2	
Winter Gardens 🏛 C1	
Yelverton Rd B2	
York Rd B3	
Zig-Zag Walks C1/C3	

Cheltenham

Albert Rd A3	Evesham Rd A3	New St B2
Albion St B3	Fairview Rd B3	North Place B2
All Saints Rd B3	Fairview St B3	Odeon 🎬 B3
Andover Rd C1	Folly Lane A2	Old Bath Rd C3
Art Gallery	Gloucester Rd . . . A1	Oriel Rd B2
& Mus. 🏛 B2	Grosvenor St B3	Overton Park Rd . . B1
Axiom Centre 🏛 . B3	Grove St A1	Overton Rd B1
Bath Parade B2	Gustav Holst	Oxford St C3
Bath Rd C2	Museum 🏛 A3	Parabola Rd B1
Bays Hill Rd B1	Hanover St A2	Park Place C1
Beechwood	Hatherley St C1	Park St A1
Shopping Centre B3	Henrietta St A2	Pittville Circus . . . A3
Bennington St . . . B2	Hewlett Rd B3	Pittville Cres A3
Berkeley St B3	High St B2/B3	Pittville Lawn A3
Brunswick St Sth . A2	Hudson St A2	Pittville Pump Room
Bus Station B2	Imperial Gdns . . . C2	& Racecourse ✦ . A3
Carlton Street . . . B3	Imperial Square . . C2	Playhouse
Cheltenham &	Information Ctr ℹ . B2	Theatre 🏛 B2
Gloucester	Keynsham Rd C3	Police Station 🚨 . B1
College A2	King St A2	Portland St B3
Cheltenham	Knapp Rd B2	Post Office 🏤 . . . B2
College C2	Ladies College 🏛 . B2	Prestbury Rd A3
Cheltenham F.C. . . A3	Lansdown Cres . . . C1	Prince's Rd C1
Cheltenham General	Lansdown Rd C1	Priory St B3
(A & E) 🏥 C3	Leighton Rd B3	Promenade B2
Clarence Square . . A2	London Rd C3	Queen St A1
Clarence St B2	Lypiatt Rd C1	Recreation Ground A2
Cleeveland St . . . A1	Malvern Rd B1	Regent Arcade . . . B2
Coach Park A2	Manser St A2	Regent St B2
College Rd C2	Market St A1	Rodney Rd B2
Colletts Dr A1	Millbrook St A1	Royal Cres B2
Corpus St C3	Milsom St A2	Royal Wells Rd . . . B2
Devonshire St . . . A2	Montpellier Gdns . C2	Sandford Lido . . . C3
Douro Rd B1	Montpellier Gr . . . C2	Sandford Park . . . C3
Duke St B3	Montpellier	Sandford Rd C2
Dunalley Par A2	Spa Rd C2	Selkirk St A3
Dunalley St A2	Montpellier St . . . C1	Sherborne Place . . B3
Everyman	Montpellier Terr . . C2	Sherborne St B3
Theatre 🏛 B2	Montpellier Walk . C2	St George's Place B2
		St George's Rd . . . B1
		St George's St . . . A1

St Gregory's 🏛 . . B2	
St James St B3	
St John's Ave B3	
St Luke's Rd C2	
St Mary's 🏛 B2	
St Matthew's 🏛 . . B2	
St Paul's Lane . . . A2	
St Paul's Rd A2	
St Paul's St A2	
St Stephen's Rd . . C1	
Suffolk Parade . . . C2	
Suffolk Rd C1	
Suffolk Square . . . C1	
Sun St A1	
Swindon Rd B2	
Sydenham	
Villas Rd C3	
Tewkesbury Rd . . . A1	
The Courtyard . . . B1	
Thirlstaine Rd . . . C2	
Tivoli Rd C1	
Tivoli St C1	
Town Hall &	
Theatre 🏛 B2	
Townsend St A1	
Trafalgar St C2	
Victoria Pl. B3	
Victoria St A2	
Vittoria Walk C2	
Wellesley Rd A2	
Wellington Rd A3	
Wellington Square A3	
Wellington St B2	
West Drive A3	
Western Rd B1	
Winchcombe St . . B3	

Exeter

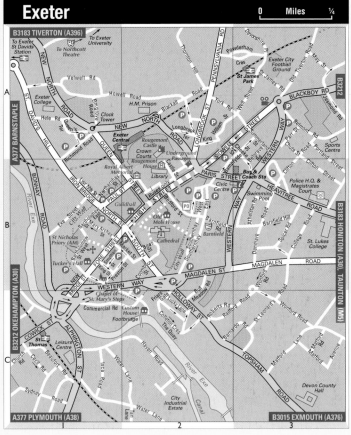

Gloucester

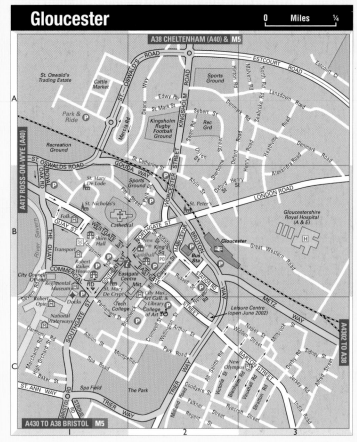

Exeter

Alphington St C1
Athelstan Rd B3
Bampfylde St B2
Barnardo Rd C3
Barnfield
  Theatre 🎭 B2
Barnfield Rd B2
Barnfield Hill B3
Bartholomew St
  East B1
Bartholomew St
  West B1
Bear St B2
Beaufort Rd C1
Bedford St B2
Belgrave Rd A3
Belmont Rd A3
Blackall Rd B2
Blackboy Rd A3
Bonhay Rd B1
Bull Meadow Rd . C2
Bus & Coach Sta.. B3
Castle St B2
Cecil Rd C1
Chapel of St. Mary's
  Steps ✦ B1
Cheeke St A3
Church Rd C1
Chute St A3
City Industrial
  Estate C2
City Wall B1/B2
Civic Centre B2
Clifton Rd B3
Clifton St B3
Clock Tower A1

College Rd B3
Colleton Cres . . . C2
Commercial Rd . . C1
Coombe St B2
Cowick St C1
Crown Courts . . . A2
Custom House 🏛 C2
Denmark Rd B3
Devon County Hall C3
Devonshire Pl . . . A3
Elmgrove Rd A1
Exe St B1
Exeter
  Cathedral ✝ . . . B2
Exeter Central
  Station ⇌ A1
Exeter City Football
  Ground A3
Exeter College . . A1
Fore St B1
Friars Gate C2
Guildhall 🏛 B2
H M Prison A2
Haven Rd C2
Heavitree Rd B3
Hele Rd A1
High St B2
Holloway St C2
Howell Rd A1
Information Ctr 🅸 . B3
Iron Bridge B1
Isca Rd C1
Jesmond Rd A3
King William St . . A2
King St B1
Leisure Centre . . C1
Library B2
Longbrook Terr . . A2

Longbrook St A2
Lower North St. . . B1
Lucky Lane C2
Magdalen Rd B3
Magdalen St B2
Market St B2
Mary Arches St . . B1
Matford Rd C3
Matford Ave C3
Matford Lane C3
May St A3
New Bridge St. . . B1
New North Rd . A1/A2
North St B1
Northcott
  Theatre 🎭 A1
Northernhay St. . . B1
Old Mols
  House 🏛 B2
Old Tiverton Rd . . A3
Paris St B2
Parr St A3
Paul St B1
Pennsylvania Rd. . A2
Police HQ &
  Magistrates
  Court 🏛 B3
Portland Street . . A3
Post Office 📮 . . . B2
Powderham Cres . A3
Preston St B1
Queen St A1
Queen's Terr A1
Radford Rd C2
Richmond Rd . . . A1
Roberts Rd C2
Rougemont
  Castle 🏰 A2

Rougemont House
  Museum 🏛 B2
Royal Albert
  Memorial Mus 🏛 B2
St David's Hill. . . . A1
St James' Park
  Station ⇌ A3
St James' Rd A3
St Leonard's Rd. . C3
St Lukes College . B3
St Nicholas Priory
  (AM) ✝ B1
St Thomas
  Station ⇌ C1
Sidwell St A2
Smythen St B1
South St B1
Southernhay East. B2
Southernhay West B2
Spicer Rd B3
Sports Centre . . . A3
Summerland St . . A3
Swimming Pool . . B3
Sydney Rd C1
Tan Lane C2
The Quay C2
Thornton Hill A2
Topsham Rd C3
Tucker's Hall 🏛 . . B1
Underground
  Passages ✦ . . . B2
Velwell Rd A1
Water Lane . . C1/C2
Well Street A3
Western Way
  . . . . . . B1/B2/A3
Wonford Rd . . B3/C3
York Rd A2

Gloucester

Albion St C1
Alexandra Rd . . . B3
Alfred St C3
All Saints Rd C3
Alvin St B2
Arthur St C2
Baker St C1
Barton St C2
Blenheim Rd C3
Bristol Rd C1
Brunswick Rd . . . C2
Bruton Way B2
Bus Station B2
Cattle Market A1
City Council
  Offices B1
City Mus., Art Gall. &
  Library 🏛 B2
Clarence St B2
College of Art . . . C2
Commercial Rd . . B1
Cromwell St C2
Deans Way A2
Denmark Rd A3
Derby Rd C3
Docks ✦ C1
Eastgate Centre . B1
Eastgate St B2
Edwy Parade . . . A2
Estcourt Close . . . A3
Estcourt Rd A3
Falkner St C2
Folk Museum 🏛 . . B1
Gloucester
  Cathedral ✝ . . . B1

Gloucester
  Station ⇌ B2
Gloucestershire
  Royal Hospital
  (A & E) 🏥 B3
Goodyere St. C2
Gouda Way A1
Great Western Rd. B3
Guildhall 🏛 B2
Heathville Rd A3
Henry Rd B3
Henry St. B2
High Orchard St. . C1
Hinton Rd A3
India Rd C3
Jersey Rd C3
King's Sq B2
Kingsholm Rd. . . . A2
Kingsholm Rugby
  Football Ground . A2
Lansdown Rd. . . . A3
Leisure Centre . . C2
Llanthony Rd C1
London Rd B3
Longsmith St B1
Malvern Rd A3
Market Parade . . B2
Merchants Rd . . . C1
Mercia Rd A1
Metz Way C3
Midland Rd C2
Millbrook St C3
Montpellier. C1
Napier St C3

National Waterways
  Museum 🏛 C1
Nettleton Rd C2
New Inn 🏛 B2
New Olympus
  Theatre 🎭 C3
North Rd A3
Northgate St B2
Oxford Rd A2
Oxford St B2
Park & Ride
  Gloucester A1
Park Rd C2
Park St. B2
Parliament St . . . C1
Pitt St B1
Police Station 🏛 . B1
Post Office 📮 . . . B2
Quay St B1
Recreation Gd . A1/A2
Regent St. C2
Regimental
  Museum 🏛 C1
Robert Opie
  Museum 🏛 C1
Robert Raikes
  House 🏛 B1
Royal Oak Rd. . . . B1
Russell St B2
Ryecroft St. C2
St Aldate St B2
St Ann Way C1
St Catherine St. . . A2
St Mark St A2
St Mary De
  Crypt 🏛 B1

St Mary De
  Lode B1
St Nicholas's 🏛 . . B1
St Oswald's Rd . . A1
St Oswald's
  Trading Estate . . A1
St Peter's 🏛 B2
Seabroke Rd A3
Sebert St A2
Severn Rd C1
Sherborne St B2
Shire Hall 🏛 B1
Sidney St C3
Southgate St . B1/C1
Spa Field C1
Spa Rd C1
Sports Ground A2/B2
Station Rd B2
Stratton Rd C3
Stroud Rd C1
Swan Rd A2
Technical College. C1
The Park C2
Transport
  Museum 🏛 B1
Trier Way C1/C2
The Quay B1
Union St A1
Vauxhall Rd C3
Victoria St C2
Wellington St C2
Westgate St B1
Widden St C2
Worcester St B2

Oxford

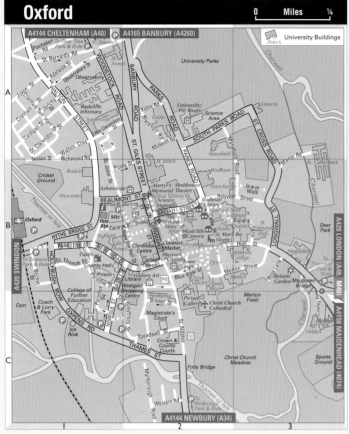

A4144 CHELTENHAM (A40) · A4165 BANBURY (A4260) · University Buildings · A4158 MAIDENHEAD (A074) · A4144 NEWBURY (A34) · A420 LONDON (A40, M40) · A420 SWINDON

0   Miles   ¼

Plymouth

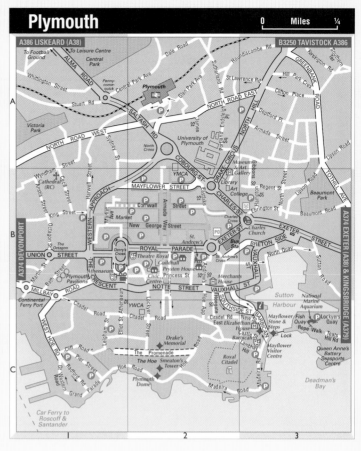

A386 LISKEARD (A38) · B3250 TAVISTOCK A386 · A374 DEVONPORT · A374 EXETER (A38) & KINGSBRIDGE (A379)

0   Miles   ¼

Oxford

Adelaide St	A1
All Souls (Coll)	B2
Apollo Theatre	B2
Ashmolean Museum	B2
Balliol (Coll)	B2
Banbury Rd	A2
Beaumont St	B1
Becket St	B1
Blackhall Rd	A2
Blue Boar St	B2
Bodleian Library	B2
Botanic Garden	B3
Brasenose (Coll)	B2
Brewer St	C2
Broad St	B2
Bus Station	B1
Cardigan St	A1
Carfax Tower	B2
Castle St	B1
Castle	B2
Catte St	B2
Cemetery	C1
Christ Church Cathedral	C2
Christ Church Meadow	C2
Christ Church (Coll)	B2
Clarendon Centre	B2
Coach & Lorry Park	C1
College of Further Education	C1
Cornmarket St	B2
Corpus Christi (Coll)	B2
County Hall	B1
Covered Market	B2
Cowley Pl	C3
Cranham St	A1
Cranham Terr	A1
Cricket Ground	B1
Crown & County Courts	C2
Deer Park	B3
Exeter (Coll)	B2
Folly Bridge	C2
George St	B1
Gt Clarendon St	A1
H M Prison	B1
Hart St	A1
Hertford (Coll)	B2
High St	B3
Hollybush Row	B1
Holywell St	B2
Hythe Bridge St	B1
Ice Rink	C1
Information Ctr	B1
Jericho St	A1
Jesus (Coll)	B2
Jowett Walk	B3
Juxon St	A1
Keble Rd	A2
Keble (Coll)	A2
Library	B2
Linacre (Coll)	A3
Lincoln (Coll)	B2
Little Clarendon St	A1
Longwall St	B3
Magdalen Bridge	B2
Magdalen St	B1
Magdalen (Coll)	B3
Magistrate's Court	C2
Manchester (Coll)	B2
Manor Rd	B3
Mansfield Rd	A3
Mansfield (Coll)	A2
Market	B1
Marlborough Rd	C2
Martyr's Memorial	B2
Merton Field	B3
Merton St	B2
Merton (Coll)	B3
Museum of Modern Art	B2
Museum of Oxford	B2
Museum Rd	A2
New College (Coll)	B3
New Inn Hall St	B2
New Rd	B1
Norfolk St	C1
Nuffield (Coll)	B1
Observatory St	A1
Observatory	A1
Old Greyfriars	B2
Oriel (Coll)	B2
Oxford Station	B1
Oxpens Rd	C1
Paradise Sq	C1
Paradise St	B1
Park End St	B1
Parks Rd	A2/B2
Pear Tree Park & Ride	A1
Pembroke (Coll)	C2
Picture Gallery	C2
Plantation Rd	A1
Playhouse	B1
Police Station	C2
Post Office	C2
Pusey St	B1
Queen's Lane	B3
Queen's (Coll)	B3
Radcliffe Camera	B2
Radcliffe Infirmary	A1
Redbridge Park & Ride	C1
Richmond Rd	A1
Rose Lane	B3
Ruskin (Coll)	A1
St Aldates	C2
St Anne's (Coll)	A1
St Antony's (Coll)	A1
St Bernard's Rd	A1
St Catherine's (Coll)	B3
St Cross Rd	A3
St Edmund Hall (Coll)	B3
St Giles St	A2
St Hilda's (Coll)	C3
St John St	B2
St John's (Coll)	A2
St Mary the Virgin	B2
St Peter's (Coll)	B1
St Thomas St	B1
Science Area	A2
Science Museum	B2
Seacourt Park & Ride	B1
Sheldonian Theatre	B2
Somerville (Coll)	A1
South Parks Rd	A2
Speedwell St	C2
Sports Ground	C3
Thames St	C2
The Oxford Story	B2
Thornhill Park & Ride	B3
Town Hall	B2
Trinity (Coll)	B2
Turl St	B2
University College (Coll)	B2
University Museum & Pitt Rivers Museum	A2
University Parks	A2
Wadham (Coll)	B2
Walton Cres	A1
Walton St	A1
Western Rd	C1
Westgate Shopping Centre	B2
Woodstock Rd	A1
Worcester (Coll)	B1

Plymouth

Alma Rd	A1
Anstis St	B1
Armada St	A3
Armada Way	B2
Art College	B2
Athenaeum St	C1
Athenaeum Theatre	B1
Barbican	C3
Barbican	C3
Bath St	B1
Beaumont Park	B3
Beaumont Rd	B3
Breton Side	B3
Bus Station	B2
Castle St	C3
Cathedral (RC)	B1
Cecil St	B1
Central Park	A1
Central Park Ave	A2
Charles Church	B3
Charles Cross Rdbt	B3
Charles St	B2
Citadel Rd	C2
Citadel Rd East	C2
Civic Centre	B2
Cliff Rd	C1
Clifton Pl	A3
Cobourg St	A2
Continental Ferry Port	B1
Cornwall St	B2
Dale Rd	A2
Deadman's Bay	C3
Deptford Pl	A3
Derry's Cross	B2
Drake Circus Rdbt	B1
Drake Circus	B2
Drake's Memorial	C2
Eastlake St	B2
Ebrington St	B3
Elizabethan House	C3
Elliot St	C1
Endsleigh Pl	A2
Exeter St	B3
Fish Quay	C3
Gibbons St	A3
Glen Park Ave	A3
Grand Parade	C1
Great Western Rd	C1
Greenbank Rd	A3
Guildhall	B2
Hampton St	B3
Harwell St	B1
Hill Park Cres	A3
Hoe Approach	B2
Hoe Rd	C2
Hoegate St	C2
Houndiscombe Rd	A2
James St	A2
Kensington Rd	A3
King St	B1
Lambhay Hill	C3
Leigham St	C1
Library	B2
Lipson Rd	A3/B3
Lockyer St	C2
Lockyers Quay	C3
Madeira Rd	C2
Market	B1
Market Ave	B1
Martin St	B1
Mayflower St	B2
Mayflower Stone & Steps	C3
Mayflower Visitor Centre	C3
Merchants House	B2
Millbay Rd	B1
Museum & Art Gallery	B2
National Marine Aquarium	C3
New George St	B2
New St	C3
North Cross Rdbt	A2
North Hill	A3
North Quay	B2
North Rd East	A2
North Rd West	A1
North St	B3
Notte St	C2
Octagon St	B1
Pennycomequick Rdbt	A2
Pier St	C1
Plymouth Dome	C2
Plymouth Pavilions	B1
Plymouth Railway Station	B3
Police Station	B3
Post Office	B2
Princess St	B2
Prysten House	B2
Queen Anne's Battery Seasports Centre	C3
Radford Rd	C1
Regent St	B3
Rope Walk	C3
Royal Citadel	C2
Royal Parade	B2
St.Andrew's Church	B2
St Andrew's Cross Rdbt	B2
St Andrew's St	B2
St Lawrence Rd	A2
Saltash Rd	A2
Smeaton's Tower	C2
Southern Terr	A3
Southside St	C2
Stuart Rd	A1
Sutherland Rd	A2
Sutton Harbour	B3
Sutton Rd	B3
Sydney St	A1
Teats Hill Rd	C3
The Crescent	B1
The Hoe	C2
The Octagon Rdbt	B1
The Promenade	C2
Theatre Royal	B2
Tothill Ave	B3
Union St	B1
University of Plymouth	A2
Vauxhall St	B2/3
Victoria Park	A1
West Hoe Rd	C1
Western App	B1
Whittington St	A1
Wyndham St	B1
YMCA	B2
YWCA	B2

Salisbury

0 Miles ¼

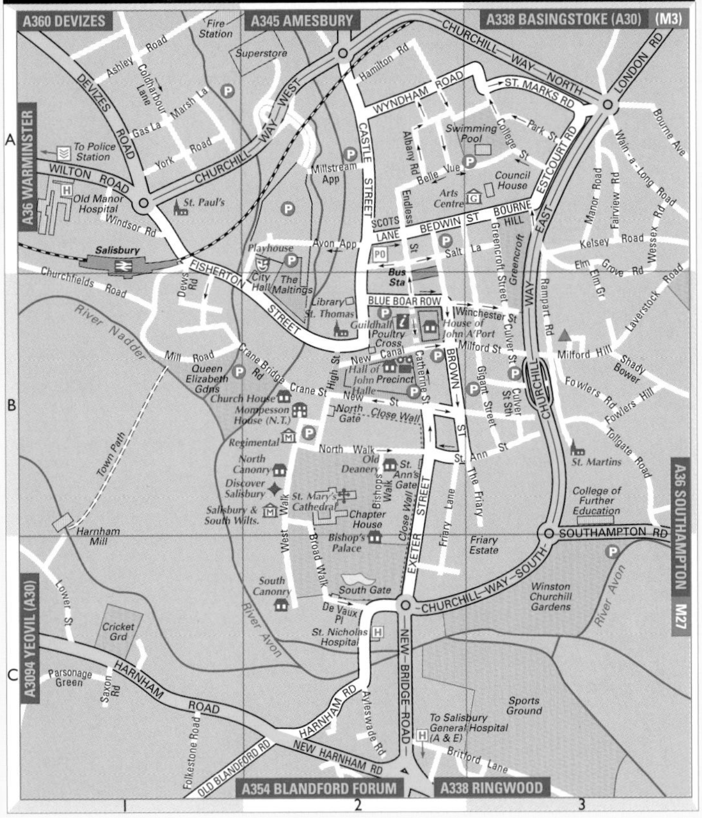
A360 DEVIZES
A345 AMESBURY
A338 BASINGSTOKE (A30) (M3)
A36 WARMINSTER
A36 SOUTHAMPTON M27
A3094 YEOVIL (A30)
A354 BLANDFORD FORUM
A338 RINGWOOD
CHURCHILL WAY NORTH
CHURCHILL WAY WEST
CHURCHILL WAY SOUTH
CHURCHILL WAY EAST
WILTON ROAD
FISHERTON STREET
CASTLE STREET
WYNDHAM ROAD
LONDON RD
SOUTHAMPTON RD
HARNHAM ROAD
NEW HARNHAM RD
NEW BRIDGE ROAD
EXETER STREET
River Nadder
River Avon
Salisbury
Old Manor Hospital
St. Paul's
Superstore
Fire Station
Playhouse
City Hall
The Maltings
Library
St. Thomas
Guildhall
Poultry Cross
Bus Sta
Swimming Pool
Council House
Arts Centre
Millstream App
Mompesson House (N.T.)
Regimental Museum
North Canonry
Discover Salisbury
Salisbury & South Wilts.
St. Mary's Cathedral
Chapter House
Bishop's Palace
South Canonry
South Gate
De Vaux Pl
St. Nicholas Hospital
Old Deanery
St. Ann's Gate
St. Martins
College of Further Education
Friary Estate
Winston Churchill Gardens
Cricket Grd
Parsonage Green
Harnham Mill
Town Path
Sports Ground
To Salisbury General Hospital (A & E)
To Police Station
Queen Elizabeth Gdns
Church House
A
B
C
1
2
3

Stratford-upon-Avon

0 Miles ¼

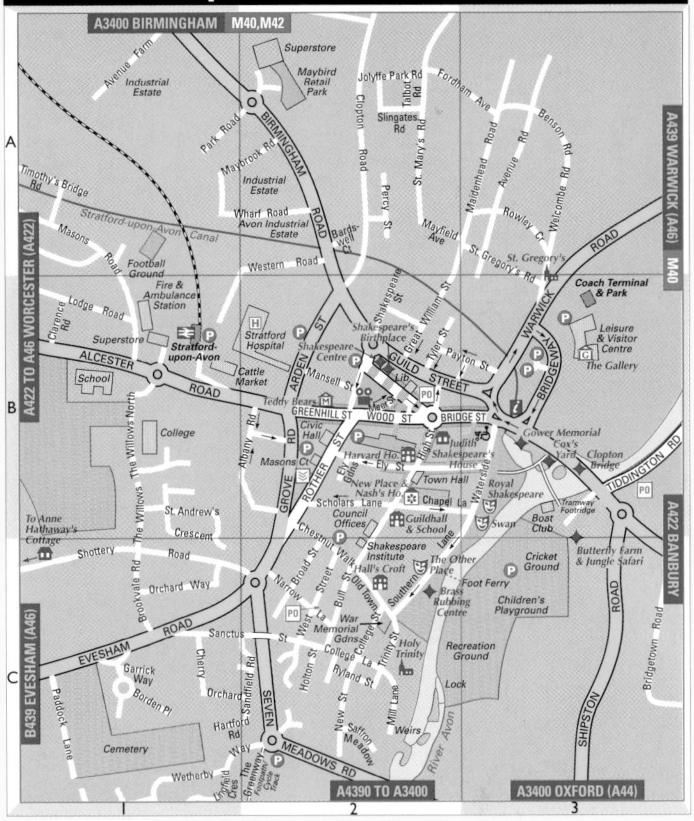
A3400 BIRMINGHAM M40,M42
A439 WARWICK (A46) M40
A422 TO A46 WORCESTER (A422)
B439 EVESHAM (A46)
A422 BANBURY
A4390 TO A3400
A3400 OXFORD (A44)
BIRMINGHAM ROAD
ALCESTER ROAD
EVESHAM ROAD
WARWICK ROAD
SHIPSTON ROAD
TIDDINGTON RD
SEVEN MEADOWS RD
Stratford-upon-Avon Canal
River Avon
Superstore
Maybird Retail Park
Industrial Estate
Avon Industrial Estate
Football Ground
Fire & Ambulance Station
Stratford-upon-Avon
Stratford Hospital
Shakespeare Centre
Shakespeare's Birthplace
Teddy Bears
Civic Hall
College
Masons Ct
Harvard Ho.
Judith Shakespeare's House
Town Hall
New Place & Nash's Ho.
Royal Shakespeare
Swan
Guildhall & School
Council Offices
Shakespeare Institute
Hall's Croft
The Other Place
Brass Rubbing Centre
Holy Trinity
War Memorial Gdns
Coach Terminal & Park
Leisure & Visitor Centre
The Gallery
Gower Memorial
Cox's Yard
Clopton Bridge
Tramway Footbridge
Boat Club
Butterfly Farm & Jungle Safari
Cricket Ground
Foot Ferry
Children's Playground
Recreation Ground
Cemetery
To Anne Hathaway's Cottage
Lock
Weirs
A
B
C
1
2
3

Salisbury

Albany Rd A2
Arts Centre A3
Ashley Rd A1
Avon Approach A2
Ayleswade Rd C2
Bedwin St A2
Belle Vue A2
Bishop's Palace C2
Bishops Walk B2
Blue Boar Row B2
Bourne Ave A3
Bourne Hill A3
Britford Lane C2
Broad Walk C2
Brown St B2
Bus Station B2
Castle St A2
Catherine St B2
Chapter House B2
Church House B2
Church of St. Thomas B2
Churchfields Rd B1
Churchill Way East B3
Churchill Way North A3
Churchill Way South C2
Churchill Way West A1
City Hall B2
Close Wall B2
Coldharbour Lane A1
College of Further Education B3
College St A3
Council House A3
Crane Bridge Rd B2
Crane St B2
Cricket Ground C1
Culver St South B3
De Vaux Place C2
Devizes Rd A1
Dews Rd B1
Discover Salisbury ✦ B2
Elm Grove B3
Elm Grove Rd A3
Endless St A2
Estcourt Rd A3
Exeter St C2
Fairview Rd A3
Fire Station A1
Fisherton St A1
Folkestone Rd C1
Fowlers Hill B3
Fowlers Rd B3
Friary Estate C3
Friary Lane B2
Gas Lane A1
Gigant St B3
Greencroft St A3
Greencroft B3
Guildhall B2
Hall of John Halle B2
Hamilton Rd A2
Harnham Mill B1
Harnham Rd C1/C2
High St B2
House of John A'Port B2
Information Ctr B2
Kelsey Rd A3
Laverstock Rd B3
Library B2
London Rd A3
Lower St C1
Manor Rd A3
Marsh Lane A1
Milford Hill B3
Milford St B3
Mill Road B1
Millstream Approach A2
Mompesson House (N.T.) B2
New Bridge Rd C2
New Canal B2
New Harnham Rd C2
New St B2
North Canonry B2
North Gate B2
North Walk B2
Old Blandford Rd C1
Old Deanery B2
Old Manor Hospital A1
Park St A3
Parsonage Green C1
Playhouse Theatre A2
Police Station A1
Post Office A2
Poultry Cross B2
Precinct B2
Queen Elizabeth Gdns B1
Rampart Rd B3
Regimental Museum B2
St Ann's Gate B2
St Ann St B2
St Marks Rd A3
St Martins B3
St Mary's Cathedral ✝ B2
St Nicholas Hospital C2
St Paul's A1
Salisbury & South Wiltshire Museum B2
Salisbury General Hospital (A & E) C2
Salisbury Station A1
Salt Lane A3
Saxon Rd C1
Scots Lane A2
Shady Bower B3
South Canonry C2
South Gate C2
Southampton Rd B2
Sports Ground C3
Swimming Pool A3
The Friary B3
The Maltings B2
Tollgate Rd B3
Town Path B1
Wain-a-Long Rd A3
Wessex Rd A3
West Walk C2
Wilton Rd A1
Winchester St B3
Windsor Rd A1
Winston Churchill Gardens C3
Wyndham Rd A2
YHA ▲ B3
York Rd A1

Stratford-upon-Avon

Albany Rd B1
Alcester Rd B1
Ambulance Station B1
Anne Hathaway's Cottage B1
Arden St B2
Avenue Farm A1
Avenue Rd A3
Avon Industrial Estate A2
Benson Rd A3
Birmingham Rd A2
Boat Club B3
Borden Place C1
Brass Rubbing Centre ✦ C2
Bridge St B2
Bridgetown Rd C3
Bridgeway B3
Broad St C2
Brookvale Rd C1
Bull St C2
Butterfly Farm & Jungle Safari ✦ C3
Cattle Market B2
Cemetery C1
Chapel Lane B2
Cherry Orchard C1
Chestnut Walk B2
Children's Playground C3
Civic Hall B2
Clarence Rd B1
Clopton Bridge ✦ B3
Clopton Rd A2
Coach Terminal & Park B3
College Lane C2
College St C2
Council Offices B2
Cox's Yard B3
Cricket Ground C3
Ely St B2
Evesham Rd C1
Fire Station B1
Foot Ferry C3
Football Ground A1
Fordham Ave A2
Garrick Way C1
Gower Memorial ✦ B3
Great William St B2
Greenhill St B2
Grove Rd B2
Guild St B2
Guildhall & School B2
Hall's Croft C2
Hartford Rd C1
Harvard House B2
High St B2
Holton St C2
Holy Trinity C2
Industrial Estate A1
Information Ctr B3
Jolyffe Park Rd A2
Judith Shakespeare's House B2
Leisure & Visitor Centre B3
Library B2
Lodge Rd B1
Maidenhead Rd A3
Mansell St B2
Masons Court B2
Masons Rd A1
Maybird Centre A2
Maybrook Rd A1
Mayfield Ave A2
Meer St B2
Mill Lane C2
Moat House Hotel B3
Narrow Lane C2
New Place & Nash's House B2
New St C2
Old Town C2
Orchard Way C1
Paddock Lane C1
Park Rd A1
Payton St B2
Percy St A2
Police Station B2
Post Office B2
Post Office B3
Post Office C2
Recreation Grd C2
Retail Park A2
Rother St B2
Rowley Cres A3
Royal Shakespeare Theatre B3
Ryland St C2
Saffron Meadow C2
St Andrew's Cres B1
St Gregory's A3
St Gregory's Rd A3
St Mary's Rd A2
Sanctus St C1
Sandfield Rd C2
Scholars Lane B2
Seven Meadows Rd C2
Shakespeare Centre ✦ B2
Shakespeare Institute C2
Shakespeare St B2
Shakespeare's Birthplace ✦ B2
Shipston Rd C3
Shottery Rd C1
Slingates Rd A2
Southern Lane C2
Stratford Hospital B2
Stratford-upon-Avon Station B1
Superstore B1
Swan Theatre B3
Talbot Rd A2
Teddy Bears Museum B2
The Gallery B3
The Greenway C1
The Other Place C2
The Willows B1
The Willows North B1
Tiddington Rd B3
Timothy's Bridge Rd A1
Town Hall B2
Tramway Bridge B3
Trinity St C2
Tyler St B2
Warwick Rd B3
Waterside B3
Welcombe Rd A3
West St C2
Western Rd A2
Wharf Rd A2
Wood St B2

Swindon

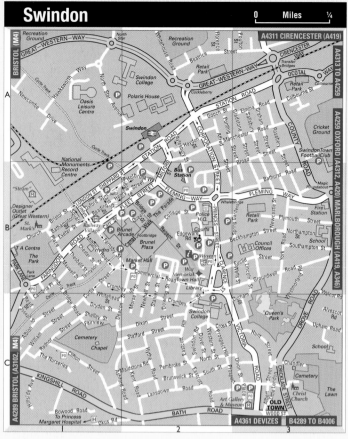

Taunton

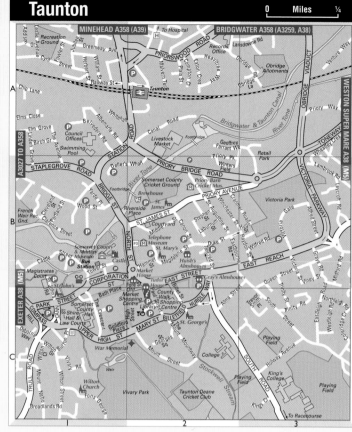

Swindon

Albert St C3
Albion St C1
Alfred St A2
Alvescot Rd A3
Art Gallery &
  Museum C3
Ashford Rd C1
Aylesbury St A2
Bath Rd C2
Bathampton St . . B1
Bathurst Rd B3
Beatrice St A2
Beckhampton St . B3
Bowood Rd C1
Bridge St B2
Bristol St B1
Broad St A3
Brunel Arcade . . B2
Brunel Plaza B2
Brunswick St C2
Bus Station B2
Cambria
  Bridge Rd B1
Cambria Place . . . B1
Canal Walk B2
Carr St B1
Cemetery . . . C1/C3
Chandler Cl C3
Chapel C2
Chester St B1
Christ Church C3
Church Place B1
Cirencester Way . . A3
Clarence St B2
Clifton St C1
Cockleberry Rdbt . A2
Colbourne Rdbt . A3
Colbourne St A3
College St B2
Commercial Rd . . B2
Corporation St . . . A2
Council Offices . . B2
County Rd A3
Courts B2
Cricket Ground . . A3
Cricklade Street . . C3

Crombey St . . B1/C2
Cross St C2
Curtis St B1
Deacon St C1
Designer Outlet
  (Great Western) . B1
Dixon St C2
Dover St C2
Dowling St C2
Drove Rd C3
Dryden St C1
Durham St C3
East St B1
Eastcott Hill C2
Eastcott Rd C2
Edgeware Rd B2
Elmina St A3
Emlyn Square . . . B1
Euclid St B3
Exeter St B1
Fairview C1
Faringdon Rd B1
Farnsby St B1
Fire Station B3
Fleet St B2
Fleming Way . . B2/B3
Florence St A2
Gladstone St A3
Gooch St A2
Graham St A3
Great Western
  Way A1/A2
Groundwell Rd . . B3
Hawksworth Way . A1
Haydon St A2
Henry St B2
Hillside Ave C1
Holbrook Way . . . B2
Hunt St C3
Hydro B1
Hythe Rd C2
Information Ctr . . . B2
Joseph St C1
Kent Rd C2
Kingshill Rd C1
Lansdown Rd C2
Library B2
Lincoln St B3

Little London C3
London St B1
Magic Rdbt B3
Maidstone Rd . . . C2
Manchester Rd . . A3
Market Hall B2
Maxwell St B1
Milford St B2
Milton Rd B1
Morse St C2
National
  Monuments
  Record Centre . . B1
Newcastle St B3
Newcombe Drive . A1
Newhall St C2
North St C2
North Star Rdbt . . A1
North Star Ave . . . A1
Northampton St . . B3
Oasis Leisure
  Centre A1
Ocotal Way A3
Okus Rd C1
Old Town C3
Oxford St B1
Park Lane B1
Park Lane Rdbt . . . B1
Pembroke St C2
Plymouth St B3
Police HQ B2
Ponting St A2
Post Office B1
Post Office B2
Post Office C1
Post Office C3
Poulton St A3
Princes St B2
Prospect Hill C2
Prospect Place . . C2
Queen St B2
Queen's Park C3
Radnor St C1
Railway
  Village B1
Read St C1
Reading St B1
Recreation Grd A1/A2

Regent St B2
Retail Park . A2/A3/B3
Rosebery St A3
St Mark's B1
Salisbury St A3
Shelley St C1
Sheppard St B1
South St C2
Southampton St . . B3
Spring Gardens . . B3
Stafford Street . . . C2
Stanier St C2
Station Road A2
"Steam" B1
Swindon
  College A2/B2
Swindon
  Station A2
Swindon
  College A2/C2
Swindon Rd C2
Swindon Town
  Football Club . . A3
T A Centre B1
Tennyson St B1
The Lawn C3
The Nurseries C1
The Parade B2
The Park B1
Theobald St B1
Town Hall B2
Transfer Bridges
  Rdbt A3
Union St C2
Upham Rd C3
Victoria Rd C3
Walcot Rd C3
War Memorial B2
Wells St B3
Western St C2
Westmorland Rd . B3
Whalebridge Rdbt B2
Whitehead St C1
Whitehouse Rd . . C1
William St C1
Wood St C2
Wyvern Theatre . . B2
York Rd B3

Taunton

Addison Gr A1
Albemarle Rd A1
Alfred St B3
Alma St C2
Bath Pl C1
Belvedere Rd A1
Billet St B2
Billetfield C2
Birch Gr A1
Brewhouse
  Theatre B2
Bridge St B1
Bridgwater &
  Taunton Canal . . A2
Broadlands Rd . . . C1
Burton Pl B1
Bus Station B1
Canal Rd A2
Cann St C1
Canon St B2
Castle B1
Castle St B1
Chip Lane A1
Clarence St B1
Cleveland St A1
Coleridge Cres . . . C3
College C2
Compass Hill C1
Compton Cl A2
Corporation St . . . B1
Council Offices . . C1
County Walk
  Shopping Centre C2
Courtyard B2
Cranmer Rd B2
Cyril St A1
Deller's Wharf . . . B1
Duke St B2
East Reach B3
East St B2
Eastbourne Rd . . . B2
Eastleigh Rd C3
Eaton Cres A2
Elm Gr A1

Elms Cl A1
Fons George C1
Fore St B2
Fowler St A1
French Weir
  Recreation Grd . B1
Geoffrey Farrant
  Wk A2
Gray's
  Almshouses . . . B2
Grays Rd A1
Greenway Ave . . . A1
Guildford Pl C1
Hammet St B2
Haydon Rd B3
Heavitree Way . . . A2
Herbert St A1
High St C2
Holway Ave C3
Hugo St B3
Huish's
  Almshouses . . . B2
Hurdle Way C2
Information Ctr . . . C2
Jubilee St A1
King's College . . . C3
Kings Cl C3
Laburnum St B2
Lambrook Rd B3
Lansdowne Rd . . . A3
Leslie Ave A1
Leycroft Rd B3
Library C2
Linden Gr A1
Livestock Market . A2
Magdalene St B2
Magistrates Court B1
Malvern Terr A2
Market House . . . B2
Mary St C2
Middle St B2
Midford Rd B3
Mount Nebo C1
Mount St C2
Mountway C2
North St B2

Northleigh Rd . . . C3
Obridge
  Allotments A3
Obridge Lane A3
Obridge Rd A3
Obridge Viaduct . . A3
Old Market
  Shopping Centre C2
Osborne Way C1
Park St C1
Paul St C2
Plais St A2
Playing Field C3
Police Station . . . B2
Portland St B1
Post Office B2
Priorswood Rd . . . A2
Priory Ave B3
Priory Barn Cricket
  Museum B2
Priory Bridge Rd. . B2
Priory Park A2
Priory Way A3
Queen St B2
Railway St A1
Records Office . . . A2
Recreation Grd . . . C3
Riverside Place . . . B2
St Augustine St . . B2
St George's C1
St James B2
St.James St B2
St John's C1
St John's Rd B1
St Mary's C1
Shire Hall & Law
  Courts C1
Somerset County &
  Military Mus . . . B1
Somerset County
  Cricket Ground. . B1
Somerset County
  Hall C1
South Rd C3
South St C3

Staplegrove Rd . . B1
Station Rd A1
Stephen St B2
Swimming Pool . . A1
Tancred St B2
Taunton Dean Cricket
  Club C2
Taunton Station . . A2
Telephone
  Museum B2
The Avenue A1
The Crescent C1
The Mount C2
Toneway A3
Tower St B1
Trevor Smith Pl . . . C3
Trinity Rd C3
Trinity St B3
Trull Rd C1
Tudor House B2
Upper High St . . . C1
Venture Way A3
Victoria Gate B3
Victoria Park B3
Victoria Parkway . B3
Victoria St B3
Viney St B3
Vivary Park C2
Vivary Rd C1
War Memorial C1
Westleigh Rd C3
Wheatley Cres . . . A3
Whitehall A1
Wilfred Rd B3
William St C1
Wilton Church . . . C1
Wilton Cl C1
Wilton Gr C1
Wilton St C1
Winchester St B2
Winters Field B2
Wood St B1
Yarde Pl B1

Torquay

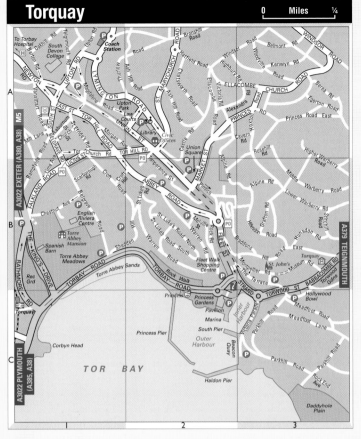

Worcester

Torquay

Abbey Rd B2	Fleet Walk	Oakhill Rd A1	Spanish Barn B1
Alexandra Rd A2	Shopping Centre B2	Outer Harbour . . . C2	Stitchill Rd B3
Alpine Rd B3	Grafton Rd B3	Parkhill Rd C3	Strand B3
Ash Hill Rd A2	Haldon Pier C2	Pavilion C2	Teignmouth Rd. . . A1
Babbacombe Rd . B3	Hatfield Rd A2	Pimlico B2	Temperance St. . . B2
Bampfylde Rd . . . B1	Highbury Rd A2	Police Station ⊠ . A1	The King's Drive . . B1
Barton Rd A1	Higher	Post Office ⊠ . . . A2	The Terrace B3
Beacon Quay C2	Warberry Rd. . . . A3	Post Office ⊠ . . . B1	Thurlow Rd A1
Belgrave Rd . . A1/B1	Hillesdon Rd B3	Post Office ⊠ . . . B2	Tor Bay B1
Belmont Rd B3	Hollywood Bowl. . C3	Princess	Tor Church Rd . . . A1
Berea Rd A3	Hoxton Rd A3	Information Ctr ⓘ . B2	Tor Hill Rd A1
Braddons Hill Rd	Hunsdon Rd. B3	Inner Harbour. . . . C3	Torbay Rd B2
East B3	Kenwyn Rd A3	Princess Gdns . . . C2	Torquay
Bronshill Rd A2	Laburnum St A1	Princess Pier C2	Museum 🏛 B3
Castle Rd. A2	Law Courts A2	Rathmore Rd B1	Torquay Station ⇌C1
Cavern Rd A3	Library A2	Recreation Grd. . . B1	Torre Abbey
Chatsworth Rd. . . A2	Lime Ave B1	Rock End Ave . . . C3	Mansion 🏛 B1
Chestnut Ave B1	Lower	Rock Rd. B2	Torre Abbey
Church St. A1	Warberry Rd. . . . B3	Rock Walk B2	Meadows B1
Civic Offices 🏛 . . A2	Lucius St B1	Rosehill Rd. A3	Torre Abbey SandsB1
Coach Station . . . A1	Lymington Rd . . . A1	St Efride's Rd A1	Torwood Gdns . . . B3
Corbyn Head C1	Magdalene Rd . . . A2	St Luke's Rd B2	Torwood St C3
Croft Hill. B1	Marina C2	St Luke's Rd	Union Square. . . . A2
Croft Rd B1	Market St. B2	North B3	Union St. A2
Daddyhole Plain. . C3	Meadfoot Lane. . . C3	St Luke's Rd	Upton Park. A1
East St A1	Meadfoot Rd C3	South B2	Upton Rd A1
Egerton Rd. A3	Melville St. B2	St Marychurch	Vansittart Rd A1
Ellacombe	Middle	Rd A2	Victoria Parade. . . C3
Church Rd A3	Warberry Rd. . . . B3	Scarborough Rd. . . B1	Victoria Rd A2
Ellacombe Rd. . . . A2	Mill Lane A1	Shedden Hill B2	Warren Rd B2
English Riviera	Montpellier Rd . . . B3	South Devon	Windsor Rd . . . A2/A3
Centre B1	Morgan Ave A1	College. A1	Woodville Rd A3
Falkland Rd B1	Museum Rd B3	South Pier C2	
Fleet St B2	Newton Rd. A1	South St. A1	

Worcester

Albany Terr. A1	Diglis Rd C2	Lychgate Centre. . B2	Shire Hall A2
Alice Otley School A2	Edgar Tower ✦ . . C2	Magistrates Court A2	Shrub Hill Rd B3
Angel Pl B2	Farrier St A2	Midland Rd B3	Shrub Hill
Angel St B2	Foregate St B2	Mill St C2	Station ⇌ B3
Athelstan Rd C3	Foregate St	Moors Severn Terr A1	South Quay B2
Back Lane South . A1	Station ⇌ B2	New Rd C1	Southfield St A2
Barbourne Rd . . . A2	Fort Royal Hill . . . C3	New St. B2	Sports Ground A2/C1
Bath Rd C2	Fort Royal Park . . C3	Northfield St A2	Stanley Rd B3
Battenhall Rd C3	Foundry St B3	Old Palace 🏛 . . . B2	The Swan
Bridge St B2	Friar St C2	Oswald's Rd A2	Theatre 🎭 A1
Britannia Square. . A1	George St B3	Padmore St B3	Tallow Hill B3
Broad St B2	Greenhill C3	Park St. C3	Tennis Walk A2
Bromwich Lane . . C1	Greyfriars 🏛 B2	Pheasant St B3	The Avenue C1
Bromwich Rd. . . . C1	Guildhall 🏛 B2	Pitchcroft	The Butts B2
Bromyard Rd C1	Henwick Rd B1	Racecourse A1	The Cross B2
Bus Station B2	High St. B2	Police Station ⊠ . A2	The Shambles . . . B2
Carden St B3	Hill St. B3	Police Station ⊠ . B2	The Tything A2
Castle St A2	Hylton Rd B1	Portland St. C2	Tolladine Rd B3
Charles St B3	Information Ctr ⓘ. B2	Post Office ⊠. . . . B2	Tudor House
Chestnut St A2	King's School. . . . C2	Quay St B2	Museum 🏛 B2
Chestnut Walk . . . A2	Lansdowne Cres	Queen St B2	Tybridge St. B1
City Walls Rd B2	Lane A3	Rainbow Hill. A3	Vincent Rd B3
Cole Hill. C3	Lansdowne Cres . A3	Recreation Ground A2	Washington St . . . A3
College St C2	Lansdowne Rd. . . A3	Rogers Hill A3	Woolhope Rd C3
Commandery 🏛 . . C3	Lansdowne Walk . A3	Royal Infirmary 🏥. B2	Worcester Bridge . B2
County Cricket	Laslett St A3	Royal Porcelain	Worcester
Ground. C1	Library, Museum	Works C2	Cathedral ✝ C2
Cripplegate Park . B1	& Art Gallery 🏛 . A2	St Dunstan's Cres C3	Worcester Royal
Croft Rd B1	Little Chestnut St . A2	St John's C1	Grammar School A2
Crowngate Centre B2	Little London A2	St Martin's Gate. . B3	Wylds Lane C3
Deansway B2	London Rd C3	St Paul's St B3	
	Lowesmoor Wharf A3	Sansome Walk . . . A2	
	Lowesmoor B2	Severn St. C2	

A

Abbas Combe *Som'set* 38 B4
Abberton *Worcs* 76 B2
Abbey *Devon* 35 D7
Abbey Dore *Heref'd* 68 A1
Abbots Bickington *Devon* 31 D7
Abbots Leigh *N Som'set* 56 B2
Abbots Morton *Worcs* 76 A3
Abbot's Salford *Warwick* 76 B4
Abbots Worthy *Hants* 53 E6
Abbotsbury *Dorset* 25 C6
Abbotsham *Devon* 31 A8
Abbotskerswell *Devon* 15 B5
Abbotsleigh *Devon* 14 F4
Abbotstone *Hants* 53 E8
Abbotswood *Worcs* 75 C7
Abbotts Ann *Hants* 52 C3
Abenhall *Glos* 69 D7
Abingdon *Oxon* 67 C6
Ablington *Glos* 71 F8
Ablington *Wilts* 51 B8
Abson *S Gloucs* 57 B6
Aconbury *Heref'd* 68 A4
Acton *Dorset* 27 E6
Acton Beauchamp *Heref'd* 74 B3
Acton Green *Heref'd* 74 C3
Acton Turville *S Gloucs* 63 F8
Adam's Green *Dorset* 37 E8
Adber *Dorset* 38 B1
Addington *Cornw'l* 9 B8
Adlestrop *Glos* 72 B3
Admington *Warwick* 77 C7
Adsborough *Som'set* 46 F5
Adscombe *Som'set* 46 D3
Adsett *Glos* 69 E8
Affpuddle *Dorset* 26 B3
Afton *Devon* 14 C4
Afton *I/Wight* 29 C7
Ailstone *Warwick* 77 B7
Aish *Devon* 14 C1
Aish *Devon* 14 D4
Aisholt *Som'set* 46 D4
Albaston *Cornw'l* 10 A4
Alcester *Dorset* 39 B7
Alcester *Warwick* 76 A4
Alcombe *Som'set* 45 B6
Aldbourne *Wilts* 60 A2
Alder Row *Som'set* 49 C7
Alderbury *Wilts* 41 A6
Alderholt *Dorset* 40 D5
Alderley *Glos* 63 D7
Aldermaston *W Berks* 61 C8
Alderminster *Warwick* 77 C7
Alderney *Poole* 27 B8
Alder's End *Heref'd* 74 E2
Alderton *Glos* 76 F3
Alderton *Wilts* 64 F1
Alderton Field *Glos* 71 A6
Aldington *Worcs* 76 D4
Aldsworth *Glos* 72 E2
Aldworth *W Berks* 61 A8
Aley *Som'set* 46 D3
Alfardisworthy *Devon* 31 D5
Alfington *Devon* 22 A4
Alford *Som'set* 48 E4
Alfrick *Worcs* 74 B4
Alfrick Pound *Worcs* 74 B4
Alhampton *Som'set* 48 E4
Alkerton *Glos* 63 A7
All Cannings *Wilts* 59 D6
Allaleigh *Devon* 14 E4
Allaston *Glos* 62 B4
Aller *Devon* 15 B5
Aller *Som'set* 47 F7
Allercombe *Devon* 22 B2
Allerford *Som'set* 45 B5
Allet *Cornw'l* 7 F6
Allington *Dorset* 24 B4
Allington *Wilts* 51 D9
Allington *Wilts* 58 A2
Allington *Wilts* 59 D6
Allowenshay *Som'set* 37 D5
Allweston *Dorset* 38 D3
Almer *Dorset* 27 A5
Alminstone Cross *Devon* 31 B7
Almondsbury *S Gloucs* 62 F3
Alne End *Warwick* 76 A5
Alney Island *Glos* 70 D2
Alphington *Devon* 21 C8
Alston *Devon* 36 F4
Alston Sutton *Som'set* 47 A8
Alstone *Glos* 70 C4
Alstone *Glos* 71 A5
Alstone *Som'set* 47 B6
Alswear *Devon* 33 B7
Altarnun *Cornw'l* 18 D1
Alton Barnes *Wilts* 59 D7
Alton Pancras *Dorset* 38 F3
Alton Priors *Wilts* 59 D7
Alvediston *Wilts* 40 B2
Alverdiscott *Devon* 32 A3
Alvescot *Oxon* 66 B2
Alveston *S Gloucs* 62 E4
Alveston *Warwick* 77 A7
Alveston Down *S Gloucs* 62 E4
Alvington *Devon* 31 B8
Alvington *Glos* 62 B4
Amberley *Glos* 64 B2
Amesbury *Wilts* 51 C8
Ameysford *Dorset* 40 F4
Ampney Crucis *Glos* 65 B6
Ampney St. Mary *Glos* 65 B6
Ampney St. Peter *Glos* 65 B6
Amport *Hants* 52 C2
Andersea *Som'set* 47 E6
Andersfield *Som'set* 46 E4
Anderson *Dorset* 26 A4
Anderton *Cornw'l* 10 E4
Andover *Hants* 52 B4
Andover Down *Hants* 52 B4
Andoversford *Glos* 71 D6
Angarrack *Cornw'l* 3 C7
Angarrick *Cornw'l* 4 C3
Angersleigh *Som'set* 36 C1
Anna Valley *Hants* 52 C3
Ansford *Som'set* 48 E4
Ansty *Wilts* 50 F4
Ansty Coombe *Wilts* 40 A1
Ansty Cross *Dorset* 39 F5
Antony *Cornw'l* 10 E3
Antron *Cornw'l* 3 E8
Apperley *Glos* 70 B3
Appledore *Devon* 35 D6
Appledore *Devon* 42 E4
Appleford *Oxon* 67 D7
Appleshaw *Hants* 52 B3
Appleton *Oxon* 67 B5
Appley *Som'set* 35 B6
Ardens Grafton *Warwick* 76 B5
Ardington *Oxon* 67 E5
Arle *Glos* 70 C4
Arlingham *Glos* 69 E8
Arlington *Devon* 43 C7
Arlington *Glos* 71 F8
Arlington Becott *Devon* 43 C7
Armscote *Warwick* 77 D7
Arne *Dorset* 27 C6
Arno's Vale *Bristol* 56 B4
Arrow *Warwick* 76 A4
Ascott d'Oyley *Oxon* 72 D5
Ascott Earl *Oxon* 72 D4
Ascott under Wychwood *Oxon* 72 D5
Ash *Devon* 14 F4
Ash *Dorset* 39 D7
Ash *Som'set* 36 B3
Ash *Som'set* 37 B7
Ash Hill *Devon* 21 F8
Ash Mill *Devon* 33 B8
Ash Priors *Som'set* 46 F3
Ash Thomas *Devon* 35 D5
Ashampstead *W Berks* 61 A8
Ashampstead Green *W Berks* 61 A8
Ashbrittle *Som'set* 35 B5
Ashburton *Devon* 14 B3
Ashbury *Devon* 19 A7
Ashbury *Oxon* 66 E2
Ashchurch *Glos* 70 A4
Ashcombe *Devon* 21 E8
Ashcott *Som'set* 47 D8
Ashcott Corner *Som'set* 47 D9
Ashe *Hants* 53 A7
Ashfield *Heref'd* 69 C5
Ashford *Devon* 14 F1
Ashford *Devon* 43 D5
Ashford Hill *Hants* 61 D8
Ashgrove *Bath/NE Som'set* 57 E6
Ashill *Devon* 36 D1
Ashill *Som'set* 36 C4
Ashington *Som'set* 37 B9
Ashleworth *Glos* 70 B2
Ashleworth Quay *Glos* 70 B2
Ashley *Dorset* 41 F5
Ashley *Glos* 64 D3
Ashley *Hants* 29 B5
Ashley *Hants* 52 E4
Ashley *Wilts* 57 C8
Ashley Down *Bristol* 56 A3
Ashley Heath *Dorset* 40 F5
Ashmansworth *Hants* 61 E5
Ashmansworthy *Devon* 31 C6
Ashmead Green *Glos* 63 C7
Ashmill *Devon* 18 A4
Ashmore *Dorset* 39 C8
Ashmore Green *W Berks* 61 C7
Ashorne *Warwick* 77 A9
Ashperton *Heref'd* 74 D2
Ashprington *Devon* 14 D4
Ashreigney *Devon* 33 D5
Ashton *Cornw'l* 3 E8
Ashton *Som'set* 47 B8
Ashton *Som'set* 47 B8
Ashton Common *Wilts* 57 E2
Ashton Hill *Wilts* 58 E4
Ashton Keynes *Wilts* 65 D6
Ashton under Hill *Worcs* 76 E2
Ashton Vale *Bristol* 56 B3
Ashwater *Devon* 18 A4
Ashwell *Som'set* 36 C5
Ashwick *Som'set* 48 B4
Askerswell *Dorset* 25 B5
Asney *Som'set* 48 D1
Asthall *Oxon* 72 E4
Asthall Leigh *Oxon* 72 E5
Aston *Oxon* 66 B3
Aston Cantlow *Warwick* 77 A5
Aston Crews *Heref'd* 69 C7
Aston Cross *Glos* 76 F1
Aston Ingham *Heref'd* 69 C7
Aston Magna *Glos* 77 E6
Aston on Carrant *Glos* 76 F1
Aston Somerville *Worcs* 76 E3
Aston Subedge *Glos* 77 D5
Aston Tirrold *Oxon* 67 E8
Aston Upthorpe *Oxon* 67 E8
Astwood *Worcs* 75 A7
Atch Lench *Worcs* 76 B3
Athelhampton *Dorset* 26 A2
Atherfield Green *I/Wight* 29 E9
Atherington *Devon* 32 B4
Atherstone *Som'set* 37 C5
Atherstone on Stour *Warwick* 77 B7
Atrim *Dorset* 24 A4
Atworth *Wilts* 58 C2
Aughton *Wilts* 61 E1
Aunk *Devon* 35 F5
Aust *S Gloucs* 62 E3
Avebury *Wilts* 59 C7
Avebury Trusloe *Wilts* 59 C6
Avening *Glos* 64 C2
Avening Green *S Gloucs* 63 D6
Aveton Gifford *Devon* 14 F1
Avington *Hants* 53 E7
Avington *W Berks* 60 C4
Avon *Wilts* 58 A4
Avoncliffe *Wilts* 57 E8
Avonmouth *Bristol* 56 A2
Avonwick *Devon* 14 D2
Awkley *S Gloucs* 62 E3
Awliscombe *Devon* 35 F7
Awre *Glos* 69 F8
Axbridge *Som'set* 55 F8
Axford *Wilts* 60 B1
Axminster *Devon* 23 A7
Axmouth *Devon* 23 B7
Axtown *Devon* 11 B6
Axworthy *Devon* 19 C6
Aylburton *Glos* 62 B4
Aylesbeare *Devon* 22 B2
Aylton *Heref'd* 74 E3
Aynho *Northants* 73 A9
Ayreville *Torbay* 14 C4
Ayshford *Devon* 35 C5

B

Babbacombe *Torbay* 15 B6
Babcary *Som'set* 48 F3
Bacchus *Glos* 70 E2
Backney *Heref'd* 69 B5
Backwell *N Som'set* 56 C1
Backwell Green *N Som'set* 56 C2
Backwell Hill *N Som'set* 56 C1
Badbury *Swindon* 65 F8
Badbury Wick *Swindon* 65 F8
Badgall *Cornw'l* 18 C1
Badger Street *Som'set* 36 C3
Badgeworth *Glos* 70 D4
Badgworth *Som'set* 47 A7
Badharlick *Cornw'l* 18 C2
Badminton *S Gloucs* 63 F8
Badsey *Worcs* 76 D4
Bagber *Dorset* 39 D5
Bagendon *Glos* 71 F6
Bagley *Som'set* 47 B9
Bagley Green *Som'set* 35 C7
Bagnor *W Berks* 61 C5
Bagpath *Glos* 63 D8
Bagpath *Glos* 64 B2
Bagshot *Wilts* 60 C3
Bagstone *S Gloucs* 63 E5
Bagwyllydiart *Heref'd* 68 B2
Bailbrook *Bath/NE Som'set* 57 C7
Baker's Hill *Glos* 69 E5
Baldhu *Cornw'l* 4 B3
Baldon Row *Oxon* 67 B8
Balingham Hill *Heref'd* 69 A5
Ball Hill *Hants* 61 D5
Ballhill *Devon* 31 B5
Ballingham *Heref'd* 68 A5
Ball's Green *Glos* 64 C2
Baltonsborough *Som'set* 48 E2
Balwest *Cornw'l* 3 D7
Bamfurlong *Glos* 70 C4
Bampton *Devon* 34 B4
Bampton *Oxon* 66 B3
Bangors *Cornw'l* 17 A9
Bank *Hants* 41 E8
Bankland *Som'set* 47 E6
Bantham *Devon* 12 D4
Banwell *N Som'set* 55 E8
Bapton *Wilts* 50 D4
Bar End *Hants* 53 F6
Barbican *Plym'th* 11 E5
Barbrook *Devon* 44 B1
Barcheston *Warwick* 77 E8
Bareppa *Cornw'l* 4 E3
Barford St. John *Oxon* 73 A7
Barford St. Martin *Wilts* 51 E6
Barford St. Michael *Oxon* 73 A7
Barkla Shop *Cornw'l* 7 E5
Barnard Gate *Oxon* 73 E7
Barnard's Green *Worcs* 75 C5
Barne Barton *Plym'th* 10 D4
Barnsley *Glos* 65 A6
Barnstaple *Devon* 43 E6
Barnwood *Glos* 70 D3
Barr *Som'set* 36 B1
Barrington *Som'set* 37 C5
Barripper *Cornw'l* 3 C8
Barrow *Glos* 70 C3
Barrow *Som'set* 48 C3
Barrow Common *N Som'set* 56 C2
Barrow Gurney *N Som'set* 56 C2
Barrow Hill *Dorset* 27 A6
Barrow Street *Wilts* 50 E1
Barrow Vale *Bath/NE Som'set* 56 D4
Barry *V/Glam* 54 C2
Barry Docks *V/Glam* 54 C2
Barry Island *V/Glam* 54 C2
Bartestree *Heref'd* 74 D1
Bartley *Hants* 41 D9
Barton *Glos* 71 B8
Barton *N Som'set* 55 E7
Barton *Torbay* 15 B6
Barton *Warwick* 76 B5
Barton End *Glos* 64 C2
Barton Gate *Devon* 43 C8
Barton on Sea *Hants* 28 B4
Barton on the Heath *Warwick* 72 A4
Barton St. David *Som'set* 48 E2
Barton Stacey *Hants* 53 C5
Barton Town *Devon* 43 C8
Bartongate *Oxon* 73 B7
Barwick *Som'set* 37 D9
Bashley *Hants* 28 A4
Bason Bridge *Som'set* 47 B6
Bastonford *Worcs* 75 B6
Batch *Som'set* 55 E6
Batcombe *Dorset* 38 F2
Batcombe *Som'set* 49 D5
Bath *Bath/NE Som'set* 57 C7
Bathampton *Bath/NE Som'set* 57 C7
Bathealton *Som'set* 35 B6
Batheaston *Bath/NE Som'set* 57 C7
Bathford *Bath/NE Som'set* 57 C7
Bathpool *Cornw'l* 18 F2
Bathpool *Som'set* 36 A3
Bathway *Som'set* 48 A3
Batsford *Glos* 77 F6
Batson *Devon* 13 E5
Batsworthy *Devon* 34 C1
Battleborough *Som'set* 47 A6
Battledown *Glos* 71 C5
Battleton *Som'set* 45 F5
Battramsley *Hants* 29 A6
Baughton *Worcs* 75 D7
Baughurst *Hants* 61 D8
Baulking *Oxon* 66 D3
Baunton *Glos* 64 B5
Baverstock *Wilts* 51 E5
Bawdrip *Som'set* 47 D6
Bay *Dorset* 49 F8
Baydon *Wilts* 60 A2
Bayford *Som'set* 49 F6
Baysham *Heref'd* 68 B5
Bayworth *Oxon* 67 B7
Beach *S Gloucs* 57 B6
Beachley *Glos* 62 D3
Beacon *Devon* 35 E8
Beacon *Devon* 36 E2
Beacon Hill *Bath/NE Som'set* 57 C6
Beacon Hill *Dorset* 27 B6
Beaford *Devon* 32 D4
Bealbury *Cornw'l* 10 B3
Bealeys *Devon* 32 C3
Bealsmill *Cornw'l* 18 E4
Beaminster *Dorset* 37 F7
Beanacre *Wilts* 58 C3
Bear Cross *Bournem'th* 27 A8
Beare *Devon* 34 F4
Bearfield *Wilts* 57 D8
Bearley *Warwick* 77 A6
Bearwood *Bournem'th* 27 A8
Beauworth *Hants* 53 F8
Beaworthy *Devon* 19 A6
Beckery *Som'set* 48 D1
Beckford *Worcs* 76 E2
Beckhampton *Wilts* 59 C6
Beckington *Som'set* 49 A8
Beckley *Hants* 28 A4
Bedchester *Dorset* 39 C7
Bedminster *Bristol* 56 B3
Bedminster Down *Bristol* 56 C3
Beechen Cliff *Bath/NE Som'set* 57 D7
Beechingstoke *Wilts* 59 E6
Beedon *W Berks* 61 A6
Beedon Manor *W Berks* 61 A6
Beenham *W Berks* 61 C8
Beeny *Cornw'l* 17 B7
Beer *Devon* 23 A6
Beer *Som'set* 47 E8
Beer Crocombe *Som'set* 36 B4
Beer Hackett *Dorset* 38 D1
Beesands *Devon* 13 D7
Beeson *Devon* 13 D7
Beetham *Som'set* 36 D3
Begbroke *Oxon* 73 E8
Beggearn Huish *Som'set* 45 D7
Belchawell *Dorset* 39 E5
Belchawell Street *Dorset* 39 E5
Bellever *Devon* 13 E3
Belluton *Bath/NE Som'set* 56 D4
Belmont *Oxon* 66 E4
Belowda *Cornw'l* 8 C2
Belstone *Devon* 20 B2
Belstone Corner *Devon* 20 A2
Bemerton *Wilts* 51 E7
Beneknowle *Devon* 14 D2
Bengeworth *Worcs* 76 D3
Benhall *Glos* 70 C4
Benham Burslot *W Berks* 61 B5
Bennacott *Cornw'l* 18 B2
Bennah *Devon* 21 D6
Benoak *Cornw'l* 9 C7
Bentham *Glos* 70 D4
Bentwichen *Devon* 44 E1
Benville Lane *Dorset* 37 F8
Bere Alston *Devon* 10 B4
Bere Ferrers *Devon* 10 C5
Bere Regis *Dorset* 26 A3
Berepper *Cornw'l* 3 F9
Berhill *Som'set* 47 D8
Berinsfield *Oxon* 67 C8
Berkeley *Glos* 63 C5
Berkeley Heath *Glos* 63 C5
Berkeley Road *Glos* 63 C6
Berkley *Som'set* 49 B8
Berkley Marsh *Som'set* 49 B8
Berriowbridge *Cornw'l* 18 E2
Berrow *Som'set* 47 A5
Berrow *Worcs* 75 F5
Berrow Green *Worcs* 74 A4
Berry Cross *Devon* 32 D2
Berry Hill *Glos* 68 E5
Berry Pomeroy *Devon* 14 C4
Berryfield *Wilts* 58 D2
Berrynarbor *Devon* 43 B6
Berwick *S Gloucs* 62 F3
Berwick Bassett *Wilts* 59 B6
Berwick St. James *Wilts* 51 D6
Berwick St. John *Wilts* 40 B1
Berwick St. Leonard *Wilts* 50 E3
Besford *Worcs* 75 D8
Bessels Leigh *Oxon* 67 B6
Bethel *Cornw'l* 8 E3
Bettiscombe *Dorset* 24 A3
Bevere *Worcs* 75 A6
Beverston *Glos* 64 D2
Bevington *Glos* 63 C5
Bewley Common *Wilts* 58 C3
Bibstone *S Gloucs* 63 D6
Bibury *Glos* 65 A7
Bickenhall *Som'set* 36 C3
Bickington *Devon* 14 A3
Bickleigh *Devon* 11 C7
Bickleigh *Devon* 34 E3
Bickleton *Devon* 42 E5
Bicklington *Devon* 43 E5
Bicknoller *Som'set* 46 D2
Bickton *Hants* 41 D5
Biddestone *Wilts* 58 B2
Biddisham *Som'set* 55 F7
Bideford *Devon* 42 F3
Bidford on Avon *Warwick* 76 B5
Bidlake *Devon* 19 C6
Bigbury *Devon* 12 C4
Bigbury-on-Sea *Devon* 12 D4
Bilbrook *Som'set* 45 C7
Billacombe *Plym'th* 11 E6
Billacott *Cornw'l* 18 B2
Billesley *Warwick* 77 A5
Bilson Green *Glos* 69 E6
Bincombe *Dorset* 25 D8
Bindon *Som'set* 35 B7
Binegar *Som'set* 48 B4
Bingham's Melcombe *Dorset* 39 F5
Binley *Hants* 53 A5
Binnegar *Dorset* 26 C4
Binsey *Oxon* 73 F8
Binton *Warwick* 77 B5
Birch Green *Worcs* 75 C7
Birch Wood *Som'set* 36 D2
Birchend *Heref'd* 74 D3
Birchgrove *Card* 54 A3
Birchill *Devon* 36 F4
Birdlip *Glos* 70 E4
Birdsend *Glos* 69 C9
Birdsmoor Gate *Dorset* 37 F5
Birdwood *Glos* 69 D8
Birlingham *Worcs* 75 D8
Birts Street *Worcs* 75 E5
Birtsmorton *Worcs* 75 E6
Biscombe *Som'set* 35 D8
Biscovey *Cornw'l* 8 E4
Bish Mill *Devon* 33 A7
Bishampton *Worcs* 76 B2
Bishop Sutton *Bath/NE Som'set* 56 E3
Bishopdown *Wilts* 51 E8
Bishops Cannings *Wilts* 58 D5
Bishop's Caundle *Dorset* 38 D3
Bishop's Cleeve *Glos* 71 B5
Bishops Frome *Heref'd* 74 C3
Bishop's Green *Hants* 61 D6
Bishop's Hull *Som'set* 36 B2
Bishops Lydeard *Som'set* 46 F3
Bishop's Norton *Glos* 70 C2
Bishop's Nympton *Devon* 33 B8
Bishop's Tawton *Devon* 43 F6
Bishopsteignton *Devon* 21 F8
Bishopston *Bristol* 56 A3
Bishopstone *Swindon* 66 F1
Bishopstone *Wilts* 40 A4
Bishopstrow *Wilts* 50 C2
Bishopswood *Som'set* 36 D3
Bishopsworth *Bristol* 56 C3
Bishopton *Warwick* 77 A6
Bisley *Glos* 64 A3
Bissoe *Cornw'l* 4 B3
Bisterne *Hants* 41 F5
Bisterne Close *Hants* 41 F7
Bittadon *Devon* 43 C5
Bittaford *Devon* 14 D1
Bittles Green *Dorset* 39 A7
Bitton *S Gloucs* 57 C5
Black Bourton *Oxon* 66 B2
Black Cross *Cornw'l* 7 C9
Black Dog *Devon* 33 E9
Black Rock *Monmouths* 62 E2
Black Torrington *Devon* 32 E2
Blackawton *Devon* 14 E4
Blackborough *Devon* 35 F6
Blackditch *Oxon* 67 A5
Blackdown *Dorset* 37 F5
Blackford *Som'set* 38 A3
Blackford *Som'set* 47 B8
Blackhorse *Devon* 22 A1
Blackhorse *S Gloucs* 57 A5
Blackland *Som'set* 44 D3
Blackland *Wilts* 58 C5
Blackmanston *Dorset* 27 D5
Blackmoor *N Som'set* 56 D1
Blackmoor *Som'set* 35 C8
Blackney *Dorset* 24 A3
Blacknoll *Dorset* 26 C3
Blackpole *Worcs* 75 A7
Blackpool *Devon* 15 F5
Blackpool *Devon* 21 F6
Blackpool Corner *Devon* 23 A8
Blackwater *Cornw'l* 4 A2
Blackwater *Dorset* 28 A2
Blackwater *Som'set* 36 C3
Blackwell *Som'set* 35 A5
Blackwell *Warwick* 77 D7
Blackwell's End Green *Glos* 70 B1
Bladon *Oxon* 73 E7
Blagdon *N Som'set* 56 E2
Blagdon *Torbay* 15 C5
Blagdon Hill *Som'set* 36 C2
Blaisdon *Glos* 69 E8
Blaise Hamlet *Bristol* 56 A3
Blaize Bailey *Glos* 69 E7
Blakeney *Glos* 69 F7
Blakeney Hill *Glos* 69 F7
Blandford Camp *Dorset* 39 E8
Blandford Forum *Dorset* 39 E7
Blandford St. Mary *Dorset* 39 E7
Blashford *Hants* 41 E5
Bleadney *Som'set* 48 B1
Bleadon *N Som'set* 55 E6
Bleak Hill *Hants* 41 D5
Bleak Street *Som'set* 49 E7
Bledington *Glos* 72 C3
Bleet *Wilts* 57 E2
Bletchingdon *Oxon* 73 D9
Blewbury *Oxon* 67 E7
Blindmore *Som'set* 36 D3
Blisland *Cornw'l* 8 A4
Blissford *Hants* 41 D6
Blockley *Glos* 77 F6
Bloxworth *Dorset* 26 B4
Blue Anchor *Cornw'l* 7 D9
Blue Anchor *Som'set* 45 C7
Blue Vein *Wilts* 57 C8
Blunsdon St. Andrew *Swindon* 65 E7
Blunt's *Cornw'l* 10 C2
Boars Hill *Oxon* 67 B6
Boasley Cross *Devon* 19 B7
Bocaddon *Cornw'l* 9 D6
Bodden *Som'set* 48 C4
Boddington *Glos* 70 C3
Bodenham Bank *Heref'd* 69 C6
Bodernham *Wilts* 41 A6
Bodieve *Cornw'l* 16 F4
Bodilly *Cornw'l* 4 D1
Bodiniel *Cornw'l* 8 B4
Bodinnick *Cornw'l* 9 E5
Bodley *Devon* 43 B8
Bodmin *Cornw'l* 8 B4
Bodrane *Cornw'l* 9 C7
Boduel *Cornw'l* 9 C7
Bodwen *Cornw'l* 8 C3
Bofarnel *Cornw'l* 9 C5
Bogtown *Devon* 19 A6
Bohemia *Wilts* 41 C7
Bohetherick *Cornw'l* 10 B4
Bohortha *Cornw'l* 5 D5
Bojewyan *Cornw'l* 2 D3
Bokiddick *Cornw'l* 8 C3
Bolberry *Devon* 12 E4
Boldre *Hants* 29 A6
Bolenowe *Cornw'l* 4 C1
Bolham *Devon* 34 D4
Bolham Water *Devon* 35 D8
Bolingey *Cornw'l* 7 E6
Bollow *Glos* 69 E8
Bolstone *Heref'd* 68 A4
Bolventor *Cornw'l* 17 E8
Bondend *Glos* 70 D3
Bondleigh *Devon* 33 F5
Bonehayne *Devon* 23 B6
Bonehill *Devon* 20 E4
Bonson *Som'set* 46 C4
Bont *Monmouths* 68 D1
Boode *Devon* 42 D5
Boomer *Som'set* 47 E5
Boreham *Wilts* 50 C2
Bosavern *Cornw'l* 2 D3
Bosbury *Heref'd* 74 D3
Boscarne *Cornw'l* 8 B3
Boscastle *Cornw'l* 17 B6
Boscombe *Bournem'th* 28 B2
Boscombe *Wilts* 51 D9
Boscoppa *Cornw'l* 8 E3
Boscreege *Cornw'l* 3 D7
Boskenna *Cornw'l* 2 F4
Bosleake *Cornw'l* 4 B1
Bossiney *Cornw'l* 17 C6
Bossington *Hants* 52 E3
Bossington *Som'set* 44 B4
Boswarthen *Cornw'l* 2 D4
Boswinger *Cornw'l* 5 B7
Botallack *Cornw'l* 2 D3
Botany Bay *Bristol* 56 A3
Botany Bay *Monmouths* 62 B2
Botely *Oxon* 67 A6
Bothampstead *W Berks* 61 A7
Bothenhampton *Dorset* 24 B4
Botley Pound *Oxon* 67 A6
Botloe's Green *Glos* 69 B8
Botternell *Cornw'l* 18 F2
Bottlesford *Wilts* 59 E7
Bottoms *Cornw'l* 2 F3
Botusfleming *Cornw'l* 10 C4
Boughspring *Glos* 62 C3
Bouldnor *I/Wight* 29 C7
Bournemouth *Bournem'th* 28 B1
Bournes Green *Glos* 64 B3
Bournside *Glos* 70 C4
Bournstream *Glos* 63 D7
Bourton *Dorset* 49 E7
Bourton *N Som'set* 55 D7
Bourton *Oxon* 66 E1
Bourton *Wilts* 59 D5
Bourton on the Hill *Glos* 72 A2
Bourton-on-the-Water *Glos* 72 C2
Bouts *Worcs* 76 A3
Boveridge *Dorset* 40 D4
Bovey Tracey *Devon* 21 E6
Bovington Camp *Dorset* 26 C3
Bow *Devon* 33 F7
Bow *Oxon* 66 D3
Bowbridge *Glos* 64 B2
Bowcombe *I/Wight* 29 C9
Bowd *Devon* 22 B4
Bowden *Devon* 14 F4
Bowden Derra *Cornw'l* 18 D2
Bowden Hill *Wilts* 58 C3
Bower Ashton *Bristol* 56 B3
Bower Hinton *Som'set* 37 C7
Bowerchalke *Wilts* 40 B3
Bowerhill *Wilts* 58 D3
Bowithick *Cornw'l* 17 D8
Bowling Green *Cornw'l* 10 A3
Bowling Green *Worcs* 75 B6
Bowlish *Som'set* 48 C4
Box *Glos* 64 B2
Box *Wilts* 57 C8
Box Hill *Wilts* 57 C8
Boxbush *Glos* 69 C7
Boxbush *Glos* 69 E8
Boxford *W Berks* 61 B5
Box's Shop *Cornw'l* 30 F4
Boxwell *Glos* 63 D8
Boys Hill *Dorset* 38 D3
Boyton *Cornw'l* 18 B3
Boyton *Wilts* 50 D4
Braddock *Cornw'l* 9 C6
Bradenstoke *Wilts* 58 A5
Bradfield *Devon* 35 E6
Bradfield *W Berks* 61 B8
Bradford *Cornw'l* 17 E7
Bradford *Devon* 31 E8
Bradford Abbas *Dorset* 38 D1
Bradford Leigh *Wilts* 58 D1
Bradford on Avon *Wilts* 57 D8
Bradford on Tone *Som'set* 35 B8
Bradford Peverell *Dorset* 25 B8
Bradiford *Devon* 43 E6
Bradley *Glos* 63 D6
Bradley Cross *Som'set* 48 A1
Bradley Green *Som'set* 46 D5
Bradley Green *Worcs* 76 A2
Bradley Stoke *S Gloucs* 62 F4
Bradlow *Heref'd* 74 E4
Bradney *Som'set* 47 D6
Bradninch *Devon* 34 F4
Bradpole *Dorset* 24 B4
Bradstone *Devon* 18 D4
Bradwell *Devon* 42 C4
Bradworthy *Devon* 31 D6
Brain's Green *Glos* 69 F7
Brampford Speke *Devon* 21 A8
Brampton Abbotts *Heref'd* 69 B6
Bramshaw *Hants* 41 C8
Bramwell *Som'set* 47 F8
Brand Green *Glos* 69 B8
Brand Green *Heref'd* 75 D5
Brandis Corner *Devon* 31 F8
Brandish Street *Som'set* 45 B5
Brane *Cornw'l* 2 E4
Branksome *Poole* 27 B8
Branksome Park *Poole* 27 B8
Bransbury *Hants* 53 C5
Branscombe *Devon* 23 C5
Bransford *Worcs* 75 B5
Bransgore *Hants* 28 A3
Brassknocker *Bath/NE Som'set* 57 D7
Bratton *Som'set* 45 B5
Bratton *Wilts* 50 A3
Bratton Clovelly *Devon* 19 B6
Bratton Fleming *Devon* 43 D7

Bratton Seymour Som'set 49 F5
Braunton Devon 42 D4
Bray Shop Cornw'l 18 F3
Braydon Side Wilts 64 E5
Brayford Devon 43 E8
Brayfordhill Devon 43 E8
Braytown Dorset 26 C3
Brazacott Cornw'l 18 B2
Brea Cornw'l 4 B1
Breach Hill Bath/NE Som'set 56 E2
Bread Street Glos 63 A8
Breadstone Glos 63 B6
Breage Cornw'l 3 E8
Bream Glos 62 A4
Breamore Hants 41 C6
Bream's Meend Glos 62 A3
Brean Som'set 55 E5
Bredenbury Heref'd 74 A2
Bredicot Worcs 75 B8
Bredon Worcs 75 E8
Bredon's Hardick Worcs 75 E8
Bredon's Norton Worcs 75 E8
Brelston Green Heref'd 68 C5
Bremhill Wilts 58 B4
Bremhill Wick Wilts 58 B4
Brendon Devon 31 D7
Brendon Devon 44 B2
Brent Knoll Som'set 47 A6
Brent Mill Devon 14 D1
Brentry Bristol 56 A3
Bretforton Worcs 76 D4
Briantspuddle Dorset 26 B3
Brickfields Worcs 75 A7
Bricklehampton Worcs 76 D2
Bridestowe Devon 19 C7
Bridford Devon 21 C6
Bridfordmills Devon 21 C6
Bridge Cornw'l 4 B1
Bridge Dorset 39 D5
Bridge End Devon 14 F1
Bridge End Devon 22 C3
Bridge End Heref'd 74 C2
Bridge End Oxon 67 D8
Bridge End Worcs 70 A2
Bridge Reeve Devon 33 D6
Bridgehampton Som'set 37 B9
Bridgend Cornw'l 9 D5
Bridgend Devon 11 F7
Bridgend Glos 63 B8
Bridgerule Devon 31 F5
Bridges Cornw'l 8 D3
Bridgetown Cornw'l 18 C3
Bridgetown Devon 14 C4
Bridgetown Som'set 45 E5
Bridgeyate S Gloucs 57 B5
Bridgwater Som'set 47 D5
Bridport Dorset 24 B4
Bridstow Heref'd 69 C5
Brierley Glos 69 D6
Brighstone I/Wight 29 D8
Brighthampton Oxon 66 B4
Brightley Devon 20 A1
Brighton Cornw'l 7 E9
Brightor Cornw'l 10 C3
Brightwalton W Berks 61 A5
Brightwalton Green W Berks 61 A5
Brightwalton Holt W Berks 61 A5
Brightwell-cum-Sotwell Oxon 67 D8
Brigmarston Wilts 51 B8
Brill Cornw'l 4 E2
Brimley Devon 21 E5
Brimpsfield Glos 70 E4
Brimpton W Berks 61 D8
Brimpton Common W Berks 61 D8
Brimscombe Glos 64 B2
Brinkley Hill Heref'd 69 A5
Brinkworth Wilts 64 F5
Brinscombe Som'set 47 A8
Brinsea N Som'set 55 D8
Brislington Bristol 56 B4
Brister End Dorset 38 D1
Bristol Bristol 56 B4
Britford Wilts 51 F8
Brithem Bottom Devon 35 D5
Brixham Torbay 15 D6
Brixton Devon 11 E7
Brixton Deverill Wilts 50 D2
Brize Norton Oxon 72 F5
Broad Blunsdon Swindon 65 D8
Broad Campden Glos 77 E6
Broad Chalke Wilts 40 A3
Broad Green Worcs 75 A5
Broad Hinton Wilts 59 A7
Broad Laying Hants 61 D5
Broad Marston Worcs 77 C5
Broad Mead S Gloucs 62 F4
Broad Oak Devon 22 B3
Broad Oak Dorset 39 D5
Broad Oak Heref'd 68 C3
Broad Parkham Devon 31 B7
Broad Street Wilts 59 E7
Broad Town Wilts 59 A6
Broadbush Swindon 65 D8
Broadclyst Devon 22 B1
Broadhembury Devon 35 F6
Broadhempston Devon 14 B4
Broadlands Devon 14 A4
Broadlane Cornw'l 4 B1
Broadmayne Dorset 26 C1
Broadmoor Glos 69 D6
Broadoak Dorset 24 A3
Broadoak Glos 69 E7
Broadrock Glos 62 C2
Broad's Green Wilts 58 C4
Broadsands Torbay 15 D5
Broadshard Som'set 37 D6
Broadstone Monmouths 62 B2
Broadstone Poole 27 A7
Broadwas Worcs 75 A5
Broadway Oxon 67 E6
Broadway Som'set 36 C4
Broadway Som'set 48 A4
Broadway Worcs 76 E4
Broadway Pound Som'set 36 C4
Broadwell Glos 69 E5
Broadwell Glos 72 B3
Broadwell Oxon 66 B2
Broadwey Dorset 25 D8
Broadwindsor Dorset 37 F6
Broadwood Kelly Devon 32 E5
Broadwoodwidger Devon 19 C5
Brockamin Worcs 75 B5
Brockenhurst Hants 41 F9
Brockham End Bath/NE Som'set 57 C6
Brockhampton Glos 71 B5
Brockhampton Glos 71 C6
Brockhampton Heref'd 69 A5
Brockhampton Heref'd 74 A3
Brockhampton Green Dorset 38 E4
Brockhollands Glos 62 A4
Brockley N Som'set 56 C1
Brock's Green Hants 61 D7
Brockscombe Devon 19 B6
Brockweir Glos 62 B2
Brockworth Glos 70 D3
Brocton Cornw'l 8 B3
Brokenborough Wilts 64 E3
Brokerswood Wilts 49 A8
Bromham Wilts 58 C4
Bromley Heath S Gloucs 57 A5
Brompton Ralph Som'set 45 E8
Brompton Regis Som'set 45 E6
Bromsash Heref'd 69 C6
Bromsberrow Glos 74 F4
Bromsberrow Heath Glos 69 A8
Bromyard Heref'd 74 B3
Brook Devon 11 A5
Brook Hants 41 D8
Brook Hants 52 F3
Brook I/Wight 29 D7
Brook Wilts 50 A2
Brook End Wilts 64 F1
Brook End Worcs 75 C7
Brookeador Devon 15 B5
Brookend Glos 62 C3
Brookend Oxon 73 C5
Brookend S Gloucs 63 B5
Brookfield Glos 75 C3
Brookgreen I/Wight 29 D7
Brookhampton Som'set 48 F4
Brookhill Hants 41 D8
Brookthorpe Glos 70 E2
Broom Warwick 76 B4
Broom Court Warwick 76 B4
Broom Hill Bristol 56 B4
Broom Hill Dorset 40 F3
Broomfield Som'set 46 E4
Broomhill Bristol 56 A4
Broom's Green Heref'd 69 A8
Brotheridge Green Worcs 75 D6
Broughton Hants 52 E3
Broughton Common Wilts 58 D2
Broughton Gifford Wilts 58 D2
Broughton Hackett Worcs 75 B8
Broughton Poggs Oxon 66 B1
Brown Candover Hants 53 D8
Browninghill Green Hants 61 E8
Brownshill Glos 64 B2
Brownston Devon 14 E1
Brownstone Devon 33 E8
Brune's Purlieu Hants 41 C6
Brunton Wilts 61 E1
Brushford Som'set 33 E6
Brushford Som'set 34 A3
Bruton Som'set 49 E5
Bryanston Dorset 39 E7
Brympton D'Evercy Som'set 37 C8
Bryngwyn Monmouths 68 F1
Buck Hill Wilts 58 B4
Buckcastle Hill Heref'd 68 B5
Buckerell Devon 35 F7
Buckfast Devon 14 B2
Buckfastleigh Devon 14 B2
Buckholt Heref'd 68 D4
Buckhorn Devon 18 A4
Buckhorn Weston Dorset 39 B5
Buckland Devon 12 D4
Buckland Devon 15 A5
Buckland Glos 76 E4
Buckland Hants 29 A6
Buckland Oxon 66 C3
Buckland Brewer Devon 31 B8
Buckland Dinham Som'set 49 A7
Buckland Filleigh Devon 32 E2
Buckland in the Moor Devon 14 A2
Buckland Manachorum Devon 11 B5
Buckland Newton Dorset 38 E3
Buckland Ripers Dorset 25 D7
Buckland St. Mary Som'set 36 D3
Buckland-tout-Saints Devon 13 C6
Bucklebury W Berks 61 B8
Bucklebury Alley W Berks 61 B7
Buckleigh Devon 42 F3
Buck's Cross Devon 31 B6
Buck's Mills Devon 31 B7
Buckshead Cornw'l 4 A4
Bude Cornw'l 30 E4
Budge's Shop Cornw'l 10 D2
Budlake Devon 34 F4
Budleigh Salterton Devon 22 D3
Budock Water Cornw'l 4 D3
Bugford Devon 43 C7
Bugle Cornw'l 8 D3
Bugley Wilts 50 C2
Bulbridge Wilts 51 E6
Bulford Wilts 51 C8
Bulford Camp Wilts 51 C8
Bulkington Wilts 58 E3
Bulkworthy Devon 31 D7
Bull Hill Hants 29 A6
Bulley Glos 70 D1
Bulls Green Som'set 49 B6
Bullyhole Bottom Monmouths 62 C1
Bulverton Devon 22 C4
Bulworthy Devon 32 A3
Burbage Wilts 60 D1
Burcombe Wilts 51 E6
Burcot Oxon 67 C8
Burcott Som'set 48 B2
Burford Devon 31 B6
Burford Oxon 72 E4
Burford Som'set 48 C3
Burghclere Hants 61 D6
Burlawn Cornw'l 8 A2
Burleigh Glos 64 B2
Burlescombe Devon 35 C6
Burleston Dorset 26 B2
Burlestone Devon 14 F4
Burley Hants 41 F7
Burley Gate Heref'd 74 C1
Burley Lawn Hants 41 F7
Burley Street Hants 41 F7
Burmington Warwick 77 E8
Burnett Bath/NE Som'set 57 C5
Burnham on Sea Som'set 47 B6
Burnt Hill W Berks 61 B8
Burnthouse Cornw'l 4 C3
Burnworthy Som'set 36 C1
Burras Cornw'l 4 D1
Burraton Cornw'l 10 D4
Burraton Coombe Cornw'l 10 D4
Burridge Devon 33 D7
Burridge Devon 36 E4
Burridge Devon 43 D6
Burrington Devon 33 C5
Burrington N Som'set 56 E1
Burrow Devon 22 B1
Burrow Devon 22 C3
Burrow Som'set 37 B6
Burrow Som'set 45 C5
Burrow Bridge Som'set 47 F7
Burstock Dorset 37 F6
Burston Devon 33 F7
Burtle Som'set 47 C8
Burtle Hill Som'set 47 C7
Burton Dorset 25 B8
Burton Dorset 28 B3
Burton Som'set 37 D8
Burton Som'set 46 C3
Burton Wilts 49 E8
Burton Wilts 57 A8
Burton Bradstock Dorset 24 C4
Bury Som'set 45 F5
Bury End Worcs 76 E4
Bury Hill S Gloucs 63 E6
Burys Bank W Berks 61 C6
Buscot Oxon 66 C1
Buscott Som'set 47 D8
Bush Cornw'l 30 E4
Bush Som'set 46 D4
Bushey Dorset 27 D6
Bushley Worcs 75 F7
Bushley Green Worcs 75 F7
Bushton Wilts 59 A6
Bussage Glos 64 B2
Bussex Som'set 47 D7
Busveal Cornw'l 4 B2
Butcombe N Som'set 56 D2
Butetown Card 54 A3
Butleigh Som'set 48 E2
Butleigh Wootton Som'set 48 E2
Butlers Marston Warwick 77 B9
Butt Green Glos 70 E3
Butterleigh Devon 34 E4
Buttermere Wilts 60 D3
Butterow Glos 64 B2
Butts Devon 21 C6
Butt's Green Hants 41 A9
Butt's Knap Dorset 39 B7
Bystock Devon 22 D2

C

Cad Green Som'set 36 C4
Cadbury Devon 34 F3
Cadbury Heath S Gloucs 57 B5
Cadeleigh Devon 34 E3
Cadgwith Cornw'l 5 H2
Cadley Wilts 59 C9
Cadley Wilts 61 E1
Cadnam Hants 41 D9
Cadoxton V/Glam 54 C2
Cadwin Cornw'l 8 C3
Caerau Card 54 A2
Caerwent Monmouths 62 D1
Caerwent Brook Monmouths 62 E1
Cainscross Glos 63 B8
Calamansack Cornw'l 4 E2
Calbourne I/Wight 29 C8
Calcot Glos 71 E7
Calcott's Green Glos 70 D1
Caldecott Oxon 67 C6
Caldicot Monmouths 62 E1
Calenick Cornw'l 4 B4
Callestick Cornw'l 7 E6
Callington Cornw'l 10 B3
Callow Heref'd 68 A3
Callow End Worcs 75 C6
Callow Hill Som'set 55 E8
Callow Hill Wilts 65 F5
Callowell Glos 64 A1
Calmsden Glos 71 F6
Calne Wilts 58 B5
Calne Marsh Wilts 58 B5
Calstock Cornw'l 10 B4
Calstone Wellington Wilts 59 C5
Calverleigh Devon 34 D3
Cam Glos 63 C7
Camborne Cornw'l 3 B9
Cambridge Glos 63 B6
Cambridge Batch N Som'set 56 B2
Cambrose Cornw'l 4 A1
Camel Hill Som'set 38 A1
Cameley Bath/NE Som'set 56 E4
Camelford Cornw'l 17 D7
Camer's Green Worcs 75 F5
Camerton Bath/NE Som'set 57 E5
Canada Hants 41 C8
Canada Common Hants 41 C8
Canford Cliffs Dorset 27 C8
Canford Magna Poole 27 A7
Cann Dorset 39 B7
Cann Common Dorset 39 B7
Cannard's Grave Som'set 48 C4
Cannington Som'set 46 D5
Cannop Glos 69 E6
Canon Frome Heref'd 74 D3
Canonstown Cornw'l 3 C6
Canton Card 54 A3
Canworthy Cornw'l 18 B1
Canworthy Water Cornw'l 18 B1
Capton Devon 14 E4
Capton Som'set 45 D8
Caradon Town Cornw'l 10 A1
Carbis Cornw'l 8 D3
Carbis Bay Cornw'l 3 C6
Carclaze Cornw'l 8 E3
Cardiff Card 54 A3
Cardinham Cornw'l 9 B5
Carey Heref'd 68 A5
Carey Park Cornw'l 9 E7
Carfury Cornw'l 2 D4
Cargreen Cornw'l 10 C4
Carhampton Som'set 45 C7
Carharrack Cornw'l 4 B2
Carisbrooke I/Wight 29 C9
Carkeel Cornw'l 10 C4
Carleen Cornw'l 3 D8
Carlidnack Cornw'l 4 E3
Carlingcott Bath/NE Som'set 57 E5
Carloggas Cornw'l 7 B8
Carn Brea Cornw'l 4 B1
Carn Towan Cornw'l 2 E3
Carne Cornw'l 5 C6
Carne Cornw'l 8 D2
Carnebone Cornw'l 4 D2
Carnhell Green Cornw'l 3 C8
Carnhot Cornw'l 4 A2
Carnkie Cornw'l 4 C1
Carnkie Cornw'l 4 D2
Carnkief Cornw'l 7 E6
Carnon Downs Cornw'l 4 B3
Carnyorth Cornw'l 2 D3
Carpalla Cornw'l 8 E2
Carter's Clay Hants 41 A9
Carterton Oxon 66 A2
Carthew Cornw'l 8 D3
Cary Fitzpaine Som'set 48 F2
Cashes Green Glos 63 A8
Cashmoor Dorset 40 D2
Cassey Compton Glos 71 D6
Cassington Oxon 73 E8
Castallack Cornw'l 2 E5
Castle Cary Som'set 48 E4
Castle Combe Wilts 58 A1
Castle Eaton Swindon 65 C7
Castle Field Som'set 47 D6
Castle Frome Heref'd 74 C3
Castle Hill Wilts 51 E7
Castlemorton Worcs 75 E5
Castletown Dorset 25 F8
Catbrain S Gloucs 62 F3
Catbrook Monmouths 62 B2
Catchall Cornw'l 2 E4
Catcomb Wilts 58 A5
Catcott Som'set 47 D7
Cathays Card 54 A3
Cathays Park Card 54 A3
Catherine Hill S Gloucs 62 E3
Catherston Leweston Dorset 24 B2
Catley Southfield Heref'd 74 D3
Catmore W Berks 67 F5
Caton Devon 14 A3
Catsgore Som'set 37 A8
Catsham Som'set 48 E3
Cattedown Plym'th 11 E5
Cattistock Dorset 25 A6
Caudle Green Glos 70 E4
Caudworthy Park Cornw'l 18 B2
Caulcott Oxon 73 C9
Caundle Marsh Dorset 38 D3
Caundle Wake Dorset 38 D3
Caute Devon 31 D8
Cawsand Cornw'l 10 E4
Cerne Abbas Dorset 38 F3
Cerney Wick Glos 65 C6
Chaceley Glos 70 A3
Chacewater Cornw'l 4 B2
Chaddlehanger Devon 19 E6
Chaddlewood Plym'th 11 D7
Chaddleworth W Berks 61 A5
Chadlington Oxon 73 C5
Chaffcombe Som'set 36 D5
Chagford Devon 20 C4
Chalbury Dorset 40 E3
Chalbury Common Dorset 40 E3
Chaldon Herring Dorset 26 D2
Chalford Glos 64 B3
Chalford Wilts 50 A2
Chalk Hill Glos 71 B8
Chalkway Som'set 37 E5
Challaborough Devon 12 C3
Challacombe Devon 43 C8
Chalmington Dorset 38 F1
Chambercombe Devon 43 B5
Chandler's Cross Worcs 75 E5
Chantry Som'set 49 B6
Chapel Allerton Som'set 47 A8
Chapel Amble Cornw'l 16 E4
Chapel Cleeve Som'set 45 C7
Chapel Hill Glos 62 B4
Chapel Hill Monmouths 62 C2
Chapel Leigh Som'set 46 F2
Chapel Plaister Wilts 57 C8
Chapel Row W Berks 61 C8
Chapel Town Cornw'l 7 D8
Chapelton Devon 32 A4
Chapmans Well Devon 18 B4
Chapmanslade Wilts 49 B8
Charatan Cornw'l 10 B2
Chard Som'set 36 E4
Chard Junction Dorset 36 F4
Chardleigh Green Som'set 36 D4
Chardstock Devon 36 F4
Charfield S Gloucs 63 D6
Chargrove Glos 70 D4
Chargy Hill Glos 70 C2
Charing Cross Dorset 40 D5
Charingworth Glos 77 E7
Charlacott Devon 43 F5
Charlbury Oxon 73 D6
Charlcombe Bath/NE Som'set 57 C7
Charlcutt Wilts 58 A4
Charlecote Warwick 77 A8
Charles Devon 43 E8
Charles Bottom Devon 43 E8
Charlestown Cornw'l 8 E3
Charlestown Dorset 25 E8
Charlinch Som'set 46 D4
Charlton Hants 52 B4
Charlton Oxon 67 E5
Charlton Som'set 36 A3
Charlton Som'set 48 C4
Charlton Som'set 49 A5
Charlton Wilts 39 B8
Charlton Wilts 59 E7
Charlton Wilts 64 E4
Charlton Worcs 76 C3
Charlton Abbots Glos 71 C6
Charlton Adam Som'set 48 F2
Charlton All Saints Wilts 41 B6
Charlton Horethorne Som'set 38 B2
Charlton Kings Glos 71 C5
Charlton Mackrell Som'set 48 F2
Charlton Marshall Dorset 39 F8
Charlton Musgrove Som'set 49 E6
Charlton on the Hill Dorset 39 F7
Charminster Bournem'th 28 B2
Charminster Dorset 25 B8
Charmouth Dorset 24 B2
Charney Bassett Oxon 66 D4
Charter Alley Hants 61 F8
Charterhouse Som'set 56 E2
Charterville Allotments Oxon 72 E5
Chase End Street Worcs 75 E5
Chase Hill Glos 63 E6
Chaselbourne Dorset 26 A2
Chastleton Oxon 72 B3
Chasty Devon 31 F6
Chavenage Green Glos 64 C2
Chawleigh Devon 33 D7
Chawley Oxon 67 B6
Chaxhill Glos 69 E8
Cheapside Worcs 76 C5
Checkley Heref'd 74 E1
Cheddar Som'set 56 F1
Cheddon Fitzpaine Som'set 46 F4
Chedglow Wilts 64 D3
Chedington Dorset 37 E7
Chedworth Glos 71 E7
Chedworth Laines Glos 71 E6
Chedzoy Som'set 47 D6
Cheglinch Devon 42 C5
Cheldon Devon 33 D7
Chelmsine Som'set 36 C1
Chelston Som'set 35 B7
Chelston Heathfield Som'set 35 B8
Cheltenham Glos 71 C5
Chelvey N Som'set 56 C1
Chelwood Bath/NE Som'set 56 D4
Chelworth Wilts 64 D4
Chelworth Lower Green Wilts 65 D6
Chelworth Upper Green Wilts 65 D6
Chelynch Som'set 49 C5
Chepstow Monmouths 62 D2
Cherhill Wilts 59 B5
Cherington Glos 64 C3
Cherington Warwick 77 E8
Cheriton Devon 44 B1
Cheriton Hants 53 F8
Cheriton Barton Devon 34 E2
Cheriton Bishop Devon 20 B5
Cheriton Cross Devon 20 B5
Cheriton Fitzpaine Devon 34 E2
Cherry Orchard Worcs 75 B7
Chesil Dorset 24 D2
Chesterblade Som'set 49 C5
Chesterton Glos 64 B5
Cheston Devon 14 D1
Chetnole Dorset 38 E2
Chetterwood Dorset 40 E2
Chettiscombe Devon 34 D4
Chettle Dorset 40 D2
Chevithorne Devon 34 C4
Chew Magna Bath/NE Som'set 56 D3
Chew Stoke Bath/NE Som'set 56 D3
Chewton Keynsham Bath/NE Som'set 57 C5
Chewton Mendip Som'set 48 A3
Chewton Place Bath/NE Som'set 57 C5
Chichacott Devon 20 A2
Chickerell Dorset 25 D7
Chicklade Wilts 50 E3
Chideock Dorset 24 B3
Chieveley W Berks 61 B6
Chilbolton Hants 52 C4
Chilcomb Hants 53 F7
Chilcombe Dorset 25 B5
Chilcompton Som'set 48 A4
Child Okeford Dorset 39 D6
Childrey Oxon 66 E4
Childswickham Worcs 76 E4
Chilfrome Dorset 25 A6
Chilhampton Wilts 51 E6
Chilla Devon 32 F1
Chilland Hants 53 E7
Chillaton Devon 19 D5
Chillington Devon 13 D6
Chillington Som'set 37 D5
Chilmark Wilts 50 E4
Chilson Oxon 72 D5
Chilsworthy Cornw'l 10 A4
Chilsworthy Devon 31 E6
Chilthorne Domer Som'set 37 C8
Chilton Devon 34 F2
Chilton Oxon 67 E6
Chilton Candover Hants 53 C8
Chilton Cantelo Som'set 38 B1
Chilton Foliat Wilts 60 B3
Chilton Polden Som'set 47 D7
Chilton Trinity Som'set 47 D5
Chimney Oxon 66 B4
Chipley Som'set 35 B7
Chippenham Wilts 58 B3
Chipping Campden Glos 77 E6
Chipping Norton Oxon 72 B5
Chipping Sodbury S Gloucs 63 F6
Chipstable Som'set 45 F7
Chirton Wilts 59 E6
Chisbury Wilts 60 C2
Chiselborough Som'set 37 C7
Chiseldon Swindon 59 A8
Chislehampton Oxon 67 C8
Chitterley Devon 34 F3
Chitterne Wilts 50 C4
Chittlehamholt Devon 33 B5
Chittlehampton Devon 33 A5
Chittoe Wilts 58 C4
Chivelstone Devon 13 E6
Chivenor Devon 42 E5
Cholderton Wilts 52 C1
Cholsey Oxon 67 E8
Cholwell Bath/NE Som'set 56 E4
Choon Cornw'l 7 F6
Christchurch Dorset 28 B3
Christchurch Glos 68 E5
Christian Malford Wilts 58 A4
Christon N Som'set 55 E6
Christow Devon 21 D6
Chudleigh Devon 21 E7
Chudleigh Knighton Devon 21 E6
Chulmleigh Devon 33 D6
Church Cove Cornw'l 5 H2
Church End Glos 63 A6
Church End Glos 70 E7
Church End Wilts 59 A5
Church Enstone Oxon 73 B6
Church Green Devon 23 A5
Church Grounds Dorset 24 A4
Church Hanborough Oxon 73 E7
Church Knowle Dorset 27 D5
Church Lench Worcs 76 B3
Church Town Cornw'l 4 B1
Churcham Glos 70 D1
Churchbridge Cornw'l 9 D7
Churchdown Devon 31 F5
Churchdown Glos 70 D3
Churchend S Gloucs 63 D6
Churchill Devon 36 F3
Churchill Devon 43 C6
Churchill N Som'set 55 D8
Churchill Oxon 72 C4
Churchill Worcs 75 B8
Churchill Green N Som'set 55 D8
Churchinford Som'set 36 D2
Churchstanton Som'set 36 D1
Churchstanton Hill Som'set 36 D2
Churchstow Devon 13 C5
Churchtown Devon 43 C8
Churscombe Torbay 15 C5
Churston Ferrers Torbay 15 D6
Chute Cadley Wilts 52 A3
Chute Standen Wilts 60 F3
Chyandour Cornw'l 3 D5
Cicelyford Monmouths 62 B2
Cinderford Glos 69 E7
Cirencester Glos 65 B5
Cladswell Worcs 76 A3
Claines Worcs 75 A6
Clandown Bath/NE Som'set 57 E5
Clanfield Oxon 66 B2
Clanville Hants 52 B3
Clanville Som'set 48 E4
Clapgate Dorset 40 F3
Clapham Devon 21 C7
Clapton Som'set 37 E6
Clapton Som'set 48 A4
Clapton Wick N Som'set 55 B8
Clapton-in-Gordano N Som'set 56 B1
Clapton-on-the-Hill Glos 72 D2
Clapworthy Devon 33 B6
Clarence Park N Som'set 55 D6
Clarken Green Hants 53 A8
Clatford Wilts 59 C8
Clatford Oakcuts Hants 52 D3
Clatworthy Som'set 45 E8
Clavelshay Som'set 46 E5
Claverham N Som'set 55 C8
Claverton Bath/NE Som'set 57 D7
Claverton Wilts 64 E4
Claverton Down Bath/NE Som'set 57 D7
Clawton Devon 18 A4
Clay Hill Bristol 56 B4
Clay Hill W Berks 61 B8
Clay Hill W Berks 61 C6
Clayhanger Devon 35 B5
Clayhanger Som'set 36 D4
Clayhidon Devon 35 C8
Clayhill Hants 41 E9
Clayland Cross Torbay 15 D5
Claypits Glos 63 A7
Clays End Bath/NE Som'set 57 D6
Clearbrook Devon 11 B6
Clearwell Glos 68 F5
Clearwell Meend Glos 69 F5
Clearwood Wilts 49 B8
Cleave Devon 36 F2
Cleers Cornw'l 8 D2
Cleeve Glos 69 E8
Cleeve N Som'set 55 C9
Cleeve Hill Glos 71 B5
Cleeve Prior Worcs 76 C4
Clench Wilts 59 D8
Clench Common Wilts 59 C8
Clevancy Wilts 59 A5
Clevedon N Som'set 55 B8
Cleveley Oxon 73 C6
Clevelode Worcs 75 C6
Clewer Som'set 47 A8
Cliff Cornw'l 9 D5
Clifford Chambers Warwick 77 B6
Clifford's Mesne Glos 69 C7
Clifton Bristol 56 B3
Clifton Devon 43 C7
Clifton Oxon 73 A8
Clifton Worcs 75 C6
Clifton Hampden Oxon 67 C7
Clifton Hill Worcs 74 A4
Clifton Maybank Dorset 38 D1
Clink Som'set 49 B7
Cloatley Wilts 64 D4
Cloatley End Wilts 64 D4
Cloford Som'set 49 C6
Closworth Som'set 37 D9
Clovelly Devon 31 B6
Clutton Bath/NE Som'set 56 E4
Clutton Hill Bath/NE Som'set 56 E4
Clyffe Pypard Wilts 59 A6

Clyst Honiton Devon 22 A1
Clyst Hydon Devon 35 F5
Clyst St. George Devon 22 C1
Clyst St. Lawrence Devon 35 F5
Clyst St. Mary Devon 22 A1
Coad's Green Cornw'l 18 E2
Coaley Glos 63 B7
Coaley Peak Glos 63 B7
Coalpit Heath S Gloucs 63 F5
Coalway Glos 69 E5
Coat Som'set 37 B7
Coate Swindon 65 F8
Coate Wilts 59 D5
Coates Glos 64 B4
Cobb Dorset 24 B1
Cobbaton Devon 43 F7
Cobbler's Plain Monmouths 62 B1
Coberley Glos 71 D5
Coburg Devon 21 E7
Cockett Hill Dorset 27 A5
Cockhill Som'set 48 E4
Cockington Torbay 15 C5
Cocklake Som'set 47 B8
Cocks Cornw'l 7 E6
Cockwood Devon 22 D1
Cockwood Som'set 46 C4
Cockyard Heref'd 68 A2
Coddington Heref'd 74 D5
Codford St. Mary Wilts 50 D4
Codford St. Peter Wilts 50 C4
Codrington S Gloucs 57 A6
Codsend Som'set 44 D4
Coffinswell Devon 15 B5
Cofton Devon 22 D1
Cogan V/Glam 54 B3
Cogges Oxon 73 F6
Coham Devon 32 E2
Colan Cornw'l 7 C8
Colaton Raleigh Devon 22 C3
Colbrooke Devon 33 F8
Colcot V/Glam 54 C2
Cold Ash W Berks 61 C7
Cold Ashton S Gloucs 57 B7
Cold Aston Glos 71 D8
Cold Green Heref'd 74 D3
Cold Harbour Wilts 50 B2
Cold Northcott Cornw'l 17 C9
Coldeast Devon 21 F6
Coldharbour Cornw'l 7 F6
Coldharbour Devon 35 D6
Coldharbour Dorset 25 D7
Coldharbour Glos 62 B3
Coldridge Devon 33 E6
Coldvreath Cornw'l 8 D2
Cole Som'set 49 E5
Cole Henley Hants 53 A6
Colebrook Devon 35 E5
Coleford Devon 33 F8
Coleford Glos 69 E5
Coleford Som'set 49 B5
Coleford Water Som'set 46 E2
Colehill Dorset 40 F3
Colerne Wilts 57 B8
Cole's Cross Dorset 37 F5
Coles Green Worcs 75 B5
Colesbourne Glos 71 E5
Colesbrook Dorset 49 F8
Coleshill Oxon 66 D1
Colestocks Devon 35 F6
Coley Bath/NE Som'set 56 E3
Collaton Devon 13 E5
Collaton St. Mary Torbay 15 D5
Collett's Green Worcs 75 B6
Collingbourne Ducis Wilts 61 E1
Collingbourne Kingston Wilts 60 E1
Collington Heref'd 74 A2
Collins Green Worcs 74 A4
Coln Rogers Glos 71 F7
Coln St. Aldwyn Glos 65 A7
Coln St. Dennis Glos 71 E7
Colscott Devon 31 D7
Colthrop W Berks 61 C7
Colt's Green S Gloucs 63 F6
Columbjohn Devon 21 A9
Colwall Heref'd 74 D4
Colwall Green Heref'd 75 D5
Colwall Stone Heref'd 75 D5
Colyford Devon 23 B7
Colyton Devon 23 B6
Combe Devon 11 E6
Combe Devon 14 B2
Combe Oxon 73 D7
Combe Som'set 47 F8
Combe W Berks 60 D4
Combe Almer Dorset 27 A5
Combe Down Bath/NE Som'set 57 D7
Combe Fishacre Devon 14 B4
Combe Florey Som'set 46 E2
Combe Hay Bath/NE Som'set 57 E6
Combe Martin Devon 43 B6
Combe Pafford Torbay 15 B6
Combe Raleigh Devon 35 F8
Combe St. Nicholas Som'set 36 D4
Combe Throop Som'set 38 B4
Combebow Devon 19 C6
Combeinteignhead Devon 15 A6
Combpyne Devon 23 B7
Combrook Warwick 77 B9
Combwich Som'set 46 C5
Come-to-Good Cornw'l 4 B4
Comeytrowe Som'set 36 B2
Comford Cornw'l 4 C2
Common Heref'd 68 D4
Common Gate Dorset 39 D5
Common Hill Heref'd 74 F1
Common Moor Cornw'l 9 B7
Common Platt Wilts 65 E7
Compass Som'set 47 E6
Compton Devon 15 C5
Compton Hants 52 F3
Compton Hants 53 F6
Compton Plym'th 11 D5
Compton W Berks 61 A7
Compton Wilts 51 A7
Compton Abbas Dorset 39 C7
Compton Abdale Glos 71 D7
Compton Bassett Wilts 59 B5
Compton Beauchamp Oxon 66 E2
Compton Bishop Som'set 55 E8
Compton Chamberlayne Wilts 51 F5
Compton Common Bath/NE Som'set 56 D4
Compton Dando Bath/NE Som'set 56 D4
Compton Dundon Som'set 48 E1
Compton Durville Som'set 37 C6
Compton End Hants 53 F6
Compton Green Glos 69 B8
Compton Greenfield S Gloucs 62 F3
Compton Martin Bath/NE Som'set 56 E2
Compton Pauncefoot Som'set 38 A2
Compton Valance Dorset 25 B6
Compton Verney Warwick 77 B9
Conderton Worcs 76 E2
Condicote Glos 72 B1
Coney Hill Glos 70 D3
Coneygar Hill Dorset 24 B4
Congdon's Shop Cornw'l 18 E2
Congresbury N Som'set 55 D8
Conham S Gloucs 56 B4
Conkwell Wilts 57 D7
Connor Downs Cornw'l 3 C7
Conock Wilts 59 E6
Constantine Cornw'l 4 E2
Constantine Bay Cornw'l 16 F2
Cookbury Devon 31 E8
Cookbury Wick Devon 31 E7
Cookhill Worcs 76 A4
Coombe Cornw'l 4 B4
Coombe Cornw'l 8 E2
Coombe Cornw'l 30 D4
Coombe Devon 21 F8
Coombe Devon 22 B4
Coombe Glos 63 D7
Coombe Som'set 37 E6
Coombe Wilts 39 B7
Coombe Wilts 51 A7
Coombe Bissett Wilts 40 A5
Coombe End Som'set 45 F7
Coombe Green Wilts 64 E3
Coombe Hill Glos 70 B3
Coombe Keynes Dorset 26 D3
Coombe Street Som'set 49 E7
Coombelake Devon 22 A3
Coombes End S Gloucs 63 F7
Copp Hill S Gloucs 63 F6
Coppathorne Cornw'l 30 F4
Copperhouse Cornw'l 3 C7
Coppleridge Dorset 39 A6
Copplestone Devon 33 F8
Copthorne Cornw'l 18 B2
Copythorne Hants 41 D9
Corfe Som'set 36 C2
Corfe Castle Dorset 27 D6
Corfe Mullen Dorset 27 A6
Corndon Devon 20 C3
Cornmeadow Green Worcs 75 A7
Cornwell Oxon 72 B4
Cornwood Devon 11 D8
Cornworthy Devon 14 D4
Corscombe Dorset 37 E8
Corse Lawn Glos 70 A2
Corsey Wilts 49 B8
Corsham Wilts 58 B2
Corsley Heath Wilts 49 B8
Corston Bath/NE Som'set 57 C5
Corston Wilts 64 F3
Corton Wilts 50 C3
Corton Denham Som'set 38 B2
Coryates Dorset 25 C7
Coryton Devon 19 D6
Coscote Oxon 67 E7
Cosmeston V/Glam 54 C3
Cossington Som'set 47 C7
Cote Oxon 66 B4
Cote Som'set 47 C6
Cotford Devon 22 B4
Cotham Bristol 56 B3
Cothelstone Som'set 46 E3
Cothill Oxon 67 C6
Cotland Monmouths 62 B2
Cotleigh Devon 35 F7
Cotleigh Devon 36 F2
Cotmaton Devon 22 C4
Cotswold Community Glos 65 C5
Cott Devon 14 C3
Cottage End Hants 53 C5
Cotteylands Devon 34 D3
Cottonworth Hants 52 D4
Couch Green Hants 53 E7
Couch's Mill Cornw'l 9 D5
Coughton Heref'd 69 C5
Coultings Som'set 46 C4
Countess Wilts 51 C8
Countess Wear Devon 21 B8
Countisbury Devon 44 B1
Courtway Som'set 46 E4
Cove Devon 34 C4
Coverack Cornw'l 5 G3
Coverack Bridges Cornw'l 4 D1
Covingham Swindon 65 F8
Cowbridge Som'set 45 C6
Cowesfield Green Wilts 41 B8
Cowgrove Dorset 27 A6
Cowhill S Gloucs 62 C4
Cowlands Cornw'l 4 B4
Cowley Devon 21 A5
Cowley Glos 71 E5
Cowley Oxon 67 B7
Cowleymoor Devon 34 D4
Cowsden Worcs 76 B1
Cowslip Green N Som'set 56 D1
Coxbridge Som'set 48 D2
Coxford Cornw'l 17 A8
Coxley Som'set 48 C2
Coxley Wick Som'set 48 C2
Coxpark Cornw'l 10 A4
Crab Orchard Dorset 40 E4
Crabtree Plym'th 11 D6
Crackington Haven Cornw'l 17 A7
Crackstone Glos 64 B2
Craddock Devon 35 D6
Cradley Heref'd 74 C4
Crafthole Cornw'l 10 E3
Cranborne Dorset 40 D3
Cranford Devon 31 B6
Cranham Glos 70 E3
Cranmore I/Wight 29 B7
Cranmore Som'set 49 C5
Crantock Cornw'l 7 C6
Crapstone Devon 11 B6
Crawley Devon 36 E3
Crawley Glos 63 C7
Crawley Hants 53 E5
Crawley Oxon 72 E5
Creacombe Devon 34 C1
Crediton Devon 34 F1
Creech Dorset 27 D5
Creech Heathfield Som'set 47 F5
Creech St. Michael Som'set 36 A3
Creed Cornw'l 8 F1
Creegbrawse Cornw'l 4 B2
Creephole Glos 63 E8
Creigau Monmouths 62 C1
Cremyll Cornw'l 10 E5
Crendell Dorset 40 D4
Cress Green Glos 63 B7
Crewkerne Som'set 37 E6
Crew's Hole Bristol 56 B4
Crick Monmouths 62 D1
Cricket Malherbie Som'set 36 D5
Cricket St. Thomas Som'set 36 E5
Crickham Som'set 47 A8
Cricklade Wilts 65 D6
Criddlestyle Hants 41 D6
Criggan Cornw'l 8 C3
Crimchard Som'set 36 E4
Crimp Cornw'l 31 C5
Crimscote Warwick 77 C7
Cripplesease Cornw'l 3 C6
Cripplestyle Dorset 40 D4
Critchell's Green Hants 41 A8
Crizeley Heref'd 68 A2
Croanford Cornw'l 8 A3
Crock Street Som'set 36 D4
Crockenwell Devon 20 B5
Crocker's Ash Heref'd 68 D4
Crockerton Wilts 50 C2
Crockerton Green Wilts 50 C2
Crockett Cornw'l 10 A3
Croford Som'set 46 F2
Croft West Cornw'l 4 A3
Crofthandy Cornw'l 4 B2
Crofton Wilts 60 D2
Cromhall S Gloucs 63 D5
Cromhall Common S Gloucs 63 E5
Crooked End Glos 69 D6
Crooked Soley Wilts 60 B3
Crooked Withies Dorset 40 E4
Crookham W Berks 61 D7
Crook's Marsh Bristol 62 F2
Cropthorne Worcs 76 D2
Croscombe Som'set 48 C3
Cross Devon 42 D4
Cross Devon 43 E7
Cross Som'set 36 D5
Cross Som'set 55 F8
Cross Ash Monmouths 68 D2
Cross Coombe Cornw'l 7 E5
Cross Hill Glos 62 C3
Cross Keys Wilts 58 B2
Cross Lanes Cornw'l 4 F1
Cross Lanes Dorset 39 F5
Cross Roads Devon 19 C6
Crosstown Cornw'l 30 D4
Crossway Heref'd 69 A6
Crossway Monmouths 68 D2
Crossway Green Monmouths 62 D2
Crossways Dorset 26 C2
Crossways Glos 68 E5
Crossways S Gloucs 63 D5
Crouch Hill Dorset 38 D3
Crouch Hill Dorset 38 D4
Croucheston Wilts 40 A4
Crow Hants 41 F6
Crow Hill Heref'd 69 B6
Crowan Cornw'l 3 D8
Crowcombe Som'set 46 D2
Crowden Devon 19 A6
Crowdhole Devon 34 C1
Crowlas Cornw'l 3 D6
Crowle Worcs 75 A8
Crowle Green Worcs 75 A8
Crownhill Plym'th 11 D5
Crowntown Cornw'l 3 D8
Crow's Nest Cornw'l 9 B8
Crows-an-wra Cornw'l 2 E3
Croyde Devon 42 D3
Croyde Bay Devon 42 D3
Crudwell Wilts 64 D4
Crugmeer Cornw'l 16 E3
Crumplehorn Cornw'l 9 E7
Crumpton Hill Worcs 75 C5
Cruse Heref'd 68 D5
Cruwys Morchard Devon 34 D2
Crux Easton Hants 61 E5
Cruxton Dorset 25 A6
Cubert Cornw'l 7 D6
Cuck Hill Som'set 55 E8
Cucklington Som'set 49 F7
Cuckold's Green Wilts 58 E4
Cuckoo's Corner Wilts 59 E5
Cuddesdon Oxon 67 B8
Cudliptown Devon 19 E7
Cudworth Som'set 37 D5
Culham Oxon 67 C7
Culkerton Glos 64 C3
Cullompton Devon 35 E5
Culm Davy Devon 35 D7
Culmstock Devon 35 D6
Culverlane Devon 14 C2
Cumnor Oxon 67 B6
Curbidge Oxon 73 F5
Curdleigh Devon 36 C2
Curgurrel Cornw'l 5 C5
Curland Som'set 36 C3
Curlott Hill Som'set 37 E6
Currian Vale Cornw'l 8 D2
Curridge W Berks 61 B6
Curry Mallet Som'set 36 B4
Curry Rivel Som'set 37 A5
Curtisknowle Devon 14 E2
Cury Cornw'l 4 F1
Cusgarne Cornw'l 4 B3
Cushuish Som'set 46 E3
Custards Hants 41 E9
Cutcombe Som'set 45 D5
Cutler's Green Som'set 48 A3
Cutmadoc Cornw'l 8 C4
Cutmere Cornw'l 10 C2
Cutsdean Glos 71 A7
Cutivett Cornw'l 10 C3
Cutts End Oxon 67 B6
Cwmcarvan Monmouths 68 F3
Cyncoed Card 54 A3
Cyntwell Card 54 A2

D

Daccombe Devon 15 B6
Daggons Dorset 40 D5
Daglingworth Glos 64 A4
Dainton Devon 15 B5
Dalwood Devon 36 F2
Damerham Hants 40 C5
Damery Glos 63 D6
Dancing Green Heref'd 69 C6
Daneway Glos 64 B3
Darbys Green Worcs 74 A4
Darite Cornw'l 9 B8
Dark Hill Glos 69 F5
Darleyford Cornw'l 9 A8
Darlingscott Warwick 77 D7
Darracott Devon 30 C4
Darracott Devon 42 D4
Darshill Som'set 48 C4
Dartington Devon 14 C3
Dartmeet Devon 20 F3
Dartmouth Devon 15 E5
Dauntsey Wilts 64 F4
Dauntsey Green Wilts 64 F4
Dauntsey Lock Wilts 64 F4
Davidstow Cornw'l 17 C8
Dawlish Devon 22 E1
Dawlish Warren Devon 22 E1
Daw's Green Som'set 26 B1
Daw's House Cornw'l 18 D3
Dawshill Worcs 75 B6
Daylesford Glos 72 B3
Dead Maids Wilts 49 B8
Dean Devon 14 C2
Dean Devon 42 C5
Dean Devon 43 B7
Dean Devon 43 B9
Dean Dorset 40 C2
Dean Hants 53 E5
Dean Oxon 73 C5
Dean Som'set 49 C5
Dean Court Oxon 67 A6
Dean Prior Devon 14 C2
Deane Hants 53 A7
Deanend Dorset 40 C2
Deanland Dorset 40 C2
Deblin's Green Worcs 75 C6
Deddington Oxon 73 A8
Deepweir Monmouths 62 E1
Deerhurst Glos 70 B3
Deerhurst Walton Glos 70 B3
Defford Worcs 75 D8
Delabole Cornw'l 17 D6
Delly End Oxon 73 E6
Demelza Cornw'l 8 C2
Denbury Devon 14 B4
Denchworth Oxon 66 D4
Dennel Hill Glos 62 C3
Deptford Wilts 50 D5
Derby Devon 43 E6
Derriford Plym'th 11 D5
Derril Devon 31 F6
Derriton Devon 31 F6
Derry Hill Wilts 58 B4
Devauden Monmouths 62 C1
Devizes Wilts 58 D5
Devonport Plym'th 10 D5
Devoran Cornw'l 4 C3
Dewlish Dorset 26 A2
Dibberford Dorset 37 F7
Didbrook Glos 71 A7
Didcot Oxon 67 D7
Diddywell Devon 42 F4
Didley Heref'd 68 A3
Didmarton Glos 63 E8
Didworthy Devon 14 C1
Dillington Som'set 36 C5
Dilton Marsh Wilts 50 A1
Dimmer Som'set 48 E4
Dimson Cornw'l 10 A4
Dinas Powis V/Glam 54 B3
Dinder Som'set 48 C3
Dines Green Worcs 75 A6
Dingestow Monmouths 68 E3
Dinghurst N Som'set 55 E8
Dinnington Som'set 37 D6
Dinton Wilts 50 E5
Dinworthy Devon 31 C6
Dipford Som'set 36 B2
Dippertown Devon 19 D5
Diptford Devon 14 D2
Ditchampton Wilts 51 E6
Ditcheat Som'set 48 D4
Ditteridge Wilts 57 C8
Dittisham Devon 15 E5
Dixton Glos 71 A5
Dixton Monmouths 68 E4
Dizzard Cornw'l 17 A8
Dobwalls Cornw'l 9 B7
Doccombe Devon 21 C5
Docklow Heref'd 74 A1
Dodbrooke Devon 13 D5
Doddiscombsleigh Devon 21 C7
Doddycross Cornw'l 10 C2
Dodington Som'set 46 C3
Dodington Ash S Gloucs 57 A7
Dodmarsh Heref'd 74 D1
Dog Village Devon 22 B1
Dogridge Wilts 65 E6
Dolemeads Bath/NE Som'set 57 D7
Dolton Devon 32 D4
Donhead St. Andrew Wilts 39 B8
Donhead St. Mary Wilts 39 B8
Doniford Som'set 46 C1
Donnington Glos 72 B2
Donnington W Berks 61 C6
Donnington Holt W Berks 61 C6
Donyatt Som'set 36 D4
Dorcan Swindon 65 F8
Dorchester Dorset 25 B8
Dorchester Oxon 67 D8
Dormington Heref'd 74 D1
Dormston Worcs 76 A2
Dorsington Warwick 77 C5
Dottery Dorset 24 A4
Doublebois Cornw'l 9 B6
Doughton Glos 64 D2
Doulting Som'set 48 C4
Dousland Devon 11 B6
Doverhay Som'set 44 B4
Dowdeswell Glos 71 D6
Dowland Devon 32 D4
Dowlish Ford Som'set 36 D5
Dowlish Wake Som'set 37 D5
Down Ampney Glos 65 C6
Down End Som'set 47 C6
Down Hatherley Glos 70 C3
Down St. Mary Devon 33 F7
Down Thomas Devon 11 E6
Downderry Cornw'l 8 E2
Downderry Cornw'l 10 E2
Downend Glos 64 C1
Downend S Gloucs 56 A4
Downend W Berks 61 A6
Downgate Cornw'l 9 A8
Downgate Cornw'l 10 A3
Downhead Som'set 38 A1
Downhead Som'set 49 B5
Downington Glos 65 C9
Downs V/Glam 54 B2
Downside Som'set 48 A4
Downside Som'set 48 C4
Downton Hants 28 B5
Downton Wilts 41 B6
Dowslands Som'set 36 B2
Doynton S Gloucs 57 B6
Drakes Broughton Worcs 75 C8
Drakewalls Cornw'l 10 A4
Draycot Cerne Wilts 58 A3
Draycot Foliat Swindon 59 A8
Draycott Glos 77 E6
Draycott Som'set 37 B8
Draycott Som'set 48 A1
Draycott Worcs 75 C7
Drayford Devon 33 D8
Draynes Cornw'l 9 B7
Drayton Oxon 67 D6
Drayton Som'set 37 B6
Drayton St. Leonard Oxon 67 C8
Draytons Som'set 37 C6
Drewsteignton Devon 20 B4
Drewston Devon 20 C4
Driffield Glos 65 C6
Drimpton Dorset 37 E6
Drinkers End Worcs 70 A2
Drive End Dorset 38 E1
Droop Dorset 39 E5
Drope V/Glam 54 A2
Druggers End Worcs 75 E5
Dry Sandford Oxon 67 B6
Drybrook Glos 69 D6
Drybrook Heref'd 69 D5
Drym Cornw'l 3 D8
Drynham Wilts 57 E2
Duck Street Hants 52 B3
Ducklington Oxon 73 F6
Dudbridge Glos 63 B8
Duddlestone Som'set 36 B2
Dudsbury Dorset 27 A8
Dulcote Som'set 48 C3
Dulford Devon 35 F6
Duloe Cornw'l 9 D7
Dulverton Som'set 45 F5
Dumbleton Glos 76 E3
Dummer Hants 53 B8
Dunball Som'set 47 C6
Dunbridge Hants 41 A9
Dundon Som'set 48 E1
Dundon Hayes Som'set 48 E1
Dundry N Som'set 56 C3
Dunfield Glos 65 C7
Dunge Wilts 58 F2
Dunkerton Bath/NE Som'set 57 E6
Dunkeswell Devon 35 E7
Dunkirk S Gloucs 63 E7
Dunkirk Wilts 58 D4
Dunley Hants 61 F6
Dunmere Cornw'l 8 B3
Dunnington Warwick 76 B4
Duns Tew Oxon 73 B8
Dunsford Devon 21 C6
Dunshill Worcs 70 A2
Dunster Som'set 45 C6
Dunster Beach Som'set 45 C7
Dunstone Devon 11 E7
Dunstone Devon 20 E4
Dunterton Devon 18 E4
Dunthrop Oxon 73 B6
Duntisborne Abbots Glos 71 F5
Duntisborne Leer Glos 71 F5
Duntisborne Rouse Glos 64 A4
Duntish Dorset 38 E3
Dunwear Som'set 47 D6
Duporth Cornw'l 8 E3
Durgan Cornw'l 4 E3
Durleigh Som'set 47 D5
Durley Wilts 60 D1
Durley Hill Bath/NE Som'set 56 C4
Durlow Common Heref'd 74 E2
Durns Town Hants 29 A5
Durrington Wilts 51 C8
Dursley Glos 63 C7
Dursley Cross Glos 69 D7
Durston Som'set 47 F5
Durweston Dorset 39 E7
Dutson Cornw'l 18 C3
Duxford Oxon 66 C4
Dyer's Common S Gloucs 62 F3
Dyffryn V/Glam 54 B1
Dyke Devon 31 B6
Dymock Glos 69 A7
Dyrham S Gloucs 57 A6

E

Earl's Common Worcs 76 A2
Earl's Croome Worcs 75 D7
Earthcott Green S Gloucs 62 E4
East Allington Devon 14 F3
East Anstey Devon 34 A2
East Anton Hants 52 B4
East Ashton Hants 53 B5
East Bloxworth Dorset 26 B4
East Bower Som'set 47 D6
East Brent Som'set 47 A6
East Buckland Devon 43 E8
East Budleigh Devon 22 D3
East Burton Dorset 26 C3
East Butterleigh Devon 34 E4
East Chaldon Dorset 26 D2
East Challow Oxon 66 E4
East Charleton Devon 13 D6
East Chelborough Dorset 37 E9
East Chinnock Som'set 37 D7
East Chisenbury Wilts 51 A7
East Cholderton Hants 52 B2
East Clevedon N Som'set 55 B8
East Coker Som'set 37 D8
East Combe Som'set 46 E3
East Compton Dorset 39 C7
East Compton Som'set 48 C4
East Cornworthy Devon 14 D4
East Coulston Wilts 58 F4
East Cranmore Som'set 49 C5
East Creech Dorset 27 D5
East Dean Glos 69 C7
East Dean Hants 41 A8
East Down Devon 43 C7
East Dundry N Som'set 56 C3
East End Dorset 27 A6
East End Glos 65 B8
East End Hants 29 A7
East End Hants 61 D5
East End N Som'set 56 B1
East End Oxon 73 A6
East End Oxon 73 D7
East End Oxon 73 E6
East End Som'set 48 A3
East End Som'set 49 B5
East End S Gloucs 57 B7
East Everleigh Wilts 59 F9
East Garston W Berks 60 A4
East Garston Woodlands W Berks 60 B4
East Ginge Oxon 67 E5
East Grafton Wilts 60 D2
East Grimstead Wilts 52 F1
East Hagbourne Oxon 67 E7
East Hanney Oxon 67 D5
East Harnham Wilts 51 F7
East Harptree Bath/NE Som'set 56 E3
East Hatch Wilts 50 F3
East Hendred Oxon 67 E6
East Hewish N Som'set 55 D7
East Holme Dorset 26 C4
East Horrington Som'set 48 B3
East Howe Bournem'th 27 A8
East Huntspill Som'set 47 C6
East Ilsley W Berks 67 F6
East Kennett Wilts 59 C7
East Knighton Dorset 26 C3
East Knowstone Devon 34 B1
East Knoyle Wilts 50 E2
East Lambrook Som'set 37 C6
East Leigh Devon 14 E1
East Leigh Devon 33 E6
East Lockinge Oxon 67 E5
East Looe Cornw'l 9 E8
East Lulworth Dorset 26 D4
East Lydford Som'set 48 E3
East Lynch Som'set 45 B5
East Lyng Som'set 47 F6
East Martin Hants 40 C4
East Mere Devon 34 C4
East Morden Dorset 27 B5
East Nynehead Som'set 35 B8
East Oakley Hants 53 B8
East Ogwell Devon 14 A4
East Orchard Dorset 39 C6
East Parley Dorset 28 A2
East Pennard Som'set 48 D3
East Portlemouth Devon 13 E5
East Prawle Devon 13 E6
East Pulham Dorset 38 E4
East Putford Devon 31 C7
East Quantoxhead Som'set 46 C2
East Rolstone N Som'set 55 D7
East Shefford W Berks 60 A4
East Stoke Dorset 26 C4
East Stoke Som'set 37 C7
East Stour Dorset 39 B6
East Stowford Devon 33 A5
East Stratton Hants 53 D7
East Street Som'set 48 D2
East Taphouse Cornw'l 9 C6
East Town Som'set 46 E2
East Town Som'set 48 C4
East Tytherley Hants 52 F2
East Tytherton Wilts 58 A4
East Village Devon 34 E1
East Water Som'set 48 A2
East Week Devon 20 B3
East Wellow Hants 41 B9
East Winterslow Wilts 52 E1
East Woodhay Hants 61 D5
East Woodlands Som'set 49 C7
East Worlington Devon 33 D8
Eastacombe Devon 43 F5
Eastbrook Som'set 36 B2
Eastbrook V/Glam 54 B3
Eastbury W Berks 60 A3
Eastcombe Glos 64 B2
Eastcott Cornw'l 31 C5
Eastcott Devon 19 D6
Eastcott Wilts 59 E5
Eastcourt Wilts 60 D1
Eastcourt Wilts 64 D4
Easter Compton S Gloucs 62 F3
Easterton Wilts 58 E5
Easterton Sands Wilts 58 E5
Eastertown Som'set 55 F6
Eastfield Bristol 56 A3

St. Ruan *Cornw'l* 5 G2
St. Stephen *Cornw'l* 8 E1
St. Stephen's *Cornw'l* 10 D4
St. Stephens *Cornw'l* 18 C3
St. Teath *Cornw'l* 17 D6
St. Thomas *Devon* 21 B8
St. Tudy *Cornw'l* 17 E6
St. Veep *Cornw'l* 9 D5
St. Wenn *Cornw'l* 8 C2
St. Weonards *Heref'd* 68 C3
St. Winnow *Cornw'l* 9 D5
Saintbridge *Glos* 70 D3
Saintbury *Glos* 76 E5
Salcombe *Devon* 13 E5
Salcombe Regis *Devon* 22 C4
Sale Green *Worcs* 75 A8
Salem *Cornw'l* 4 B2
Saleway *Worcs* 75 A8
Salford *Oxon* 72 B4
Salford Priors *Warwick* 76 B4
Salisbury *Wilts* 51 E8
Salisbury Street *Dorset* 39 C5
Salperton *Glos* 71 C7
Saltash *Cornw'l* 10 D4
Salterton *Wilts* 51 D7
Saltford *Bath/NE Som'set* 57 C5
Saltmead *Card* 54 A3
Saltrens *Devon* 32 B2
Salwayash *Dorset* 24 A4
Sambourne *Wilts* 50 C2
Sampford Arundel *Som'set* 35 C7
Sampford Brett *Som'set* 45 C8
Sampford Chapple *Devon* 32 F5
Sampford Courtenay *Devon* 33 F5
Sampford Moor *Som'set* 35 C7
Sampford Peverell *Devon* 35 D5
Sampford Spiney *Devon* 11 A3
Sancreed *Cornw'l* 2 E4
Sand *Som'set* 47 B8
Sandbanks *Poole* 27 C7
Sandford *Devon* 34 F1
Sandford *Dorset* 27 C5
Sandford *Hants* 41 F6
Sandford *N Som'set* 55 E8
Sandford on Thames *Oxon* 67 B7
Sandford Orcas *Dorset* 38 B1
Sandford St. Martin *Oxon* 73 B7
Sandhills *Dorset* 38 D3
Sandhills *Dorset* 38 F1
Sandhurst *Glos* 70 C2
Sandleford Close *W Berks* 61 C6
Sandleheath *Hants* 40 D5
Sandplace *Cornw'l* 9 D8
Sandway *Dorset* 49 E7
Sandy Gate *Devon* 22 A1
Sandy Lane *Wilts* 58 C4
Sandy Way *I/Wight* 29 D9
Sandygate *Devon* 21 F7
Sandylake *Cornw'l* 9 C5
Sandypark *Devon* 20 C4
Sandyway *Heref'd* 68 B3
Sanford Batch *N Som'set* 55 E8
Sanham Green *W Berks* 60 C3
Sapperton *Glos* 64 B3
Sarsden *Oxon* 72 C4
Satterleigh *Devon* 33 B6
Saul *Glos* 69 F8
Saunton *Devon* 42 D4
Saveock *Cornw'l* 4 A3
Scarcewater *Cornw'l* 8 E1
School Green *I/Wight* 29 C6
School House *Dorset* 36 F5
Scorrier *Cornw'l* 4 B2
Scorriton *Devon* 14 B2
Scotland End *Oxon* 73 A5
Scowles *Glos* 68 E5
Sea *Som'set* 36 D4
Sea Mills *Bristol* 56 A3
Seaborough *Dorset* 37 E6
Seagry Heath *Wilts* 64 F4
Seaton *Cornw'l* 10 E2
Seaton *Devon* 23 B6
Seaton Junction *Devon* 23 A6
Seatown *Dorset* 24 B3
Seavington St. Mary *Som'set* 37 D5
Seavington St. Michael *Som'set* 37 C6
Sector *Devon* 23 A8
Sedbury *Glos* 62 D2
Sedgeberrow *Worcs* 76 E3
Sedgecroft *Devon* 36 F4
Sedgehill *Wilts* 50 F2
Seend *Wilts* 58 D3
Seend Cleeve *Wilts* 58 D3
Seend Row *Wilts* 58 D3
Sellack *Heref'd* 68 B5
Sellick's Green *Som'set* 36 C2
Sells Green *Wilts* 58 D3
Selsey *Glos* 63 B8
Selworthy *Som'set* 45 B5
Semington *Wilts* 58 D2
Semley *Wilts* 50 F2
Sennen *Cornw'l* 2 E3
Sennen Cove *Cornw'l* 2 E3
Serrington *Wilts* 51 D6
Setley *Hants* 41 F9
Seven Ash *Som'set* 46 E3
Seven Springs *Glos* 71 D5
Sevenhampton *Glos* 71 C6
Sevenhampton *Swindon* 65 D9
Severn Beach *S Gloucs* 62 F2
Severn Stoke *Worcs* 75 D7
Sevington *Wilts* 55 A2
Seworgan *Cornw'l* 4 D2
Shadwell *Glos* 63 C7
Shaftesbury *Dorset* 39 B7
Shaggs *Dorset* 26 D4
Shakesfield *Glos* 69 A7
Shalbourne *Wilts* 60 D3
Shalcombe *I/Wight* 29 C7
Shaldon *Devon* 15 A6
Shalfleet *I/Wight* 29 C8
Shalford *Som'set* 49 E6
Shallowford *Devon* 13 E3
Shapridge *Glos* 69 D7
Shapwick *Dorset* 40 F1
Shapwick *Som'set* 47 D8
Sharcott *Wilts* 59 E8
Sharnhill Green *Dorset* 38 E4
Sharpness *Glos* 63 B5
Sharpstone *Bath/NE Som'set* 57 E7
Sharptor *Cornw'l* 9 A8
Shaugh Prior *Devon* 11 C6
Shave Cross *Dorset* 24 A3
Shaw *Swindon* 65 E7
Shaw *W Berks* 61 C6
Shaw *Wilts* 58 C2
Shaw Common *Glos* 69 B7
Shear Cross *Wilts* 50 C2
Shearston *Som'set* 47 E5
Shebbear *Devon* 32 E1
Sheepscombe *Glos* 70 E3
Sheepstor *Devon* 11 B6
Sheepwash *Devon* 32 E2
Sheffield *Cornw'l* 2 E5
Shefford Woodlands *W Berks* 60 B4
Sheldon *Devon* 35 E7
Shellingford *Oxon* 66 D3
Shellthorn *Som'set* 46 E4
Shepherds *Cornw'l* 7 E7
Shepherd's Patch *Glos* 63 B6
Shepperdine *S Gloucs* 62 C4
Shepton Beauchamp *Som'set* 37 C6
Shepton Mallet *Som'set* 48 C4
Shepton Montague *Som'set* 49 E5
Sherborne *Dorset* 38 C2
Sherborne *Glos* 72 E2
Sherborne Causeway *Dorset* 39 B6
Sherfield English *Hants* 41 B8
Sherford *Devon* 13 D6
Sherford *Som'set* 36 B2
Shernal Green *Worcs* 75 A8
Sherrard's Green *Worcs* 75 C6
Sherrington *Wilts* 50 D4
Sherston *Wilts* 64 E2
Sherston Parva *Wilts* 64 E2
Sheviock *Cornw'l* 10 D3
Shifford *Oxon* 66 B4
Shillingford *Devon* 34 B4
Shillingford *Oxon* 67 D8
Shillingford Abbot *Devon* 21 C8
Shillingford St. George *Devon* 21 C8
Shillingstone *Dorset* 39 D6
Shilton *Oxon* 72 F4
Shilvinghampton *Dorset* 25 D7
Shinner's Bridge *Devon* 14 C3
Shipham *Som'set* 55 E8
Shiphay *Torbay* 15 B5
Shiplate *N Som'set* 55 E7
Shippon *Oxon* 67 C6
Shipston on Stour *Warwick* 77 D8
Shipton *Glos* 71 D6
Shipton Bellinger *Hants* 52 B1
Shipton Gorge *Dorset* 24 B4
Shipton Moyne *Glos* 64 E2
Shipton Oliffe *Glos* 71 D6
Shipton on Cherwell *Oxon* 73 D8
Shipton Solers *Glos* 71 D6
Shipton under Wychwood *Oxon* 72 D4
Shirehampton *Bristol* 56 A2
Shirenewton *Monmouths* 62 D1
Shirley *Hants* 28 A3
Shirwell *Devon* 43 D6
Shirwell Cross *Devon* 43 D6
Shobley *Hants* 41 E6
Shobrooke *Devon* 34 F2
Shop *Cornw'l* 16 F2
Shop *Cornw'l* 30 D4
Shop *Devon* 31 D7
Shopnoller *Som'set* 46 E3
Shoreditch *Som'set* 36 B2
Shorley *Hants* 53 F8
Shorncote *Glos* 65 C5
Short Street *Wilts* 49 B8
Shorta Cross *Cornw'l* 10 D1
Shortacombe *Devon* 19 C7
Shorthampton *Oxon* 73 C5
Shortlanesend *Cornw'l* 7 F7
Shorton *Torbay* 15 C5
Shortstanding *Glos* 68 E5
Shortwood *Glos* 64 C1
Shortwood *S Gloucs* 57 A5
Shorwell *I/Wight* 29 D9
Shoscombe *Bath/NE Som'set* 57 E6
Shoscombe Vale *Bath/NE Som'set* 57 E6
Shottery *Warwick* 77 A6
Shoulton *Worcs* 75 A6
Shrewton *Wilts* 51 C6
Shrivenham *Oxon* 66 E1
Shroton *Dorset* 39 D6
Shucknall *Heref'd* 74 D1
Shurdington *Glos* 70 D4
Shurton *Som'set* 46 C4
Shute *Devon* 23 A7
Shute *Devon* 34 F2
Shute End *Wilts* 51 F8
Shuthonger *Glos* 75 E7
Shutta *Cornw'l* 9 E8
Sid *Devon* 22 C4
Sidbrook *Som'set* 46 F5
Sidbury *Devon* 22 B4
Sidcot *N Som'set* 55 E8
Siddington *Glos* 65 C5
Sidford *Devon* 22 B4
Sidmouth *Devon* 22 C4
Sigford *Devon* 21 F5
Signet *Oxon* 72 E3
Silford *Devon* 42 F3
Sillaton *Cornw'l* 10 C3
Silver Street *Glos* 63 B7
Silver Street *Som'set* 35 B8
Silver Street *Som'set* 48 E2
Silverton *Devon* 34 F4
Silverwell *Cornw'l* 7 F5
Simonsbath *Som'set* 44 D2
Sinton Green *Worcs* 75 A6
Sion Hill *Bath/NE Som'set* 57 C6
Siston *S Gloucs* 57 A5
Sithney *Cornw'l* 3 E8
Sithney Green *Cornw'l* 3 E8
Sitterton *Dorset* 26 B3
Sixpenny Handley *Dorset* 40 C2
Skenfrith *Monmouths* 68 C3
Skilgate *Som'set* 45 F6
Skinner's Bottom *Cornw'l* 4 A2
Skinners Green *W Berks* 61 C6
Slad *Glos* 70 F3
Slade End *Oxon* 67 D8
Slades Green *Worcs* 75 F7
Sladesbridge *Cornw'l* 8 A3
Slapton *Devon* 13 C7
Slaughterford *Wilts* 55 B1
Sledge Green *Worcs* 75 F6
Sleight *Dorset* 27 A6
Slepe *Dorset* 27 B5
Slerra *Devon* 31 B6
Slimbridge *Glos* 63 B6
Sling *Glos* 69 F5
Slipperhill *Cornw'l* 18 E2
Sloncombe *Devon* 20 C4
Slough Green *Som'set* 36 B3
Small Way *Som'set* 48 E4
Smallbrook *Devon* 21 A7
Smallbrook *Glos* 62 B3
Smallridge *Devon* 36 F3
Smannell *Hants* 52 B4
Smeatharpe *Devon* 36 D1
Smith End Green *Worcs* 75 B5
Smithaleigh *Devon* 11 D7
Smithincott *Devon* 35 D6
Snapper *Devon* 43 E7
Sneachill *Worcs* 75 B8
Sneedham's Green *Glos* 70 E2
Sneyd Park *Bristol* 56 A3
Snig's End *Glos* 70 B1
Snitterfield *Warwick* 77 A7
Snowshill *Glos* 76 F4
Sodom *Wilts* 64 F5
Soho *Som'set* 49 B5
Soldon Cross *Devon* 31 D6
Sollers Hope *Heref'd* 69 A6
Somerford *Dorset* 28 B3
Somerford Keynes *Glos* 64 C5
Somerton *Oxon* 73 B8
Somerton *Som'set* 47 F1
Sopley *Hants* 28 A3
Sopworth *Wilts* 63 E8
Sorley *Devon* 13 C5
Souldern *Oxon* 73 A9
Soundwell *S Gloucs* 57 A5
Sourton *Devon* 19 B7
South Allington *Devon* 13 E6
South Baddesley *Hants* 29 A7
South Barrow *Som'set* 48 F4
South Bockhampton *Dorset* 28 A3
South Bowood *Dorset* 24 A3
South Brent *Devon* 14 C1
South Brewham *Som'set* 49 D6
South Cadbury *Som'set* 38 A2
South Cerney *Glos* 65 C5
South Chard *Som'set* 36 E4
South Cheriton *Som'set* 38 B3
South Common *Devon* 36 F4
South End *Hants* 40 D5
South End *W Berks* 61 B8
South Fawley *W Berks* 66 F4
South Gorley *Hants* 41 D6
South Hill *Cornw'l* 10 A2
South Hill *Som'set* 48 F1
South Hinksey *Oxon* 67 B7
South Hole *Devon* 30 C4
South Huish *Devon* 12 D4
South Knighton *Devon* 14 A4
South Leigh *Oxon* 73 F6
South Littleton *Worcs* 76 C4
South Marston *Swindon* 65 E8
South Milton *Devon* 12 D4
South Molton *Devon* 33 A7
South Moreton *Oxon* 67 E8
South Newington *Oxon* 73 A7
South Newton *Wilts* 51 E6
South Perrott *Dorset* 37 E7
South Petherton *Som'set* 37 C6
South Petherwin *Cornw'l* 18 D3
South Pill *Cornw'l* 10 D4
South Pool *Devon* 13 D6
South Poorton *Dorset* 24 A5
South Radworthy *Devon* 44 E1
South Row *Oxon* 67 E6
South Stoke *Bath/NE Som'set* 57 D6
South Tawton *Devon* 20 B3
South Tehidy *Cornw'l* 3 B9
South Tidworth *Hants* 52 B1
South Town *Devon* 22 D1
South Twerton *Bath/NE Som'set* 57 D6
South Weirs *Hants* 41 F8
South Wheatley *Cornw'l* 18 B1
South Widcombe *Bath/NE Som'set* 56 E3
South Wonford *Devon* 31 E7
South Wonston *Hants* 53 D6
South Wraxall *Wilts* 57 D8
South Zeal *Devon* 20 B3
Southam *Glos* 71 B5
Southbourne *Bournem'th* 28 B2
Southbrook *Dorset* 26 B3
Southbrook *Wilts* 49 E8
Southcott *Devon* 32 C1
Southcott *Devon* 42 F4
Southcott *Wilts* 59 E8
Southdown *Bath/NE Som'set* 57 D6
Southend *Glos* 63 C6
Southend *Oxon* 67 B8
Southend *Wilts* 59 B8
Southerton *Devon* 22 B3
Southington *Hants* 53 B7
Southleigh *Devon* 23 B6
Southmarsh *Som'set* 49 E6
Southmead *Bristol* 56 A3
Southmoor *Oxon* 66 C4
Southover *Dorset* 24 C4
Southover *Dorset* 25 B7
Southrop *Glos* 65 A9
Southtown *Som'set* 36 C4
Southtown *Som'set* 48 D3
Southway *Plym'th* 11 C5
Southway *Som'set* 48 C2
Southwell *Dorset* 24 D2
Southwick *Som'set* 47 B7
Southwick *Wilts* 58 E1
Southwood *Som'set* 48 E3
Sowden *Devon* 22 D1
Sowton *Devon* 22 A1
Sparkford *Som'set* 38 A2
Sparkwell *Devon* 11 D7
Sparnon Gate *Cornw'l* 4 B1
Sparsholt *Hants* 53 E5
Sparsholt *Oxon* 66 E3
Spaxton *Som'set* 46 D4
Spearywell *Hants* 52 F3
Speedwell *Bristol* 56 B4
Speen *W Berks* 61 C6
Speen Hill *W Berks* 61 C6
Spelsbury *Oxon* 73 C6
Spetchley *Worcs* 75 B7
Spetisbury *Dorset* 39 F8
Spirthill *Wilts* 58 A4
Splatt *Cornw'l* 16 E3
Splatt *Cornw'l* 18 C1
Splatt *Som'set* 46 D4
Splottlands *Card* 54 A3
Spreyton *Devon* 20 A4
Spriddlestone *Devon* 11 E6
Springbank *Glos* 70 C4
Sprytown *Devon* 19 C5
Stable Green *Devon* 33 D5
Staddiscombe *Devon* 11 E6
Stafford's Green *Dorset* 38 B2
Stag's Head *Devon* 43 F8
Stalbridge *Dorset* 38 C4
Stalbridge Weston *Dorset* 38 C4
Stallen *Dorset* 38 C2
Stanbridge *Dorset* 40 F3
Stanbrook *Worcs* 75 C6
Standen Manor *W Berks* 60 C3
Standerwick *Som'set* 49 A8
Standish *Glos* 70 F2
Standish Moreton *Glos* 70 F1
Standlake *Oxon* 66 B4
Standon *Hants* 53 F5
Stanford Bishop *Heref'd* 74 B3
Stanford Dingley *W Berks* 61 B8
Stanford in the Vale *Oxon* 66 D3
Stanley *Wilts* 58 B4
Stanley Downton *Glos* 63 B8
Stanley Green *Poole* 27 B7
Stanley Hill *Heref'd* 74 D3
Stanley Pontlarge *Glos* 71 A5
Stanmore *Hants* 53 F6
Stanmore *W Berks* 61 A6
Stanpit *Dorset* 28 B3
Stanton *Glos* 76 F4
Stanton Drew *Bath/NE Som'set* 56 D3
Stanton Fitzwarren *Swindon* 65 D8
Stanton Harcourt *Oxon* 67 A5
Stanton Prior *Bath/NE Som'set* 57 D5
Stanton St. Bernard *Wilts* 59 D6
Stanton St. Quintin *Wilts* 58 A3
Stanton Wick *Bath/NE Som'set* 56 D4
Stantway *Glos* 69 E8
Stanway *Glos* 71 A7
Stapehill *Dorset* 40 F4
Staple *Som'set* 46 C2
Staple Cross *Devon* 35 B5
Staple Fitzpaine *Som'set* 36 C3
Staple Hill *S Gloucs* 57 A5
Stapleford *Wilts* 51 D6
Staplegrove *Som'set* 36 A2
Staplehay *Som'set* 36 B2
Stapleton *Bristol* 56 A4
Stapleton *Som'set* 37 B7
Stapley *Som'set* 35 D7
Staplow *Heref'd* 74 D3
Star *Som'set* 55 E8
Starcross *Devon* 22 D1
Start *Devon* 13 C7
Startley *Wilts* 64 F4
Stathe *Som'set* 47 F7
Staunton *Glos* 68 E4
Staunton *Glos* 70 B1
Staverton *Devon* 14 C3
Staverton *Glos* 70 C3
Staverton *Wilts* 58 D2
Staverton Bridge *Glos* 70 C3
Stawell *Som'set* 47 D7
Stawley *Som'set* 35 B6
Steanbow *Som'set* 48 D3
Steart *Som'set* 46 C5
Steeple *Dorset* 27 D5
Steeple Ashton *Wilts* 58 E3
Steeple Aston *Oxon* 73 B8
Steeple Barton *Oxon* 73 B7
Steeple Longford *Wilts* 51 D5
Stembridge *Som'set* 37 B6
Stenalees *Cornw'l* 8 D3
Stenhill *Devon* 35 D6
Stennack *Cornw'l* 3 C6
Stepaside *Cornw'l* 8 E1
Sterridge *Devon* 43 B6
Stert *Wilts* 59 E5
Sterte *Poole* 27 B7
Steventon *Hants* 53 B7
Steventon *Oxon* 67 D6
Stewley *Som'set* 36 C4
Stibb *Cornw'l* 30 D4
Stibb Cross *Devon* 31 D8
Stibb Green *Wilts* 60 D1
Sticker *Cornw'l* 8 E2
Sticklepath *Devon* 20 B2
Sticklepath *Devon* 43 E6
Sticklepath *Som'set* 45 D7
Sticklinch *Som'set* 48 D3
Stifford's Bridge *Heref'd* 74 C4
Stileway *Som'set* 48 C1
Stinchcombe *Glos* 63 C6
Stinsford *Dorset* 26 B1
Stitchcombe *Wilts* 60 C1
Stithians *Cornw'l* 4 C2
Stoborough *Dorset* 27 C5
Stoborough Green *Dorset* 27 C5
Stock *N Som'set* 55 D9
Stock Green *Worcs* 76 A2
Stock Wood *Worcs* 76 A3
Stockbridge *Hants* 52 D4
Stockcross *W Berks* 61 C5
Stockham *Oxon* 66 E4
Stocking *Heref'd* 69 A6
Stockland *Card* 54 A2
Stockland *Devon* 36 F2
Stockland Bristol *Som'set* 46 C4
Stockleigh English *Devon* 34 E1
Stockleigh Pomeroy *Devon* 34 F2
Stockley *Wilts* 58 C5
Stocklinch *Som'set* 37 C5
Stocklinch Ottersey *Som'set* 37 C5
Stockton *Wilts* 50 D4
Stockwitch Cross *Som'set* 37 B8
Stockwood *Bristol* 56 C4
Stockwood *Dorset* 38 E1
Stockwood Vale *Bath/NE Som'set* 56 C4
Stoford *Som'set* 38 D1
Stoford *Wilts* 51 D6
Stogumber *Som'set* 46 D1
Stogursey *Som'set* 46 C4
Stoke *Devon* 14 A1
Stoke *Devon* 30 B4
Stoke *Hants* 53 A5
Stoke *Plym'th* 10 D5
Stoke Abbott *Dorset* 37 F7
Stoke Bishop *Bristol* 56 A3
Stoke Cannon *Devon* 21 A8
Stoke Charity *Hants* 53 D6
Stoke Climsland *Cornw'l* 18 F4
Stoke Cross *Heref'd* 74 B2
Stoke Edith *Heref'd* 74 D2
Stoke Farthing *Wilts* 40 A4
Stoke Fleming *Devon* 15 F5
Stoke Gabriel *Devon* 14 D4
Stoke Gifford *S Gloucs* 62 F4
Stoke Hill *Devon* 21 B8
Stoke Lacy *Heref'd* 74 C2
Stoke Orchard *Glos* 70 B4
Stoke Rivers *Devon* 43 E7
Stoke St. Gregory *Som'set* 47 F6
Stoke St. Mary *Som'set* 36 B3
Stoke St. Michael *Som'set* 49 B5
Stoke sub Hamdon *Som'set* 37 C7
Stoke Trister *Som'set* 49 F6
Stoke Villice *N Som'set* 56 D3
Stoke Wake *Dorset* 38 E5
Stokeford *Dorset* 26 C4
Stokeinteignhead *Devon* 15 A6
Stokenham *Devon* 13 D7
Stolford *Som'set* 46 B4
Ston Easton *Som'set* 56 F4
Stone *Glos* 63 C5
Stone *Som'set* 48 E3
Stone Allerton *Som'set* 47 A8
Stone End *Glos* 70 D1
Stone Hill *S Gloucs* 56 B4
Stonebridge *N Som'set* 55 E7
Stone-edge-Batch *N Som'set* 56 B1
Stonehall *Worcs* 75 C7
Stonehouse *Glos* 63 A8
Stonehouse *Plym'th* 10 E5
Stonesfield *Oxon* 73 D6
Stoney Cross *Hants* 41 D8
Stoney Stoke *Som'set* 49 E6
Stoney Stratton *Som'set* 49 D5
Stoneyard Green *Heref'd* 74 D4
Stoneyford *Devon* 22 C3
Stony Cross *Devon* 32 A3
Stony Cross *Heref'd* 74 C4
Stony Knaps *Dorset* 36 F5
Stoodham *Som'set* 37 C6
Stoodleigh *Devon* 34 C3
Stoptide *Cornw'l* 16 E3
Stormore *Wilts* 50 B1
Stormsdown *Devon* 14 A3
Storridge *Heref'd* 75 C5
Stoughton Cross *Som'set* 47 B8
Stoughton Cross *Som'set* 47 B8
Stoulton *Worcs* 75 C8
Stour Provost *Dorset* 39 B5
Stour Row *Dorset* 39 B6
Stourpaine *Dorset* 39 E7
Stourton *Warwick* 77 E8
Stourton *Wilts* 49 E7
Stourton Caundle *Dorset* 38 C4
Stout *Som'set* 47 E8
Stoven *S Gloucs* 63 F5
Stowe *Glos* 62 A3
Stowe Green *Glos* 68 F5
Stowell *Som'set* 38 B3
Stowey *Bath/NE Som'set* 56 E4
Stowfield *Glos* 69 D5
Stowford *Devon* 19 C5
Stowford *Devon* 22 C4
Stowford *Devon* 43 C8
Stowford *Devon* 43 F7
Stow-on-the-Wold *Glos* 72 B2
Stradbrook *Wilts* 50 A3
Straight Soley *Wilts* 60 B3
Strand *Glos* 69 E8
Strangford *Heref'd* 69 B5
Strangways *Wilts* 51 C7
Stratford *Worcs* 75 E7
Stratford Castle *Wilts* 51 E7
Stratford Tony *Wilts* 40 A4
Stratford-upon-Avon *Warwick* 77 A7
Stratton *Cornw'l* 30 E4
Stratton *Dorset* 25 B7
Stratton *Glos* 64 B5
Stratton St. Margaret *Swindon* 65 E8
Stratton-on-the-Fosse *Som'set* 49 A5
Stream *Som'set* 45 D8
Streatley *W Berks* 67 F8
Street *Devon* 23 C5
Street *Som'set* 36 E5
Street *Som'set* 48 D1
Street *Som'set* 49 A5
Street End *N Som'set* 56 E1
Street on the Fosse *Som'set* 48 D4
Streetway Lane *Dorset* 39 F5
Stretch Down *Devon* 33 D9
Stretcholt *Som'set* 47 C5
Strete *Devon* 14 F4
Stretton Grandison *Heref'd* 74 D2
Stretton on Fosse *Warwick* 77 E7
Stringston *Som'set* 46 C3
Stroat *Glos* 62 C3
Stroud *Glos* 64 A2
Stroud Green *Glos* 70 F2
Stroud Green *W Berks* 61 C6
Stubhampton *Dorset* 39 D8
Stubhampton Down *Dorset* 39 D8
Stuckton *Hants* 41 D6
Studland *Dorset* 27 D7
Studley *Wilts* 58 B4
Sturminster Common *Dorset* 39 D5
Sturminster Marshall *Dorset* 27 A6
Sturminster Newton *Dorset* 39 D5
Suckley *Worcs* 74 B4
Suckley Green *Worcs* 74 B4
Suckley Knowl *Worcs* 74 B4
Sudbrook *Monmouths* 62 E2
Sully *V/Glam* 54 C3
Summercourt *Cornw'l* 7 D8
Summerlands *Som'set* 37 C8
Summertown *Oxon* 73 F9
Sunningwell *Oxon* 67 B7
Sunnymead *Oxon* 73 F9
Sunrising Estate *Cornw'l* 9 E8
Sunton *Wilts* 61 E1
Sutcombe *Devon* 31 D6
Sutcombemill *Devon* 31 D6
Sutton *Cornw'l* 10 A1
Sutton *Devon* 13 D5
Sutton *Oxon* 67 A5
Sutton *Som'set* 48 E4
Sutton Benger *Wilts* 58 A3
Sutton Bingham *Som'set* 37 D8
Sutton Courtenay *Oxon* 67 D7
Sutton Green *Oxon* 73 F7
Sutton Mallet *Som'set* 47 D7
Sutton Mandeville *Wilts* 50 F4
Sutton Montis *Som'set* 38 B2
Sutton Poyntz *Dorset* 25 D9
Sutton Row *Wilts* 50 F4
Sutton Scotney *Hants* 53 D6
Sutton under Brailes *Warwick* 77 E9
Sutton Veny *Wilts* 50 C2
Sutton Waldron *Dorset* 39 C7
Sutton Wick *Bath/NE Som'set* 56 E3
Sutton Wick *Oxon* 67 D6
Swainswick *Bath/NE Som'set* 57 C7
Swallowcliffe *Wilts* 50 F4
Swallowfields *Devon* 14 C3
Swampton *Hants* 53 A5
Swanage *Dorset* 27 E7
Swanbridge *V/Glam* 54 C3
Swanley *Glos* 63 C6
Swarraton *Hants* 53 D8
Sway *Hants* 29 A5
Sweetham *Devon* 21 A7
Sweets *Cornw'l* 17 A8
Sweetshouse *Cornw'l* 8 C4
Swell *Som'set* 36 B5
Swerford *Oxon* 73 A6
Swimbridge *Devon* 43 E7
Swimbridge Newland *Devon* 43 E7
Swinbrook *Oxon* 72 E4
Swindon *Glos* 70 B4
Swindon *Swindon* 65 E8
Swineford *S Gloucs* 57 C5
Swinesherd *Worcs* 75 B7
Swinford *Oxon* 73 F7
Swinley Green *Worcs* 70 A2
Swinmore Common *Heref'd* 74 D3
Swyre *Dorset* 25 C5
Syde *Glos* 71 E5
Sydenham *Som'set* 47 D6
Sydenham Damerel *Devon* 19 E5
Sydling St. Nicholas *Dorset* 25 A7
Sydmonton *Hants* 61 E6
Symonds Yat *Heref'd* 68 D5
Symondsbury *Dorset* 24 B3
Synderford *Dorset* 37 F5
Syreford *Glos* 71 C6

T

Tackley *Oxon* 73 C8
Tadden *Dorset* 40 F2
Taddington *Glos* 71 A7
Taddiport *Devon* 32 C2
Tadley *Oxon* 67 E7
Tadwick *Bath/NE Som'set* 57 B6
Talaton *Devon* 22 A3
Talbot Village *Bournem'th* 27 B8
Talbot's End *S Gloucs* 63 D6
Talewater *Devon* 22 A3
Talskiddy *Cornw'l* 8 B1
Tal-y-coed *Monmouths* 68 D2
Tamerton Foliot *Plym'th* 10 C5
Tangier *Som'set* 36 B2
Tangley *Hants* 52 A3
Tanis *Wilts* 58 D4
Tarlton *Glos* 64 C4
Tarnock *Som'set* 47 A7
Tarr *Som'set* 46 E2
Tarrant Crawford *Dorset* 39 F8
Tarrant Gunville *Dorset* 39 D8
Tarrant Hinton *Dorset* 39 D8
Tarrant Keyneston *Dorset* 39 F8
Tarrant Launceston *Dorset* 40 E1
Tarrant Monkton *Dorset* 40 E1
Tarrant Rawston *Dorset* 39 E8
Tarrant Rushton *Dorset* 39 E8
Tarrington *Heref'd* 74 D2
Taston *Oxon* 73 C6
Tatworth *Som'set* 36 E4
Taunton *Som'set* 36 A2
Tavistock *Devon* 19 F6
Taw Green *Devon* 20 A3
Tawstock *Devon* 43 F5
Taynton *Glos* 69 C8
Taynton *Oxon* 72 E3
Tedburn St. Mary *Devon* 21 B6
Teddington *Glos* 71 A5
Tedstone Delamere *Heref'd* 74 A3
Tedstone Wafre *Heref'd* 74 A3
Teffont Evias *Wilts* 50 E5
Teffont Magna *Wilts* 50 E4

Tegiskey Cornw'l 5 A8
Teign Village Devon 21 D6
Teigncombe Devon 20 C3
Teigngrace Devon 21 F7
Teignmouth Devon 15 A6
Tellisford Som'set 57 E7
Temple Cornw'l 9 A5
Temple Wilts 49 C8
Temple Cloud Bath/NE Som'set 56 E4
Temple Cowley Oxon 67 B7
Temple Grafton Warwick 76 B5
Temple Guiting Glos 71 B7
Templecombe Som'set 38 B4
Templeton Devon 34 D2
Templeton Bridge Devon 34 D2
Terhill Som'set 46 E3
Terras Cornw'l 8 E1
Tetbury Glos 64 D2
Tetbury Upton Glos 64 C2
Tetcott Devon 18 A3
Tevorrick Cornw'l 8 A1
Tewkesbury Glos 70 A3
Thatcham W Berks 61 C7
The Banks Wilts 58 A5
The Barton Wilts 59 A6
The Batch Som'set 48 A2
The Batch S Gloucs 57 B5
The Bourne Worcs 76 A2
The Butts Som'set 49 B7
The Camp Glos 70 F4
The Cleaver Heref'd 68 B4
The Common Oxon 72 B4
The Common Wilts 52 E1
The Common Wilts 64 E5
The Eaves Glos 62 A4
The Fence Glos 62 A2
The Flat Glos 69 D9
The Folly Som'set 48 A3
The Folly W Berks 61 C6
The Fox Wilts 65 E7
The Frenches Hants 41 B9
The Gibb Wilts 57 A8
The Graig Monmouths 68 F4
The Green Glos 71 B5
The Green Hants 52 F2
The Green S Gloucs 57 B5
The Green Warwick 77 A7
The Green Wilts 50 E2
The Green Wilts 50 E4
The Grove Worcs 75 D7
The Ham Wilts 50 A2
The Hill Worcs 75 E6
The Holt Hants 61 D8
The Holt W Berks 60 B3
The Hoo Glos 77 E6
The Hook Worcs 75 D6
The Kendals Dorset 49 F8
The Knapp S Gloucs 63 D5
The Leigh Glos 70 B3
The Linleys Wilts 58 C2
The Marsh Wilts 65 F6
The Moors Heref'd 68 A4
The Mount Dorset 24 A4
The Mount Hants 61 D5
The Mythe Glos 75 F7
The Narth Monmouths 62 A2
The Oval Bath/NE Som'set 57 D6
The Park Glos 70 B4
The Park Glos 70 C4
The Park N Som'set 55 A8
The Pill Monmouths 62 E1
The Pitts Wilts 40 A4
The Point Devon 22 D1
The Pound Glos 69 A8
The Purlieu Glos 63 A5
The Quarry Glos 63 C6
The Ramplings Worcs 75 F7
The Reddings Glos 70 C4
The Rhydd Heref'd 68 A3
The Ridge Wilts 58 C2
The Rocks S Gloucs 63 F7
The Roundabout S Gloucs 62 E4
The Row Oxon 73 E7
The Scarr Glos 69 B8
The Shoe Wilts 57 B8
The Slade W Berks 61 C7
The Spa Wilts 58 D3
The Stocks Wilts 58 D3
The Strand Wilts 58 E3
The Thorn Heref'd 68 C5
The Tynings Glos 70 D4
The Verne Dorset 24 D2
The Wrangle Bath/NE Som'set 56 E2
Theale Som'set 48 B1
Theobald's Green Wilts 58 C5
Thicket Mead Bath/NE Som'set 57 E5
Thickwood Wilts 57 B8
Thorley I/Wight 29 C7
Thorley Street I/Wight 29 C7
Thornbury Devon 31 E8
Thornbury Heref'd 74 A2
Thornbury S Gloucs 62 D4
Thornbury Park S Gloucs 62 D4
Thorncross I/Wight 29 D8
Thorndon Cross Devon 19 B7
Thorne Coffin Som'set 37 C8
Thorne St. Margaret Som'set 35 B6
Thornecombe Dorset 37 F5
Thornend Wilts 58 A4
Thorney Som'set 37 B6
Thorney Hill Hants 28 A4
Thornfalcon Som'set 36 B3
Thornford Dorset 38 D2
Thorngrove Som'set 47 E7
Thornhill Wilts 59 A6
Thornhill Head Devon 31 C8
Thornicombe Dorset 39 F7
Thorns Beach Hants 29 A8
Thorverton Devon 34 F3
Three Ashes Som'set 49 B5
Three Burrows Cornw'l 4 A2
Three Hammers Cornw'l 18 C1
Three Horse Shoes Devon 21 A8
Three Legged Cross Dorset 40 E4
Threemilestones Cornw'l 4 B3
Threewaters Cornw'l 8 B3
Throckmorton Worcs 76 C2
Throop Dorset 26 B3
Throwleigh Devon 20 B3
Thrupe Som'set 48 B4
Thrupp Glos 64 B2
Thrupp Oxon 66 C2
Thrupp Oxon 73 D8
Thrushelton Devon 19 C5
Thruxton Hants 52 B2
Thruxton Heref'd 68 A2
Thurdon Cornw'l 31 D5
Thurlbear Som'set 36 B3
Thurlestone Devon 12 D4
Thurloxton Som'set 46 E5
Tibberton Glos 69 C9
Tibberton Worcs 75 A8
Tichborne Hants 53 E8
Tickenham N Som'set 55 A9
Tickmorend Glos 64 C1
Tidcombe Wilts 61 E2
Tiddington Warwick 77 A7
Tideford Cornw'l 10 D2
Tideford Cross Cornw'l 10 C2
Tidenham Glos 62 C3
Tidmington Warwick 77 E8
Tidnor Heref'd 74 E1
Tidpit Hants 40 C4
Tigley Devon 14 C3
Tilland Cornw'l 10 C2
Tillers Green Glos 69 A7
Tilsdown Glos 63 C7
Tilshead Wilts 51 B5
Tiltups End Glos 64 C1
Timbercombe Som'set 46 E4
Timberscombe Som'set 45 C6
Timsbury Bath/NE Som'set 57 E5
Tincleton Dorset 26 B2
Tinhay Devon 18 C4
Tinkers Hill Hants 52 B4
Tintagel Cornw'l 17 C6
Tintern Parva Monmouths 62 B2
Tintinhull Som'set 37 E8
Tiptoe Hants 28 A5
Tipton Cross Devon 22 B3
Tipton St. John Devon 22 B3
Tirley Glos 70 B2
Tisbury Wilts 50 F3
Titchberry Devon 30 A4
Titcomb W Berks 60 C4
Tithill Som'set 46 F3
Titson Cornw'l 30 F4
Tiverton Devon 34 D4
Tivington Som'set 45 B5
Tockenham Wilts 58 A5
Tockenham Wick Wilts 65 F5
Tockington S Gloucs 62 E4
Todber Dorset 39 B5
Toddington Glos 71 A6
Todenham Glos 77 E7
Tog Hill S Gloucs 57 B6
Tolborough Cornw'l 17 E8
Toldish Cornw'l 8 D1
Tolgus Mount Cornw'l 4 B1
Tolladine Worcs 75 A7
Tolland Som'set 46 E2
Tollard Farnham Dorset 40 C2
Tollard Royal Wilts 40 C1
Toller Fratrum Dorset 25 A6
Toller Porcorum Dorset 25 A6
Toller Whelme Dorset 37 F8
Tollerford Dorset 25 A6
Tolpuddle Dorset 26 B2
Tone Som'set 35 B7
Tone Green Som'set 35 B8
Tonedale Som'set 35 B7
Toot Baldon Oxon 67 B8
Toothill Swindon 65 F7
Topsham Devon 22 C1
Torbay Torbay 15 C6
Torbryan Devon 14 B4
Torcross Devon 13 D7
Torfrey Cornw'l 9 E5
Tormarton S Gloucs 57 A7
Torpoint Cornw'l 10 D4
Torquay Torbay 15 C6
Torr Devon 11 C8
Torr Devon 11 E7
Torre Som'set 45 C7
Torre Torbay 15 B6
Tortworth S Gloucs 63 D6
Tosberry Devon 31 B5
Totford Hants 53 D8
Totland I/Wight 29 C6
Totnell Dorset 38 E2
Totnes Devon 14 C4
Tottens Wilts 41 A7
Touches Som'set 36 E4
Toulton Som'set 46 E3
Towan Cornw'l 16 F2
Towan Cross Cornw'l 6 F5
Towednack Cornw'l 3 C5
Towerhead N Som'set 55 E8
Town Street Glos 70 B2
Townlake Devon 19 E5
Town's End Dorset 26 A4
Town's End Dorset 27 D6
Town's End Dorset 38 E1
Towns End Hants 61 E8
Towns End Som'set 38 C4
Town's End Som'set 46 C2
Town's End Som'set 49 B5
Townsend Bath/NE Som'set 56 E3
Townsend Oxon 66 E4
Townsend Som'set 36 D5
Townsend Som'set 47 E7
Townsend Som'set 48 A2
Townsend S Gloucs 62 F3
Townsend Wilts 58 E4
Townshend Cornw'l 3 D7
Townwell S Gloucs 63 D5
Traboe Cornw'l 4 F2
Tracebridge Som'set 35 B6
Tram Inn Heref'd 68 A3
Trapshill W Berks 60 D4
Travelmond Cornw'l 9 C7
Treaddow Heref'd 68 C4
Treamble Cornw'l 7 D6
Treator Cornw'l 16 E3
Trebahwartha Cornw'l 4 E3
Trebarber Cornw'l 7 C8
Trebartha Cornw'l 18 E2
Trebarvah Cornw'l 3 E6
Trebarvah Cornw'l 4 D2
Trebarwith Cornw'l 17 C6
Trebeath Cornw'l 18 C2
Trebehor Cornw'l 2 F3
Trebetherick Cornw'l 16 E3
Treble's Holford Som'set 46 E2
Treborough Som'set 45 D7
Trebudannon Cornw'l 7 C8
Trebullett Cornw'l 18 E3
Treburley Cornw'l 18 E3
Treburrick Cornw'l 7 A8
Trebyan Cornw'l 8 C4
Trecrogo Cornw'l 18 D3
Tredarrup Cornw'l 17 B8
Tredaule Cornw'l 18 D1
Tredavoe Cornw'l 2 E5
Tredington Glos 70 B4
Tredington Warwick 77 D8
Tredinnick Cornw'l 2 D4
Tredinnick Cornw'l 9 B6
Tredinnick Cornw'l 9 D7
Tredrizzick Cornw'l 16 E4
Tredworth Glos 70 D2
Treen Cornw'l 2 C4
Treen Cornw'l 2 F3
Treesmill Cornw'l 8 D4
Tre-Essey Heref'd 68 C4
Treffany Hill Cornw'l 9 D7
Tregada Cornw'l 18 D3
Tregadillet Cornw'l 18 D2
Tre-gagle Monmouths 68 F4
Tregajorran Cornw'l 4 B1
Tregare Monmouths 68 E2
Tregarland Cornw'l 9 D8
Tregarne Cornw'l 4 F3
Tregaswith Cornw'l 7 C8
Tregatta Cornw'l 17 C6
Tregavarras Cornw'l 5 B7
Tregear Cornw'l 7 E8
Tregeare Cornw'l 18 C1
Tregellist Cornw'l 16 E5
Tregenna Cornw'l 17 F6
Tregeseal Cornw'l 2 D3
Tregonce Cornw'l 16 F3
Tregonetha Cornw'l 8 C2
Tregonhawke Cornw'l 10 E4
Tregonna Cornw'l 8 A1
Tregony Cornw'l 5 B6
Tregoodwell Cornw'l 17 D7
Tregorrick Cornw'l 8 E3
Tregoss Cornw'l 8 C2
Tregowris Cornw'l 4 F3
Tregrehan Mills Cornw'l 8 E3
Tregullon Cornw'l 8 C4
Tregunna Cornw'l 16 F4
Tregunnon Cornw'l 18 D1
Tregurrian Cornw'l 7 B8
Trehan Cornw'l 10 D4
Trehemborne Cornw'l 7 A8
Treheveras Cornw'l 7 F7
Trehill V/Glam 54 B1
Trehunist Cornw'l 10 C2
Trekeivesteps Cornw'l 9 B7
Trekelland Cornw'l 18 D3
Trekelland Cornw'l 18 E2
Trekenner Cornw'l 18 E3
Treknow Cornw'l 17 C6
Trelan Cornw'l 5 G2
Trelash Cornw'l 17 B8
Trelassick Cornw'l 7 E8
Treleigh Cornw'l 4 B2
Treligga Cornw'l 17 D6
Trelights Cornw'l 16 E4
Trelill Cornw'l 17 E5
Trelinnoe Cornw'l 18 D3
Trelion Cornw'l 8 E1
Trelissick Cornw'l 4 C4
Trellech Monmouths 62 A2
Trelleck Cross Monmouths 62 B2
Trelleck Grange Monmouths 62 B1
Trelonk Cornw'l 5 B5
Trelowia Cornw'l 10 D1
Trelowth Cornw'l 8 E2
Trelowthas Cornw'l 7 F8
Treluggan Cornw'l 5 C5
Tremail Cornw'l 17 C8
Tremaine Cornw'l 18 A1
Tremar Cornw'l 9 B8
Trematon Cornw'l 10 D3
Trembraze Cornw'l 9 B8
Tremollett Cornw'l 18 E2
Tremore Cornw'l 8 C3
Tremorfa Card 54 A4
Trenale Cornw'l 17 C6
Trenance Cornw'l 7 B8
Trenance Cornw'l 7 C7
Trenance Cornw'l 8 A1
Trenant Cornw'l 9 B7
Trenarren Cornw'l 8 F3
Trenarrett Cornw'l 18 D1
Trenault Cornw'l 18 D2
Trencreek Cornw'l 7 C7
Trendeal Cornw'l 7 E8
Trendrean Cornw'l 7 D7
Treneague Cornw'l 8 A2
Trenear Cornw'l 4 D1
Treneglos Cornw'l 17 C9
Trenewan Cornw'l 9 E6
Trengune Cornw'l 17 B8
Trenhorne Cornw'l 18 E2
Treninnick Cornw'l 7 C7
Trenode Cornw'l 9 D8
Trenoweth Cornw'l 4 D3
Trent Dorset 38 C1
Trentishoe Devon 43 B7
Trenwheal Cornw'l 3 D8
Trequite Cornw'l 17 E5
Trerank Moor Cornw'l 8 D2
Trerose Cornw'l 4 E3
Trerulefoot Cornw'l 10 D2
Tresawle Cornw'l 5 A5
Tresawsen Cornw'l 7 F6
Trescowe Cornw'l 3 D7
Tresean Cornw'l 7 D6
Tresevern Croft Cornw'l 4 C2
Tresham S Gloucs 63 D7
Tresillian Cornw'l 5 A5
Treskillard Cornw'l 4 C1
Treskinnick Cross Cornw'l 17 A9
Tresmeer Cornw'l 18 C1
Tresowes Green Cornw'l 3 E7
Tresoweshill Cornw'l 3 E7
Tresparrett Cornw'l 17 B7
Tresparrett Posts Cornw'l 17 B7
Trespeane Cornw'l 18 D1
Tressinney Cornw'l 17 D7
Treswithian Cornw'l 3 B8
Treswithian Downs Cornw'l 3 B8
Trethevy Cornw'l 17 C6
Trethewey Cornw'l 2 F3
Trethosa Cornw'l 8 E1
Trethowel Cornw'l 8 E3
Trethurgy Cornw'l 8 D3
Tretire Heref'd 68 C4
Trevadlock Cornw'l 18 E2
Trevalga Cornw'l 17 C6
Trevance Cornw'l 8 A1
Trevanger Cornw'l 16 E4
Trevanson Cornw'l 8 A2
Trevarrack Cornw'l 3 D5
Trevarren Cornw'l 8 C1
Trevarrian Cornw'l 7 B8
Trevarrick Cornw'l 5 B7
Trevarth Cornw'l 4 B2
Treveal Cornw'l 7 D6
Treveighan Cornw'l 17 E6
Trevellas Cornw'l 7 E5
Trevemper Cornw'l 7 D7
Treverbyn Cornw'l 8 D3
Treverbyn Cornw'l 9 B7
Treverva Cornw'l 4 D3
Trevescan Cornw'l 2 F3
Trevethan Cornw'l 4 B2
Trevia Cornw'l 17 D6
Trevilla Cornw'l 4 C4
Trevillian Cornw'l 17 B8
Trevilson Cornw'l 7 D7
Treviscoe Cornw'l 8 D1
Trevithal Cornw'l 2 E5
Trevivian Cornw'l 17 C8
Trevoll Cornw'l 7 D7
Trevone Cornw'l 16 E2
Trevowah Cornw'l 7 D6
Trew Cornw'l 3 E8
Trewalder Cornw'l 17 D6
Trewarlett Cornw'l 18 D3
Trewarmett Cornw'l 17 C6
Trewarne Heref'd 68 D4
Trewassa Cornw'l 17 C7
Treween Cornw'l 18 D1
Trewellard Cornw'l 2 D3
Trewen Cornw'l 18 D2
Trewen Heref'd 68 D4
Trewennack Cornw'l 4 E1
Trewetha Cornw'l 16 D5
Trewethern Cornw'l 16 E5
Trewidland Cornw'l 9 D8
Trewint Cornw'l 10 C1
Trewint Cornw'l 17 A8
Trewint Cornw'l 18 D1
Trewithian Cornw'l 5 C5
Trewoodloe Cornw'l 10 A2
Trewoofe Cornw'l 2 E4
Trewoon Cornw'l 8 E2
Treworga Cornw'l 5 B5
Treworlas Cornw'l 5 C5
Treworthal Cornw'l 5 C5
Treyarnon Cornw'l 16 F2
Trickett's Cross Dorset 40 F4
Tricombe Devon 23 A6
Trill Devon 23 A7
Trimstone Devon 42 C4
Trinity Devon 34 E4
Triscombe Som'set 46 D3
Trispen Cornw'l 7 E7
Troan Cornw'l 7 D8
Trolway Heref'd 68 C3
Troon Cornw'l 3 C9
Troswell Cornw'l 18 B2
Trow Devon 23 C5
Trow Green Glos 69 F5
Trowbridge Card 54 A4
Trowbridge Wilts 58 E1
Trowle Common Wilts 58 E1
Trudoxhill Som'set 49 C7
True Streek Devon 14 C4
Trull Som'set 36 B2
Trumpet Heref'd 74 E3
Truro Cornw'l 4 B4
Truscott Cornw'l 18 C3
Trusham Devon 21 D7
Truthwall Cornw'l 3 D6
Trythogga Cornw'l 2 D5
Tubney Oxon 67 C5
Tuckenhay Devon 14 D4
Tuckermarsh Devon 10 B4
Tuckingmill Cornw'l 3 B9
Tuckingmill Cornw'l 18 B1
Tuckingmill Wilts 50 F3
Tuckton Bournem'th 28 B2
Tudorville Heref'd 69 C5
Tuffley Glos 70 D2
Tufton Hants 53 B6
Tumpy Green Glos 63 B6
Tunley Bath/NE Som'set 57 E5
Tunnel Hill Worcs 75 D6
Turfdown Cornw'l 8 B4
Turfmoor Devon 36 F3
Turkdean Glos 71 D8
Turleigh Wilts 57 D8
Turlin Moor Poole 27 B6
Turmer Hants 41 E5
Turnchapel Plym'th 11 E5
Turner's Green W Berks 61 C7
Turners Puddle Dorset 26 B3
Turner's Tump Glos 69 D6
Turnworth Dorset 39 E6
Tutnalls Glos 62 B4
Tutshill Glos 62 C2
Tutts Clump W Berks 61 B8
Tutwell Cornw'l 18 E4
Twelveheads Cornw'l 4 B3
Twerton Bath/NE Som'set 57 D6
Twigworth Glos 70 C2
Twinhoe Bath/NE Som'set 57 E6
Twitchen Devon 44 E2
Two Bridges Devon 13 F2
Two Burrows Cornw'l 7 F5
Two Mile Oak Cross Devon 14 B4
Twyford Dorset 39 C7
Twyning Glos 75 E7
Twyning Green Glos 75 E8
Twyn-yr-odyn V/Glam 54 B2
Twyn-y-Sheriff Monmouths 68 F2
Tyneham Dorset 26 D4
Tyning Bath/NE Som'set 57 E5
Tyntesfield N Som'set 56 B2
Tytherleigh / Tythecott Devon 31 C8
Tytherington Som'set 49 B7
Tytherington S Gloucs 63 E5
Tytherington Wilts 50 C3
Tytherleigh Devon 36 F4
Tywardreath Cornw'l 8 E4
Tywardreath Highway Cornw'l 8 D4

U

Ubley Bath/NE Som'set 56 E2
Uckinghall Worcs 75 E7
Uckington Glos 70 B4
Udley N Som'set 56 D1
Uffcott Wilts 59 A7
Uffculme Devon 35 D6
Uffington Oxon 66 E3
Ugborough Devon 14 D1
Ugford Wilts 51 E6
Uley Glos 63 C7
Ullcombe Devon 36 E2
Ullenwood Glos 70 D4
Ullingswick Heref'd 74 C1
Ulwell Dorset 27 D7
Umberleigh Devon 32 B5
Underdown Devon 20 B4
Underwood Plym'th 11 D6
Up Cerne Dorset 38 F3
Up Exe Devon 34 F3
Up Hatherley Glos 70 C4
Up Mudford Som'set 38 C1
Up Somborne Hants 52 E4
Up Sydling Dorset 38 F2
Upavon Wilts 59 F8
Upcott Devon 32 E4
Upcott Som'set 26 B1
Upcott Som'set 34 A3
Uphall Dorset 37 F9
Upham Devon 34 E2
Uphempston Devon 14 C4
Uphill N Som'set 55 E6
Uplands Glos 64 A2
Upleadon Glos 69 B9
Uploders Dorset 24 A5
Uplowman Devon 35 C5
Uplyms Devon 23 B8
Upottery Devon 36 E2
Upper Basildon W Berks 61 A8
Upper Brailes Warwick 77 E9
Upper Broadheath Worcs 75 A6
Upper Buckenhill Heref'd 69 A5
Upper Bucklebury W Berks 61 C7
Upper Burgate Hants 41 C5
Upper Canada N Som'set 55 E7
Upper Canterton Hants 41 D8
Upper Cheddon Som'set 46 F4
Upper Chicksgrove Wilts 50 F4
Upper Chute Wilts 61 E2
Upper Clatford Hants 52 C4
Upper Coberley Glos 71 D5
Upper Colwall Heref'd 75 D5
Upper Egleton Heref'd 74 C2
Upper End Glos 71 E8
Upper Enham Hants 52 A4
Upper Fivehead Som'set 36 B4
Upper Framilode Glos 69 E8
Upper Godney Som'set 48 C1
Upper Green Monmouths 68 D1
Upper Green W Berks 60 D4
Upper Grove Common Heref'd 68 B5
Upper Ham Worcs 75 C7
Upper Ham Worcs 75 E7
Upper Heyford Oxon 73 B8
Upper Hill S Gloucs 63 C5
Upper Howsell Worcs 75 C5
Upper Inglesham Swindon 65 C9
Upper Kilcott Glos 63 E7
Upper Lambourn W Berks 66 F3
Upper Langford N Som'set 56 E1
Upper Ley Glos 69 D8
Upper Littleton N Som'set 56 D3
Upper Lydbrook Glos 69 D6
Upper Milton Oxon 72 D4
Upper Milton Som'set 48 B2
Upper Minety Wilts 64 D5
Upper Moor Worcs 76 C2
Upper Morton S Gloucs 63 D5
Upper Oddington Glos 72 B3
Upper Pennington Hants 29 A6
Upper Quinton Warwick 77 C6
Upper Ratley Hants 41 B9
Upper Seagry Wilts 64 F3
Upper Siddington Glos 65 C5
Upper Slackstead Hants 52 F4
Upper Slaughter Glos 72 C2
Upper Soudley Glos 69 E7
Upper Stanton Drew Bath/NE Som'set 56 D4
Upper Street Hants 41 C5
Upper Strensham Worcs 75 E8
Upper Studley Wilts 58 E1
Upper Swell Glos 72 B2
Upper Town Heref'd 74 C1
Upper Town N Som'set 56 C2
Upper Town Wilts 58 A4
Upper Upham Wilts 60 A1
Upper Vobster Som'set 49 B6
Upper Waterhay Wilts 65 D6
Upper Welland Worcs 75 D5
Upper Weston Bath/NE Som'set 57 C6
Upper Wick Glos 63 C6
Upper Wick Worcs 75 B6
Upper Wilcove Cornw'l 10 D4
Upper Wolvercote Oxon 73 E8
Upper Woodford Wilts 51 D7
Upper Woolhampton W Berks 61 C8
Upper Wootton Hants 61 F8
Upper Wraxhall S Gloucs 57 B7
Upper Wyche Worcs 75 D5
Uppincott Devon 34 F2
Uppington Dorset 40 E3
Upthorpe Glos 63 B7
Upton Cornw'l 9 A8
Upton Cornw'l 30 F4
Upton Devon 13 D5
Upton Devon 35 F6
Upton Dorset 26 D1
Upton Dorset 27 B6
Upton Hants 60 E4
Upton Oxon 67 E7
Upton Oxon 72 E3
Upton Som'set 45 F6
Upton Som'set 47 F9
Upton Warwick 76 A5
Upton Wilts 50 E2
Upton Bishop Heref'd 69 B7
Upton Cheney S Gloucs 57 C5
Upton Crews Heref'd 69 B6
Upton Cross Cornw'l 9 A8
Upton Hellions Devon 34 E1
Upton Lovell Wilts 50 C3
Upton Noble Som'set 49 D6
Upton Pyne Devon 21 A8
Upton St. Leonards Glos 70 E3
Upton Scudamore Wilts 50 B2
Upton Snodsbury Worcs 76 B1
Upton upon Severn Worcs 75 D7
Upwey Dorset 25 C8
Urchfont Wilts 59 E5
Uton Devon 21 A6

V

Valley Truckle Cornw'l 17 D6
Vellanoweth Cornw'l 3 D6
Vellow Som'set 46 D1
Velly Devon 31 B5
Venn Devon 14 F3
Venn Devon 31 B6
Venn Green Devon 31 D7
Venn Ottery Devon 22 B3
Venny Tedburn Devon 21 A6
Venterdon Cornw'l 18 F4
Venton Devon 11 D7
Venton Devon 20 B3
Ventongimps Mill Cornw'l 7 E6
Vernham Dean Hants 60 E3
Vernham Row Hants 60 E3
Vernham Street Hants 60 E4
Vertington Som'set 49 F6
Verwood Dorset 40 E4
Veryan Cornw'l 5 C6
Veryan Green Cornw'l 5 B6
Victoria Cornw'l 8 C2
Victoria Park Dorset 25 C8
Viney Hill Glos 63 A5
Vinny Green S Gloucs 57 A5
Virginstow Devon 18 B4
Viscar Cornw'l 4 D2
Vobster Som'set 49 B6
Vole Som'set 47 A7

W

Wadborough Worcs 75 C8
Waddeton Devon 15 D5
Waddicombe Devon 44 F4
Waddon Devon 21 E7
Waddon Dorset 25 C7
Wadebridge Cornw'l 8 A2
Wadeford Som'set 36 D4
Wadswick Wilts 58 C1
Wadwick Hants 53 A5
Wagg Som'set 47 F8
Waggs Plot Devon 36 F4
Wainhouse Corner Cornw'l 17 A8
Wakeham Devon 14 F1
Walcombe Som'set 48 B3
Walcot Swindon 65 F8
Walcot Warwick 77 A5
Walditch Dorset 24 B4
Wales Som'set 38 A1
Walford Heref'd 69 C5
Walham Glos 70 C4
Walhampton Hants 29 A6
Walkford Dorset 28 B4
Walkhampton Devon 11 B6
Wall Cornw'l 3 C8
Wall Mead Bath/NE Som'set 57 E5
Waller's Green Heref'd 74 E3
Wallingford Oxon 67 E8
Wallisdown Poole 27 B8
Wallow Green Glos 63 C8
Wallston V/Glam 54 B2
Wallsworth Glos 70 C2
Walpole Som'set 47 C6
Walrow Som'set 47 B6
Walson Monmouths 68 C2
Walton Som'set 48 D1
Walton Warwick 77 B8
Walton Cardiff Glos 70 A4
Walton Elm Dorset 39 C5
Walton Park N Som'set 55 B8
Walton St. Mary N Som'set 55 B8
Walton-in-Gordano N Som'set 55 B8
Wambrook Som'set 36 E3
Wanborough Swindon 65 F9
Wanderwell Dorset 24 B4
Wanson Cornw'l 30 F3
Wanstrow Som'set 49 C6
Wanswell Glos 63 B5
Wantage Oxon 67 E5
Wapley S Gloucs 57 A6
Warborough Oxon 67 D8
Warbstow Cornw'l 17 B9
Warbstow Cross Cornw'l 17 B9
Warden Hill Glos 70 C4
Ware Devon 23 B8
Wareham Dorset 27 C5
Warfleet Devon 15 E5
Warkleigh Devon 33 B5
Warleggan Cornw'l 9 B6
Warleigh Bath/NE Som'set 57 D7
Warminster Wilts 50 C2
Warminster Common Wilts 50 C2
Warmley S Gloucs 57 B5
Warmley Hill S Gloucs 57 B5
Warmwell Dorset 26 C2
Warndon Worcs 75 A7
Warndon Worcs 75 A7
Wash Common W Berks 61 D6

Washaway *Cornw'l* 8 B3
Washbourne *Devon* 14 E3
Washbrook *Som'set* 47 A8
Washfield *Devon* 34 C3
Washford *Som'set* 45 C7
Washford Pyne *Devon* 33 D9
Wasperton *Warwick* 77 A8
Watchet *Som'set* 45 C8
Watchfield *Oxon* 66 E1
Watchfield *Som'set* 47 B6
Watcombe *Torbay* 15 B6
Water *Devon* 20 D5
Water Eaton *Oxon* 73 E9
Watercombe *Dorset* 26 D2
Waterditch *Hants* 28 A3
Waterend *Glos* 69 E9
Waterfall *Hants* 29 B6
Watergate *Cornw'l* 17 D7
Watergore *Som'set* 37 C6
Waterhead *Devon* 14 F1
Waterlane *Glos* 64 B3
Waterlip *Som'set* 49 C5
Waterloo *Cornw'l* 9 A5
Waterloo *Poole* 27 B7
Waterloo *Worcs* 75 E8
Watermoor *Glos* 65 B5
Watermouth Castle *Devon* 43 B6
Waterrow *Som'set* 35 A6
Watledge *Glos* 64 B1
Watley's End *S Gloucs* 63 F5
Watton *Dorset* 24 B4
Wawcott *W Berks* 60 C4
Way Village *Devon* 34 D2
Way Wick *N Som'set* 55 D7
Waye *Devon* 14 A3
Wayend Street *Heref'd* 74 E4
Wayford *Som'set* 37 E6
Waytown *Devon* 31 B7
Waytown *Dorset* 24 A4
Weacombe *Som'set* 46 C2
Weald *Oxon* 66 B3
Wearde *Cornw'l* 10 D4
Weare *Som'set* 47 A8
Weare Giffard *Devon* 32 B2
Wearne *Som'set* 47 F8
Webbington *Som'set* 55 E7
Webb's Heath *S Gloucs* 63 B5
Wedhampton *Wilts* 59 E6
Wedmore *Som'set* 47 B8
Week *Devon* 14 C3
Week *Devon* 33 F6
Week *Devon* 43 F6
Week Green *Cornw'l* 18 A1
Week St. Mary *Cornw'l* 18 A1
Weeke *Hants* 53 E6
Weethley *Warwick* 76 A4
Weir Green *Glos* 70 D1
Weir Quay *Devon* 10 B4
Weirend *Heref'd* 68 C5
Welcombe *Devon* 30 C4
Welford *W Berks* 61 B5
Welford on Avon *Warwick* 77 B5
Well Cross *Devon* 14 D1
Well Head *Wilts* 49 E8
Well Town *Devon* 34 E3
Welland *Worcs* 75 E5
Wellesbourne *Warwick* 77 A8
Wellhouse *W Berks* 61 B7
Wellington *Som'set* 35 B7
Wellington Heath *Heref'd* 74 D4
Wellisford *Som'set* 35 B6
Wellow *Bath/NE Som'set* 57 E6
Wellow *I/Wight* 29 C7
Wellow Wood *Hants* 41 B8
Wells *Som'set* 48 B2
Wellswood *Torbay* 15 C6
Welsford *Devon* 31 B5
Welsh Bicknor *Heref'd* 69 D5
Welsh Newton *Heref'd* 68 D3
Welstor *Devon* 14 A2
Welton *Bath/NE Som'set* 57 E7
Wembdon *Som'set* 47 D5
Wembury *Devon* 11 F6
Wembworthy *Devon* 33 E6
Wendron *Cornw'l* 4 D1
Wenfordbridge *Cornw'l* 17 E6
Wenvoe *V/Glam* 54 B2
Wernheolydd *Monmouths* 68 E1
Wern-y-cwrt *Monmouths* 68 E1
Werrington *Cornw'l* 18 C3
West Allington *Wilts* 13 D5
West Amesbury *Wilts* 51 E2
West Anstey *Devon* 44 F3
West Ashford *Devon* 42 E5
West Ashton *Wilts* 58 E2
West Bagborough
  Som'set 46 E3
West Bay *Dorset* 24 B4
West Bexington *Dorset* 25 C5
West Bourton *Dorset* 49 F7
West Bradley *Som'set* 48 D3
West Buckland *Devon* 43 B6
West Buckland *Som'set* 35 B8
West Camel *Som'set* 38 B1
West Chaldon *Dorset* 26 D2
West Challow *Oxon* 66 E4
West Charleton *Devon* 13 D6
West Chelborough *Dorset* 37 E8
West Chinnock *Som'set* 37 D7
West Chisenbury *Wilts* 51 A7
West Coker *Som'set* 37 D8
West Compton *Dorset* 25 B6
West Compton *Som'set* 48 C2
West Creech *Dorset* 26 D4
West Curry *Cornw'l* 18 B2
West Dean *Wilts* 52 F2
West Down *Devon* 42 C5
West End *Dorset* 39 F8
West End *Glos* 64 C2
West End *N Som'set* 55 C9
West End *Oxon* 67 B5
West End *Oxon* 67 E8
West End *Som'set* 36 D5
West End *Som'set* 48 A3
West End *Som'set* 48 F1
West End *S Gloucs* 63 E6
West End *Wilts* 39 B8
West End *Wilts* 40 B2
West End *Wilts* 58 A4
West End *Worcs* 76 E4
West Grafton *Wilts* 60 D1
West Grimstead *Wilts* 41 A7

West Hagbourne *Oxon* 67 E7
West Hanney *Oxon* 67 D5
West Harnham *Wilts* 51 F7
West Harptree
  Bath/NE Som'set 56 E3
West Hatch *Som'set* 36 B3
West Hatch *Wilts* 50 F3
West Hay *N Som'set* 55 D9
West Heath *Hants* 61 E8
West Hendred *Oxon* 67 E5
West Hewish *N Som'set* 55 D7
West Hill *Devon* 22 B3
West Hill *N Som'set* 55 A9
West Hill *N Som'set* 56 A1
West Hill *Wilts* 58 C2
West Holme *Dorset* 26 C4
West Horrington *Som'set* 48 B3
West Howe *Bournem'th* 27 A8
West Howetown *Som'set* 45 D5
West Huntspill *Som'set* 47 C6
West Hurn *Dorset* 28 A2
West Ilsley *W Berks* 67 F6
West Kennett *Wilts* 59 C7
West Kington *Wilts* 57 A8
West Kington Wick *Wilts* 57 A8
West Knighton *Dorset* 26 C1
West Knoyle *Wilts* 50 E2
West Lambrook *Som'set* 37 C6
West Lavington *Wilts* 50 A5
West Leigh *Devon* 33 E6
West Littleton *S Gloucs* 57 A7
West Lockinge *Oxon* 67 E5
West Looe *Cornw'l* 9 E8
West Luccombe *Som'set* 45 B5
West Lulworth *Dorset* 26 D4
West Lydford *Som'set* 48 E3
West Lydiad *Heref'd* 74 D1
West Lyn *Devon* 44 B1
West Lyng *Som'set* 47 F6
West Malvern *Worcs* 75 C5
West Melbury *Dorset* 39 B7
West Milton *Dorset* 24 A5
West Monkton *Som'set* 46 F5
West Moors *Dorset* 40 F4
West Morden *Dorset* 27 A5
West Mudford *Som'set* 38 B1
West Newton *Som'set* 47 F5
West Ogwell *Devon* 14 A4
West Orchard *Dorset* 39 C6
West Overton *Wilts* 59 C7
West Panson *Devon* 18 B3
West Parley *Dorset* 27 A8
West Pennard *Som'set* 48 D2
West Pentire *Cornw'l* 7 C6
West Porlock *Som'set* 44 B4
West Pulham *Dorset* 38 E4
West Putford *Devon* 31 C7
West Quantoxhead
  Som'set 46 C2
West Sandford *Devon* 33 F9
West Shepton *Som'set* 48 C4
West Stafford *Dorset* 26 C1
West Stoke *Som'set* 37 C7
West Stoughton *Som'set* 47 B8
West Stour *Dorset* 39 B5
West Stowell *Wilts* 59 D7
West Stratton *Hants* 53 C7
West Taphouse *Cornw'l* 9 C6
West Tolgus *Cornw'l* 4 B1
West Town
  Bath/NE Som'set 56 D2
West Town *Devon* 21 A7
West Town *Devon* 31 B6
West Town *N Som'set* 56 C1
West Town *Som'set* 48 D2
West Tytherley *Hants* 52 F2
West Tytherton *Wilts* 58 B4
West Wellow *Hants* 41 C8
West Wembury *Devon* 11 F6
West Wick *N Som'set* 55 D7
West Winterslow *Wilts* 52 E1
West Woodhay *W Berks* 60 D4
West Woodlands *Som'set* 49 C7
West Worlington *Devon* 33 D8
West Yatton *Wilts* 55 A4
West Yeo *Som'set* 47 E6
Westbourne *Bournem'th* 27 B8
Westbrook *W Berks* 61 B5
Westbrook *Wilts* 58 C4
Westbury *Wilts* 50 A2
Westbury Leigh *Wilts* 50 A2
Westbury on Trym *Bristol* 56 A3
Westbury Park *Bristol* 56 A3
Westbury-on-Severn *Glos* 69 B8
Westbury-sub-Mendip
  Som'set 48 B2
Westcombe *Som'set* 48 F1
Westcombe *Som'set* 49 D5
Westcot *Oxon* 66 E3
Westcote *Glos* 72 C3
Westcott *Devon* 21 C5
Westcott *Devon* 35 F5
Westcott Barton *Oxon* 73 B7
Westcourt *Wilts* 60 D1
Westdowns *Cornw'l* 17 D6
Westend *Glos* 70 F1
Westend *Oxon* 73 C5
Westend *S Gloucs* 62 D4
Westend Town *S Gloucs* 57 B7
Westerleigh *S Gloucs* 57 A6
Westerleigh Common
  S Gloucs 63 F6
Westerleigh Hill *S Gloucs* 57 A6
Westfield
  Bath/NE Som'set 57 F5
Westfield *Heref'd* 74 C4
Westfields *Dorset* 38 E4
Westford *Som'set* 35 B7
Westhall Hill *Oxon* 72 E3
Westham *Dorset* 25 E8
Westhay *Som'set* 47 C8
Westhide *Heref'd* 74 D1
Westholme *Som'set* 48 C3
Westlake *Devon* 11 E8
Westlea *Swindon* 65 F7
Westleigh *Devon* 35 C6
Westleigh *Devon* 42 F4
Westmancote *Worcs* 76 E1
Weston *Bath/NE Som'set* 57 C6
Weston *Devon* 23 C5
Weston *Devon* 35 F7
Weston *Dorset* 24 D2
Weston *W Berks* 60 B4

Weston Bampfylde
  Som'set 38 A2
Weston Beggard *Heref'd* 74 D1
Weston Colley *Hants* 53 D7
Weston Mill *Plym'th* 10 D5
Weston Park
  Bath/NE Som'set 57 C6
Weston Subedge *Glos* 77 D5
Weston Town *Som'set* 49 C6
Weston under Penyard
  Heref'd 69 C6
Westonbirt *Glos* 64 E2
Weston-in-Gordano
  N Som'set 55 B8
Weston-on-Avon *Warwick* 77 B6
Weston-super-Mare
  N Som'set 55 D6
Westonzoyland *Som'set* 47 D7
Westover *Hants* 52 C4
Westowe *Som'set* 46 E2
Westown *Devon* 35 D7
Westport *Som'set* 37 B5
Westra *V/Glam* 54 B2
Westridge Green *W Berks* 61 A8
Westrip *Glos* 63 A8
Westrop *Swindon* 65 D9
Westrop *Wilts* 58 B2
Westward Ho! *Devon* 42 F3
Westwell *Oxon* 72 E3
Westwells *Wilts* 58 C2
Westwood *Devon* 22 A2
Westwood *Devon* 34 F1
Westwood *Wilts* 57 E8
Wexcombe *Wilts* 61 E2
Weycroft *Devon* 36 F4
Weyhill *Hants* 52 B3
Weymouth *Dorset* 25 E8
Whaddon *Glos* 70 E2
Whaddon *Glos* 71 C5
Whaddon *Wilts* 41 A6
Whaddon *Wilts* 58 D2
Whatcote *Warwick* 77 D9
Whatley *Som'set* 36 E5
Whatley *Som'set* 49 B6
Wheal Baddon *Cornw'l* 4 B3
Wheal Busy *Cornw'l* 4 B2
Wheal Frances *Cornw'l* 7 E6
Wheal Rose *Cornw'l* 4 B2
Wheatenhurst *Glos* 70 F1
Wheathill *Heref'd* 48 E3
Wheatley *Devon* 21 B8
Wheatley *Oxon* 67 A8
Wheatridge *Glos* 70 D3
Wheddon Cross *Som'set* 45 D5
Whelford *Glos* 65 C8
Wherry Town *Cornw'l* 2 E5
Wherwell *Hants* 52 C4
Whetley Cross *Dorset* 37 F7
Whichford *Warwick* 77 F9
Whiddon *Devon* 43 E6
Whiddon Down *Devon* 20 B3
Whimble *Devon* 31 F7
Whimple *Devon* 22 A2
Whipcott *Devon* 35 C6
Whipsiderry *Cornw'l* 7 C7
Whipton *Devon* 21 B8
Whitbourne *Heref'd* 74 A4
Whitbourne Ford *Heref'd* 74 A4
Whitchurch *Bristol* 56 C4
Whitchurch *Card* 54 A3
Whitchurch *Devon* 11 A5
Whitchurch *Hants* 53 B6
Whitchurch *Heref'd* 68 D4
Whitchurch *Warwick* 77 C7
Whitchurch Cannonicorum
  Dorset 24 A2
Whitcombe *Dorset* 26 C1
White Ball *Devon* 35 C6
White Cross
  Bath/NE Som'set 56 E4
White Cross *Cornw'l* 4 F1
White Cross *Cornw'l* 7 D8
White Cross *Wilts* 49 E7
White End *Glos* 70 B2
White Hill *Wilts* 49 E8
White Lackington *Dorset* 26 A1
White Ladies Aston *Worcs* 75 B8
White Ox Mead
  Bath/NE Som'set 57 E6
White Rocks *Heref'd* 68 C2
White Stone *Heref'd* 74 D1
Whitebrook *Monmouths* 62 A2
Whitechurch *Som'set* 38 B4
Whitecliff *Glos* 68 E5
Whitecroft *Glos* 62 A4
Whitecross *Cornw'l* 3 D6
Whitecross *Cornw'l* 8 A2
Whitecross *Dorset* 24 A4
Whitefield *Dorset* 27 B5
Whitefield *Som'set* 45 F8
Whitehall *Devon* 35 D7
Whitehall *Devon* 43 D5
Whitelackington *Som'set* 37 C5
Whiteleaved Oak *Heref'd* 75 E5
Whitelye *Monmouths* 62 B2
Whitemoor *Cornw'l* 8 D2
Whiteoak Green *Oxon* 73 E5
Whiteparish *Wilts* 41 B8
Whites *Som'set* 47 E6
Whiteshill *Glos* 70 F2
Whiteshill *S Gloucs* 56 A4
Whitestaunton *Som'set* 36 D3
Whitestone *Devon* 21 B7
Whitestone *Devon* 42 B4
Whitestone Cross *Devon* 21 B8
Whiteway
  Bath/NE Som'set 57 D6
Whiteway *Glos* 64 C1
Whiteway *Glos* 70 E4
Whiteworks *Devon* 11 A8
Whitfield *Heref'd* 68 C5
Whitfield *S Gloucs* 63 D5
Whitford *Devon* 23 A7
Whitleigh *Plym'th* 10 C5
Whitley *Wilts* 58 C2
Whitminster *Glos* 70 F1
Whitmoor *Devon* 35 D6
Whitmore *Dorset* 40 E4
Whitnage *Devon* 35 C5
Whitnell *Som'set* 46 D4
Whitney Bottom *Som'set* 36 D4
Whitsbury *Hants* 41 C5
Whitstone *Cornw'l* 18 A2
Whittington *Glos* 71 C6

Whittonditch *Wilts* 60 B2
Whitway *Hants* 61 E6
Wick *Bournem'th* 28 B3
Wick *Devon* 35 F8
Wick *Som'set* 46 C4
Wick *Som'set* 47 F8
Wick *Som'set* 48 D2
Wick *Som'set* 55 F6
Wick *S Gloucs* 57 B6
Wick *Wilts* 41 B6
Wick *Worcs* 76 C2
Wick Hill *Som'set* 58 B4
Wick St. Lawrence
  N Som'set 55 C7
Wick Street *Glos* 70 F3
Wickham *W Berks* 60 B4
Wickham Green *W Berks* 60 B4
Wickham Heath *W Berks* 61 C5
Wickhamford *Worcs* 76 D1
Wicklane *Bath/NE Som'set* 57 E5
Wickridge Street *Glos* 70 B2
Wicksgreen *Glos* 70 E1
Wickwar *S Gloucs* 63 E6
Widcombe
  Bath/NE Som'set 57 D7
Widcombe *Som'set* 36 C2
Widdenham *Wilts* 58 B1
Widecombe in the Moor
  Devon 20 E4
Widegate's *Cornw'l* 9 E7
Widemouth Bay *Cornw'l* 30 F4
Widewell *Plym'th* 11 C5
Widham *Wilts* 65 E6
Widworthy *Devon* 23 A6
Wigbeth *Dorset* 40 E3
Wigborough *Som'set* 37 C6
Wiggaton *Devon* 22 B4
Wigginton *Oxon* 73 A6
Wigley *Hants* 41 C9
Wilcot *Wilts* 59 D7
Wildhern *Hants* 52 A4
Wildmoor *Oxon* 67 C6
Wilkin Throop *Som'set* 38 B3
Willand *Devon* 35 D5
Willand *Som'set* 36 D1
Willand Moor *Devon* 35 D5
Willersey *Glos* 76 E5
Willesleigh *Devon* 43 E6
Willesley *Glos* 64 E2
Willestrew *Devon* 19 E5
Willett *Som'set* 46 E2
Willingcott *Devon* 42 C4
Willington *Warwick* 77 E8
Williton *Som'set* 45 C8
Willsbridge *S Gloucs* 57 B5
Willtown *Som'set* 37 B1
Wilmcote *Warwick* 77 A6
Wilmington
  Bath/NE Som'set 57 D5
Wilmington *Devon* 23 A6
Wilminstone *Devon* 19 E6
Wilsford *Wilts* 51 D7
Wilsford *Wilts* 59 E6
Wilson *Heref'd* 68 C5
Wilton *Cornw'l* 69 C5
Wilton *Som'set* 36 B2
Wilton *Wilts* 51 E6
Wilton *Wilts* 60 D2
Wiltown *Devon* 35 C8
Wimborne Minster *Dorset* 27 A7
Wimborne St. Giles *Dorset* 40 D3
Wimpstone *Warwick* 77 C7
Wincanton *Som'set* 49 F6
Winchcombe *Glos* 71 B6
Winchester *Hants* 53 F6
Wincombe *Wilts* 39 B7
Windcross *Glos* 69 A7
Windmill *Cornw'l* 16 F2
Windmill Hill *Bristol* 56 B3
Windmill Hill *S Gloucs* 63 B4
Windmill Hill *Som'set* 36 C4
Windmill Hill *Worcs* 75 C8
Windrush *Glos* 72 C2
Windsoredge *Glos* 64 B1
Winford *N Som'set* 56 C2
Winfrith Newburgh *Dorset* 26 D3
Wingfield *Wilts* 57 E8
Winkfield *Som'set* 33 E5
Winkton *Dorset* 28 A3
Winkton Common *Dorset* 28 B3
Winnall *Heref'd* 68 A3
Winscombe *N Som'set* 58 E8
Winsford *Som'set* 45 E5
Winsham *Devon* 42 D4
Winsham *Som'set* 36 E5
Winsley *Wilts* 57 D8
Winson *Glos* 71 F7
Winstone *Glos* 71 F5
Winswell *Devon* 32 D2
Winter Well *Som'set* 36 B3
Winterborne Clenston
  Dorset 39 F6
Winterborne Herrington
  Dorset 26 C8
Winterborne Houghton
  Dorset 39 F6
Winterborne Kingston
  Dorset 26 A4
Winterborne Monkton
  Dorset 25 C8
Winterborne Stickland
  Dorset 39 F6
Winterborne Whitechurch
  Dorset 39 F6
Winterborne Zelston
  Dorset 26 A4
Winterbourne *S Gloucs* 62 E4
Winterbourne *W Berks* 61 B5
Winterbourne Abbas
  Dorset 25 B7
Winterbourne Bassett
  Wilts 59 A6
Winterbourne Dauntsey
  Wilts 51 E8
Winterbourne Down
  S Gloucs 57 A5
Winterbourne Earls *Wilts* 51 E8
Winterbourne Gunner *Wilts* 51 D8
Winterbourne Monkton
  Wilts 59 B6
Winterbourne Steepleton
  Dorset 25 C7
Winterbourne Stoke *Wilts* 51 C6
Winterhay Green *Som'set* 36 C5

Winton *Bournem'th* 28 B1
Wishanger *Glos* 70 F4
Witchampton *Dorset* 40 E2
Witcombe *Som'set* 37 B7
Witham Friary *Som'set* 49 C6
Withacott *Devon* 31 C8
Witheridge *Devon* 33 D9
Withiel *Cornw'l* 8 B2
Withiel Florey *Som'set* 45 E6
Withielgoose Mills *Cornw'l* 8 B3
Withington *Glos* 71 D6
Withington *Heref'd* 74 D1
Withington Marsh *Heref'd* 74 D1
Withleigh *Devon* 34 D3
Withybrook *Som'set* 49 B5
Withycombe *Som'set* 45 C7
Withycombe Raleigh
  Devon 22 D2
Withyditch
  Bath/NE Som'set 57 E6
Withypool *Som'set* 44 D3
Withywood *Bristol* 56 C3
Witney *Oxon* 73 E6
Wittensford *Hants* 41 D8
Wiveliscombe *Som'set* 45 E8
Wixford *Warwick* 76 B4
Woath *Dorset* 24 A4
Wofferwood Common
  Heref'd 74 B3
Wolborough *Devon* 15 A5
Wolleigh *Devon* 21 E6
Wolvercote *Oxon* 73 F8
Wolverstone *Devon* 35 F7
Wolverton *Hants* 61 E8
Wolverton *Hants* 49 E7
Wolverton Common *Hants* 61 E8
Wonderstone *N Som'set* 55 E6
Wonford *Devon* 21 B8
Wonson *Devon* 20 C3
Wonston *Dorset* 38 E4
Wonston *Hants* 53 D6
Wood *Som'set* 36 E4
Wood Bevington *Warwick* 76 B4
Wood End *Heref'd* 74 D2
Wood Stanway *Glos* 71 A7
Wood Street *Wilts* 59 A6
Woodacott *Devon* 31 E7
Woodacott Cross *Devon* 31 E7
Woodborough *Wilts* 59 E7
Woodbridge *Devon* 23 A5
Woodbridge *Devon* 38 D4
Woodbury *Devon* 22 C2
Woodbury Salterton
  Devon 22 C2
Woodchester *Glos* 64 B1
Woodcock *Wilts* 50 C2
Woodcombe *Som'set* 45 B5
Woodcott *Hants* 61 F5
Woodcroft *Glos* 62 C2
Woodcutts *Dorset* 40 C2
Woodfalls *Wilts* 41 B6
Woodfield *Glos* 63 B6
Woodford *Cornw'l* 30 D4
Woodford *Devon* 14 E3
Woodford *Glos* 63 C5
Woodford *Plym'th* 11 D6
Woodford *Som'set* 45 D8
Woodford *Som'set* 48 C2
Woodgate *Devon* 35 C7
Woodgreen *Hants* 41 C6
Woodhill *N Som'set* 56 A1
Woodhill *Som'set* 47 F7
Woodhouse *Hants* 41 B9
Woodhouse Down
  S Gloucs 62 E4
Woodington *Hants* 41 B9
Woodlake *Dorset* 26 B4
Woodland *Devon* 11 D8
Woodland *Devon* 14 B2
Woodland Head *Devon* 21 A5
Woodlands *Dorset* 40 E4
Woodlands *Som'set* 46 C3
Woodlands *Som'set* 48 D2
Woodlands St. Mary
  W Berks 60 A3
Woodleigh *Devon* 14 F2
Woodley *Devon* 19 E5
Woodmancote *Glos* 63 C7
Woodmancote *Glos* 71 B5
Woodmancote *Glos* 71 F6
Woodmancott *Hants* 53 C8
Woodmanton *Devon* 22 C2
Woodmarsh *Wilts* 57 E2
Woodminton *Wilts* 40 B3
Woodrow *Dorset* 38 E4
Woodrow *Dorset* 39 D5
Woodsend *Wilts* 60 A1
Woodsford *Dorset* 26 B2
Woodside *Hants* 29 B6
Woodspeen *W Berks* 61 C5
Woodstock *Oxon* 73 D7
Woodtown *Devon* 31 B8
Woodville *Dorset* 39 B6
Woodwalls *Dorset* 37 E8
Woody Bay *Devon* 43 B8
Woodyates *Dorset* 40 C3
Wookey *Som'set* 48 B2
Wookey Hole *Som'set* 48 B2
Wool *Dorset* 26 C3
Woolacombe *Devon* 42 C4
Woolaston *Glos* 62 C3
Woolaston Common *Glos* 62 C3
Woolaston Slade *Glos* 62 B3
Woolaston Woodside *Glos* 62 B3
Woolavington *Som'set* 47 C7
Woolfardisworthy *Devon* 33 E8
Woolfardisworthy *Devon* 34 E1
Woolgarston *Dorset* 27 D6
Woolhampton *W Berks* 61 C8
Woolhope *Heref'd* 74 E2
Woolhope Cockshoot
  Heref'd 74 E2
Woolland *Dorset* 39 E5
Woollard *Bath/NE Som'set* 56 D4
Woollaton *Devon* 32 D2
Woolley *Bath/NE Som'set* 57 C6
Woolley *Cornw'l* 30 D3
Woolley *Wilts* 57 D8
Woolley Green *Wilts* 58 D1
Woolmersdon *Som'set* 47 E5
Woolminstone *Som'set* 37 E6
Woolridge *Glos* 70 C2
Woolsbridge *Dorset* 40 E5

Woolsgrove *Devon* 33 F8
Woolston *Cornw'l* 10 B1
Woolston *Devon* 13 D5
Woolston *Som'set* 46 D1
Woolston *Som'set* 48 F4
Woolston Green *Devon* 14 B3
Woolstone *Glos* 71 A5
Woolstone *Oxon* 66 E2
Woolton Hill *Hants* 61 C5
Woolvers Hill *N Som'set* 55 D7
Woolverton *Som'set* 57 F7
Woon *Cornw'l* 8 D3
Wootton *Heref'd* 74 E1
Wootton *Hants* 28 A4
Wootton *Oxon* 67 B6
Wootton *Oxon* 73 D7
Wootton Bassett *Wilts* 65 F6
Wootton Courtney
  Som'set 45 C5
Wootton Fitzpaine *Dorset* 24 A3
Wootton Rivers *Wilts* 59 D8
Wootton St. Lawrence
  Hants 61 F8
Worcester *Worcs* 75 A7
Worgret *Dorset* 27 C5
World's End *W Berks* 61 A6
Worle *N Som'set* 55 D7
Worlebury *N Som'set* 55 D6
Worley *Glos* 64 C1
Wormbridge *Heref'd* 68 A2
Wormelow Tump *Heref'd* 68 A3
Wormington *Glos* 76 E3
Worminster *Som'set* 48 C3
Worrall Hill *Glos* 69 E6
Worston *Devon* 11 E7
Worth *Devon* 32 F2
Worth *Devon* 34 F4
Worth *Devon* 44 E3
Worth *Som'set* 48 B2
Worth Matravers *Dorset* 27 E6
Worthy *Som'set* 44 B4
Wortley *Glos* 63 D7
Worton *Wilts* 58 E4
Worton Common *Wilts* 58 E4
Wotter *Devon* 11 C7
Wotton *Glos* 70 D2
Wotton under Edge *Glos* 63 D7
Wrafton *Devon* 42 D4
Wrangaton *Devon* 14 D1
Wrangway *Som'set* 35 C7
Wrantage *Som'set* 36 B4
Wraxall *N Som'set* 56 B1
Wraxall *Som'set* 48 D4
Wrigwell Hill *Devon* 14 B4
Wrington *N Som'set* 56 D1
Writhlington
  Bath/NE Som'set 57 E6
Wroughton *Swindon* 65 F8
Wyastone Leys *Heref'd* 68 D4
Wych *Dorset* 24 B4
Wyck Rissington *Glos* 72 C2
Wyegate Green *Glos* 62 A3
Wyesham *Monmouths* 68 E4
Wyke *Dorset* 39 A5
Wyke Champflower
  Som'set 49 E5
Wyke Green *Devon* 23 A8
Wyke Regis *Dorset* 25 E8
Wylye *Wilts* 50 D5
Wymans Brook *Glos* 70 C4
Wynford Eagle *Dorset* 25 A6
Wynn's Green *Heref'd* 74 C2
Wyre Piddle *Worcs* 76 C2
Wytham *Oxon* 73 F8

Y

Yafford *I/Wight* 29 D8
Yalberton *Torbay* 15 D5
Yalway *Som'set* 46 E4
Yanley *N Som'set* 56 D3
Yanworth *Glos* 71 E7
Yarberry *N Som'set* 55 E7
Yarcombe *Devon* 36 E2
Yarford *Som'set* 46 F4
Yarford *Som'set* 46 F4
Yarkhill *Heref'd* 74 D2
Yarley *Som'set* 48 B2
Yarlington *Som'set* 49 F5
Yarmouth *I/Wight* 29 C7
Yarnacott *Devon* 43 E7
Yarnbrook *Wilts* 58 F2
Yarner *Devon* 21 E5
Yarnscombe *Devon* 32 A4
Yarnton *Oxon* 73 E8
Yarrow *Som'set* 47 B7
Yate *S Gloucs* 63 F6
Yate Rocks *S Gloucs* 63 F6
Yatesbury *Wilts* 59 B6
Yattendon *W Berks* 61 B8
Yatton *N Som'set* 55 C8
Yatton Keynell *Wilts* 58 A2
Yawl *Devon* 23 B8
Yeabridge *Som'set* 37 C6
Yealmpton *Devon* 11 E7
Yearsett *Heref'd* 74 B4
Yelford *Oxon* 66 B4
Yelland *Devon* 42 E4
Yelverton *Devon* 11 B6
Yenston *Som'set* 38 B4
Yeo Mill *Devon* 34 A1
Yeo Park *Devon* 11 E7
Yeoford *Devon* 21 A5
Yeolmbridge *Cornw'l* 18 C3
Yeovil *Som'set* 37 C9
Yeovilton *Som'set* 37 B9
Yetminster *Dorset* 38 D1
Yettington *Devon* 22 C3
Yondertown *Devon* 11 D7
Yondover *Devon* 24 B4
Yorkley *Glos* 69 F6
Yorkley Slade *Glos* 69 F6

Z

Zeal Monachorum *Devon* 33 F7
Zeals *Wilts* 49 E7
Zelah *Cornw'l* 7 E7
Zennor *Cornw'l* 2 C5
Zoar *Cornw'l* 5 G3